Coronado:
The Enchanted Island

by Katherine Eitzen Carlin
and Ray Brandes

Edited by Bruce Linder

4th Edition
Coronado Historical Association

Copyright © 2015 by the Coronado Historical Association.
All rights reserved. No part of this book may be reproduced or transmitted in any form whatsoever without prior written permission from the publisher except in the case of brief quotations embodied in critical articles and reviews.

Fourth Edition (revised) New Material Included: Text, Photographs.
Material Excluded: Text, photographs. First published 1987

Published by
Coronado Historical Association
1100 Orange Avenue
Coronado, CA 92118
www.coronadohistory.org

Carlin, Katherine Eitzen ; Brandes, Ray ; Linder, Bruce, editor.

Coronado: The Enchanted Island / Carlin, Katherine Eitzen (1903 – 1986); Brandes, Ray (1924 - 2014)

ISBN 978-0-9969705-1-8
Library of Congress Control Number: 2015956674

1. Coronado (Calif.) – History. 2. Hotel del Coronado (Coronado, Calif.)--History.
3. Naval Air Station North Island (Calif.) 4. Coronado Naval Amphibious Base (Calif.)
5. Babcock, Elisha, 1848-1922. 6. Spreckels, John Diedrich, 1848- 1926 7. Historic Buildings – California -- Coronado. 8. Coronado (Calif.)--Social life and customs--Pictorial works.
9. San Diego-Coronado Bridge (Coronado and San Diego, Calif.)

Notice: The information in this book is true and complete to the best of our knowledge.
It is offered without guarantee on the part of the editor or the Coronado Historical Association.
The editor and the Coronado Historical Association disclaim all liability
in connection with the use of this book.

Manufactured in the United States
Copies may be ordered from
Coronado Historical Association
1100 Orange Avenue
Coronado, CA 92118
619. 435.7242

Table of Contents

Chapter 1	The Golden Age of Exploration	1
Chapter 2	Planning & Developing the Peninsula 1886-1887	13
Chapter 3	The Promise Fulfilled: The Hotel del Coronado – 1888	35
Chapter 4	John D. Spreckels and the Renaissance of the Crown City 1889-1900	53
Chapter 5	A Time of Optimism before the Road to War 1900-1914	75
Chapter 6	1915-1929 World War I and the Roaring Twenties	113
Chapter 7	1930-1944 The Depression and World War II	157
Chapter 8	1945-1959: The Post War Years & A Growing Village	197
Chapter 9	The Coming of the Bridge 1960-1969	227
Chapter 10	The Opening of the Second Century	257
The Coronado Almanac		299
Bibliography		313
Index		321

Key to photo credit abbreviations:

Coronado Historical Association = *CHA*

Coronado Public Library = *CPL*

Leslie Crawford Collection = *LCC*

(CHA)

(CHA)

FOREWORD

It's been said that Coronado has more history per square inch than any other community in San Diego County. This reputation that has been building for over 125 years and *Coronado: The Enchanted Island* is the single best authority of that wonderful past.

Coronado is a community rich in heritage, community pride, and small town atmosphere and equally rich in promise for the future. Our inspiring future, as we all know, is directly built upon the firm foundation of the community's past.

Katherine Eitzen Carlin, who nurtured the original vision for this book, described its goal as "the telling of the story of our people, their names, accomplishments, and contributions." But history, indeed, never sleeps and that story of Coronado has now been refined and expanded through this, its fourth impressive edition. More than anything, a Fourth Edition is proof of the depth and complexity of the Coronado story … and of its boundless fascination for readers across so many years.

The First Edition of this iconic history was published in 1987, begun by Katherine and finished by historian Dr. Ray Brandes upon her untimely passing. A Second Edition followed in 1988, fostered by Coronado's inspiring and peerless team of Nancy Cobb and Gerry MacCartee. Ten years later a Third Edition appeared in expanded format, carefully crafted by CHA Executive Director Cindi Malinick and Kelly Purvis.

Today's Fourth Edition (released after a further seventeen years), capitalizes on new advances in historical research to present a more vibrant and complete volume. The Fourth Edition injects many fresh and exciting new images, introduces a first-time-ever "Coronado Almanac," and corrects the occasional factual inaccuracies from previous editions that have been reported by both the CHA staff and folks in town. The Fourth Edition has been compiled through the efforts of a highly experienced Editorial Committee that included Pam Crooks, Leslie Crawford, Candice Hooper and myself. This volume's impact, clarity, and eye-catching page craft is due principally to Laurie Berg. The unwavering support of the Coronado Public Library was particularly noteworthy. Extra thanks is also due to the untiring efforts of Rebecca Baker, Kathy Crawford, Kirstin Dahlquist, Christine Donovan, Jamie Edmonds, Susan Enowitz, Christian Esquevin, Jon Froomin, Jean McKey, Kelly Purvis, Denise Wald, Stephanie Washburn, and Kitt Williams.

The front cover proudly still carries the signature lettering identifying Enchanted Island's first authors — as it should. One of the goals of this edition was to retain the unique tone and flow of the original Carlin/Brandes narrative from 1987. Where we have added important new elements of Coronado's history that were not included in earlier volumes, we have clearly indicated these additions through the use of subtle background shading in the flow of text.

We think that our fresh new account of Coronado's treasured past is an important addition to the historical record and has earned a place on every Coronadan's bookshelf.

Bruce Linder
Executive Director, Coronado Historical Association

(CHA)

(CHA)

PREFACE

THIS STORY is the history of a development—a city and hotel—inspired by a real estate boom, an ocean beach, and the added attraction of an excellent year-round climate.

A California development sounds uninteresting and commonplace. There were, and still are, many developments—too many. Some think, but Coronadans believe, that their city was, and is, a place unique. Due to its isolation in the ferry days, the Island City was exclusive—not in the manner of snobbism, although there was reason. There was a great deal of wealth and social prestige nestled within its realm. The islanders were bound to a common interest: their loyalty to their own Coronado and the great Hotel, the hub of the city's existence.

Due to the highly advertised hostelry, the climate, and the beach, fascinating personages visited the city: royalty, presidents, educators, musicians, artists, literary men, high military officials, statesmen, heads of industries, financiers, medical men, sportsmen, early aviators, theatrical personalities, movie stars and rich playboys. Probably no other small town in America has hosted so many VIP's. The majority rested at the Hotel del Coronado, while others rented or owned homes for the winter season. Eventually a number of these visitors became permanent residents.

In the summer months our neighbors, the San Diegans, as well as many other vacationers, particularly those from the Imperial Valley and Arizona, spent their idle moments on the sands of Coronado's Tent City.

Another contribution to the Island's colorful background came from its proximity to Mexico. Coronado has inherited much from its border friends—their appealing music, food, art, and street names.

And being near the border, Coronadans enjoyed horse racing from the years of the old Tijuana Race Track to the new Agua Caliente turf. During its heyday of the 1920s and 1930s, racing peoples compared Agua Caliente to Monte Carlo. The glamour and accessibility of the tracks along with gambling, bull fights, and Hollywood stars, had a tremendous influence on Coronado tourism as did its internationally famous polo games right on its own local field.

Other contributing factors to the development of Coronado which involve the entire San Diego area, are the military installations at North Island and the Amphibious Base, which often label Coronado "Navy Town." The combination of all these elements has been instrumental in molding Coronado's life style: a place for the active, the retired, the young and the old, who have gathered here from all over the nation—even from all over the world.

Some of our citizens go back for several generations of living in this island town, some are native sons and daughters. Others are a transient group, bringing their traditions with them. This is evident in the types of architecture: New England, Southern, Mid-western, English, French, Spanish. Then, too, scattered all over town are the little "beach cottages" which, in their simple way, convey their own meaning–the early settlers' homes, workers of the Coronado Beach Company.

From the day the Bay Bridge opened, on August 2, 1969, connecting our "Island" to the mainland and the last pilings disappeared from the old ferry landing, I have felt that Coronado is no longer the same place. The event marked a new era. The whole concept of our town changed. Newcomers are taking up residence who know little about the history of "the Beach"; old timers are dying off, carrying their tales and their memories with them.

During Coronado's existence numerous booklets, magazine articles and newspaper columns have published articles about the town, glamorizing the ferries, street cars, Tent City, and the famous Hotel. They tell of the "village" atmosphere which citizens sought to maintain, the fact that the doors were left unlocked and the police station closed at midnight. Stories grew rosier with time. Much, however, is left unwritten.

A real need has existed for a history of Coronado—factual and exciting—which deals with the community's development through the years, with dates of happenings, our political victories and defeats. (The telling of the story of our people, their homes, accomplishments and contributions-is a book that can be used for reference and one that can also be enjoyed.) I took up that task. Being a resident of this "Island" since February 1, 1928, 1 too, have memories of bygone days and a devotion to my adopted home town. As a founding member of the Coronado Historical Association, Inc., in charge of artifacts and historical files, including all of Coronado's newspapers from the first issue in May 1887, I have developed an engrossing interest in local history. By researching these crumbling, yellowed pages, I discovered many things that I did not know. It became fascinating, like detective work-hunting for the clues. Still some mysteries exist that have not, and may never be solved. Records of those early years about Coronado Beach are scanty.

Sometimes I strayed from Coronado to include San Diego and area history. The two are so closely related that they are almost inseparable. The tie between San Diego and Coronado has always existed even though the "Island" fought to break away and become a separate city, and Coronado did succeed in establishing its own local incorporated government in 1890.

I have tried to objectively present the struggles that our city government and its citizens have encountered in their efforts to develop our tight little island in the way the various individuals thought it should go, trying to please everyone—which cannot be done—and yet hoping to keep the town "a nice place in which to live." Due to Coronado's very limited amount of land and its isolation as a peninsula, every bit of development has become a major issue, particularly since World War II. Beach preservation, the Hog Ranch sale (Coronado Cays), providing a golf course, the Port District suit, school enlargements, zoning, the Navy Housing, high rise condominiums, the Bay Bridge, tidelands usage, Glorietta Bay plan, traffic control, city planning—these controversial problems have often baited antagonisms among citizens which would not have reached such magnitude had Coronado been able to expand normally to provide for the inevitable future growth.

Katherine Eitzen Carlin

INTRODUCTION

I HAD NO CHANCE to meet Katherine Carlin. We spoke to one another over the telephone about our village and sometimes asked questions about mutual friends or about events that shook our memories loose. She put some ten years of her life into gathering the research to build this book about a place with which she had fallen in love. It is unfortunate that she was called away before she could finish her work.

I took the editorial liberty of extracting from her original introduction an apologia wherein she explained that she was not a professional writer or researcher, and that her goal was simply to help preserve the history of Coronado. Mrs. Carlin needed to make no such apology. She gathered information from newspapers and periodicals; she interviewed "old-timers," she drew on first-hand knowledge of events.

If there is one trait which historians acquire, it is to tell the truth. To get at that truth, we could not avoid colliding head on with issues which have contributed to changing our village. We chose not to skirt unfortunate events which have changed Coronado, like many other early coastal resort towns, in ways we would not have preferred. At the same time, we preferred neither to become anecdotal, nor to hurt anyone by dredging up events unnecessary to the story. Progress is evolutionary; change becomes necessary. While we cannot live in the past, that does not mean we should not have a a remembrance bank.

While Mrs. Carlin and I had mutual historical interests, hers were primarily political and social. She had a grasp of the politics of the city. She and her husband entertained and socialized to the degree that they were extremely well-known. I, on the other hand, am antisocial to a point, perhaps an outgrowth of purpose in life. Time for me is a precious commodity. Time must be used purposefully so as to leave something worthwhile behind when one is gone. Each of us is here to achieve something.

Much of my work as an archaeologist has helped me to think a great deal about man's past. My role as a professor-historian has given me the time to use that past in looking at the future.

This book about Coronado represents a blending of ideas. We hope that the mixture of research, experiences, and writing will bring back a flood of memories for every person who has come to know the Enchanted Island. In our mind's eye we saw a community which has an enduring coastal charm, where people have been concerned about the quality of life. We thought of Coronado as a village where visitors have always been welcome. We know that we were all visitors when we first arrived.

Coronadans will recognize that a detailed history of their village would have been impossible in a volume this size. The authors found the task impossible to include everything that probably should have been written about. Much more could have been related about the interminable story of the the bridge/tunnel, or the many people who made contributions of some sort that were important. We restrained ourselves when editorializing crept into our work. The volume, therefore, is our way of piecing together a story-teller's story about a village that has a memory. Like most people, this story has its flaws and its blemishes, but the book is about a place we care for and the people who have made it that way.

Unquestionably the major turning point in local history came at the time where Mrs. Carlin first felt this book should end-with the coming of the bridge. I chose, however, to drive beyond the San Diego-Coronado Bay Bridge to see what has happened since 1969. That bridge was completed nearly thirty years ago. The questions remaining to be answered included: what the future holds for the village? what kind of changes may be predicted? who will be the recipients of the change?

Coronado: The Enchanted Island tells a story, but there are lessons to be learned from the transformation of the village. The impacts caused by the bridge, the added military installations, and the freeways are not immutable. Coronado began in the minds of Babcock, Story, and Spreckels as a quiet resort village.

Coronado will not again be the village it was in the 1920s and 1930s. It can never be. Coronadans should know, however, that they are far better off than they have ever been, even with changes that have impinged the island's natural state.

Villagers can insure their future by the creation of an aesthetically beautiful civic center with a city hall, school buildings, police and fire stations, and public meeting halls that reflect a place with class and a remarkable heritage. Coronado needs a "blueprint" for its Renaissance put together by the proud people who understand what the city should have, not done in haste, not done the cheapest way possible. We should never concede that freeways, highrises, condominiums and apartment houses are the future of this village.

There are changes taking place at this very moment that can return the village of the 1920s to a remarkable place to live that will be consistent with the 21st century. The recreational/ tourist additions to the parameter of the island will help the image of a seacoast resort village. Resolution of the traffic and the noise and air pollution are top priorities if we are to protect the unique qualities of the village we love. It is the responsibility of every person who values Coronado to insist on a "Blueprint for Coronado's Quality" so that our children and their children will know that we kept the Enchanted Island for them.

Ray Brandes, Ph.D.
1998

(CHA)

(CHA)

To Everyone Who Has Felt the Magic of
This Enchanted Island
and
especially to Mary and Tom Carlin.

Nancy Cobb and Gerry MacCartee
fostered this book.

Chapter I

The Golden Age of Exploration

There is an old, old...legend, that Point Loma, on the southwest corner of the United States, is the oldest part of the earth, and that Coronado Beach, protected by its sheltering arms...was given the first selection of all good things intended for the world.

— From a booklet published in 1902: "Hotel del Coronado"

SPONSORED BY DR. AND MRS. OWEN PECK

IN THE YEAR 1542, after the Golden Age of Exploration had opened in the New World, the vessels of the navigator Juan Rodríguez Cabrillo, sailing under the Spanish flag, anchored in a port he named San Miguel, now called San Diego. In Cabrillo's time, Coronado was a combination of two islands, with a swampy area called the Spanish Bight separating the North Island and the South Island.

> Cabrillo was the first explorer to "discover" San Diego and Coronado in the European sense, and Cabrillo's flagship, the galleon San Salvador, can be seen as the "founding ship" of Coronado and California. She predated the Mayflower, the founding ship of Pilgrim New England, by 80 years. Cabrillo stayed five days, interacted with the local Indians, and thoroughly explored the bay and lands surrounding it, including Coronado. The ship returned a second time–for six days–on its voyage back to Mexico. Coronado and San Miguel Bay soon began to appear on a hundred different Spanish charts of California and the Pacific.

(Image above: Maritime Museum of San Diego)

Undeveloped North Island and Coronado as seen from Point Loma. (Coronado Public Library/Leslie Crawford Collection – CPL/LCC)

There is a long spit coming from the embayment of the Sweetwater and Tijuana rivers. This is the natural sand source; as water is transported north along the Silver Strand the sand is deposited, which makes Coronado technically a peninsula.

On November 8, 1602, Sebastian Vizcaíno, another Spanish explorer, sailed past the four rocky islands approximately seventeen miles from the mainland. He named the four islands "Las Islas Coronadas," symbolizing the "Crowned Four," in honor of four martyred brothers who were canonized as saints by the church in Rome in that calendar date.

When his vessels entered the port to the northeast of Las Islas Coronadas, he called it "San Diego de Alcalá," for St. James of Alcalá–Saint Didacus of the Roman Catholic Church. At some place in the harbor, the crew went ashore in a small boat, "pitched a tent to serve as a church," and gave thanks with a Mass. They found a spring of fresh water at the western end of the North Island. The chronicler was the first to describe this "low, flat land just east of the Channel entrance," and he wrote of the natives, the wild life and the flora.

Vizcaíno's voyage marked the end of an era, because for 167 years no other European stood on the San Diego shoreline.

These sailors, and the conquistadores who traveled inland from Tenochtitlan (Mexico City), sought riches and wealth. Like their ancestors, they had read works such as *Las Sergas de Esplandían*, written by Garcí Rodríguez de Montalvo in 1500, which told of the Amazon Queen, Calafía, who ruled over an idyllic place called "California." These men searched for passageways to the East Indies, for the "Seven Cities of Gold," and "Mountains of Gold."

Vessels from many nations, having taken a circuitous route from Mazatlan to the Philippines, were carried by the Japanese currents back to California and down the coastline, until they reached their point of origin. Legends say that pirate ships, anchored in the sheltered coves of the nearby Las Islas Coronadas, lay in wait for the Manila galleons loaded with treasures from the East. Not until 1769, with the threat of Russian encroachment on North American soil, did the Spanish government awaken to the necessity of occupying the region. In that year, two land expeditions left Loreto in Lower California, and three sea expeditions sailed from San Blas and La Paz, both heading for San Diego, where on July 7, 1769, the first city in California was founded. The incredible loss of men, and the hardships endured by the priests, soldiers and artisans who made those journeys are better painted in a larger portrait of San Diego and California history.

This book can only bring some speculation about early peoples who lived on the island of Coronado. Between 1918 and 1921, Howard O. Welty, principal of University Heights School in San Diego, wrote to Dr. A.L. Kroeber of the University of California that he had made an archaeological survey of Coronado, assisted by Mr. Joseph Jessop. They found temporary Indian campsites and some arrowheads during their search. Shell mounds, left by Indians discarding seafood, were discovered, as well as a number of identified Indian sites scattered along the peninsula. In all, he documented seventeen sites on the bay front, near the ferry landing, and drew sketches and plans. Nels Nelson, a renowned anthropologist who worked for the federal government, also found evidence on the peninsula of man's past in this era.

Unquestionably, the spring at the southwest corner of North Island attracted natives. Author Max Miller, who wrote a number of books, including *I Cover the Waterfront* and *Harbor of the Sun*, noted in the *San Diego Union* (August 7, 1966), "We found the Lost North Island Spring in 1928." [It was filled in with cement by the U.S. Army during World War I.] Miller maintained that the spring had been used by Russian sea otter hunters; thus it became known, perhaps mythologically, as the "Russian Spring."

Since wildlife was a source of dietary needs, the natives snared rabbits, gophers and other varieties of fauna, which ran wild. Adventurers wrote of ducks and many other kinds of birds; they told of wildcats, martens and other animals. They wrote of the abundance of fish, lobsters and other edible sea life. In a historical novel, called *Lewey and I*, written by William H. Thomes in 1846, the author wrote:

> We drifted over to Spanish Bight. The shore was alive with fowl—brant, white geese, curlew waders, millets, dowitchers, and snipe—and a variety that would make an Eastern sportsman crazy. There were quail and doves.

In the early 1930's, Arthur Woodward, an archaeologist, reported finding artifacts on the Silver Strand. It is likely that Diegueño Indians sought out the game, wild berries, roots and greens on the islands, and that they harvested the bonito, flounder and halibut.

In the *Coronado Journal* of October 1, 1964, Colonel Alexander J. Kirby, USN (Ret.), and Dr. Spencer L. Rogers, a San Diego State University archaeologist, wrote: "Recent excavations in front of the Glorietta Bay Motel reveal large deposits of shells left by prehistoric visitors, with the deposits 12 to 15 feet below the present ground level." They referred to them as La Jollan Indians, a name applied by anthropologists, and noted that "...at least 18 different kinds of shells were identified in the mounds as well as turtle shells, sea urchins, crabs, and pine nut shells brought over from the mainland." Kirby wrote, "Old timers said the edges of middens could be seen along the bank before the highway was built, and that the hillside extended to about the middle of the present roadway." Dr. Rogers said that Coronado, even in prehistoric times, must have been a fine place to live.

Kumeyaay Indians traveled to the coast each summer, seeking cooler weather, and the abundant small game, fish and shellfish found there. Dozens of middens (piles of discarded shells) left by the Native-Americans were discovered on Coronado. (Engraving published by Schott, Sorony and Co., 1857)

While Spain's California frontier first began with missions, presidios (walled cities) and pueblos (townsites), California's land and climate also

Mexican Grant.

 Pio Pico, constituted Governor of the Department of California.

WHEREAS, Don Pedro Carillo has laid claim to, for the benefit of himself and family, the land known by the name of the Island or Peninsula in the Port of San Diego, having performed the necessary investigation previously concerning it, making use of the powers conferred on me, in name of the Mexican Nation. I have determined by a Decree of this day to grant him the land designated, declaring him the proprietor of it by the present letters, in conformity with the law of the 18th of August, 1824, and the regulation of the 21st of November, 1828, subject to the approval of the Excellent Departmental Assembly and under the following conditions:

1st. He can fence it without prejudice to the paths, roads or outlets, or rights of way. He shall enjoy it free and exclusively, making use of and cultivating it as best pleases him.

2nd. He shall request of the competent Judge, judicial possession in virtue of this dispatch by which the boundaries shall be marked out.

3rd. The land which is granted to him consists of two square leagues, and is bounded on the north by the Bay of San Diego, which is between it and the town, on the east by the point of land on the Ranch of San Augustin Metijo, on the south by the Ocean and on the west by the Bay, or where vessels anchor. The dispatch will explain the plan.

The Judge that gives possession will have it measured according to law.

Consequently, I order, that, considering the present title, firm and valid, it may be recorded on the proper book and be delivered to the interested party for his security and for any other purpose.

Given in the City of Los Angeles on this common paper for want of the stamped, on the 15th of May, 1846.

Signed: PIO PICO,
                    JOSE MATIAS MORENO.

This superior dispatch is recorded in the proper book.

This superior dispatch is recorded on the page turned or doubled over in
                    MORENO.
the proper book, at the Sub-Prefecture under my charge.
                    JOSE R. ARGUELLO,

Recorded in Book O of Deeds for San Diego County, at page 2.

(The above is a translation as recorded in Book A of Deeds, at page 5.)

ABSTRACTED BY
THE SAN DIEGO TITLE AND ABSTRACT CO.

Translation of the Land Grant from Mexican Governor Pio Pico to Don Pedro Carrillo on May 15, 1846, for "the Island or Peninsula in the Port of San Diego." (Coronado Public Library – CPL)

Looking toward Point Loma with the Spanish Bight and North Island in the upper right side of the picture. Spanish bayonet (commonly known as yucca), sumac, manzanita, other native shrubs were cleared off the land and burned in huge bonfires which could be seen from across the bay. (Coronado Historical Association – CHA)

provided appealing prospects for good farming and ranching. Settlers came, primarily out of Mexico, prepared to start life over again on the new frontier. Rancheros brought cattle and goods overland from Mexico.

Even while California remained under Spanish control, trading and vessels from many countries of the world sought refuge in the harbor. After the year 1830, hide houses were built on the beach across from North Island, on the inner side of Point Loma, by whalers on ships that had sailed out of the harbors of New England.

One account relates that "San Diego Bay was filled with female whales passing between Ballast Point [a spit of land across from North Island] and that thin sliver of sand on North Island that marks the eastern turning point of the harbor...that La Playans [residents on the other side] could not cross the narrow entrance to bring water from 'Russian Springs,' as they sometimes did." As late as the 1840s, San Diego was a favorite spot for female whales during calving season, when scores of them could be seen spouting and basking in the sunlight.

> Shore whaling flourished between the 1850s and 1870s in La Playa on Pt. Loma, and at North Island's Whaler's Bight, and became Coronado's first industry. Whaling companies pursued whales off the coast, during the winter and early spring every year when they migrated south to southern Mexican waters. Whalers from stations in San Diego Bay would intercept these whales, kill them and tow the carcasses back to the bay to render them for whale oil and other products.
>
> In the late 1850s, Whaler's Bight came into use for the repair of ships, but also as a "parking" area for dead whales, awaiting processing at Ballast Point. In 1873, however, the Army evicted the whalers from Ballast Point to begin building a major fort. Whale companies shifted their operations to La Playa and North Island with the Packard Company, while the Wall-Plummer Company set up shop in Whaler's Bight. These operations featured tryworks ovens, dormitory shanties, warehouses, shops and various vats, tubs, and lumber piles. Whaling became Coronado's very first industry. Whaling in Coronado continued until probably 1886, when demand for whale oil plummeted in the face of cheaper petroleum products, and the whale stations were abandoned.

Companies such as the New England, John Company Brothers, and Packard Brothers and Company were among those who built hide houses, and whose hide and tallow business flourished. Boston ships, especially those of the J. Bryant Sturgis Company, brought in groceries, hardware, ploughs, quinine, and dishes, which they traded for hides and furs.

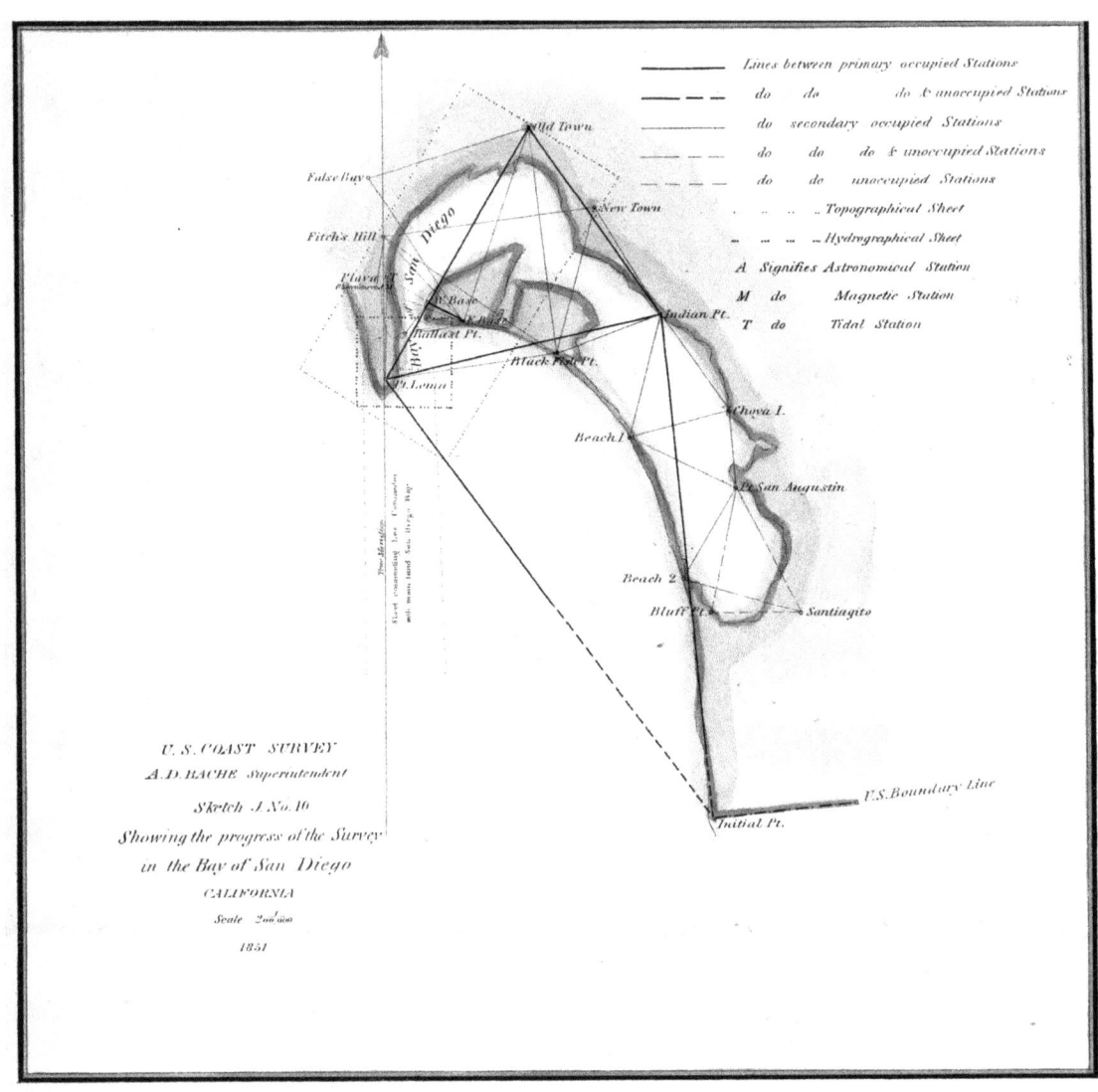

U.S. Coast Survey / A.D. Bache superintendent; sketch J. no. 10 showing the progress of the survey in the Bay of San Diego California, 1851. Probably the first formal map of Coronado in the American era. (CPL).

Between 1810 and 1821, disenchanted peoples in Mexico carried out a revolution against the Spanish Crown. By 1821, Mexico had become an independent republic, and the Governors of Mexican California awarded most of the "Spanish" land grants, large tracts of land previously held by Spain. The grant, which Coronadans are most interested in, came into being at this time.

Pedro C. Carrillo was born in Santa Barbara in 1817. Captain William G. Dana, husband of Josefa Carrillo took Pedro, his nephew, to Boston where he would be able to study for a law degree. When he returned to California, Pedro Carrillo settled in San Diego. He married Josefa Bandini, and was deeded the Coronado peninsula as a "wedding gift" by Governor Pio Pico on May 15, 1846. (Pedro Carrillo and Josefa Bandini would have several children, and were the grandparents of motion picture actor Leo Carrillo.)

Pedro Carrillo and his amigos rode on horseback around the strand, where to the southwest they could see Las Islas Coronadas; as they crossed the Spanish Bight to reach the North Island, they saw the pointed finger of land called Punta Loma. "Symbolically, he pulled up the grass and broke the branches of shrubs on his property. After he had destroyed a small patch of vegetation, Don Pedro turned and threw a stone in each of the four cardinal directions. These acts indicated that for the first time this land was separate from the public domain."

Land surveys had always been required, and Captain Henry Delano Fitch made the map of the Pueblo of San Diego in August 1845. The deed described Coronado as: on the north, the bay or estero of the port of San Diego; between the rancho and the town at the east, the point or end of land of the Rancho San Agustin Melijo; on the south, the Pacific Ocean; and at the west, the anchorage for ships in the channel of the harbor. The deed indicated the size as two square leagues.

In Carrillo's time, the two "islands," North and South, were covered with underbrush, shrubs, sagebrush, reeds, grasses, wild flowers and a few large trees. Under Carrillo's ownership, his cattle and sheep drank the peninsula water from the Russian Spring. One vaquero said that the lemonade berry trees were ten to twenty feet high and that their trunks were eight to fifteen inches thick. Century plants grew in profusion. When North Island was being cleared of brush by the Coronado Beach Company in the late 1880s, the vegetation which remained was stripped from the land.

The year 1846 has been called "The Year of Decision," because so many worldwide historical events occurred in those twelve months. In 1846, in the beginning days of the War with Mexico, the captain of the American sloop-of-war, *Cyane*, anchored in the bay between La Playa and Coronado, and sent sailors and Marines ashore to capture the city. San Diego was one of the focal points of the war because of its harbor and townsite, called Old Town. So began the American era for Coronado.

One of the first Americans to arrive was Bezer Simmons, a native of Woodstock, Vermont, captain of a trading ship. Soon, he and Carrillo struck a deal. On October 20, 1846, the two men signed papers turning North and South Island over to Simmons for $1,000 in silver.

> *[This transaction was undoubtedly connected with the American conquest–perhaps to ensure Simmons' investment in the suddenly-volatile land market. Simmons was familiar with "The Peninsula" from stops in San Diego harbor, and had begun investing during the "buyers market" created as a result of land title disputes between Mexican and American laws. Simmons also bought prime investment property from another Mexican landowner on the shores of San Francisco Bay. At the opening of the California Gold Rush in 1849, Simmons, his wife Laura, and her brother Frederick Billings traveled across the Isthmus of Panama, and along the coast to San Francisco. Shortly afterwards, brother-in-law Billings and lawyer Archibald Peachy joined in partnership with Simmons, purchasing a one-sixteenth interest in "The Peninsula" for $5.00. —ed.]*

A San Francisco law firm formed by Billings, Peachy, and Henry W. Halleck (who would later become a noted Civil War general), managed Bezer Simmons' estate upon his death. Partners in the firm continued to hold title to land of "The Peninsula" (even after the dissolution of the firm in 1861) until 1885, sharing partial investments with others, including James R. Bolton of San

An outing on North Island, showing what most of Coronado and North Island looked like before building began. (CPL)

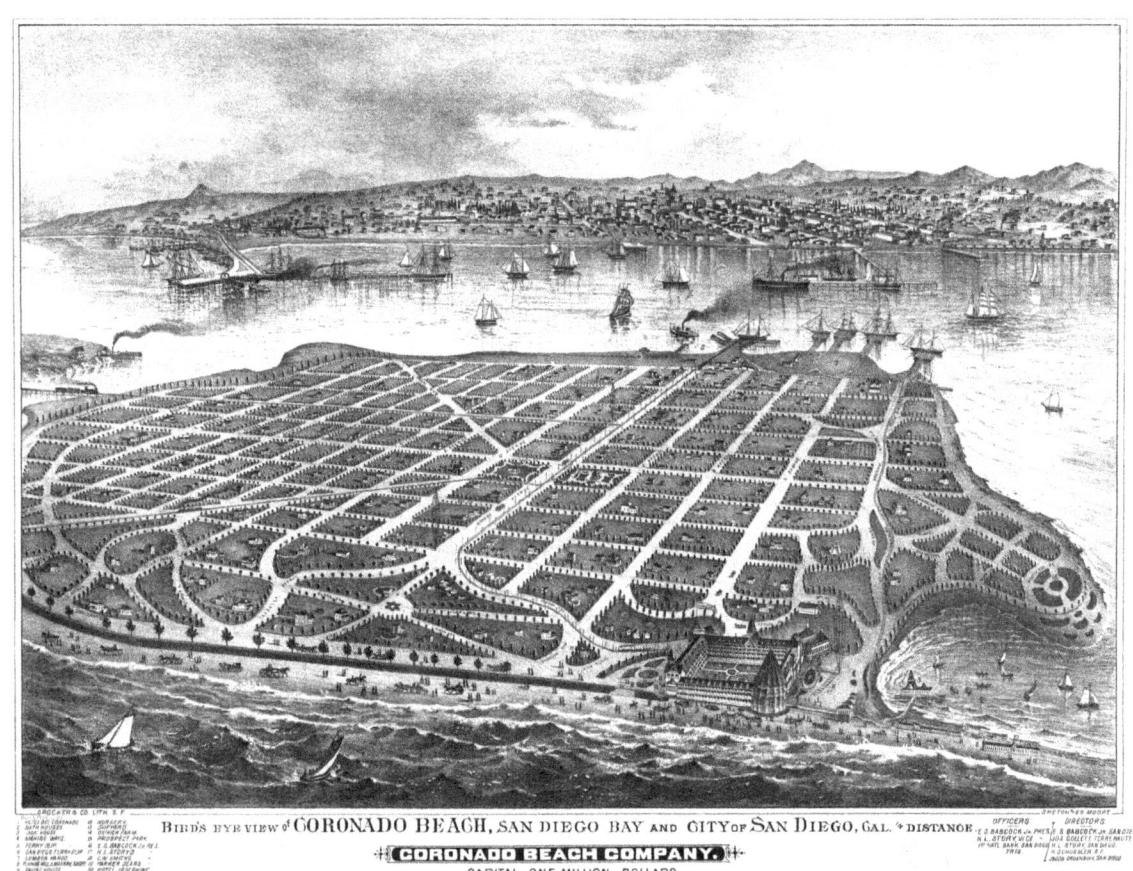

First published map of the proposed new resort, 1886. Over 100,000 copies were printed for distribution. This map was commissioned by the Coronado Beach Company for marketing purposes. The map shows city blocks in the center grid measuring 300 by 500 feet, surrounded by irregularly shaped blocks on the perimeter. The core of the "master planned" community concept that Coronado has enjoyed ever since. (Library of Congress)

Francisco, an investor in land interests including Santa Cruz Island, and millionaire William H. Aspinwall, founder of the Pacific Mail Steamship Company, and the first operator of steam-powered passenger ships up the coast of California.

In 1855, Captain J.C. Bogart, an agent for the Pacific Mail Steamship Company, wanting to experiment with agriculture, leased ground on the peninsula and planted barley and wheat. According to the *San Diego Herald* of November 17, 1855, the experiment was meant to remedy "the evil arising from a dry climate and long-continued drought" in San Diego. A team of men planted the grain before the fall rains, on the theory that the grain would begin growing after the first rain, and would mature in the spring. But lack of rainfall and the inability to irrigate properly caused the experiment to fail.

With portions of the land being sold, the Courts required a plot map be made of the Island, or Peninsula of San Diego; this was done in June and July 1867. That document determined the quantity of land within the boundaries was 4,185.46 acres, or less than one square league. The courts affirmed that the claimants at this time were Peachy and Aspinwall, and that the grant was:

> Lot numbered forty in Township seventeen South of Range three West, Lot Numbered thirty-seven in Township eighteen South of Range three West, and Lot numbered thirty-eight in Township eighteen South of Range two West of the San Bernardino Meridian

The Peninsula was used from time-to-time for various purposes. In 1874, woodcutters leased the land "for the exclusive purpose of removing and selling wood," leaving only the scrub brush and cactus. In the early 80s, Captain Enos Wall set up his iron pots and other gear for a modest whaling station on North Island. In these pots, with a capacity of 150 gallons each, the owner received pieces of butchered whales, and processed oil from the marine mammals.

The fallow land on the islands lay ready for development, but for some twenty years after the survey was finished, little changed except that the value of the land increased.

In 1867, an economic boom hit the region when Alonzo Erastus Horton purchased a considerable amount of land in San Diego and began to sell real estate, especially that at the foot of Fifth Street. That boom caught the ears of Coronado property owners Billings and Aspinwall, who were in New York City in 1872. They had already begun to read "Chamber of Commerce" style pamphlets extolling the climate, opportunities for farming, and healthful atmosphere. They took advantage of those glowing stories to negotiate sale of the peninsula to Charles F. Holly of New York City, a business acquaintance of the two men. Holly paid $110,850 for the land, with a heavy mortgage held by Aspinwall, Peachy and Billings.

> *[The partners foreclosed on Holly's loan after only four years, with Holly losing his investment. George W. Granniss, a managing partner for a San Francisco law firm overseeing ownership, managed the subsequent affairs of the peninsular land for the firm. —ed.]*

Just as lands of "The Peninsula" were being prepared for sale to new investors, a chance letter published by the *San Diego Union* on June 28, 1885, captures the moment with an expansive vision for a new master-planned community and resort: "Do the people know what a magnificent sea-beach lies over across from their city [San Diego]? A great, broad, solid beach of clear white sand, upon which roll phalanx after phalanx of splendid breakers, extending up and down for miles. Some day, when San Diego wakes up, she will discover that mine of wealth and health and pleasure over across "The Peninsula" and, establishing a ferry, people will go over in crowds."

The growth in California during the 1880s was fostered by the coming of the railroads. Cheap and fast transportation attracted the unemployed Easterners, health seekers, real estate promoters, and a variety of merchants and tradespeople. Their arrival sparked an economic boom, fed by

The Silver Strand, 1898. The train tracks extending to the beach were used to carry boulders to and from the jetty that still exists. The large building in the foreground was a short-lived natural history museum; the building behind housed the salt water plunge baths. (CHA)

Key players in Coronado history survey Coronado Beach. The four men on the left side of the photo are from L to R: Elisha Babcock, Harry Titus, Alonzo Horton, and Hampton Story. (CHA)

more rapid transportation of goods and supplies, and an era of unbounded construction. By 1885, Hampton L. Story, Elisha S. Babcock Jr., and Jacob Gruendike, had created a partnership to pursue ownership of the peninsula, and the dream of the Enchanted Island began.

Hampton L. Story left Cambridge, Massachusetts for Chicago, in 1856. There he opened a music store, served in the Union Army during the Civil War, and afterwards, farmed in Kansas. He returned to Chicago, and formed a partnership called the Story and Clark Piano Co. Determined to take life easier, he vacationed in San Diego, where he bought some farm land in the Chollas Valley. By 1885, he had spent half a dozen summers and winters in San Diego. Ready to retire, he gave his son his share of the Chicago business and moved permanently to San Diego.

Here, he met Elisha S. Babcock Jr., a native of Evansville, Indiana. Babcock had joined the Union Army just after graduation from high school, and upon discharge went to work for the Evansville and Terre Haute Railroad. From menial jobs, Babcock worked his way up the ladder, until he and others were in a position to purchase and reorganize the railroad as a syndicate. In 1879, he helped found the Cumberland Telegraph and Telephone Company, a subsidiary of Bell Telephone Company. As its first president, Babcock oversaw the expansion of the company into other states. But he had serious bronchial problems, and needed to spend winters in other places. By 1883-1884 he found his perfect climate in San Diego. Here, Babcock could also pursue his intense interest in fishing and hunting jack rabbits, quail, etc., for which North Island had already become noted. The story goes that during one of his frequent "hunting expeditions," the plan to turn the peninsula into a resort began to be formulated.

Jacob Gruendike had come to San Diego from Oregon, where he had owned a cattle ranch. By 1873, he was known in the county as a rancher and cattle grower. He became involved in plans to bring the Texas and Pacific Railroad to San Diego. By 1886-1887, Gruendike was president of the First National Bank, president of the San Diego Water Company, owner of the Pacific Livery Stable and was involved in the general merchandising business. He was also an organizer of the San Diego Street Car Company, along with Hampton Story, Milton Santee, and R.A. Thomas.

To accomplish their plan to acquire "The Peninsula," Gruendike, Hampton and Story needed to find a suitable go-between, who could negotiate with George W. Granniss to obtain the land. They selected Major Levi Chase, a prominent lawyer who had come to San Diego in 1868. Chase had already proved his mettle by negotiating the purchase of land grants with similar problems. Colonel G. G. Brandt also assisted with the difficult negotiations.

> In 1885, George W. Granniss was faced with these eager investors, when suddenly a second investment syndicate, led by S. R. Johnson of Omaha, surfaced, visited "The Peninsula," and began to arrange funds. This group's vision for a resort hotel on the ocean, and a ferry to connect to the beach, was similar. But their investigation concluded the title was in question, particularly since multiple speculators had a hand in the land at different times, and because there were questions about the Holly foreclosure that had brought Granniss to the forefront of ownership.
>
> In September 1885, in order to solidify title, Granniss filed quit claim deeds from numerous former owners of "The Peninsula" (and their descendants) with the County recorder, conveying to him clean title to the property.

The sale was negotiated, and on November 19, 1885, Gruendike, Babcock and Story bought the entire tract from Granniss for $110,000. There remained one other matter to be resolved. Babcock wanted two of his former Indiana business partners to be a part of the plan to develop "The Peninsula," and invited them to come to San Diego.

Heber Ingle, Babcock's brother-in-law, came from Evansville, Indiana. (His wife was the sister of Mrs. Elisha J. Babcock, Jr.) Ingle took an active part in business and social activities from that time forward. He became the first president of the Cuyamaca Club, and his son, John Gerald, would become a prominent real estate developer. Josephus Collett, of Terre Haute, Indiana, the last major investor, was a railroad stockholder of several western lines as well as a building contractor. He had served as president of the Rose Polytechnic School in Terre Haute. Like his new partners, Collett had considerable wealth for these times. At this juncture, Babcock, Story, and Gruendike sold Ingle and Collett one-fourth of the land in equal shares for $27,500.23.

On April 7, 1886, in the San Diego County Clerk's office, the five proprietors filed articles of incorporation for the Coronado Beach Company. Capital stock was one million dollars. The stage was now set to plan and develop the peninsula in 1886-1887.

1181 — POINT LOMA, SAN DIEGO, CALIFORNIA.

Chapter 2

Planning & Developing the Peninsula 1886-1887

SPONSORED BY MICHEL AND PATRICIA DABBAR

HAMPTON LOVEGROW STORY visualized building the village on the North Island, since it lay near the harbor channel, where visitors would have a terrific view of the entrance to San Diego Bay and Point Loma. The idea was to build a resort on the order of a planned community. In the 1870s, a County surveyor, Myron G. Wheeler, mapped both North and South Islands. However, the syndicate determined that because the "island" was so close to San Diego, a new topographical survey should be carried out on South Island. The new survey would replace the one completed in the 1870s, and would ensure the preciseness of the land ownership. In retrospect the decision proved wise, because upon inspection and borings, an extremely hard bedrock was discovered on the ocean shore. This base would provide an ideal foundation for the proposed hotel; in fact, this was the key factor in deciding to build the hotel on the South Island.

On December 9, 1885, the steam yacht *Della*, with owners H.L. Story as engineer and Elisha S. Babcock as captain, sailed toward Coronado, pulling a barge with forty Chinese laborers aboard, who would begin work on developing the peninsula. The *Della*, named for Story's wife Adella, was a modest 21-foot steam launch. Formerly a sailboat, the *Della* had originally been brought to San Diego by rail, to strictly serve as Story's pleasure craft.

(Image above: CPL / LCC)

Steam launch Adella (or 'Della') was owned by Hampton Story and provided the first scheduled ferry service to Coronado for visitors and workers. Occasionally, it towed a second boat containing additional passengers. (CHA)

Orange Avenue and ferry wharf, 1887. The Oxford Hotel is large building in upper right; the Beach Company building is under construction in upper left. (CPL)

The laborers first built a boarding house for the construction workers, near the place where the *Della* landed at the foot of Orange Avenue. A second building erected nearby became the Coronado Beach Company's superintendent's office. It was later moved, because when the plat map of the island was finished, the building stood in the middle of Orange Avenue! The Chinese workers graded a "driveway" around the island. They planted sixty acres of barley so that hay would be available when the horses arrived. Story and Babcock obtained a machine to which six horses were attached to clear away the smaller brush. The brush they burned made the evening sky glow, letting San Diegans across the bay know the development of the great resort had begun. Large clumps of sumac were left undisturbed, as were the dwarf mahogany (which may have been manzanita) and a form of cactus known as the Spanish bayonet, along with a variety of other native vegetation on the island.

No sooner had the land platting begun, when it became the focus of disagreement between the owners. Babcock wanted straight avenues and streets in a grid pattern like the Benjamin Franklin Plan, while Story wanted an irregular plotting with circular parks, fashioned on the hub of a spoked wheel, as in the Hispanic tradition. The compromise they reached formed the description outlined in a pamphlet called "Coronado Beach" (1886), and a map titled "Coronado Beach and San Diego, California" (1886):

> The outside of the plat would have irregular-shaped blocks and lots, and leave the center regular. The first plan showed three sides of the South 'island,' excluding the side nearest San Diego, with serpentine avenues and streets. The scheme gave a frontage unequalled for effect, displayed in the architecture of the proposed cottages and villas to a far greater advantage than regular blocks. The area along the Spanish Bight, the inlet between North and South "islands," had sharp curves until modified later into one continuous drive. In the center, they designed blocks 300-feet wide and 500-feet long, and marked off rectangular lots, 25 by 140 feet, in each block. An alley, 25 feet wide, subdivided each block to serve the prospective business portion of the resort.

Work on the land progressed, but the turnover in labor became an enormous problem because the economic boom of the period had sparked an unprecedented demand for building skills. Workers moved around constantly from job-to-job looking for better pay. In March 1886, Babcock hired some 50 to 75 local Native Americans, but they didn't last long because everywhere in the San Diego region employment opportunities were excellent. Advertisements for workers appeared in newspapers across the country, even in Babcock's hometown of Evansville, Indiana. Eventually, he contracted with The Seven Companies of San Francisco, a Chinese organization in California that supplied more than a hundred men.

The lack of housing became a problem for such a large labor force; to solve it tents were erected. Men of various nationalities lived together in the first days of development, and the newspaper reported, "It was not an uncommon sight to see a wagon full of men with a black driver, whites, Chinese, and Mexicans riding along laughing and talking with each other in his own way." Many could not speak English. Wages were a dollar per day, and while the men were not organized politically, they knew they were working hard, with long-enough days to justify more pay. On one occasion, workers threatened to quit if they did not get $1.25 a day. The scale is seen when one compares that to the cost of renting a home for $12 a month, or building one for $400 to $600.

In January 1886, with the plats of the island newly completed, only a name was lacking before the map of the fledgling resort was ready for the lithographer. Accordingly, San Diego newspapers announced a naming contest with a $50 prize offered by the owners. Soon a flood of mail brought

Railway track down Orange Avenue, February 1887. (CPL)

such names as Belulah, Belvedere, Brooklyn, Bella Marine, Corona, Estrella, Ingleside Beach, Welcome City, Shining Shore, Campobello, Hiawatha, Serraland, La Frontera and Villamar. Stuart Stanley, a retired British Indian agent, who at one time hoped to become a member of the syndicate, was given the honor of choosing the name. He selected "Miramar," the name given to Maximillian's resort on the Adriatic Sea.

No sooner had the name been announced on January 23, than the public lambasted Stanley, the land owners, and the people who had sent in the ludicrous names. The owners retreated and solved the problem by borrowing the now-anglicized name "Coronado" or "Coronado Beach," from the nearby Mexican Islands, meaning "the Crowned One," which seemed a fitting title for what would become the Crown of Pacific resorts.

Toward the end of January, a nursery was set up on the island and workers began to plant according to the plat scheme. Orange Avenue, 140-feet wide, became the main road and was planted with orange trees. Two diagonal streets, Palm and Olive, cut through the island, were 100-feet wide, and received appropriate vegetation for their names. The main part of the island was divided into alphabetical avenues and numerical streets each 80-feet wide.

Irregular streets were given Spanish names, while the three boulevards were named for their location: Bay, Ocean, and West. In April 1887, four-foot palm trees were set out between the rows of orange trees on Orange Avenue. The orange trees didn't last long because jackrabbits gnawed them down faster than they could grow. Wind and smoke from the trains also disturbed the trees. When the street was graded in 1889, the orange trees were removed; cypress, pines and palms replaced them.

ORIGINAL CORONADO STREET NAMES

Orange, Olive and **Palm Avenues:** for those trees planted there.

Isabella Avenue: for Isabella Babcock, wife of Elisha Babcock, Jr.

Adella Avenue: for Adella Story, wife of Hampton Story.

Ada Place: for Hampton Story's daughter. Later changed to **R.H. Dana Place** for Richard Henry Dana, who first mentioned the peninsula in his book, *Two Years before the Mast* (1837).

Churchill Place: first called Bachelor Row, was renamed for General Mendal Churchill, who built a large home on Block 10 in 1897.

Star Park Circle: named for the original star-shaped floral design planted within the park.

Inez Place: once called Clarita Row, after a friend of Babcock & Story.

Tolita: named for a beautiful Spanish girl, whose father owned some of the Long Beach oil fields.

San Luis Rey: once called Anita Row, after a friend of Babcock and Story.

Bay Boulevard: when it was paved in 1916, it became Glorietta Boulevard.

Marina Avenue: originally named **Glorietta**; to avoid confusion, the name changed to "Marina" when "Bay" was renamed "Glorietta." **Marina** was the name on the waterfront at the San Francisco Exposition, leading the Board of Trustees to think the name appropriate, since that street led to the ocean in Coronado.

Alameda: originally ran into "K" Avenue; because of that fact, on August 23, 1919, citizens petitioned to drop "K" Avenue.

West Boulevard: ran along the west side of the island by the Spanish Bight, from Ocean to First Street, but was the street was eliminated when the race track was built in 1891.

Over the years, there have been petitions from citizens who sought to change the names of Coronado streets to reflect more of the Spanish heritage, but these attempts always failed. For instance on January 7, 1924, First Street was renamed "Cabrillo Esplanade." While that was pleasing to the ear, it created too much confusion by the elimination of a numbered street. The change lasted only a short time. At later dates, other changes were made in street naming:

Olive Lane, in Block 23, is a name given to an alley.

Pendleton Road, an alley, is named for General Joseph H. Pendleton, USMC.

Encino, Adella, Loma and **El Chico** were also such desirable alleys that they were renamed "Lanes."

Among the problems faced by gardeners in the layout of the island were the rabbits, who managed to get to their plants and shrubs almost as soon as they were planted. A lack of water also plagued the builders of the resort. Beginning in 1886, the Coronado Water Company, with Babock and Story as owners, was organized. Water prospectors came onto the island to search for likely spots for artesian wells. One site was selected on Block 141, the highest spot on the island, located between Third and Fourth streets, "F" and "G" Avenues. Steam-powered, well-boring apparatus sank a 12-inch pipe, gradually decreasing to an eight-inch pipe. At 420 feet deep, only brackish water, which rose to within 40 feet of the surface, was found. The $11,000 project was abandoned.

> A trusted supply of water was paramount for the new, master-planned Coronado resort. With none to be found on the Island, Babcock turned to John Gruendike (one of the Coronado Beach Company investors, and owner of the San Diego Water Company) to connect a pipe under the bay to Old Town, in order to tap San Diego River water. Babcock and Gruendike joined together to form the San Diego and Coronado Water Company, which built a second water line down the Strand to service the expected residential development at Coronado Heights. That line was later extended to the Otay River Valley.

Another important planning consideration was transportation: how to get people from one place to another. In late January 1886, laborers received a Victor road grader needed to help clear large clumps of sumac, to make way for a street railway that could carry a 50-seat excursion car and a steam locomotive. Workers constructed streetcar tracks up Orange Avenue, from the wharf landing to the grounds of the proposed hotel, to carry building supplies that were too heavy for mule teams and wagons to transport. One of the problems facing this system was the rise in elevation between Second and Fifth Streets. Laborers eventually leveled this section by literally cutting through the earth, forming embankments, on either side of Orange Avenue, still visible today. When the heavy rails arrived, shipped from England, the first railroad track on the Avenue was completed. That same year, the Coronado Beach Railroad system was incorporated, with $24,000 capital.

The railways constructed for the Coronado Beach Company seemed to be laid down all at once; during 1887, they did virtually lay all these tracks in this order:

> The railroad down Orange Avenue–from the ferry wharf to the Hotel del Coronado site– was finished in February 1887.

> The Belt Line, or Strand Railway, followed the Strand Road south from Coronado before curving around the head of San Diego Bay, leading up to the City of San Diego; that line may have been the most important, in terms of transportation of very heavy supplies.

> The Pomona Avenue line, which connected with the Belt Line railroad near the curve of Glorietta Bay (by the Boat House), was finished in August. A bit later, that line ran to First Street, to the north end of Alameda Boulevard, and then to the Fourth Street trestle bridge leading to North Island.

> The trestle bridge ("cable road") railroad was begun in June. By August, the engineers had finished plans, and on September 6th, R.E. Osgood & Company signed a contract to do the job. This was, in fact, a continuation of the Belt Line Railway, which later became a roadway for motor vehicles at the end of Fourth Street.

On April 16, 1886, the San Diego and Coronado Ferry Company, again headed by Babcock and Story, filed its Articles of Incorporation for sole right to the ferry business from San Diego to Coronado. Hampton Story traveled to San Francisco to order a ferry large enough to handle their increased transportation needs. Thus, construction began. The vessel *Coronado* was built from plans drawn by C. C. Bemis, U.S. Inspector of Steam Vessels.

Meanwhile, the Company allowed their idea for a $300,000 hotel to "leak out," getting help from such noted newspaper moguls as Harrison Gray Otis of the *Los Angeles Daily Times*, who declared, "...the hotel would be the finest thing, not excepting Del Monte at Monterey." Pamphlets were distributed calling attention to the proposed hotel, and promoting the idea that people would come and live permanently around the "inn."

The Coronado Beach Company planned a grand celebration for the 4th of July weekend in 1886, as part of their promotion of the resort. Preparations impressed everyone, as Babcock and Story arranged for a bandstand and seats to be erected for military exercises, speeches, and introductions of dignitaries. The street railway company carried up to 60 people each trip, but some 3,500 people virtually swamped the transportation facilities. In the morning, military exercises held the attention of the crowd; after lunch, sightseers headed for the beach.

Meanwhile, Babcock and Story made ready-to-sell lots on the peninsula, and hired Colonel William H. Holabird as general agent for the Coronado Beach Company. Holabird, a native of Vermont, had served in the Vermont Volunteer Infantry during the American Civil War, as did Hampton Story. He came to San Diego at Story's urging, and is sometimes referred to as the "Father of the Boom," because of the extraordinary skills he showed in advertising Southern California to the rest of the nation.

W.H. Holabird became the organizational man for the publicity that would offer the peninsula land for sale to the public. He carefully laid out a system to provide railroad passengers with colorful reading material about the island. In very short order, he had copies of the property map and literature describing Coronado distributed in nearly every city and town in the United States and Canada and even, it is said, in Europe. He organized excursions, and brought the annual encampment of the "Grand Army of the Republic"—a fraternal organization of Civil War veterans—to Coronado.

The Coronado Railroad transported visitors, with fresh, salty wind in their hair, from the Ferry Landing to the Hotel del Coronado, and also up the Strand from San Diego. (CPL)

By August 10, 1886, Holabird's work began to draw people to the island in numbers. The *Coronado*, the first official village ferryboat, constructed with state-of-the-art technology, docked at the foot of Orange Avenue, waiting to be put into service. Designed to carry 13 horse teams and over 600 people, she was steam-engine powered, had side paddle wheels and a wooden hull. She made her first run on August 19, with Captain Donald R. McDonald.

At a cost of $15,000, ferryboat *Coronado* proved her worth over the years. Between 1886 and 1888, before the railroad was completed around the Strand, she transported hundreds of workmen, wagons, and heavy equipment used in the construction of the town and the Hotel. Retired in 1922, she was sold to a motion-picture company, disguised as a Spanish galleon, blown up, and sunk in the silent film, *Captain Blood*.

At the same time Holabird was spreading the word about the island paradise, the Coronado Beach Company was busy with improvements, including building a dance pavilion and a bandstand to entertain visitors and, hopefully, interest them in buying a lot. The San Diego City Guard Band gave concerts at the beach. A tent, which held 1,500 people, was made available for picnics, celebrations, and religious services. By September, a water system was in place and plants and trees set out were easily irrigated. This impressed visitors as they moved closer to the sales offices.

Organizers and auctioneers of the Pacific Coast Land Bureau, regarded by Coronado Beach Company officials as the premier land development agency, handled the auction. The president of the company, Wendell Easton, set the date of the first land auction for November 13, 1886. Titles to property in Coronado, examined in preparation for this book, indicate that a few lots were sold as early as June and July 1886, but the main auction was designed to sell as much of the property as possible.

Easton put Robert J. Pennell, who had come to San Diego in 1885, in charge as agent for the Land Bureau. Pennell had photographed Coronado in July 1886 for a county exhibit, and knew the property. A shrewd salesman, Pennell did his job well, inviting prospective investors to pick up

Coronado Beach Company stables were located near the bay on lower Orange Ave, next to the Oxford Hotel, 1887. (CHA)

On November 13, 1886, the Coronado Beach Company held a public auction to sell lots on Coronado Beach. More than 6,000 people came to Coronado for the event. A large tent by the beach was erected for the auction, and a free lunch of coffee and sandwiches was served. By the end of the day, 350 lots had sold for a total of $110,000. Maj. Levi Chase, the lawyer who negotiated the purchase of the peninsula for Babcock and Story, bought the first oceanfront lot. (CHA)

a map and examine the property. Each parcel had a red flag, which identified the specific lot and block number.

The day before the auction, Babcock filed an official map of Coronado Beach, North and South Island at the County Recorder's office. When the document was filed, it contained a number of reservations, giving exclusive rights to the Coronado Beach Company: for water, gas, sewer and other pipes, electric telegraph and telephone, other wires or overhead cables or underground of the same; exclusive rights to operate streetcar or railroad lines; to remove shade and other trees along the same; the right to fix and establish grades to alter streets; and finally, all rights to fishing and bathing. Other riparian rights were also granted on their property.

Deeds, once prepared and transferred, could not be changed as to the above restrictions; and each deed contained a clause that forbid making or selling intoxicating liquor. The Coronado Beach Company decided that since there were no law enforcement officers on the island, it would be a more desirable and safer place to live if liquor were prohibited. At the same time, the Women's Christian Temperance Union was being heard everywhere.

However, Coronado Beach did have its liquor. A story, told in strictest confidence by an elderly woman whose stepfather ran the bar for Elisha Babcock, has it that Babcock, as a desperate means of keeping workmen on their jobs, provided them a cold beer after a hard workday; he set up a workman's bar in a building near the Hotel del Coronado (somewhere in the bushes behind the present El Cordova Hotel)!

Meanwhile, Holabird had been touring the East, meeting tour agencies and Chambers of Commerce, distributing literature wherever he could, working especially with ticket agents of railroad lines. When November 13, 1886 arrived, over 6,000 visitors crossed the bay, impressed with the transportation system and improvements made. Water spouted from fountains among the trees along Orange Avenue as visitors moved to the auction site area, somewhere near the present Hotel del Coronado. At 11 a.m. Easton and Pennell moved to the auction block.

Bidding began at $500 and moved up to $1,600. Major Levi Chase bought the first lot on the ocean, near the site of the proposed hotel. Before the day ended, the Land Bureau had sold 350 lots for a total of $110,000. Aside from the auction sales, the Coronado Beach Company and the Land Bureau devised a system going forward to provide a uniform scale of prices. And anyone who would build within six months would get a 25% discount on the price of the lot. In November, an additional $72,000 in sales helped to pay off some of the mortgage still due George W. Granniss.

Elisha S. Babcock, Jr. (CHA)

On December 10, 1886, Postmaster N. Moser opened a temporary office where people could come and pick up their mail. Visitors stayed at the Orange Avenue Hotel, the first place of its kind on the beach, located on the northeast side of Third Street and Orange Avenue. Meals were 25 cents, and lodging was $5.50 to $6.50 per week. Now, with the town laid out and the lots selling, it was time for the next phase of resort development—building the Hotel del Coronado itself.

To design the grand hostelry, Elisha Babcock called on the Reid Brothers, prominent architects in Evansville, Indiana. Babcock had been associated with James William Reid and his brother Merritt in earlier times. When he and the other investors bought the peninsula and determined to build the resort hotel, Babcock wished to put the task into the hands of his trusted architect friends. James was born in 1851, his brother Merritt four years later, in New Brunswick, Canada. While they had established their reputation in the Midwest as talented architects, the Hotel del Coronado, and other buildings in Coronado and San Diego, would lead them to San Francisco by 1905. They achieved world-wide fame there for designing such buildings as the Fairmont Hotel and the Cliff House.

Hampton L. Story (Hotel del Coronado Heritage Department)

Babcock, Story and Herbert Ingle met James Reid at the Santa Fe Depot in San Diego in December 1886. Brother Merritt remained in Evansville and kept their busy practice going. They took James for a ride around the island to let him see what a glorious site it was for a luxury hotel. Anxious to get underway, the three owners told him the building had to start at once; offices were ready and equipped to do the job.

Babcock and Story put the architect to work preparing a description of the peninsula and hotel for a prospectus. The grand hotel would be built around a court... a garden of tropical trees, shrubs and flowers...balconies should look down on this court from every story...

James Reid prepared sketches and from these drew up a lumber order, which he and Ingle took to San Francisco. The idea was to give a full view of the ocean, the bay and the village from the hotel resort. Reid said the structure would cover nearly three times as much ground as the famous Hotel del Monte at Monterey. To speed up the project, all agreed to forego preparing final blueprints, and instead to work from preliminary drawings.

Work was begun on a brick kiln, a planing mill, a metal and repair shop, and a small iron works before the lumber arrived.

Borings were made a few feet down to bedrock that would carry the concrete. By March 12, 1887, work on the foundation had begun. To provide a hard support for the stone foundation, a layer of coarse gravel and cement were spread over the bottom of the excavation. One hundred barrels of cement were used every day, eventually totaling 14,000. A small office was erected for the temporary use of the architects. Workers lived in tents around the jobsite, while the Reid Brothers are said to have built a Victorian bungalow for their own residence at 1111 Loma Avenue.

After James Reid came to Coronado, his younger architect brother Watson E. Reid, and an engineer named Ingersoll, arrived to add their skills to the building of the giant structure. Short of labor and materials, they used apprentice carpenters and laborers as they went along.

On March 19, 1887, the official ground-breaking ceremony took place. Mrs. Babcock, Mrs. Story and Miss Clara Ingle turned the shovels of earth.

The lumber ordered in San Francisco was largely redwood, but included Douglas fir, cedar, hemlock and pine that was cut and shipped from the firm of Dolbeer and Carson. It was floated to Coronado Beach in log rafts, lightered on Glorietta Bay and unloaded near the hotel site, where the wood was planed. The planing mill kept 50-60 woodworkers busy planing and finishing lumber, while the furnace consumed the scraps. At one point, a million feet of lumber was scattered about the grounds, and more arrived all the time. The use of redwood and a complete sprinkling system made the hotel as fireproof as any building in the country at the time. Nonetheless, the foremen were extremely careful and would not let workers smoke.

Near the lumber mill were the machine shops, where iron workers used the newest and most improved machinery. The engine which operated the lathes and band saws in the mill, also worked the forges and hammers in the machine shop.

The Coronado Brick Company, built in late 1886 and owned by the Coronado Beach Company, had its kilns going night and day. Coronado clay was used to provide the building material, not only for the Hotel; large orders were shipped to other cities as well. The company operated near Glorietta Bay, and a small cove nearby became a popular place for swimming and picnics. In time, the Brick Company was turning out 150,000 bricks per day. The Hotel fireplaces and chimneys were made of these bricks, and they were also used in homes built in Coronado during this period.

Over 250 men were employed in all phases of the Hotel construction; seven men alone drafted detailed plans. An emphasis was placed on installing outdoor electric lights so there could be day

"A" Avenue, 1888, looking toward San Diego Bay. Tents provided temporary housing for residents. (CHA)

and night labor shifts. Throughout the construction period, the Hotel had electricity, the current furnished by cable laid on the bottom of the bay. A huge electrical plant was set up at the Hotel, powered by a Corliss engine built in Providence, Rhode Island. After the Hotel and power house were completed, the bay line was abandoned. The Hotel del Coronado provided the entire city with electricity until 1922, when it again turned to San Diego for power.

W.N. Thomas, an electrician with the Mather Electric Company of Chicago, supervised installation of lighting at the Hotel. The Hotel engine room contained five dynamos that ran almost 2,000 interior incandescent lights and 30 exterior arc lights. Twenty-eight wires ran from the engine room to the Hotel's basement under the breakfast room. A fusible plug protected each lamp. The mammoth Hotel could boast that the incandescent electric light plant was the largest local installation of its kind in the world.

> As an area of low-tide mud banks and extreme shallowness, Glorietta Bay was originally named Glorietta Bight. In 1888, the Coronado Beach Company contracted with Bates, Amburg, and McAdams of Chicago to dredge a 10-foot deep channel through Glorietta Bight to a circular turning basin, near the newly built Boathouse. For the first time, this new channel allowed recreational boating to serve the hotel's guests, and would later aid Tent City waterfront development. Soil from dredging was deposited for the future Tent City, and to round the end of the bay.

When that project was finished, the dredger set to work on the Spanish Bight, the shallow body of water separating North and South Island, dredging it to a depth which allowed the lumber vessels to moor there. The sand was utilized to provide boulevards along the shore. A Von Schmidt dredger, which worked on the hydraulic principle, was used. With this machine, mud could be discharged on the bank, or on a lighter (barge), through large iron pipes with ball and socket joints. While the cost of the enormous mud-eater was about $100,000, it assisted greatly in speeding up the process of dredging. In September, the dredger cut the bank near the new ferry boat yard, to ease the launching of vessels being built for the Coronado Beach Company. In the coming year, the Beach Company signed contracts with Bates and Amburg Company of Chicago for the building of an immense dredger, with six times the capacity of the Von Schmidt dredger at the Coronado Ship Yard.

In 1886, the new steam powered, side-paddle ferry Coronado makes its first run. At a cost of $15,000, the ferry could carry 600 people and 13 horse teams. (CPL)

On May 16, 1887, the first issue of the *Coronado Evening Mercury* was printed. For a time, the newspaper offices were located in the basement of the Coronado Beach Company's building at First and Orange; later the owners leased a tent on "J" Avenue, and then a lean-to shack on Orange Avenue near Third Street. Managing Editor Robert William Hornbeck and Business Manager Frederick E.A. Kimball published a very special first edition. (Hornbeck had served his newspaper apprenticeship in Ohio; Kimball learned the trade in New Hampshire, and would later found the *San Diego Evening Tribune*.) By the second week, the paper boasted 500 subscribers, and was delivered on horseback by Hugh Gwynn Foster.

Coronado's first public school was erected in 1887 on the corner of Seventh Street and D Avenue. (CPL)

One architect familiar to early Coronadans was Joseph F. Falkenham, who designed a number of homes on the peninsula during the year 1887, and had an office at Third and "F". He built a home for J.H. Hartupee at 924 "H"; for W.H. Forman at Tenth and "F"; H.G. Dow at 1004 Isabella Avenue (with a stable); for the postmaster J.D. Brownlee at Third and "G"; and for H.S. Ballou, a six-room cottage at the corner of "C" Avenue and Orange Avenue. In May, Falkenham completed plans for George Foster's home at the corner of Sixth and "B". Other builders put up cottages, such as the two for R. R. Campion near Eighth and Orange. These two cottages were later moved to 1109 and 1111 Ninth Street. Some homes were moved across the bay on barges, or moved up the Strand on wagons pulled by horses. Among these, the homes at 54 Tenth Street, and a cottage at 1540 Glorietta Boulevard are still on the peninsula.

Of course, there were still a number of people living in tents on Coronado Beach, either workers or families, waiting for houses to be completed. While advertising continued to mention Coronado's climate and charms, the site was still a place of tents. Tent structures were important to the times.

The first school opened on January 25, 1887, in a tent at Seventh and "D". While the Hotel was being built, Mrs. Emma Garrison operated a big tent restaurant on the Hotel grounds, to serve an enormous number of dirty, tired, hungry and usually lonely men who worked there. (By the time the Hotel began to serve meals, Mrs. Garrison and her son had built a two-story barn on the Silver Strand, and with her herd of milch cows from Santa Paula, California, ran Coronado's first dairy farm, providing islanders with fresh milk.) Mrs. Garrison didn't operate the only restaurant. D.C. Fox served meals at his Coronado Restaurant, also situated in a tent, located near the present-day El Cordova Hotel. He asked people to provide newspapers and magazines and, by June 1887, also had Coronado's first "Reading Room" lit by electricity. He was known to have served wine to his most avid readers.

The first mail delivery to islanders proved frustrating, because it came by horse-drawn cart. By February 1887, a post office was opened in the corner of a store J.A. Mathewson had rented for his grocery business, near Third and Orange. But on June 4th, 1887, Uncle Sam gave Coronado Beach a post office. The local paper reported, "There are a thousand people who receive a hundred letters a day and many pounds of printed matter." Since homes and businesses had no street addresses for some time, mail had to be picked up at the Post Office. The first postmaster, N. Moser, resigned within a month. He was followed by Jonathan D. Brownlee, who resigned in December 1887.

Townspeople lacked entertainment; dances at the pavilion near the hotel construction site were their only outlet. They wanted a place to meet, dance and encourage social life, so a "Hall Group" met in May 1887, and proposed putting up shares of stock for a two-story building. The committee asked Joseph Falkenham to prepare plans, but the money could not be raised. Since they would not be using it, Coronado Beach Company officials asked if the Hall Group would like to contribute to have the 50 x 80-foot floor on the second story of its new building at First and Orange, finished for a public meeting hall,. James Reid calculated the costs, including making the second story fire-proof and capable of carrying the weight of many people. By November, Coronado had its new meeting place, and most town events were held there until the Hotel's combination theater and ballroom opened. The town newspaper was printed in the basement of the building; the third floor was leased as a first-class rooming house, christened the "Bay View House."

In May, a site was located for a marine railway and dry dock on the northeast shore at North Island. The Marine Ways was financed by William Wallace Stewart of San Diego, and designed to take a 1,000 ton vessel for repairs. In time, the Ways would be sold to John D. Spreckels, whose clientele owned every conceivable kind of vessel.

Coronado's first telephone was connected by line construction around the Strand. In early May of 1887, lines were brought to the Spanish Bight and the Marine Ways. Around the same time, the first submarine transbay cable was laid between San Diego and Coronado, which furnished service through the San Diego exchange.

Among the first ventures at the Marine Ways (the Coronado Iron Works) was the construction of a ferry, named *Silver Gate*, in 1888. Christian Telson, a ship builder from Babcock's hometown of Evansville, Indiana, was chosen to oversee its design. He had worked at the Navy Yard in Portsmouth, Virginia, and his last job had been to scuttle the USS *Merrimac*, to prevent her from falling into enemy hands. Telson was taken as a prisoner of war, and promptly put to work raising the sunken vessel. He then had the job of converting her to the CSS *Virginia*.

In August, 20 ships' carpenters arrived from Chicago and St. Louis to work on the ferry. The machine foundry, located near the ship yard on the waterfront of the island, on the bayside, provided the metal work for the ferry. Due to delays, the *Silver Gate* was not launched until April Fools' Day 1888–seemingly an appropriate date! Reporters swore the vessel was jinxed from the start. She was extremely slow responding to the helm, and rammed into the pilings at the slip while trying to dock, knocking passengers to the deck. Coronado's maritime writer, Jerry MacMullen, blamed the ferry's problems on the genius who had tried to improve the blueprints. She was decommissioned two years later, a failure.

Toward the end of the year, the Beach Company reported it had prepared plans for a commodious ferry house, with a large waiting room and ticket offices. Passengers would board the ferry's upper deck by means of a bridge.

Coronado was a favorite place for swimming and bathing, especially during the summer months. Boats and trains carrying visitors were filled to capacity on every trip. People rented bathing suits and used tent showers to wash off the salt water. A yachting fraternity, a forerunner of the present day Coronado Yacht Club, began late in 1887, and was called the "Coronado Boating Club." Its members sailed Glorietta Bay in their shallow-draft "swan boats." The "Glorietta Silver Band" formed with 14 pieces; the band instruments belonged to the City, paid for by subscription. On Sundays, the men performed at different places around the island. Much of the entertainment took place at the pavilion, although concerts, games, suppers, and other gatherings took place at the Town Hall.

The "Glorietta Club," a social organization, was formed, "By Invitation Only." As a rebuttal to that group, a "Good Time Club" was organized for anyone who wanted to have fun!

The "Coronado Lyceum," a discussion group, met in the school tent for a while, and then moved to the pavilion. The first subject debated was the question of "prohibition," which took two evenings. The "Ladies Mutual Escort Association" was formed by young ladies in town. The *Mercury* was asked to publicize that the organization was for women only. Men could deliver ladies to the meeting and take them home afterward, but they were excluded from what occurred inside.

Such sedate recreation was not all that went on in those early days, however. For example, in November, two friends, Tom Wing and Ah Gow, who worked at Coronado Beach, had a grudge

Left: The ferry wharf and station were under construction in 1888. (CPL)

Right: Ferry house completed, 1888. The ferry 'Silver Gate' is visible to the left, the ferry 'Benicia' to the right. The Coronado Beach Railroad provided transportation from the ferry landing to the hotel grounds. (CHA)

Ferry 'Coronado' sailing to San Diego. Ferry 'Silver Gate' is at the dock. (CPL)

over a gambling game. At 10 pm on November 15, 1887, Ah Gow was near the First Street lumber yard when he was felled by a blow and knocked unconscious. Tom Wing did the job with the flat of a shovel behind Gow's right ear. Frightened by what he had done, Wing sought help. He and a friend dragged Gow to the bay and took him by boat to the Stingaree District, the redlight district of San Diego. Gow recovered from his scalp wound, and Wing apologized by paying him the gambling debt he owed.

Land sales boomed during the summer months of 1887, and the Coronado Beach Company gave price reductions of 20% to those who could buy a lot and build a home before September 15. The Beach Company, which even loaned money (charging interest), preferred to keep speculators out, with the land settled as a place for people to live. Among the promotional inducements were free ferry rides for prospects; free railroad excursions from Los Angeles and San Francisco; and a tour by horse and carriage around the island for potential clients. As the lots sold, some were bought by real estate companies; some individuals bought lots and then sold them to such companies. Real estate branch offices included the B.L. Muir & Company near Star Park; Woolwine, Spring & Nerney at Orange and "B"; and Ross & Dow at the head of Orange Avenue.

The Victorian boathouse in Glorietta Bay, completed in July 1887, provided on-the-job training for unskilled laborers at the Hotel. Soon after, a bathhouse was connected to the boathouse, providing a simple row of dressing rooms heated by machinery. People could rent bathing suits for 35 cents. There were floats and ropes for protection of the swimmers.

Built in the same Victorian style as the future hotel, the boathouse, Coronado's oldest landmark, was completed in July 1887. (CHA)

Down by the ferry landing, a great deal of activity was also taking place. The shipyard, ferry landing and streetcar lines served as a focal point for everything and everyone who came to the island. In July 1887, the Oxford Hotel was built at First and Orange by Ben S. Miller, a retired cattleman from the Indian Territory. At street level were a barber shop and a drugstore. G.W. Peters managed a livery stable known as the Circle Bar Stable. In 1912, the Oxford would be moved near the Hotel del Coronado, be redesigned by John D. Spreckels' architect Eugene Hoffman, and serve as living quarters for female workers at the Hotel del Coronado. In 1983, through preservation efforts of M. Larry Lawrence, the Hotel del Coronado Corporation moved the Oxford to the Hotel Del grounds, where it was integrated into an office building.

Hotel Josephine, designed by the famed Reid brothers and built in 1887, was located between Third and Fourth Streets on Orange Avenue. After Coronado was incorporated as a city in 1890, the new city's board of trustees held its first meetings here. The building was torn down in 1915. (CHA)

By July 1887, Miller also broke ground for the Hotel Josephine on Orange Avenue, between Third and Fourth Streets. The three-story, Eastlake-style building, designed by James Reid, had offices, stores and some 65 sleeping rooms.

> *[From Josephine's tops floors, one could look toward Point Loma with unobstructed views or peer down on ferries coming and going. To differentiate itself from the Hotel Del, Josephine advertised its value as a "First Class Family Hotel." Businessmen, house builders, and long-term residents were just as likely to be seen on Josephine's wide and comfortable verandas as vacationers. Competition with the Hotel Del caused the Josephine to be sold in 1901 to Mr. and Mrs. A. L. Reed, who renovated and renamed it Hotel Iturbide (after a palace in Mexico City and a famous hotel in Ensenada). The hotel ultimately went bankrupt in 1908, and for a year in 1909 briefly held the California Military Institute (school) for boys. The building was torn down in 1915 after a fire, with its salvageable wood, siding and fixtures distributed among an expanding community.—ed.]*

Another of the earliest hotels built in this period was a tall narrow wooden building with Victorian trim, called the Nadeau House. Architect J.F. Nadeau and his real estate partner designed and built the three-story frame building on the east side of Orange Avenue, near the corner of Second or Third Streets, at a cost of $6,000. By November, a two-story addition was made to the rear. A year later a fire nearly destroyed the building, but Nadeau rebuilt it. The Coronado Beach Company eventually acquired and moved it to Ynez Place, where it was used as a rooming house for male workers at the Hotel. In 1912, it was demolished to make way for a parking lot for Coronado's Post Office.

Dr. Wiltschek also built a hotel on Orange Avenue, between Fifth and Sixth Streets, near the middle of the block, utilizing G. Van Swansenberg & Company as architects. The hotel, named Wilhelmina House, probably for Queen Wilhelmina I of the Netherlands, was a three-story building which cost $5,000. It offered "special diets for the infirm" and "home cooking," although it was open to anyone. It was later moved to 1323 Orange Avenue.

During 1887, the Coronado Beach Company tried to work out a financial arrangement with people owning property along Orange Avenue, to grade and pave the streets because of the dust. The Company couldn't shoulder the costs alone, so wooden plank sidewalks were built from First to Fourth on Orange, as an alternative. By October the Company had used 37,000 feet of plank for sidewalks three-feet wide. (According to Kenneth W. Bandel, when these boardwalks were later replaced with cement, townspeople used the boards to build fences.) As a result, Orange Avenue was not completely paved until 1912; in the interim, more street lights were added, and, to help hold down the dust, shrubbery was planted down the center strip.

On July 8, 1887, John D. Spreckels, who founded a company of shipping and commission merchants that operated vessels between San Francisco and Hawaii, arrived in San Diego on board his yacht, the *Lurline*. The son of Claus Spreckels, the "Sugar King" of Hawaii and San Francisco, John D., and his brother Adolph, formed a partnership known as the Spreckels Brothers Commercial Company.

Buildings were being built quickly to accommodate businesses and employees of the Coronado Beach Company. City blocks were becoming defined, though paths across empty lots are still visible. The nursery in the lower left was owned by the Beach Company and provided plants and food for the guests at the Hotel del Coronado. (CHA)

By mid-1887, the entire country had begun to feel the results of a worldwide depression. The construction business, which brought many people to this area, fell apart. Banks folded and some businesses closed their doors. Babcock had thought monies from the land sales would be enough to complete the Hotel and carry out its operations. Unfortunately, many of the purchasers could not meet their obligations. Babcock's letters revealed his financial predicament. He frequently wrote to Spreckels, stating the problems and asking for help. Babcock had become acquainted with Spreckels, since his ships had carried cement and other supplies and goods to Coronado. Although one might have the impression that Spreckels later appeared suddenly in San Diego, instead it seems that Spreckels lent Babcock money when he first came to Coronado Beach in 1887, and may have come purposely to do so. Spreckels even purchased seven lots along Ocean Boulevard for himself and his brothers, at a total cost of $24,000.

In mid-August 1887, the *Coronado Evening Mercury* published a list of hundreds of purchasers of Coronado Beach lots, including the names of the states and cities in which they lived. Many of these names would become well-known in Coronado later on. As they came to look at their properties, visitors always managed to find the three nurseries then located on the island. The Beach Company Nursery, also called the "Botanical Gardens," was managed by Superintendent Edgar Sharp, "who possessed an encyclopedial (sic.) knowledge of the botanical world." Fred W. Koeppen, a native of Germany, took over the nursery and built a cottage on the grounds to be near his work. One section was devoted entirely to growing palm trees, with over 30 varieties from all over the world; one for edible plants and other species, which produced fibers and leaves for the making of furniture, baskets, and Panama hats. Across the road from the Botanical Garden, on "D" Avenue, was a large flower garden owned by the Beach Company, where roses and other flowers were cultivated, primarily for the Hotel del Coronado.

The S.G. Blaisdell & Son Nursery, later with Kate Sessions, located between Second and Third, "B" and "C," advertised bedding plants and ornamental and shade trees, including 7,000 camphor, cypress, pine, and eucalyptus trees. J.C. Bailey's Place, the third nursery, took up all of Block 117, which was bordered by Fourth and Fifth Streets, "A" and Pomona Avenues. Bailey, the son of a missionary minister, was born and raised in the Sandwich [Hawaiian] Islands. He was educated in the States and brought his four sons to Coronado in 1886. He introduced many plants and trees from foreign countries, and cultivated over 600 banana trees and 90 coconut palms which he sold to the Beach company.

Pioneer horticulturist Kate Sessions, later called "The Mother of Balboa Park" for her early landscaping efforts in that reserve, loved Coronado. In 1884, she spent her first Thanksgiving in San Diego enjoying a picnic with friends on a Coronado beach. In November 1886, she attended the Coronado Beach Company lot sale, purchasing 32 lots with business partner S.G. Blaisdell (see above). Although the partnership was shortly dissolved, she retained her property (13 lots) near the ferry landing, building her first nursery and living on the island for a time. She was quite involved in landscaping of the Hotel Del. By 1889, Kate was managing the Hotel's botanical gardens, creating huge flower arrangements for the Hotel's public spaces, and selling flowers from a quaint vine-covered lathhouse in the courtyard. During the same period, she was managing a flower shop in downtown San Diego and a nursery in Balboa Park. The time spent crossing back and forth on the ferry became an issue, so she gradually sold her interests in Coronado to focus on her San Diego businesses. She remained friends with many people on the island, including John D. Spreckels who gave her a life-long pass on his San Diego Electric Railway Company.(CHA)

In addition to its nursery, the Coronado Beach Company also owned a vegetable garden that occupied the whole block bordered by "E" and "F," Sixth and Seventh, later known as "Cutler Field." Fresh vegetables, fruits, and melons were grown here for the Hotel's use.

Since no house numbers had been put up yet, when anyone asked where someone lived, they were given the block number. These same visitors were amazed at the amount of home construction going on, beginning in September 1887. Prices ranged from $3,000 to $5,000, dependent upon the location and size of the house. The Coronado newspaper carried an advertisement for the "California Model Cottage," prefabricated houses made of redwood, finished and packed together, so all a buyer had to do was provide paint, nails, and labor.

The architects who had come to Southern California in the 1880s, brought their plans and ideas with them from the East and Midwest, and built Victorian, Eastlake, and Craftsman-style homes, many which can still be found in Coronado today.

The Coronado Beach Company took advantage of Admission Day in 1887, to stage another extravaganza for potential property buyers. An aeronaut, Professor Emil Melville, was hired to make a balloon ascent to a height of 250 feet, where he would perform acrobatic feats. Without warning, the balloon descended into Glorietta Bay, and Melville, who had taken the precaution to wear a life preserver, came down in knee-deep mud to be rescued by onlookers!

Work meanwhile continued on the grand hostelry. Plans called for two, three, four and five story sections, decorative towers, bay windows, and dormers around the courtyard. Edward H. Davis, one of the draftsmen, said, "...the hotel never did seem to stop growing...it was amazing how many rooms were not even shown on the original plans."

By September 1887, teams of men were excavating a tunnel to connect the Hotel with the power house and the laundry. The 200-foot tunnel, which still exists today, provided routing for water, steam, gas, and electrical lines. Bricklayers, meanwhile, finished the cupular chimney for the two Hazeltine boilers in the laundry. Visitors were taken on tours through the tunnel to the ice house, to watch the making of artificial ice. In time, so much ice was being produced that it was sold elsewhere in the County to enable shipment of fruits, vegetables and perishable products.

When visitors came across the bay to Coronado, they rode in a trolley up the middle of Orange Avenue, glimpsing the Hotel del Coronado in the distance. (CPL/LCC)

Men at the planing mills continued to turn out woodwork for the Hotel, including 3,100 window frames and doors. Meanwhile, artists were at work preparing frescos on certain walls of the private dining, sitting, and parlor rooms. Eighty rail cars of furniture were shipped to the Hotel from New York, Utica, Detroit, Grand Rapids, Indianapolis, and Chicago. As areas of the Hotel were finished, decorators went to work following the plans for furnishing.

The Coronado Beach Company set November 11, 1887, as the anniversary celebration of its founding, even though the 13th represented the actual date of the original auction. November 13, 1887 fell on a Sunday, and no one felt it socially acceptable to have celebrations on the Sabbath. So on the 11th, 600 guests assembled at the Coronado Beach Company Public Hall at First and Orange. There were the usual speeches, followed by music provided by the Phoenix Military Band. Guests then took the streetcar line to the pavilion for a raffle, socializing and refreshments. At 11 p.m. the crowd returned to the Company's reception room, where 100 couples danced the hours away.

The Hotel was nearing completion, and it became apparent in November that staff to coddle and serve the guests would soon be needed. Manager John B. Seghers hired 100 of his old Chicago employees; another 150 came from Boston, New York and Philadelphia. They were quartered at the Hotel Josephine, with a chance to begin a new life in California. The first dinner for the staff was cooked at the Hotel on December 7, 1887; the next evening the new employees had a big dance at the pavilion to become better acquainted.

On the 1st of December 1887, a Pacific storm brought wind and heavy rains, which raised havoc with tents and temporary shanties. Mrs. Garrison's cooking tent at the pavilion flew off in rags, and the tent at Mr. Campbell's Ostrich Farm came down. By mid-month, however, a light rainstorm cleared the air and Coronado Beach was covered with slender blades of grass intermingled with lovely wild flowers. A reporter commented on the number of people who came by boat from San Diego, to see and gather them. The flowers were so plentiful that school children were taken to North Island for nature study classes.

On December 25th, Manager Seghers served the first Christmas dinner at the Hotel del Coronado. The Hotel had not yet opened to the public, but this was a special occasion for some 25 people. Among those present were Mr. and Mrs. Hampton L. Story, Mr. and Mrs. Elisha S. Babcock Jr., Dr. and Mrs. Clark, and architect James Reid. By the end of the year, workers were clearing the grounds and the beach of scrap building material and debris, so lawns could be planted. The owners gave thanks to the workers, and looked optimistically toward 1888, and the opening of the Hotel del Coronado. The island resort, at the end of its first full year, had grown considerably and seemed destined to fulfill its promise of paradise.

Hôtel del Coronado, Calif.

Chapter 3

The Promise Fulfilled: The Hotel del Coronado – 1888

SPONSORED BY MICHEL AND PATRICIA DABBAR

BY 1888, CORONADO appeared to be on its way toward becoming a quaint resort town, although Elisha Babcock and the Coronado Beach Company had, in their eagerness to develop the island, encouraged industries without regard for long-range consequences. The planing mill, lumber yard, brick kiln, and shipyard all worked to full capacity. The new railroad connections around the Strand, combined with the building boom, assured that other factories and foundries would come. Babcock encouraged them, stubbornly holding to the idea that in order to get people to settle on the island, they would have to have employment. Kate Field, a noted authoress and lecturer of her day, spoke out against that idea, saying of Coronado: "You have a little gem here – a beautiful place – but I don't like the notion of foundries, factories, machine shops, and oil refineries coming here."

In addition, North Island, had the Marine Railway and Drydock Company, and an oil refinery. The Marine Ways had been established by William Wallace Stewart and Capt. William Bell in 1888, as San Diego's first shipyard. The shipyard featured rails leading down into the water, a powerful steam engine and a huge hauling chair, where ships in need of repair could be drawn up onto the land to be worked upon. The Spreckels Brothers soon bought the enterprise, and Spreckels ferries (and his yachts) were constant customers. The Marine Ways stood until the end of World War I, when the Navy built their first carrier pier on that site.

(Image above: CPL / LCC)

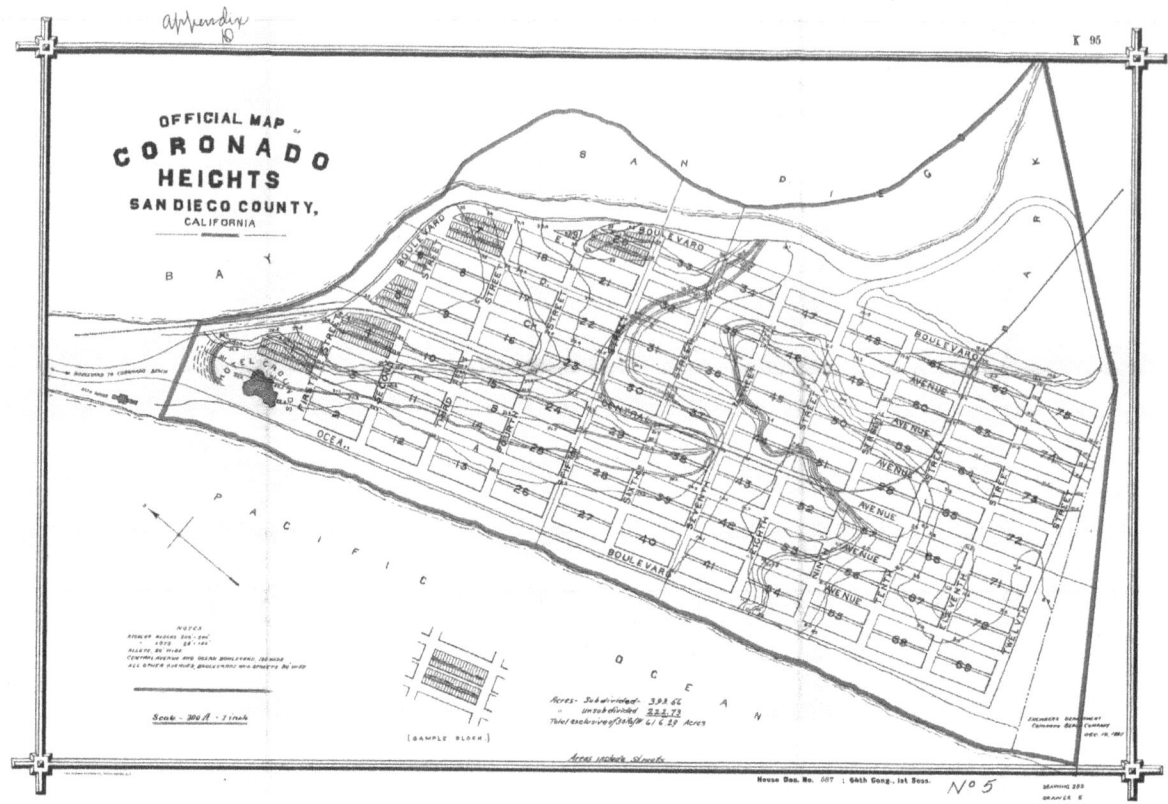

Coronado Beach Company tried to develop another small community called Coronado Heights, located at the southern end of the strand, just south of present-day Coronado Cays. Lots sold briskly, but an economic depression settled in and the project never got off the ground. The property is now only accessible to U.S. Navy personnel who use the land for training purposes. (CPL/LCC)

Still, the plan was to eventually also divide North Island into lots for residential development. By January 1888, a fine lithograph map was completed, looking very much like the street layout of Coronado Beach. A graded drive was completed along the bluff, which overlooked the beach across from Point Loma. By summer, builders Judd and Jackson secured a contract to build a "Swiss-type house with a broad veranda around the structure" for Superintendent William Bell of the Marine Ways.

At the same time, an undeveloped area at the southern end of the peninsula, where the Strand widens, had been acquired by the Coronado Beach Company and named Coronado Heights. A community similar to Coronado Beach was planned, and by the end of 1887, the land was subdivided into lots. Since water hadn't been located, a water main piped the liquid from Coronado down the Strand, to the proposed new village. Hampton L. Story personally supervised the tree planting, overseeing placement of 1,000 pepper, cypress, and eucalyptus trees grown at the Coronado Beach nursery.

The Coronado Beach Company made plans for auction sales of the Heights property. However, the sale was held up until the railroad and a driving road could be built to provide better transportation than the small wharf that existed on the bay side. Over a hundred railroad workmen of various nationalities lived in tents at the Heights. Proof of Company optimism lay in the opening of a post office and a small railroad station there.

The railroad from Coronado Heights to Coronado was completed during the 1887 Christmas season, and advertising for the auction began. Special train excursions ran from Los Angeles and San Francisco for the event. On December 31, 1887, a record 11,000 people arrived by various means at the site. John B. Seghers, manager of the Hotel del Coronado, provided a free luncheon set up under a large tent. As the newspaper in Coronado went to press, it reported sales totaling

$150,000. The auction then continued after dark in the theater room of the Hotel del Coronado until 7 p.m. when sales reached $181,550. Lots were disposed of at reasonable prices, because the Company was anxious for the Heights to develop. Not a single mishap occurred; even the weather, which had been stormy a few days before was nice.

But at the end of 1887, a nationwide Depression hit San Diego, which had a population of nearly 40,000 people. The economic boom had brought street car lines, gas, electricity, telephones, financial institutions, large mercantile establishments, good hotels, fine churches, schools, and culture. Yet the bubble still burst. Thousands of parcels of land were abandoned by their owners, many of whom had only made small down payments. When taxes were not paid, the property was sold at auction by the sheriff. The bust marked the end of Coronado Heights and North Island as residential sites, neither of which really got off the ground before the hard times hit.

> It was during this time that one of the most brilliant and interesting marketing schemes in Coronado history took place. But it was also a scam. With the depression impacting the number of hotel visitors and sales of residential lots in Coronado (which the Coronado Beach Company was depending on to pay off its loans), Elisha Babcock began to promote the quality and medicinal value of Otay Valley well water that his Coronado Water Company was having pumped through pipes to serve Coronado and its hotel. The model he followed was that of Waukesha, Wisconsin, famed for its mineral spring water that attracted flocks of tourists to that small resort town. Babcock's water soon became known as "Coronado Waukesha Water."

Babcock erected a big, barn-like structure on Coronado Heights, and opened the Coronado Waukesha Water and Bottling Works. The "miraculous cure" water was pumped in from pipes already laid across the bay. It bubbled up into a cement vat in a very impressive manner, and for a time the enterprise kept him busy, but with little profit.

> Through an avalanche of advertisements, Babcock stimulated intense interest in this specialty water, especially in its medicinal qualities. Babcock began shipping the water (for a profit) to Los Angeles and San Francisco, and built a new ice house on the grounds of the Hotel Del, to provide ice cubes of Coronado Waukesha Water for Hotel guests. It was all a wonderful venture that substantively lifted the reputation and aura of exclusivity, for both the young community of Coronado and the Hotel Del. It was also mostly a clever deception, as the

Pavilion(s) overlooking beach were used to 'sell people' on the project during construction. At the site of their proposed hotel, Babcock and Story built a large pavilion with windows on the west side for protection from the wind, allowing visitors to view the site in comfort. (CHA)

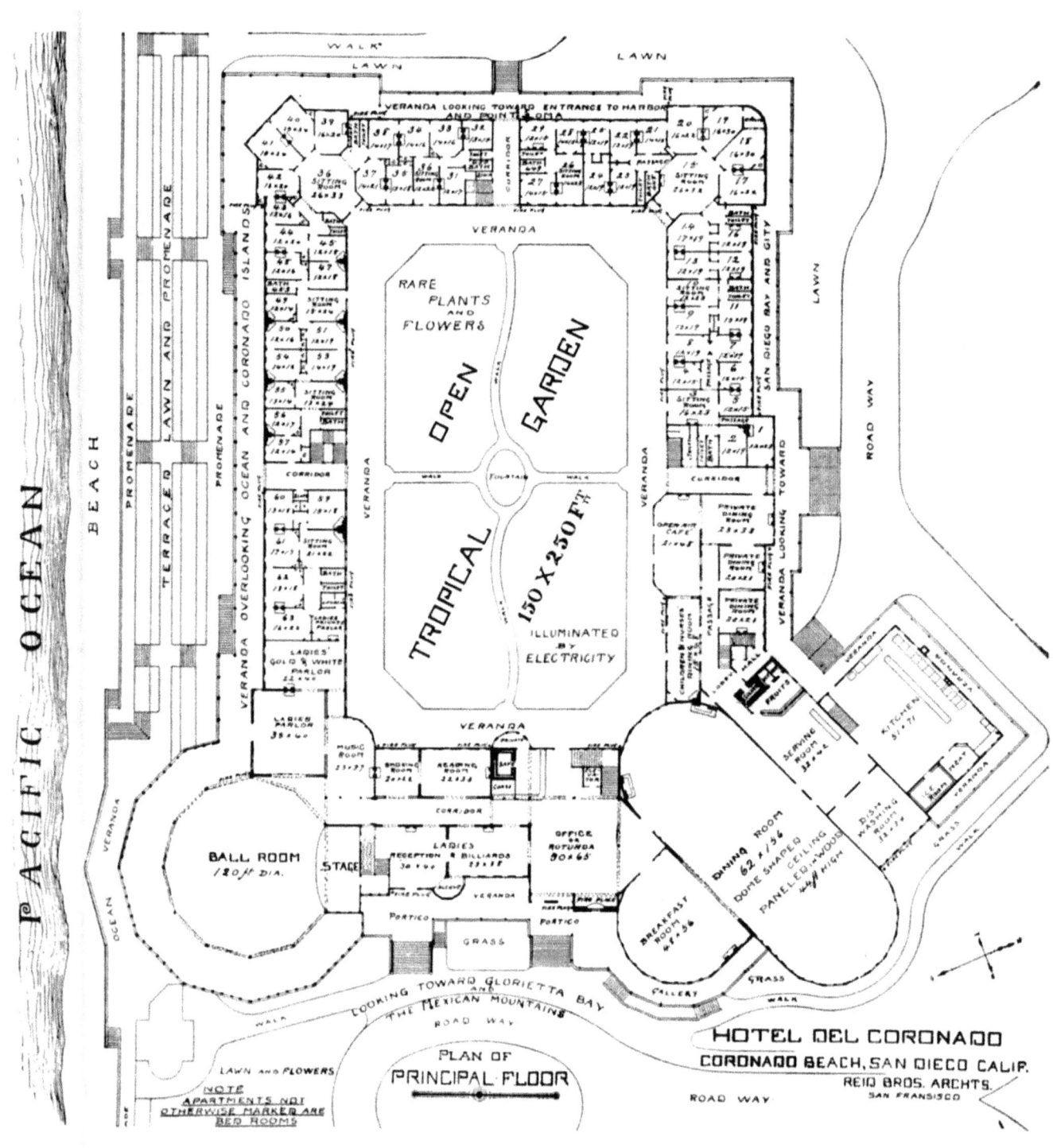

Plan of the Main Floor of the Hotel Del Coronado, Reid Brothers, Architects. (CPL)

water was mainly just plain utility water. Coronado Waukesha Water labeling ended in mid-1890, once John D. Spreckels and his brother gained controlling interest in the Coronado Beach Company.

The economic crunch may have been the reason the Coronado *Daily Mercury* became a weekly. In August 1888, the paper credited the financial wizardry of Babcock and Story for preventing the community from suffering the woes of the Depression. They also reported that Coronado was still on the move. The planing mill had added an evening shift, and the machine shop ran day and night. J.J. Lutz and F. Hahn, who had begun foundry operations on January 11th, made sewer tops and manhole covers for the City of San Diego, and gratings for the ferry gates. M.R. Vanderkloot's Coronado Foundry and Machine Company also prospered, at the junction of Second and Soledad Place. Vanderkloot, born in the Netherlands in 1860, learned the business with his parents in Chicago.

San Diego and Coronado Ferry Company ferry, "Benicia," served passengers from July of 1888 until July of 1903, when she was replaced. (CPL)

The Coronado Milling Company filed papers of incorporation in mid-January 1888, to manufacture and sell flour, corn meal, milling material and general products. In the same month some 450 tons of bituminous rock were unloaded at the Coronado wharf by the Bituminous Rock and Paving Company of Coronado. The material was used for paving purposes. Twenty-five men paved the walks and streets near the ferry slips and on the grounds of the Hotel del Coronado, at a cost of $150,000. The sidetrack for the Belt Line Railroad, south of the Hotel del Coronado, was completed near the Hotel laundry, and opened in January 1888. The railroad carried 780 people daily almost from the start. This sidetrack enabled Coronado visitors, especially railroad and banking tycoons, to come to Coronado in their private rail cars, towed by the local train. George Mortimer Pullman, president of the Pullman Palace Car Company, arrived at the hotel in a private car. Once a car arrived, it could be shunted off to the sidetrack rails to await the owner's departure.

The huge dredger continued to employ a full workforce of men to deepen Glorietta Bay. Part of the bay shore, close to the Boathouse was filled in to provide a good road bed for Pomona Avenue. On one occasion, the dredger got caught under the edge of the Boathouse and almost lifted it up. The plan called for a bulkhead all around the area and to dredge out the shallow Glorietta Bay water, allowing a craft to sail directly up to something resembling a quay wall. Too many "experts" complained, however, that the moving around of the sand and clay would eventually ruin the entire bay, so the plan was halted for a time. What did emerge was an area known as "the flats," a section of Coronado, in and around Stingray Point, regarded as undesirable, despite its fine view of the bays. It was used mostly as farm land and for cattle raising. Glorietta Boulevard was created by dredging on the north and east sides, and the Coronado Beach Company set out trees and flowers.

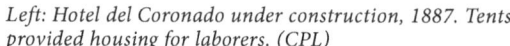
Left: Hotel del Coronado under construction, 1887. Tents provided housing for laborers. (CPL)

A northeast view of the Hotel Del Coronado, now obscured by another building. (CPL)

The Hotel Del Coronado under construction. Photo taken from the top of Boat House. (CPL)

Not all the activity in town was related to construction. S. Hoyte Averill owned a dry goods store, which he sold to J.F. Burton in early 1888. Islanders no longer had to cross the bay to shop at the famous Marston store. Averill carried books, magazines and stationery. And H.F. Prien, following Mr. J. A. Mathewson's lead, prepared to open a store in the Hotel, as soon as lodging became available for the public.

Two incidents occurred during 1888, which illustrate the fact that Coronado did not yet feel a need for law enforcement on the island. Mrs. James Blake of San Diego had tired of being the second wife and mother of James Blake's four children by his first marriage. Those details, coupled with his laziness and cruelty, brought her to find employment at the Coronado Bakery owned by Mr. and Mrs. Jacob Reusch on Adella Avenue, near the present El Cordova Hotel. Mr. Blake boated over to Coronado with a pistol, grabbed his ex-wife by the throat, and dragged her across the street. She broke away and ran back into the bakery, with Mr. Blake in hot pursuit. Reusch intervened, at which point Blake shot him in the ribs, the bullet coming out by the breastbone. Blake was overpowered and held until Deputy Sheriff Miller arrived on the ferry to take custody. Dr. W. F. Bailey, the Coronado Beach Company's physician, dressed Reusch's wounds. Mr. Reusch was up and driving his delivery wagon within a few days, but Blake's fate is unknown.

At the Oxford Hotel, an old-fashioned shooting occurred. An innocent man became involved when Bertha Moore, a pretty waitress at the hotel, encouraged jealousy over her affections for two friends: Watson and Spencer. On a particularly big night, Watson, dancing boisterously, kicked Spencer. Spencer, wearing a Scandinavian Rifles uniform, went across the hall, on the way accidentally dropping a bayonet. Watson picked it up and threw it at Spencer, who drew a revolver and fired, hitting T.E. Farnsworth, who unfortunately chose that moment to step between the two men. He took a bullet and died a short time later. Spencer and Watson were arrested by San Diego Police Chief Joseph Coyne. As a result of his crime, Spencer served some time in prison.

Dr. R.E. Armstrong was the first doctor on Coronado Beach, building a home at Third and "F." Dr. F.G. Powers, who lived at the corner of Ninth and "E", opened his office in a drugstore at the Oxford Hotel. Dr. Powers was also the official Coronado Beach Company's physician, replaced by Dr. W. F. Bailey in December 1887.

However, Coronado had no hospital at that time. Many diseases were prevalent and tuberculosis was quite common on the Island. Children were lost to typhoid, diptheria, smallpox, whooping cough and measles. As early as 1887, a sanitarium was established by a Dr. Barnes, in a large frame house known as "the Ross House," which he leased on the block between Adella and "A," Ninth and Tenth Streets.

The Coronado Athletic Club was organized in early 1888, with 40 members. They set up a sort of gym at Fifth and Orange, where new members had to pass initiation tests such as climbing a greasy pole. Fellowship was important to the athletes. In January 1888, Coronado had a baseball team–the Coronado Baseball Club–which played teams like the one from the San Diego Commercial College. Their first game ended with a tie score of 14 to 14, called due to darkness. The Hotel del Coronado also had a team, the "Hall Boys and Waiters," which gave the employees something to do when not working. In July, the "Dreadnaughts" organized. They took their baseball seriously, and even had a constitution and by-laws. An early baseball diamond was set up near the intersection of Pomona and Glorietta.

Yacht racing in the late 19th century preoccupied many Coronadans. At 1 p.m. on January 2, 1888, four yachts, E.S. Babcock's the *Teaser*; the *Kittie B.*, owned by Amos Pettingill; *The Volunteer*, owned by Robert Steadman; and the *Allie*, with Captain Parker at the helm, left the starting line on Glorietta Bay with the signal gun. Enthusiasts wanting to see the championship race won by the Allie, crowded every vantage point on both sides of the bay.

Babcock and Story had invested heavily in improvements on the Peninsula, because they believed that the land they owned lay outside the city limits of San Diego and, therefore, would remain exempt from city taxation. On September 17, 1886, however, the City of San Diego Board of Trustees, acting as the Board of Equalization, assessed the property but made no move to collect taxes. San Diego based its jurisdiction over the Peninsula on an interpretation of the municipal boundaries defined as "An Act to Reincorporate the City of San Diego," in the Statutes of California Passed at the Twenty-First Session of the Legislature, 1875-1876, published by the State Printing Office in Sacramento in 1876.

The Reincorporation Act referred to the pueblo survey made in 1858 as a basis for the municipal boundaries of San Diego. According to the field notes taken during the survey, all the land known as North and South Island lay within the corporate limits of San Diego, except for the waterfront line in San Diego Bay. In 1877, the City of San Diego tried to tax George W. Granniss, a Peninsula owner at the time, but the Superior Court of San Diego County ruled the land to be outside of municipal limits. Until 1886, San Diego did not make another attempt to challenge that ruling.

In 1887, Coronado residents didn't believe the Peninsula was a part of San Diego, and petitioned the Board of Supervisors of San Diego County to establish a school district on Coronado Beach. The Board of Supervisors did establish an independent school district, and on June 4, 1887, Coronado held its first election to select school trustees. Legal voters needed to be residents for one year in the state, six months in the county, and 90 days in the voting precinct. This meant that five legal voters unanimously elected a three-man board. In order to provide for the 75 Coronado school children, the Trustees sought approval to issue a $40,000 bond for a schoolhouse. That bond election attracted eight voters who passed the issue unanimously.

Coronado's third schoolhouse on Sixth Street between E and F Avenues. Opened in 1888, at a cost $17,000, with four rooms and a library on the first floor, four rooms on the second floor. Photo taken about 1905. (CPL)

Elisha Babcock became an early champion of a local school system, motivated in part by the pull of "great schools" to potential buyers of residential lots in Coronado. His vision for schools stressed high quality, entrusting school management to a local board of school trustees, and locating schools at the exact geographic center of the community, to allow children to walk or bike directly to school.

While other complications arose, the amount was settled, and the Coronado Beach Company bought all the bonds and sold the land for the schoolhouse at well below market value. On August 1, 1887, the Coronado Beach Company deeded all the lots on Blocks 91 and 92 to the Coronado School District—the blocks just west of the plaza, bounded by Sixth and Seventh Streets and "E" and "F" Avenues.

Early in 1887, the present school district was formed. On January 24, 1887, Coronado's first public school began in a wood-floored tent at Seventh and "D" for seven pupils. By the end of the term, attendance had reached 50 children in eight grades. The block on which the school was to be built, was selected because it was near the geographical center of the island. Architects Comstock and Trotsche of San Diego drew plans for the new one-and-a-half story schoolhouse. In the meantime, the fall term approached with 75 children. But problems arose over issuance of the school bonds, which delayed the architects. To relieve overcrowding at the Public School Tent, a temporary building (Coronado's second public schoolhouse) was put up at the southeast corner of Seventh and "E."

The January 31, 1888 issue of the *Coronado Evening Mercury* described the opening of "the elegant new school-house north of the Plaza" for its first batch of 86 students. The schoolhouse featured five classrooms, washrooms, library, closets, "a number of large blackboards," verandas and porches. Three rooms were readied with Miss Mabel Cassiday's section located on the southeast corner of the building; Professor W. J. McLean (who acted as Principal) on the southwest corner, and Miss Lizzie Armstrong in the northeast room. Over 240 desks and seats were provided, and each room had a number of large blackboards. Coronado residents had good reason to be proud of their school as the term opened

> *[This attractive schoolhouse would operate continuously until the 1930s. One afternoon each month was set aside for patriotic and general exercises at the school that included patriotic recitations and instruction in the principals of government and the duties and dignities of American citizenship. The American flag was raised to the highest point of the school building on the day of these exercises—ed.]*

During January 1888, workmen hurried to finish construction of the Hotel del Coronado, now several months behind schedule. Some of these delays were due to unexpected accidents such as the explosion of steam pipes, the delay in shipment of the electric light apparatus, and installation of features not originally planned. In January, Superintendent of Plumbing, G. F. Kendall, put 160 ingenious fire extinguishers into the Hotel, far superior to any kind known. With his simple design, a valve could only be turned one way, thus easily managed by a child.

The circular Grand Ballroom, also known as the Theater Room, was 120 feet in diameter and overlooked the Pacific through tall, narrow windows. Its superstructure rose to a height of 57 feet. This cone-shaped opening above the dance floor was the underside of the large cupola on the south wing. The ballroom was wooden-walled with supporting wooden columns around the outside of the dance floor. Above, a balcony encircled the elegant room so spectators could watch dancers below. (The balcony still exists today, although covered by an acoustical ceiling.) A low railing separated the dance floor from the surrounding area where tables and chairs were set up by the windows. On the left as one entered, was a large stage where orchestras played their tunes.

Since the Hotel had been built so close to the water's edge, the contractors soon realized it was necessary to have some protection from high tides, waves, and storms. A substantial and lasting bulkhead of rocks was built, and a jetty of heavy boulders ran for some distance out into the ocean to break the force of the sea. The rocks were hauled from the back country by train, via the railway along the Strand.

Impatient islanders hoped for new residents sufficient to support incorporation of Coronado as an independent municipality. In solidarity, the Coronado Beach Company and Coronado residents refused to pay city taxes assessed by San Diego in 1887. The cloud of taxation hung over the heads of Coronado investors about the same time the economic bubble began to burst in southern California. Land values in Coronado suffered as they had elsewhere, but Coronado had just begun what Babcock called a stable industrial base for her economy.

Another foundry was planned for Coronado by the South Halsted Street Iron Works of Chicago. Sumner W. Bugbee established a factory to make strawboard fabricated cottages. Strawboard, straw saturated with a composition which gave it strength and solidity, was used for the inside. Bugbee claimed this material was stronger than lumber. He intended to build cottages at a selling price of $250 to $5,000. The burst of the bubble brought his operation to a halt. But O.B. Hannah then started building his portable cottages, which sprang up all over the beach. These homes, constructed of sheets of board glued together–somewhat like plywood–were made in sections, which two men could build one in a day.

The Coronado shipyard finished the tugboat *Santa Fe*, which sailed out into the bay on a trial trip on February 12, 1888. New businesses also kept coming into the bay town. Wells Fargo and Company opened an express office at Averill's Book Store, in the 100 Block of Orange Avenue, and the Coronado Transfer company made deliveries of mail for the Express Company.

The first ferry building began to rise in early February 1888. Stained glass sparkled in the windows. The roof was ornamented by two beautiful turrets. Two dormer windows were built in the roof over the ticket office. It had a frontage of 75 feet toward the south, a length of 120 feet and cost $7,000 upon completion. The main waiting room included the ticket office and water closets for men and women. The architects, Nelson Alanson Comstock and Carl Trotsche, had designed nearly 60 buildings in the region, including the Villa Montezuma, the Sherman-Gilbert House, the Timken residence, and Coronado's own school house. Comstock, called the "Knight of the jigsaw and lathe," was a native of Jackson, Michigan, and Trotsche a native of Germany.

By January 26, 1888, a few guests had rooms at the unfinished Hotel del Coronado. Three days later, 75 special guests were admitted. The delay in the formal opening scheduled on February 19, 1888, was caused by freight blockades of all transcontinental rail lines, which blocked delivery of furniture and fixtures.

On February 2, 1888, the breakfast room opened with a sunny southeastern exposure through numerous windows. For several weeks it served as the main dining room. Meanwhile, the Corliss steam engine was put in motion to test the 1,850 incandescent electric lights in this and other rooms.

Planing mill workers made the solid oak mantel for the main Hotel office, 19-feet wide by 13-feet high, and by March, it was in the process of being embellished with oaken carvings, fretwork, circles, and crosses.

A "male" dormitory was built as quarters for employees of the Hotel and other workers of the Coronado Beach Company. The structure, designed by the Reid Brothers, was first built on Block 43

The exquisite Crown Room was an architectural wonder, said to be designed like a railroad trestle, spanning 160 feet long by 60 feet wide by 33 foot high, without any pillars to interrupt the view. This historic room has hosted presidents, dignitaries and royalty. (CPL)

The Coronado Beach Railroad provided transportation from the ferry landing to the hotel grounds. The car could be opened to a fresh breeze or closed up in a matter of moments, maximizing comfort for riders. (CHA)

on Pomona Avenue near the bay. Containing fifty large rooms, the structure was moved a year later to Lot 9, Block 4 on Ynez Place, and called "The Barracks" (which existed until 1975).

As the finishing touches were put to the Hotel, James Reid supervised the planting of the patio. Guests could walk about on the broad pavements of artificial stone, which intersected (at that time) a blue-grass carpeted rectangle, and admire the blooming lilies, fuchsias, daisies, tulips and marguerites mingled among the numerous palms, ferns, mandrakes, bananas, caladiums and other foliage. A fountain sprayed in the center of the patio.

Parallel with the great Crown Dining Room, and to the west of it, with an entrance on the patio side, was the children's dining room, done in pastel colors with crisp white ruffled curtains at the windows. Special meals were prepared and served to the young guests within this bright room until World War II, when the Hotel was taken over almost entirely by the military.

From the first of February 1888, "special guests" had entered the "Queen of the Beach." Every edition of both Coronado and San Diego newspapers published lists of persons who had registered at the Hotel. On Valentine's Day, 1888, a short article in the *Coronado Evening Mercury* stated:

> The formal opening of the Hotel del Coronado will not take place until after the Lenten season. However, the hotel has opened informally, and in a few days the main dining room will be opened.

When the Hotel del Coronado first opened, the lobby had no rug—only the tile flooring—and furnishings were very simple. The Hotel was a sportsman's paradise; guests came in with strings of fish and bags of game, tossing them down on the floor. The hotel became a mecca for outdoor lovers.

Printed on envelopes from the prestigious Hotel Del Coronado. (CPL/LCC)

Large trunks arrived for the ladies, filled with pretty clothes and hats, but all they needed at Coronado Beach were riding habits, yachting dresses, tennis outfits and modest bathing suits.

The Hotel had opened its doors without ceremony on January 28, 1888, but for reasons not well understood—shipments of furnishings were still delayed. Painting, paving, and planting also continued. The work, in fact, would go on for two more years before its actual completion, but guests swarmed over the Hotel delighted with its appearance and the warm February sunshine. The first special guest was Nelson Morris, a millionaire cattle king, who had a suite of nine rooms, enough for his wife and children, plus their nursemaid and other servants. A second apartment went to Donald A. Sweet, assistant to the vice-president of the Atchison, Topeka and Santa Fe Railroad. Hotel advertisements in the Los Angeles Times specified that the hotel was "opened to receive guests on February 15, 1888.

So, while some give the opening date as February 14, 1888, others claim it to be the 19th when the grand dining room was opened. The next day the paper reported, "This vast and elegant room with its wealth of appointments, is a rare sight, especially under the brilliant incandescent lights that illuminate it. The polished floors, over which an army of trained servants noiselessly glide, the high inlaid ceilings, the snowy linen and the glitter of the silver and glassware combined, made a most charming picture."

The most handsome guest room described in the Hotel was the bridal chamber, furnished in solid natural mahogany. Prevailing colors in upholstery and tapestry were pale blue and cream. The most elegant "Turkish steam bath rooms" on the Pacific Coast were also being constructed; furniture arrived for the reading room, and the 24 billiard tables and six ten-pin bowling alleys were finished.

Hotel management declared the formal opening would come after Lent, when an informal ball would be held on Washington's birthday, February 22nd. That evening an "informal little ball" did take place with music furnished by an orchestra from the East, under the leadership of Charles Leuders.

This porch overlooked the beach and was protected from the elements. (CPL/LCC)

In February, 1888, the first convention ever held at the Hotel consisted of several hundred female school teachers from the states of Illinois, Indiana, Wisconsin, Iowa, and New York. They arrived by excursion train and were ushered into the Hotel for breakfast. After a welcoming speech, the ladies took the Orange Avenue streetcars, with two open and five new closed cars, to the ferry wharf, where they boarded the steamers *Tortuga* and *Roseville*, for an excursion around the water ways.

A long-awaited Natural History Museum (Coronado's first museum), located between the Bath House and the Hotel del Coronado, and designed by the Reid Brothers, was opened. The company had already purchased thousands of dollars worth of animal, vegetable, and mineral specimens, maps, pictures, curios, and rarities of all kinds. Ten train carloads full of material arrived from Rochester, New York, comprising zoological, botanical and ornithological specimens. Among the articles were fossils, skeletons of animals, including the skeleton of a 48-foot whale, skeletal portions of prehistoric animals, gold nuggets, rocks and stone, stuffed animals, birds and reptiles, relief maps, and views of volcanic regions. During the museum's existence, a huge stuffed sea turtle hung head downward from the gabled peak of the building, always attracting the attention of visitors. By July 1888, the Museum had crowds passing daily through its turnstiles. However, costing $56,000, the museum never proved to be a financial success, and within two years was demolished.

All over the Island on President Washington's birthday, the American flag began to appear—on the Hotel, ferry boats, the bathhouse, and Babcock's yacht *Isabel*. Sunbathers, swimmers, and players on Coronado's first tennis court were enjoying the climate. Others sailed to Ensenada on the steamer *Montserrat*, where they shopped, ate and returned to Coronado for a late dinner at the Hotel Josephine and dancing at the Hotel del Coronado.

Coronado was still one of the seven cities in California that prohibited the sale of liquor. However, the *Evening Mercury* of March 6, 1888, explained that, while everyone understood the policy, it was very important for the Hotel bar to be open. They assured readers that tight limits would be set so as not to abuse the sales.

In the Spring of 1888, real estate offices opened their sales campaigns with advertising across the country; in one 24-hour period 1,400 persons passed through the ferry turnstiles to Coronado. Several frame business buildings were erected at the corner of Orange and Fifth Street, each containing a large storeroom on the first floor and eight lodging rooms above. Opposite the Hotel del Coronado, Willis C. Vajen and Col. William H. Holabird had buildings designed for stores and offices.

Mr. and Mrs. R.J. Chard of London opened a candy factory on the east side of Orange between First and Second in 1888; and Mr. O. B. Hannah began a box factory known as the Coronado Fruit Package Company, located on the bay front, east of the wharf. He intended to supply the whole of Southern California with boxes for packing fruit. That business prospered for a few years, while logs received were cut down by machinery and made into packing crates. The workers were so busy that money prizes were offered to those who could assemble the largest number of wooden boxes in one day. A Coronado shell factory was even started to provide curiosities in the way of sea shells and other interesting novelties for visitors to Coronado. Abalone shell, whole or cut for jewelry, proved to be the most sought-after item. Buttons and ornamental inlay work were shipped to places such as Liverpool, England.

For a time Coronado remained pastoral, with cattle, horses, dogs, cats, and jack rabbits roaming the town at will, prompting a warning posted for Coronado residents on March 21, 1888:

> Those persons permitting stock of any kind to run at large upon the Beach are notified that the Coronado Beach Company hereafter will protect the property from damage and depredation by such stock and will take possession, impound, and hold the same until all damages done by and expenses of impounding the same, shall be liquidated in full by the owner or owners.

Babcock signed the poster and commented that the fleas coming from these animals had plagued "Coronadites" to the point of exasperation. Other insects, such as monstrous-sized moths, accumulated by the hundreds around the Hotel del Coronado lights used outside during the construction, irritating the workers during the evening working hours.

Babcock and Story had their hands full after the Coronado Beach Company announced in March 1888 that mechanics would have to continue to work 10 hours a day. On March 2, 1888, 50 machinists, blacksmiths and helpers working at the Coronado machine shops, quit work at 5 o'clock instead of 6 o'clock as required. Babcock and Story looked upon this labor difficulty as equivalent to a resignation on the workers part, so pay checks were made out to them promptly. The men said it was their privilege to quit; they knew they would not be re-employed. Master Mechanic Barnes claimed this wasn't a problem, because he had hired other men. Then, at the Hotel del Coronado, 27 carpenters and 14 painters quit their jobs, and were paid off. Even as the labor difficulties plagued the Hotel over matters that might have been resolved with more patient management, no delay in finishing the construction took place because men stood in line to be hired for work.

When the Hotel del Coronado opened, Babcock felt he had to have a private office near the ballroom/theatre. It was to be of architecture similar to the main hotel. The office, furnished in hardwood, was an "architectural gem." In August, he moved into this attractive cupola-roofed building and used these quarters until it was taken over by the hotel physician, Dr. Raffaele Lorini, who used the structure for nearly 25 years.

On June 6, 1888, the Belt Line Railroad from San Diego made its first test run around the head of the bay. After June 13th, trains began making regular trips, which was a big help to Coronadans since the ferry stopped running at an early hour in the evening. Ten bridges were built along the line, the largest of which was 300 feet in length. Until this railroad around the Strand was finished, all of the supplies to build the town of Coronado had come by water.

The Belt Line helped the Hotel, when it finally held its "Grand Ball" (or "Opening Ball") on Saturday, June 23, 1888, by bringing many people around the bay. Between 300 and 400 invitations were accepted to the Ball; tables were decorated with tempting dishes and during the evening of dancing and socializing, guests made their way from table to table. The program of twelve dances was printed in the Coronado *Evening Mercury* of June 25, 1888.

Hotel Del Coronado visitors sitting beachside on a patio next to the Ball Room. (CPL/LCC)

The month of July 1888, brought the start of construction on a round house large enough to accommodate engines and cars near the ferry house. Two oil storage tanks also were constructed near First Street and Prospect Place, to hold up to 250,000 gallons of oil. A building for train cars and carpenter shops was built between "B" and "C" and First and Second Streets. Several other buildings were "located by the ferry." They belonged to the Coronado Beach Company; all of these had to do with construction or repairs to Company equipment.

On the 4th of July, a very special Independence Day parade was held. The ladies took special pride in their "Liberty" float, embellished by 38 radiant women with Miss Clara Hill, post office clerk, representing the Goddess of Liberty. All the way along Orange Avenue, shops and homes were decorated with flags and bunting. Professor Ward's float featured natural history specimens from the Museum in the procession, including a mounted lion and a rhino. The parade moved along Orange, around the newly-planted Star Park (where a fountain had been placed) to Loma, and then to the front of the Hotel del Coronado.

People boarded ferries at San Diego to come see the celebration. The Belt Line also did a good business. Onlookers estimated 11,000 people saw the parade, including 400 excursionists from Los Angeles. In the afternoon, the Hotel put on a daylight pyrotechnic display on the grounds. Lined up to be set off one by one, were Prismatic Lights, Blazing Sun, Caprice Wheel and Roman Candles. However, a spark dropped into one of the boxes and set off everything at once. Hotel

The Ostrich Farm was located on "A" Avenue between Eighth and Ninth Streets, 1887. (CPL)

employees worried about a fire; horses became frightened, people scrambled from the ground and ran screaming, but no one was hurt.

The much-talked of Coronado Beach horserace track became a reality by the 4th of July 1888, when the first races were run. The track, laid out by Surveyor Morley, was situated on the point of land to the east of Glorietta Bay and southeast of the Hotel, a mile in length. The plan included a large grandstand and stables. Those less inclined to such strenuous activities, could use a circulating library started by a new arrival, Miss Sawyer of Boston, who had 500 volumes in her collection. Books could be "borrowed" for five cents a day.

Coronado needed more bay transportation, and in the summer of 1888, the ferry boat *Benicia*, built in 1881, was purchased at Martinez, California, at a cost of $9,600.. She had operated there as a cattle boat, and was steam-engine powered, with a walking beam drive, side paddle wheels, and a wooden hull. First towed by the *Santa Fe* to the Marine Ways, she was repaired, painted and readied to carry passengers. The *Benicia* operated until July 4, 1903, when she was dismantled and abandoned. In those early years, the Coronado Beach Company operated the ferries *Coronado*, *Silver Gate*, and *Benicia*.

In August 1888, George Neale bought the Coronado Dairy Farm, moving the stock from the Silver Strand to Block 113, between Fifth and Sixth, Glorietta and Pomona, where he built a barn. He intended to go into stock raising on a large scale. Mrs. Emma Garrison had gone back into the cafe business at Orange Avenue (between the present La Avenida and El Cordova hotels). In July 1888, the Coronado Republican Club met at the Oxford Hotel, with A.D. Eldridge as President. Three months later, on September 21, the Democrats held their own organizational meeting (with better attendance), electing architect Joseph Falkenham, president; 23 Democrats signed the roll of the club. On November 6th, polls opened at 6 a.m. for Coronado's participation in its first National Election. At 7 p.m. the polls closed. Counting began at once, but was not completed until 5:00 a.m. There were 249 votes polled, with Benjamin Harrison getting 154 and Grover Cleveland 87. That night a large crowd gathered at the rotunda of the Hotel del Coronado to listen to the returns that were received by telegraph.

With the rail line around the Strand, and the first post office at the Oxford Hotel, two mail runs per day arrived at the Beach. Henry F. Prien, the druggist, was also Postmaster, and in that year the Post Office also became a money order office. Late in the year the Postmaster relocated himself to].A. Mathewson's new grocery store on the northwest side of Orange and Second. Maude Mathewson Messner, Mathewson's daughter said, "The Post Office was in the front corner of the store and the pot-bellied stove in the back."

The days around Thanksgiving 1888, brought outings and entertainment for Coronadans. Members of the Philharmonic Society invited friends to make an excursion to Point Loma. A commodious yacht, the *San Diego*, carried 40 persons to Ballast Point, while the fourteen piece Glorietta Silver Coronet Band livened up the afternoon. At Ballast Point, they feasted, ascended to the lighthouse, and then returned to Coronado.

December 1888, on the other hand, proved to be a bad month for some homeowners. A number of fires pointed up the need for a fire department. On the 9th, a fire burned a home at First Street and "I" belonging to H.M. Reynolds. The cottage, valued at $1,500 was a total loss. The *Mercury* reported that "the fire only emphasizes the fact of Coronado's lack of protection against fire." Near the end of the month, the J.E. Roberts' two-story frame house on the corner of Sixth and "C," which Joseph Falkenham had designed, was destroyed. The San Diego Fire Department was called, and came on the ferry, but owing to the time for crossing, and the muddy condition of Coronado streets, they could not get to the scene in time. This was the fifth of the December fires, and the urgency for a fire department again became apparent.

The *Mercury* took the task unto itself to call a public meeting at the old school house to take up the question of forming a volunteer fire company. In the interim, the Coronado Beach Company issued orders for placement of fire plugs along Orange Avenue, with 15 more at different points in Coronado. The Company also provided some 2,000 feet of hose. Company officials voiced the importance of a locally-based fire department. By the first week in January 1889, beach residents had organized a hose company with a hose cart, and kept a horse harnessed at the stable every night.

In a very real sense, Coronado was isolated from the San Diego city government, especially

Looking to the west, down the promenade. In times of heavy surf, the ocean came up to the walkway, and the Hotel shuddered from the vibrations. (CPL)

after the boom. During this era, the Coronado Beach Company had opposed incorporation of the City of Coronado. On December 12, 1888, the Supreme Court of the State held that the Peninsula, even though it was not included within the limits of the lands patented to San Diego, was within the city limits, and so subject to assessment and taxation. The court also ruled that people who could vote in San Diego elections had to be residents of the city and, therefore, subject to taxation. The Court said, "It is, topographically, almost as much in the heart of the city as if the latter enclosed it on all sides, as in a circle," referring to the Peninsula.

A Citizens Committee composed of W.H.C. Ecker, F.W. Noble, George Foster, Charles S. Wilcox, and Samuel P. Duzan met in January 1889, to address the Supreme Court decision. That Committee, supported by Babcock and the Coronado Beach Company, appealed for a precise definition of city boundaries. As arguments continued, the Committee stated that in the previous two years they owed San Diego delinquent taxes amounting to about $50,000, and that the City of San Diego had not spent "the smallest . . . fraction of American coin" for any benefits in Coronado. At the same time, they listed over four million dollars spent in Coronado by private and corporate means to build the town site, which included the Hotel del Coronado, mills and factories, street cars and railroads, ferries, approaches and landings, streets and tree plantings, and a number of public buildings.

Chalmers Scott went to Sacramento carrying the interests of the Coronado Beach Company and the Citizens' Committee, arguing against the new San Diego charter. In ensuing arguments, Senator William W. Bowers had pressure from the Coronado Beach Company and San Diego. A compromise was reached, in which the Company forgot its opposition to the freeholders charter in exchange for a segregation amendment to an earlier Reincorporation Act. On March 16, 1889, the legislature approved an amendment to the 1876 law, now called the "Coronado Segregation Bill," which defined the waterfront boundary of San Diego as ship's channel and, on the same day, approved the city's new charter.

As May 1889 came and went, petitions to the San Diego County Board of Supervisors asking for an election to incorporate Coronado went on deaf ears. All Coronadans could do was continue to advertise and be visited by Easterners, who brought their enthusiasm and money with them. Many tourists said they wouldn't have come as far south if the beach town and the Hotel del Coronado did not exist.

Other changes were on the horizon for Coronado, however. Due largely to the Depression, the Hotel reportedly lost $60,000 in the first three months of business, and matters became so bad that Babcock had to lay off some employees. Some of the other Coronado Beach Company incorporators sold or exchanged their stock, for they thought the handwriting was on the wall. Babcock went to the East coast to interest an English syndicate in purchasing the San Diego and Coronado Water Company. During this era, English capitalists had begun to invest in a variety of American business interests, such as banking, cattle ranching and railroads. Babcock felt the time had come to bring new ideas and energy into the area.

Chapter 4

John D. Spreckels and the Renaissance of the Crown City 1889-1900

SPONSORED BY MILLIE AND GUNDER CREAGER

ON JULY 26, 1889, JOHN DIEDRICH SPRECKELS bought H.L. Story's one-third interest in the Coronado Beach Company. He paid $511,050 for 3,057 shares in every Coronado Beach Company enterprise, including Story's stock in the railways. At the same time, Jacob Gruendike put his shares on the market. Elisha Babcock remained as principal manager of the major corporation, while Josephus Collett retained the third largest share. John D. Spreckels became Vice President, and he and his brothers gained controlling interest in the company.

The Spreckels' acquisition of the Hotel del Coronado was no historical accident. The acquisition has led to strong assumptions that the possession was in actuality an amenable foreclosure. This may be true. Babcock's correspondence showed the Spreckels' interests had made considerable loans to Babcock two years prior to the acquisition. The Articles of Incorporation were filed April 18, 1892, when all of the Spreckels' interests were consolidated, including North Island, reflecting strong commitments to Coronado's development.

(Image above: CPL / LCC)

Right: John Dietrich Spreckels was the most important player in Coronado's early history. By 1892, Spreckels owned the Hotel del Coronado, North Island, and most of the Coronado beach property. He kept the Hotel del Coronado solvent, donated a public library, land for schools, built two homes, and the Spreckels building on Orange Avenue, leaving a lasting legacy. (Wikimedia Commons) Left: John Spreckels' grandchildren from son, Claus. Left to right: Claus, Claire, Tookie and Frank. (CHA)

Even though taxes were being assessed on Peninsula residents, San Diego would still not give Coronado any municipal benefits. Coronado had neither a fire department nor a police department. The Coronado Beach Company continued to carry the load of street improvements, paid its share of taxes, and maintained the parks and vegetation. Exasperated because of the annoying correspondence from the San Diego Tax Collector's Office, citizens of Coronado paid their taxes, but resented lack of any support by San Diego.

The County assessed Coronado Beach for support of the San Diego School District, yet did not share in the additional financial burden of Coronado's school, except for maintenance of the school building. Since no high school existed on the Peninsula, parents also had to bear the expense of sending their children across the bay for their education.

In March 1890, with San Diego still refusing to consider segregation, the Coronado Citizens Committee asked the San Diego Common Council to submit to an election dealing with the question of Coronado Beach exclusion by changing municipal boundaries. The *San Diego Union* stood by their City, with editorials clearly supporting the actions of the Supreme Court against such a move.

The Hotel and Coronado continued to be a large draw for tourists who spent money not only on the Peninsula, but in San Diego where they visited and shopped. Millionaires, who otherwise could have gone elsewhere for their rest and recreation, were attracted to the resort and some of them built vacation or permanent homes in Coronado. None of these economic gains seemed to impress the San Diego Common Council, which continued efforts to prevent segregation. Then a new force came on the horizon.

The United States government wanted to focus its military at certain points on the Pacific coast, and suggested North Island would be a good military and naval station. The federal government took the stand that if the Beach Company would cooperate, within two years they could begin to build "the most gigantic military and naval station on the globe." While the U.S. wanted to pay only one-tenth the value of the land for the military, citizens felt that South Island property values would increase rapidly. In September 1890, a bill went to the Senate Committee on Military Affairs to acquire title of not more than 1,000 acres on North Island to build quarters for a twelve-company military post. Several ranking military officers wrote to the *San Diego Union* to encourage "the owners of North Island to convey a good title of the property to the United States because San Diego is one of the points to which the United States Government has naturally turned its attention."

> *[The year 1890 saw the very first published mention in San Diego of the region's interest in pursuing federal monies to build permanent bases for the Navy and Marines. North Island was mentioned in several cables between San Diego and Washington, as was the dream of seeking harbor improvements and dredging. Little came of this immediately — the parties were wide apart in their visions, and most of the press reporting of the period did not convey the complete story. The Spreckels brothers (who held title to all of North Island) were adamantly opposed to surrendering North Island, and felt the Navy's Pacific Squadron was tiny and didn't need bases beyond those at Mare Island (San Francisco) and Puget Sound.—ed.]*

Near the end of the year 1890, a party of engineers surveyed and made soundings for the U.S. Government near what is now Zuñiga Shoal, a spit of land jutting north/south from North Island into the Pacific Ocean, in preparation for lengthening and deepening the entrance to the harbor. Currents were taking sand from Zuñiga Shoal and filling up the only channel into San Diego Bay. Engineers recommended a rock jetty to hold the wayward sands in place. To put in place the required 200,000 tons of rock, a railroad would have to be run down Coronado's Orange Avenue to Seventh and then out Olive to the Ocean. From that point the line would continue to North Island. Clearly, the federal government had already thought in terms of development of the harbor and coastal environment.

Papers throughout the County did their part to encourage the use of the harbor by the U.S. as a permanent naval base, emphasizing the economic importance of the naval presence. An admiral said that the federal government "should appropriate one million dollars which should be expended at once for heavy guns and the erection of adequate fortifications," and recommended that all ships fitted at Mare Island Naval Shipyard should rendezvous in San Diego for drill. Moving toward that goal in 1891, government engineers looked at Zuñiga Point, seeking money for a 7,500 foot jetty

John Spreckels moved to Coronado after the San Francisco earthquake and wanted his new house to be earthquake-proof. Spreckels hired architect Harrison Albright, known for designing structures with reinforced concrete. (CHA)

(which took eleven years to build). By December 24, 1892, word had come that the jetty could be constructed at once. The cost estimates reached half a million dollars.

In 1893, a parcel of land, 18.05 acres in size at the far southwest tip of North Island, was acquired by condemnation by the U.S. Government from the Coronado Beach Company. In that year, contractor Silas R. Smith drove the first pilings for the gigantic railroad project, which called for a double-track trestle to accommodate a track on which the huge rocks would be hauled on flat cars up the Strand and through Coronado to be dumped overboard at the jetty site. The spur railroad tracks completed, the tons of rock were put into the ocean. To prevent the rocks from sinking in the sand, they were deposited on willow "mattresses," each forty by sixty feet and weighted to the bottom with the rocks.

> Zuñiga Point is the most southwesterly point of North Island pointing out into the Pacific Ocean. The point may have been named by Spanish explorer Sebastian Vizcaino for his sponsor Gasper de Zuñiga, Conde of Monterey; but, in any event, has regularly appeared on charts reaching back to the 1780s labeling a dangerous shoal at the entrance to San Diego Bay. Construction of a breakwater at Zuniga Point was considered in order to reduce the hazards of navigation at the harbor entrance, and to protect the harbor channel from sand being washed into it. Surveys began as early as 1886. A 7,500-foot "rubble-mound breakwater was designed, and 18.85 acres of land at Zuñiga was condemned and transferred from the Coronado Beach Company to the US Government for a cost of $13,942. The work began in 1894 with construction of a double-railed trestle out over the water. Rock would be delivered by flat car and dumped overboard to the side.
>
> By October 1896, 311,000 tons of rock had been deposited on the breakwater, placed on willow mattresses to prevent the rocks from sinking into the soft sand. The rock came from nearby Sweetwater quarry and willow brush from the San Luis Rey River near Oceanside. The rocks were hauled from the Sweetwater River to downtown San Diego, around the southern end of San Diego Bay and up the Silver Strand, across Coronado (Orange Avenue to Seventh Street to Olive Avenue to Ocean Boulevard), across the sand spit into North Island, and then to Zuniga Point. In the final breakwater phase, quarried rock from the Coronado Islands was barged to the site.
>
> The government officially completed Zuñiga Jetty on July 24, 1904, at a total cost of $542,850. In the ten years of the project, one laborer lost his life. It was described as a "magnificent engineering feat," not only for its labor intensive construction, but for its immediate impact on stabilizing the harbor's difficult navigation channel, and allowing for a measured program of harbor dredging that helped spur development and bring prosperity to San Diego Bay.

The news that the U.S. Navy was moving into the region in strength only reinforced San Diego's decision to hold firm against segregation (*i.e., separation of Coronado from the City of San Diego*). Coronadans, now enraged at the inaction of San Diego City government, held the largest public meeting ever on the peninsula to hear resolutions favoring segregation. Attempts to have the State Supreme Court resolve the issue failed, but the court did order the San Diego Common Council to schedule an election to consider the exclusion of Coronado. The City set a special election for October 6, 1890.

Arguments for both sides filled the newspapers and the public debated the question. Coronadans went to the polls in force and voted. San Diego voters held for segregation by a vote margin of 482 votes (of 2,672 votes cast). In Coronado, the vote was much more of a landslide, 235-4. Coronadans virtually went wild; the band turned out, gunpowder was ignited in front of the newspaper office, ferry whistles blew, streetcars clanged bells, and Babcock thanked all those who had helped Coronado, as he led a torchlight parade up Orange Avenue.

The City government and management became a more somber body, and the Citizens Committee prepared a statement of what the village needed in improvements. While segregation had come, the question of incorporation had not. Segregation meant only separation from the City of San Diego. The next step of incorporation implied forming an independent City. On November 8, 1890, the Board of Supervisors of San Diego County ordered an election for the incorporation of the City of Coronado as a sixth-class City.

Coronado voted for incorporation on December 6, 1890. When the polls closed at 6 p.m., the result showed 206 people had cast their ballots, with a majority of 60 in favor of incorporation. When the Secretary of State finally recognized the vote on December 11, 1890, the City of Coronado officially came into being, just four years after the first auction of lots on the beach. Coronado would now be governed by a Board of Trustees. Elected to office that December, were M.R. Vanderkloot, J.H. Hartupee, E.S. Babcock, Jr., A.M. McConoughey, and J.W. Bean. Positions appointed by the Board were H.G. Dow as Clerk; Carl I. Ferris as Treasurer; Samuel P. Duzan, Recorder; and as City Marshal and Pound Keeper, W.W. Stevens. They held their first meeting at the Hotel Josephine on December 15, 1890, at which time the Trustees elected Babcock as Chairman of the Board.

John D. Spreckels loved the Hotel del Coronado as he did the Peninsula, and invested a great deal of money in additional amenities. After he took charge, the refurbishing of the main floor of the Hotel began with the installation of "rich, thick ripe-red carpets, great deep inviting divans, and big, wide alluring armchairs." The oak pillars, the paneling, and the balcony balustrade gave a new appearance of that of an English palace. With these, and other alterations by Spreckels, the Hotel interior seemed much less masculine, and became more elegant and graceful.

At the onset of the year 1890, Coronado had 450 residences. A mile-long street railway followed Orange Avenue from the ferry to the Hotel. Cottages, with their gardens, gave the appearance of a countryside resort. A racetrack, a museum, an ostrich farm, the Hotel labyrinth, good roads for driving carriages and many other attractions awaited lucky visitors.

Gus A. Thompson, "the coachman" for the Babcocks was African-American and someone very special to Coronado. He had come from Henderson, Kentucky, and soon became a familiar island fixture. In his reminiscences, he would recall the first luncheon served to the stock holders of the Coronado Beach Company, prior to the opening of the Hotel, and the day he met the Hotel's first lady guest at the ferry, a woman from Indianapolis. When he drove passengers in the omnibus, the *Santa Fe*, he studied faces and people, and remembered the distinguished actress Madam Helena Modjeska. Gus became so successful, he purchased his own livery stable near the corner of 8th and "C," and when his son was born two years later, Gus drove him up and down Orange Avenue in one of the carriages from his company.

There were other stables in Coronado. Colquitt and Momand operated one on Glorietta between Anita Row (San Luis Rey) and Jacinto Place. With the popularity of horseback riding, the necessity for stables, sufficient horses, hunting and bridal paths became a responsibility of the Hotel staff, and a stable with horses available for the guests was located on the grounds.

Yachting had become one of Coronado's foremost sports. As early as February 1888, a fleet of 12 new sailboats were in demand by Hotel guests and local residents. In April, a friendly race took place from the Coronado Boat House to National City, around a marked buoy and back to the Boat House. Not only were there races, but moonlight rowing parties with picnic suppers as well. Sailing parties, and also tugboat trips to North Island, Roseville, La Playa, Point Loma, and the Coronado Islands, gained favor, too.

The Grand Army of the Republic (GAR), had taken part in the City's Fourth of July parade in 1888. The G.A.R. was a society of veterans who fought for the Union during the American Civil

War. In 1890, they encamped on Coronado Beach on the east side of the island facing San Diego Bay. They had reviews, parades, drills and boating, and three formal dances in the Hotel ballroom. The encampment attracted 15,000 people who enjoyed themselves so much they returned several more times in the 1890s.

The pier at the Hotel was referred to as "the iron pier," because iron railroad rails were laid across the pilings before placing the planks on top. The pier was intended to make it possible for those who loved fishing to go out 100 feet further over the ocean. In 1891 and in 1892, other longer piers would be built to replace portions of the first one washed away by high waves. By 1892, the Coronado pier was over 400 feet long! For the most part, these piers were used for fishing or strolls. Small vessels could also tie up while visitors made the rounds. Rock and rubble were piled into cribs, structures of wood and wire alongside the pier, to create a buffer against ocean waves.

The "fire department" had stood on wobbly legs since May 1887, when the Veteran Hose Company, a volunteer group, was organized by R.H. Bierce. The Company failed due to lack of equipment and fire hydrants. A second hose company was formed in January 1889, with a promise of a hose, a hose cart, and a horse that would be kept harnessed at a stable every night in the event of a fire. In February 1892, the local paper announced the placement of hydrants, and two months later the *Coronado Mercury* posted an editorial related to the "Hose and Ladder Company," about a third fire company organized through the efforts of more volunteers. A grand ball was held at the Orange Avenue Hotel to raise funds for the company, and E.S. Babcock offered the Fire Company use of the former Catholic Chapel at First and Orange as Coronado's first fire house (later, the Mexican Village Restaurant).

The "police department" likewise lay in infancy. B.R. Pattleton became Deputy for Coronado Beach in May 1888. Ben Miller was made Constable in that year; in 1890, W.H. Holcomb was

Fire Company in front of first firehouse, 1895. (CPL)

appointed Constable for Coronado, with T. Whaley as his Deputy. These men came across the bay from San Diego, until the incorporation of the City. In 1890, W.W. Stevens became the first Constable appointed for the township by its own City Board of Trustees. His salary was $460 per year.

There had been a few disturbances and crimes prior to 1890, but a more serious offense occurred on October 7th that year, when a masked man appeared at the doorway of the Coronado Beach Company's building and fired at the night watchman. Hennessey, the watchman, drew his pistol and returned fire, wounding the would-be robber. He was taken to the Oxford Hotel to Dr. Bowditch Morton, but shot through the lungs, the man died. He was identified as a felon named Grady, who had served a term in a Texas penitentiary. On his deathbed, he gave directions for finding money he had buried in Coronado. While many searched for it, the loot was never found. This was his second attempt to steal receipts locked in the Ferry Company vaults.

In December, 1890, after Samuel P. Duzan's planing mill in Coronado went broke as a result of the Depression, the Mechanic's Mill building was leased to an out-of-town company for operation of a soap factory. That factory, known as the Southern California Soap Company, was capitalized at $50,000. Workmen installed machinery intending to make about 10,000 pounds of soap per day, employing 15 people. For a time, they manufactured medicated and toilet soaps, printers' soaps, and filled parlor soap needs. The quantity often proved sufficient to ship to other places such as New York.

House moving became prevalent in Coronado. Not only were houses moved around the Peninsula almost like a game of checkers, but were brought from other cities across the bay via barge. The home of Dr. William A. Edwards was moved in this fashion to 1132 Isabella. Marjorie Massey said her cottage at 1540 Tenth Street was moved from National City in 1887. Many Coronado houses are no longer in their original locations.

During this era, due to the economic bust, the Hotel del Coronado reported itself almost empty of guests and, therefore was looking for ways to attract vacationers. Spreckels had a new indoor plunge pool built of wooden construction near the Hotel, which also contained 70 changing rooms for bathers. Complete with a copper-lined slide and tropical plants placed about, the interior pool was quite attractive. Noted as "a plunge for the elite," the pool also became a place for water polo, the rage at the time among the sports minded. The plunge lasted until 1934, when the Hotel's outdoor pool was installed.

> The Coronado Public Library began in 1890, as a group endeavor to do good works in Coronado. The Young People's Society of Christian Endeavor, based at the Presbyterian Church, supplied reading materials to residents and visitors and helped form the Coronado Library and Free Reading Room Association on December 6, 1890. The YMCA and the Coronado Magazine Club donated reading matter. Other items were purchased through donated funds. Early documents mention that "a room was rented," apparently on Orange Avenue, in a building owned by A. W. Corbett. When he wanted the space back for his shop, the Library moved to the Nadeau House Hotel, on Orange Avenue, between Second and Third Streets. In October 1892, the Coronado Free Library at the Nadeau House closed in preparation for a move to the Hamilton Building, a general store at the northwest corner of Fifth and Orange.
>
> The Library would reopen some three months later in a combined space with the Coronado Athletic Club, and the manager of both would be J. E. Roberts. Mrs. Elisha Babcock was an early supporter of the Coronado Free Library, and after some discussions with Library Board members, sought a more stable (and more affordable) solution for the Library. Accordingly, her husband offered the Del's former Spring House Pavilion for use as a library space.

This building was originally the Beach Pavilion before being moved to the north side of the Hotel del Coronado. The building then served as Coronado's first library from 1895 until 1908, when John Spreckels donated a new library to Coronado. (CPL)

To make the Hotel reading room in the pavilion more appealing to visitors, Miss Nordhoff supervised redecoration. She was the daughter of noted author Charles Nordhoff, whose family wintered at the Hotel that year. Mrs. Babcock had originally collected books and magazines for the room. Soon after, the pavilion was moved to the end of the streetcar line on Orange Avenue, near Glorietta Boulevard. A Victorian car-stop shelter known as Park Station, had been added to the side of the building. E.S. Babcock installed a mineral water "spring" encircled by vines, potted plants, and water pitchers within the reopened library, which was furnished rent free courtesy of the Coronado Beach Company. Citizens complained, however, that the project was not centrally located. The new facility at the Del opened on March 4, 1895 as the Coronado Beach Library.

The City Board of Trustees met regularly at the Josephine Hotel on Orange Avenue, paying $5 per month for use of the hall. They set up committees for Finance, Streets and Sewers, Fire and Water, Parks and Shade Trees, and Public Buildings, Wharves and Waterfront. The City Clerk was paid $30 per month, while the Marshal, who also served as pound keeper, earned $60 per month. A.H. McConoughey was appointed City Attorney, and the Recorder was Samuel P. Duzan.

Among the ordinances enacted on January 5, 1891, by the Board were those that dealt with the unlawful discharge of any kind of weapon, including slingshots and propulsion devices. Citizens could not use fireworks except on holidays, as permitted by the President of the Board. The Trustees made it unlawful for any person to drive a horse team or animal in the public streets faster than six miles per hour. To entertain residents and attract people from across the bay, the Trustees authorized the building of a new bandstand at the Plaza on Orange Avenue, now known as Spreckels Park, during July 1891.

Land problems plagued the Coronado Board of Trustees. The *Coronado Mercury* was quick to point out in February 1891 that the City of San Diego had tried to sell Coronado property on which it claimed taxes were due. At the auction, the only bids made were by "The Real Estate Security

Investment Company," which had no legal existence, and was formed solely to extort money from property owners through fraud and intimidation. Soon after the so-called tax sale, residents received letters telling them that their property had been sold, and that they should call at the tax collector's office to settle the costs. Then two men posted notices on vacant lots with the intent to seize the lands, signed with the name of Charles F. Paehler, County Tax Collector. Paehler, however, made a tactical error by not giving notice of the delinquent taxes in the newspapers prior to taking the properties, in accord with certain Codes of California. He was advised that he had illegally seized the properties, and could not secure titles. Homeowners relaxed at the good news.

By 1892, despite the recession, Coronado had grown, with the population rising to 1,200. There were three Hotels, including the Hotel del Coronado, three public parks, plus many varieties of trees ornamenting the City streets. The City had a foundry, a large planing mill, a soap manufactory, a fruit package factory, and other business interests. Wharves projected into the harbor and invited commercial activity.

Religious denominations included Methodist, Presbyterian, Catholic, Episcopal and Baptist, with the first three having churches in place. Presbyterians met on the island first during December of 1887, to arrange a Sunday School. The Presbyterian Church of Coronado was organized March 18, 1888, and first services were held in the schoolhouse tent. Later they were conducted in the "Lillian Block" on Orange Avenue and Sixth Street, until the completion of the present church edifice in November 1890. (In this era, a building, in architectural terms, was customarily called a 'block'). The new church was erected on the northeast corner of 10th and "C," a gift of Isabella Babcock in memory of her parents, John and Susan Graham. James W. Reid, architect for the Hotel del Coronado, designed the fine Victorian-Gothic Revival building with its stained glass windows, fish scale shingles, and lancet windows.

In 1887, the Baptists also held their first service in the school tent. By the 1890s, services were conducted at a Baptist Mission at the Orange Avenue Hotel, on the corner of Third and Orange. On

President Harrison (in top hat, center) on steps of Hotel, 1891. (CPL)

January 11, 1894, the Mission had moved from the Orange Avenue Hotel to the corner of Fifth and Orange.

By July 1887, the First Methodist Church, designed by Joseph Falkenham, was under construction on the northeast side of Seventh and "E" at a cost of $12,000. The Methodists began meeting as early as May of that year. During the pastorate of Reverend Alfred Inwood (1888-1890), the church was completed and dedicated. It was moved to Seventh and "D" in 1916, and demolished August 7, 1962, when the present building was erected on the site.

In 1887, the Catholic Church bought several lots at the corner of Palm and "H." These were later disposed of since not properly located for a church site. A temporary Catholic "chapel" was established in one of the buildings belonging to the Coronado Beach Company at 124 Orange Avenue (later, site of the Mexican Village Restaurant). Father Antonio D. Ubach of San Diego conducted services. When the chapel was no longer adequate to hold the numbers of people, Mr. and Mrs. T.J. Fisher gave land at Seventh and "C" for a church. On Easter Sunday, 1891, a little frame house of worship was dedicated, called Sacred Heart Church.

In 1919, Louis John Gill presented his rendering of the new Church of the Sacred Heart. Construction began at Seventh and "C"; the church was not planned to be large, with a seating capacity of but 400. Gill, following the lead of the Bishop, planned an edifice that would be dignified, plain, artistic inside and out, with every surface line, cover, or emblem having a meaning and purpose in the Catholic worship. The church was dedicated with a high pontifical mass on Thanksgiving Day, 1920.

Services were conducted once again in the old school house tent on February 12, 1888, for the Episcopal Church! A few months later, they met at the Josephine Hotel. A fundraising drive for a new church was underway, when Charles T. Hinde bought four lots at Ninth and "C." James W. Reid was engaged to design the Gothic Revival church of hand-hewn granite stone, quarried in Santee. The building was completed for $19,693.83, with the cornerstone laid September 19, 1894, in memory of Hinde's twelve-year old daughter, Camilla, who had died of influenza. In May 1896, ladies of the Episcopal Church contributed about $575 to buy and install the pipe organ by Robert E. Pilcher of Louisville, Kentucky. The organ had 24 registers and 835 pipes. In 1902, Captain Hinde provided a large frame rectory of 4,000 square feet at 926 "C" Avenue, which became the home of the Rector Spalding and his family. The same year, Captain Hinde donated funds for construction of the parish hall.

Teachers at Coronado's first formal schoolhouse, c. 1900. (CHA)

In 1892, an Easterner reading a local paper during this time would certainly have gotten the impression that Coronadans' principal interests lay in recreation. That same year, four young Coronado girls, who started rowing on the bay for pleasure organized a Rowing Club named "ZLAC" taken from the first letters of their given names. The "Z" was for Zulette Lamb, while the Polhamus sisters, Lena, Agnes, and Caroline furnished the "LAC." When the family moved to San Diego in 1894, they took the club with them. In March 1894, some "girls" of Coronado organized two football teams, playing several times that year.

The U.S. Naval boat races were held on the bay south of the Hotel del Coronado between the crews of the USS *San Francisco* and the USS *Charleston*.

The Carey/Hizer house on Loma Avenue in 1890. Chez Loma Restaurant has inhabited the house for many years. (CHA)

These included cutters with twelve oars, gigs with six oars, dinghies with four oars, whaleboats with six oars, and single sculls. Bicycle racing enthusiasts held events at the Coronado Driving Park (the Coronado Race), usually with bicycles rented from Holland's Bicycle Shop located near the Hotel del Coronado.

An Athletic Club was organized on July 21, 1892, when a crowd gathered at a hall at Fifth and Orange to make the organization official. Those attending elected officers and drew up a constitution and bylaws. Among the sports included was the Gun Club, whose members hunted game in the back country, in Lower California, and on North Island. Members of that club included Captain J.S. Sedam; A. B. Daniels of Denver; George Sturges of Chicago; C. Bidwell of Buffalo; Tomas T. Hillman of Birmingham; J.T. Hayden, President Whitney National Bank of New Orleans; Paul Morton, 2nd Vice President of AT & SF Railway, Chicago; General Nelson A. Miles, U.S. Army; Captain C. F. Goodrich, USN; Lieutenant E.P. Jessop, USN.; and Dr. Edward E. Beeman of chewing gum fame. These men, who participated in sports whenever they happened to be in Coronado, and other noted amateurs and professionals, competed for prizes.

Dr. Raffaele Lorini wrote articles for the *Coronado Journal* after his retirement in May 1929, and told of the rabbit drives, horseback riding, gym club, rod and reel clubs, and fishing organizations, which originated on the peninsula. The Hotel del Coronado sponsored many events for its visitors and the residents of Coronado. In January 1892, management arranged a concert by the band from the Navy flagship, USS *San Francisco*, and some 2,000 people crossed the bay to hear the music. The Hotel sponsored rabbit hunts on North Island and shooting forays for duck, quail and doves.

On January 30, 1892, the Hotel held a "Leap Year Party" at the Lillian Lodging House, owned by O.L. Manner, a native of Denmark. It was one of Coronado's earliest buildings, located at the corner of Sixth and Orange. Later the building was moved next door to the fire house. Eventually, it was moved to the polo grounds, where, after remodeling, the structure became a clubhouse for the Coronado Stables and Riding Club. The men so enjoyed themselves, they suggested a Leap Year dance every year. San Diegans did all they could to encourage tourists to come to Coronado. For example, the *San Diego Union*, in its January 1, 1892 edition, ran a front page headline calling it "Peerless Coronado," with a sketch of the Hotel del Coronado.

Still, there was reason for potential vacationers to pause, when, on the evening of February 23, 1892, an earthquake hit the region, causing houses to creak. The shaking lasted about forty seconds, followed by smaller tremors at intervals throughout the night and into the next day. The earthquake, centered in Baja California, took guests at the Hotel by complete surprise and made headlines, as news spread of people running from the Hotel in their night clothes. Some ladies fled to the ferry landing, only to find that the last vessel had left for the night. The earthquake did not prevent delegates of the Eighth Annual Editorial Association from arriving in Coronado on Sunday, May 15, 1892. Traveling from all over the country, the party numbered 800, the largest convention held up until that time. They arrived via a pleasant ride on the Belt Line Railroad.

The Coronado Beach School was the first private school in Coronado, attended by children who lived at the Hotel as well as children of wealthier families in town. In addition to regular class work, students learned French and attended dance class in the hotel ballroom. (CPL)

In the summer months of 1892, the Hotel Del provided facilities for a Coronado Beach Summer School, established by a prominent San Diego attorney, Daniel Cleveland, and Dr. George E. Abbott, then house surgeon at the Hotel. Instructors were mainly from Stanford and the University of California. A booklet from the Coronado Beach Library stated that the climate in Coronado was invigorating, and would "repay" tired teachers with renewed health. The Coronado Beach Company provided rooms for lectures, study and laboratories, besides offering the museum, the botanical gardens, the ocean and a bay rich in marine life. Unfortunately, the first summer school established in California operated for only three years, and then did not reopen.

Charles Hinde home, c. 1900, on the 900 block of "C" Avenue. Today, it is owned by the Presbyterian Church and known as the Kirk House. (CHA)

The Seaport News, a San Diego publication, on November 26, 1892, described the Hotel del Coronado as a matchless summer and fall resort, listing temperatures for the season and carrying information about "a hundred ways of diversion," while in Coronado. It chose to overlook the near-tragic event that occurred in September, when the platform of the Boat House gave way during aquatic sports. About fifty people standing on it were thrown out into the bay. Women screamed and men yelled, while cooler heads began working a rescue; and not a single person was lost.

City business was carried out by elected officials who dispensed decisions not unlike those required today. They established a law that would fine those caught driving across vacant lots. The citizens' newly-gained right to vote took on mammoth proportions, however, in an election of City officials on April 11, 1892. The election became affectionately called, "The Citizens," (residents and taxpayers) versus "the Hotel Boys," (Mr. Spreckels, Mr. Babcock, his friends, and employees of the Hotel). Heaping verbal abuse on one another, the two factions fought over the desires of Babcock to charge rent for use of his water company, and the reservation of certain "public properties," which Babcock claimed as his. As reported, "he [claims to own] everything from Sheol below, to Heaven above the place of ground he proposes...to deed to the City," [the strip of ground in the center of Orange Avenue].

The results showed (after somewhat questionable voting, when some ballots were thrown out) that voters elected M.R. Vanderkloot, J.Walter Bean, J.Y. Jackson, Samuel T. Green and Thomas J. Fisher to the Board of Trustees, with Vanderkloot as President of the Board. For the first time, Coronado was released from dominance of the original Coronado Beach Company of Babcock's time. But the Hotel del Coronado came out ahead, with several of the "Hotel Boys" elected as Trustees. All met to celebrate at the nearest bar with no hard feelings. The local newspapers carried the accounts. *The Mercury,* was operated under Frederick E.A. Kimball until September 1892. This same firm published the short-lived newspaper, *The Seaport News.* A partner, T.B. Beasley, was a well-known artist living at the Hotel Josephine, who created numerous pen and ink sketches for both papers.

During the boom era, a rapid building of streetcar lines had taken place. When the boom collapsed, the primary rail lines went out of business or were converted into electric lines, except the National City & Otay, and the San Diego, Old Town & Pacific Beach Railways.

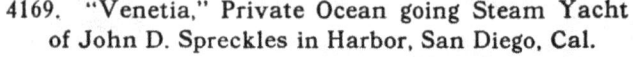

John D. Spreckels' luxurious ocean-going yacht, 'Venetia,' at 226 feet long, was an impressive sight anchored in the bay. He sailed it regularly between San Diego and San Francisco. (CPL/LCC)

On January 30, 1892, the entire San Diego Street Car Company went into the hands of the John D. and A.B. Spreckels Company, including the Coronado line. They incorporated these as the San Diego Electric Railway Company. Coronado street cars ordered from the J.G. Brill Company had numbers in the "forty" series, to avoid conflict with those in other places where the Spreckels lines already ran. In 1892, the Orange Avenue section was re-tracked from the ferry to the Hotel del Coronado and wired, so it could be converted to an electric road. During that time, while the cars were out of commission, a four-horse bus connected with the ferry boats. The first electric car barn was built on the northwest side of Orange Avenue near First Street.

To make the trip around the Strand a bit easier for horse and buggy traffic, the Board of Supervisors authorized a contract to apply a 20-foot wide top coating of clay for a distance of three miles from the Hotel, going southward. But, shifting sands and the narrowness of the road proved to be unsatisfactory, and within a few years a new topping had to be provided. With more traffic, more roads were needed so, in the summer of 1893, construction began on a boulevard around San Diego Bay, starting at Coronado. The road permitted construction workers, or people out for a ride, to travel around the two islands. It led to North Island along the oceanfront sand spit across the Spanish Bight—the only access available between the two islands that could be used for horses.

Early in 1893, the State Supreme Court affirmed the decision of the Lower Court, which ended all disputes concerning the legal segregation of Coronado from San Diego. The City Trustees now felt that citizens would not hesitate to buy bonds when issued and home seekers would buy more readily. It was hoped the decision would end further annoyances and disruptions between the two cities. Yet Coronado citizens continued to complain throughout the year about the techniques the County Assessor, and the unfairness of the system used for assessment and taxing. The major complaint seemed to be that assessments were doubled between 1892 and 1893, and that lots were being assessed for more than their cash value. Meanwhile, City records show the Trustees struggled with the problems of assessing Coronado Beach properties and citizen's properties, and trying to figure out how to balance the City budget using the tax base.

The Hotel del Coronado received full-page New Year's Day coverage in the *San Diego Union* in 1893, with a sketch of the Hotel and of the Coronado saltwater swimming tanks. In describing the idyllic place, a reporter called Coronado, "The [place with] absolute absence of saloons and gambling resorts, and the presence of many pretty little churches, whose spires here and there show above the trees..."

The Coronado Mercury, quoted from a speech delivered by General Eli Huston Murray at the Hotel del Coronado's 7th anniversary celebration, honoring the founders of Coronado: "Babcock, Story, Gruendike, Ingle, and Collett, but particularly noting the indomitable pluck of Babcock who, standing by his guns in the days of dire distress, snatched victory from often times impending disaster." Coronado's growth seemed unprecedented in 1893, with tourist-aimed literature referring to Coronado as a "Model City." Marshall Field, a multimillionaire dry goods merchant from Chicago, built a house on Ocean Boulevard that year; it was later moved to San Diego, barged by way of the Spanish Bight.

The City Board of Trustees recognized that Coronado had been hit by a Depression, and that Coronado needed investments or money loaned to the City at a reasonable interest. The Trustee duties were particularly trying and onerous. With a deficiency in the treasury, the existence of an unjust and excessive tax assessment, and the certainty of meeting a heavy water tax, some thought the obstacles insurmountable.

Trustee actions were varied in 1893. They gave permission to the National Guard of California to set up a practice rifle range along Glorietta Bay, somewhere between Third and Sixth Streets. In January, the Diamond Carriage & Livery Company, owned by Arnold Babcock, son of Elisha Jr., sprinkled the streets under City contract. Financed by the City, the paving of Orange Avenue got under way. Conglomerate gravel delivered from San Diego was used for the job, and proved a great success for an outlay of $55,000. Trustees reported that work continued on the Zuñiga jetty, as a large quantity of rock was delivered to North Island by the railroad. By the end of April 1894, the jetty had been constructed, measuring 2,464 feet despite high tides impeding work, and a derrick and other equipment being damaged.

The police department needed attention. There were two Marshals in early 1894, T.J. Fisher and D. McCollister; then in May, John H. Hartupee was appointed Marshal, with a salary of $900 per year. These lawmen had no office other than their own home. By this time, the telephone had come to Coronado. If the Marshal happened to be away, he notified the Hotel del Coronado's switchboard where he could be contacted.

Just prior to segregation, Coronado had been part of the San Diego school system, and did not have its own high school.

> *[High-school level instruction was carried out at Russ High School (later San Diego High).—ed.]*

Russ serviced all of San Diego, including Pt. Loma and La Jolla. When segregation occurred, a Coronado School District was formed and with Trustees selected, Professor Hugh J. Baldwin became head of Coronado's school. So many students were enrolling in 1893 that double sessions were held. Problems concerning securing title to the school property were aired at "City Hall" on October 13, 1894, as a report from the Board of School Trustees was read. While the matter took several years to resolve, an election to authorize purchase of the school block was held and approval given.

> *[No state requirement existed for schooling beyond the 8th Grade until the 1920s. Beyond 8th Grade, Coronado parents had three choices for their children: attend Coronado schools in a college-prep track, attend Coronado schools in a vocational training track, or enroll in Russ High School, necessitating daily ferry trips.—ed.]*

Coronado's first high school instruction began in 1890 or 1891, and the first high school commencement exercises were celebrated with two graduates, Misses Caroline M. Polhamus and N. Elizabeth McQuown, in June 1894 at the Hotel del Coronado. Miss Polhamus delivered an essay entitled, "Opportunities of the Young Woman of Today," and music was provided by the Hotel Del Coronado orchestra.

Between 1894 and 1912, Coronado held regular high school commencements for just two to six students each year. However, diplomas were not Coronado-specific, as Coronado fell under the oversight of the San Diego County Superintendent of Schools.

Good news came to Coronado's educational system when the State University at Berkeley, by vote of its academic council, granted the privilege of entitling graduates of Coronado High School to enter the University without examination. Various professors of the University of California had made an inspection of the high school.

At North Island, the Coronado Beach Company put in 100 acres of grain as fodder for livestock. George Neale, owner of Coronado's dairy farm, grew crops of barley there and took his cattle to graze. School children were taken to the Spanish Bight to find shell fish and other sea life, while sportsmen from the Hotel rode horses to hunt small game such as jackrabbits and quail, often following a pack of greyhounds.

At the Hotel Del Coronado, Kate Sanborn wrote *A Truthful Woman in Southern California*, and declared, "Every recreation is found in this little [Hotel Del Coronado]," mentioning innumerable sports and recreation. She also noted the "many athletic, fine-looking men, who ride daringly to kill [the game at North Island]." A building first used as a real estate office, located between the Hotel and the Spanish Bight, was fixed up and served as a dressing room for bathers along the beach. Visitors took a Hotel horse and carriage along the firm, wet sand at the water's edge. In April, a daughter of Jefferson Davis stayed at the Hotel, while in August, Ulysses S. Grant, III and Jesse R. Grant and their families checked in.

At the site of the still undeveloped Coronado Heights, the Beach Company put in 100 acres of grain, while a party from the U.S. Engineer Corps collected data for a proposed government erection of gun batteries. Plans as outlined, with estimates and surveys nearly finished, included three first-class batteries of six guns each to be placed at the Heights, at Point Loma and at the shore end of Zuñiga jetty. What occurred with the Army is not known, but during the next decade, land at the Heights was leased to various persons for farming, raising crops of wheat and rye. The large

Anderson's Bakery in 1911, now 956 Orange Avenue. Mr. Anderson is on right, Bud and Clare in wagon. This building is still standing in back of a present-day bakery. (CHA)

warehouse which had been used for the questionable Waukesha Bottling Works was used to store some of the grain.

On April 21, 23, and 24, 1894, the Coronado Beach Company decided to hold a Spanish fiesta at the Coronado Race Track (later known as the Polo Grounds) to bring people to the island community. The production was managed by Señor Don Marco Forster (of the Rancho Santa Margarita family), Don Tomás Alvarado and Pio Pico. Charles Fletcher Lummis, editor of *The Land of Sunshine* and *Out West* magazines, gave a complete account of the fiesta for *Harper's Weekly*, as did the *Coronado Seaport News*. Orange Avenue and Fifth Street were decorated with streamers and flags, as was the Hotel del Coronado. Between April 21 and 24, a number of American Indians appeared, as did Mexicans in native costumes, riding on horseback competing in horsemanship. Long distance races were held, and all sorts of competition, much like a rodeo. Shops at the edge of the field gave participants a chance to exhibit and sell their jewelry, rugs, pottery and other goods. While it brought temporary relief from thoughts of the recession, it also helped to bring dollars to the town, and when Miss Annie Kimball took over the *Coronado Mercury* in May, she and her manager/editor, George Cox, anticipated a second such fiesta the following year.

In July 1894, the Coronado School Board of Trustees met and elected Mrs. E.S. Newcomb as Chairman of the Board and John H. Brouwer as District Clerk. Certain school statistics were given such as the average attendance of 161, an increase of 60 over the previous year. The total expense for maintaining the schools was $2,905, about $900 less than the previous year. The Board, with Principal Hugh J. Baldwin, selected its corps of teachers for the next year: Miss M.F. Taylor, grammar grades; Miss Adella Meyer, fifth and sixth grades; Miss Blanche Boring, primary grades; with high school and kindergarten teachers to be selected.

One of the major arguments during the year concerned a special school tax. The opposition to a tax of $1,000 for public schools, levied by the City of Coronado, arose when people questioned the School Board. Citizens felt the Board was being too extravagant, that the school had too many teachers, and salaries were too high. Some opposed continuation of the high school, while others felt there was no need for a kindergarten. These matters were not resolved during the year.

On the first day of the New Year, 1895, the *San Diego Union* featured a sketch of the Hotel del Coronado and wrote of the winter visitations, portraying a number of fine homes belonging to luminaries such as Charles T. Hinde, resident partner of the Spreckels Brothers Commercial Company; K.H. Wade, general manager of the Southern California Railroad; J. Malcom Forbes, the Boston millionaire and owner of the Pacific Beach Railroad; General W.E. Webb; and Charles Nordhoff, a well-known author.

The *Coronado Weekly Mercury* was published until July 25, 1896 when the Kimballs moved to Tucson, Arizona. Until that time the editor kept an eye on Capt. Robert D. Israel, former Point Loma (Cabrillo) Lighthouse Keeper, who was building a home near the race track, and the "Band of Mercy," which performed to provide money for a public fountain where horses, dogs, cats, birds, and people could drink. The fountain was located near the ferry landing. *The Mercury* also took note of the fact that Architect Irving J. Gill was to be chairman of the Committee on Floats for the 4th of July Parade.

The Board of Trustees created an ordinance prohibiting chickens and other fowl from running at large, which meant Coronadans had to take up the Anglo-Saxon tradition of fencing their properties. The Trustees also passed Town Ordinance No. 63, regulating use of bicycles and tricycles on the streets, stipulating bikes on the right hand side of the street and trikes on the sidewalk.

One unifying force among all communities in the region, despite the desire to remain independent of the City of San Diego, was the burst of enthusiasm that arose over "women's rights." Women of San Diego, Coronado, Oceanside, National City, Escondido, Fallbrook, Ramona, Julian, El Cajon, and other places organized a County Central Committee with Mrs. Freeland as the representative from Coronado. Their intent was to organize suffragettes throughout the City and County so they could freely hold meetings and circulate campaign literature. While a few years would pass before their efforts came to fruition, these women kept up the campaign until they got the vote. Women also took on a strong role when they created the Village Improvement Society, credited not only with beautifying many of the roads and drives, but with placing Coronado's pavilion public library upon a more substantial foundation.

> Capt. Charles T. Hinde, President of the Library Board of Trustees, oversaw a series of fundraisers to maintain the Library and its collections. A water polo match was held at the Del's Bath House in March 1896, and balls were held in March 1896 and 1897. John D. Spreckels provided the "spring house" (former pavilion) to be used for the Coronado Library "rent free."

Part of the inspiration for the many forms of recreation available on the island was an early desire of the Coronado Beach Company to give its many employees sufficient activities close to home to relieve the monotony of the long working hours. The Company still had among its subsidiary companies the Coronado Machine Shop, located near the bay, south of the ferry landing. Cars of the Coronado Belt Line Railroad were entirely built there and many coaches and cars were repaired.

Later in the year of 1895, the federal government announced that negotiations had closed for land on the Coronado sand spit. The report indicated the government had purchased 50 acres of land on the isthmus, south of the Hotel del Coronado, and would place upon it 16 modern mortars,

12-inches in diameter, capable of defending the harbor of San Diego against the approach of any kind of war vessel. The total cost of the work was estimated to be about $400,000.

> In 1897, funds were finally appropriated to build fortifications at Ballast Point to protect the entrance to the harbor, while plans were cancelled for installation of guns south of the Hotel del Coronado. Across from Ballast Point on North Island, at the head of the Zuniga jetty, Fort Pio Pico was also built. It contained two three-inch rapid-fire guns, with these gun emplacements referred to as Battery James Meed. These guns continued to protect San Diego and Coronado throughout World War I, with Fort Pio Pico decommissioned in 1919. In addition, on January 1, 1897, contracts were let for gun fortifications and torpedo casements on Ballast Point, and a battery of big guns on Point Loma's seaward side. While most of the construction on Point Loma was carried out, plans for fortifications on the Silver Strand were not, because Congress never appropriated the funds.

To replace the now-discontinued *Mercury* newspaper, Edwin N. Sullivan, who owned several other papers, started a weekly called the *Coronado Ozone* in 1897, which existed only briefly. It did not cover much of the local news, containing primarily advertising.

The big news of 1897, was the development of Coronado's first golf course, a project of the Coronado Beach Company. It was a nine-hole course on level land, across Glorietta Bay from the future site of Tent City, near the corner of present-day Glorietta Boulevard and Anita Row (San Luis Rey). It is said to have had grass greens, the first in the state. There was a five-year lease on the golf course, and lessees agreed to pay rent of one dollar per year, all State and County taxes, and all street improvements. E.S. Babcock, Jr. was President; B.W. McKenzie, Vice President; Usher F. Newlin,

This photo of the Hotel del Coronado lobby in the 1890s, shows the fine furnishings shipped from the east coast. The lobby was known as the Gallery. (CPL)

Secretary/Treasurer; Directors were J. Clyde Hizar and W. S. Goodless. A number of tournaments were held on this course, including some for ladies.

> The first mention of a tournament at the course was in October 1897, when Colonel Davis and Miss Pratt set the mixed-players record there with an 82 score, an event followed by a "rabbit chase on North Island." In January 1898, W. C. Peet of New York was elected president of the Coronado Golf Club organization at a membership meeting in the parlors of the Hotel Del. In April 1898, the turf from the Hotel's courtyard was replaced and transferred to the links of the golf club.

When Andrew Ervast, an engineer, arrived in San Diego, Babcock soon hired him; in fact, Babcock gave Ervast almost free reign to undertake tasks at hand. Ervast became City Engineer for Coronado from 1897 to 1915, and oversaw the Ocean Boulevard seawall. He arranged for a jetty constructed out into the ocean just below the Hotel del Coronado, in hopes of changing the course of currents so as to protect the Hotel and its diminishing beach. Following the same method used for the Zuñiga jetty, railroad tracks were constructed out into the ocean. Rocks from the back country were used for the jetty, loaded on flatcars and hauled by the Belt Line Railway around the Strand. Eventually the jetty provided a place from which to fish and a cove for swimming. Later Ervast would become engineer for the Spreckels companies from 1915 to 1932, designing such structures as the old Adams Avenue streetcar barn in San Diego.

In 1897, the City paid five cents a head for gophers dead or alive; (in August 1930 the City raised the official gopher bounty to a dime.) Many youngsters supported themselves by buying a few traps and setting them each day.

The year 1897 proved extremely dry. Some trees died while others were endangered. The Board ordered heavier watering all over the island. Trenches were dug around the trees and filled with water. Nonetheless, a number of them died and had to be replaced after the drought ended, but that would be two years away. One annoyance, according to citizens who brought their protestations to the Trustees, was a cow ranch on Block 34 (between Ninth and Tenth, "F" and "G." The Trustees told the owners to clean up their "ranch" or move elsewhere—meaning out-of-town! Board business that year also included an agreement to pay rent on the firehouse for three months at a cost of $15.

Progress was made on a new home for Giles Kellogg, opposite the Hotel Josephine. In "antique Spanish style," the place had 15 rooms and was expected to be ready by Christmas. Notably, it stood on the highest point in Coronado, on Fourth Street, with commanding views of the Hotel Del, Pt. Loma, and the ferry landing. The home was later relocated to Fourth and "A" Avenue before World War II, and demolished in 2014. The Josephine itself was serving as a home for tourists and permanent visitors. An Episcopal minister, the Reverend Cossitt, was building a new home on Adella; he had been long-time rector of the Episcopal church in Utica, New York, but his failing health caused him to move to the balmy climate. General Mendal Churchill also broke ground for his new mansion on the vacant lot at Block 10, across from the Hotel Del.

In February, a brilliant tableaux put on at the Hotel to benefit the Coronado Library was seen by hundreds of people. Visitors watched water polo at the Coronado Bath House, trolled for barracuda and Spanish mackerel, and played golf matches.

In 1898, scarcely a note appeared referring to the William Randolph Hearst-inspired U.S. conflict with Spain in Cuba and the Philippines, which resulted in the Spanish-American War. On May 4th, however, all residents of Coronado capable of bearing arms were requested to meet at the Hotel to form a local reserve. A number of men volunteered to serve in branches of the service and retired officers returned to active duty. Many American-owned yachts were commandeered and refitted for war. All navy ships were ordered to replace their existing brilliant white paint for the lead-gray color used during the Civil War, making them less visible at sea.

> Warship visits to San Diego Bay increased notably, and many folks, in both San Diego and Coronado, witnessed the fact that the Navy was becoming a valued member of the community and a contributor to the social fabric of the region. The Hotel Del chose this time to produce a glossy pamphlet that mentioned the Navy in glowing terms, noting that Hotel guests "could attend weekly receptions on board the U.S. cruisers of the Pacific White Squadron, some of which are usually riding at anchor in the harbor."

The War, which ended in December, had brought some prominence to San Diego. Vessels carrying war munitions and supplies docked in San Diego en route to the battle scene. Naval ships in the ocean near Coronado became a frequent sight, as they took on supplies and men. However, socially-minded Coronadans focused more attention on the colorful dances for ship's officers held in the flag-draped ballroom of the Hotel del Coronado.

No work was done on the jetties near the Hotel Del during this year, nor in 1899, as the war came first. Meanwhile, much of what had been constructed on both the Zuñiga and Hotel sites was washed away. Erosion problems began immediately.

One other important event did take place, however. On May 5, 1898, Dr. William A. Edwards of San Diego signed a contract with the Coronado Beach Company to locate a building on Block 4, lots 2 and 3 (on Adella near Orange Avenue) to function as a permanent hospital. The Beach Company agreeed to add a kitchen, porches and household plumbing with sewer connection.

Elisha Babcock stayed on as manager of the Hotel del Coronado after John Spreckels became the owner. (CPL/LCC)

Vegetable gardens were planted on the grounds. Electric lighting and bells would operate on the circuit of the Hotel del Coronado. Edwards agreed to pay $1,200 a year to rent the sanitarium.

> *[The terms "hospital" and "sanitarium" were used interchangeably during this era.—ed.]*

Since the City was highly advertised as a health resort, the Coronado Beach Company was so eager for a hospital or sanitarium that they combined several buildings to make the new structure. What has been commonly called in more recent times the "Hotel Annex," was, in fact, Coronado's first hospital.

> *[The Hotel del Coronado, since its inception, had a permanent onsite staff doctor; this nearby facility provided services from surgery and care of injuries, to simple recuperation.—ed.]*

In 1899, adapting to provisions of a new state law, the City placed tax monies in the Library account for the first time. By 1901, the City assumed the salary of the librarian and the cost of building upkeep, but all reading material still depended on donations.

In less than 15 years, Coronado's South Island had grown from a sand and sagebrush covered landscape into a beautiful resort town, whose reputation was almost solely based on its glamorous Victorian Hotel. Yet, as a residential community it had hopes of achieving much more.

John D. Spreckels proved to be the "saving grace" for the island as he continued to provide financing for many of the public utilities and transportation. At this point, he still resided in San Francisco because he and his brothers held other business interests there, and in Hawaii. However, Coronado would take on new meaning for John Diedrich Spreckels, as he saw the tiny resort village on the brink of becoming a full-blown town.

12768 TENT CITY, CORONADO BEACH, CALIF.   DETROIT PUBLISHING CO

Chapter 5

A Time of Optimism before the Road to War 1900-1914

SPONSORED BY BRUCE & BETSY GILL

"TEDDIE'S WAR WITH SPAIN" (as Theodore Roosevelt and his war had become known) had ended, and the military settled back into the routine of peacetime service with infrequent maneuvers, and around-the-world travel intermingled with social affairs at ports of call. Coronado was a proven party town, and gatherings at the Hotel del Coronado were frequent. As the military rubbed elbows with millionaires, both became charmed by the tiny village. Alvin B. Daniels, a Denver banker, wrote that he had spent two winters in Coronado, commenting that it was far superior to the Riviera and the health resorts of Southern France.

However, the town had to be able to sustain itself when there were downturns in tourism. Year-round recreation became important. When the first golf links, across Glorietta Bay from Tent City, became too small, the Coronado Beach Company opened an 18-hole course between Alameda, then "K" Avenue, and the Spanish Bight, extending from the west end of Ocean Boulevard to San Diego Bay at 1st Street. A contract between the "Coronado Golf Club" and the Schaniel Brothers Company of San Diego was negotiated on April 29, 1901. (At that time, there was a large race track on land just north of Fourth Street and the Spanish Bight, with stables at the corner of Fourth and Alameda.)

(Image above: CPL / LCC)

Country Club on Ocean Blvd., c. 1902. (CPL)

The par 72 course, designed by Alex Smith, the Coronado Golf Club's professional, was 5,318 yards long, covering three miles. Part of it formed a ladies' course of nine holes, 2,055 yards long. Putting greens, twenty feet in diameter, were initially made of asphalt covered with a thin coat of sand, known as "sand greens." Rectangular driving platforms were filled with hardened earth encased by four boards 6" to 8" high. Beside each driving platform was a white wooden stand: a tee box, resembling a flower box. This held two metal-lined compartments, one for water and one for sand. The golfer dampened a bit of sand with the water and set up a little pointed mound on which to place his ball for the drive. Caddies were plentiful at 50 cents for an 18-hole round. The two-story Club House was located on Glorietta Avenue (later renamed Marina Avenue) near the end of Ocean Boulevard. At that time, it was the logical place for the Club since transportation to the golf course was furnished for guests from the Hotel on electric-powered buses.

Across from the golf course, on the tiny triangular Block 27 near the ocean, stood the Japanese Tea Garden, with buildings about where Alameda Boulevard and Marina Avenue intersect. George T. Marsh, landscape architect for San Francisco's Golden Gate Park, leased that block from the Coronado Beach Company for 20 years, at an annual fee of one dollar. On this property, he built an authentic Japanese Tea Garden, complete with attractive, native-type buildings, trees, and blossoms where players from the nearby golf course could drop in for a cup of tea at the 19th hole. The project was the idea of Spreckels, who did much to furnish recreation for his Hotel guests. Jinrikishas, pulled by Japanese coolies, could be hired to take visitors along an unpaved Ocean Boulevard, to and from the Tea Garden. Not only was it colorful, but the rickshaws provided a fascinating setting for pictures that could be sent home by the tourists.

For indoor amusement, Trustees voted to allow slots in the Hotel, but they had to be licensed. The Hotel register shows that the machines were in the red the entire time: all seven slots, one 50-cent machine, one musical machine and one weight machine. By 1915, most had been scrapped as "worthless."

One other Spreckels inspiration was "Camp Coronado," later known as Tent City, established in 1900, just south of the Hotel. A summer campground, it provided tents available for rent, and offered such attractions as a large bathhouse, the open plunge with a sand bottom and a restaurant. Events had been scheduled so people could vacation, even if just for a weekend. A booklet-type circular, the *Tent City News*, served as a type of newspaper, carrying programs about band concerts, water sporting events, hours of Sunday church services, news of visitors, and some advertisements.

Spreckels always kept in mind the larger picture of his business ventures. He related one business to another. To him, Tent City was a place to adventure, and rest, but it was also located at the end of the transportation lines he owned.

In the late 1890s, George Marsh leased land from John Spreckels and built a Japanese Tea Garden, introducing Japanese culture to Coronado Beach. There were actually two different gardens. The first was next to the Coronado Country Club at the end of Ocean Boulevard, destroyed by the big storm of 1905. The second was across the street from the Hotel del Coronado, behind the Spreckels Mansion. Marsh is best known for his Japanese Tea Garden in Golden Gate Park. The top image is of the first Tea Garden in 1904, bottom image is of second one. (CPL)

The dance pavilion at Tent City was the largest pavilion on the West Coast, also serving as a bowling alley and skating rink. It was torn down in 1939, when Tent City permanently closed. (CHA)

Originally, it was said, Tent City was a joint business venture between the Spreckels interests and a Los Angeles tent-and-awning manufacturer named Swanfeldt, whose name was stenciled on the tents. There was a choice of white, or red and white striped, ranging from family size to a small single. All tents had wooden floors and were furnished. Each had one bedstead or more, a three-legged "spider" for a wash basin and pitcher, a dresser, and a chair. If cooking facilities were wanted, a kerosene stove was set up in a "cook tent" in the rear for an extra $5 a month – complete with a few pots, some crockery, and flatware – but no guarantee against fire. Most tents rented for $4.50 per week at that time.

The *San Diego Union* of January 1, 1901, reported that over 500 persons lived in the tents during the previous season, and 68,139 people attended evening concerts, dances and other attractions. The advertising of Camp Coronado was thorough, and systematically done by the Santa Fe Railroad and the Coronado Beach Company.

Each year, Tent City opened its season with more attractions and improvements. Down the center of Tent City ran Main Street, which was paralleled by Ocean Front and Bay Front, intersected by numbered streets. At each corner of Main Street was a big white barrel with a spigot, kept filled with ice, making ice water. In the center of each block was a community sink for dishwashing and some laundering. Tubs of water were put at various places in which to wash off sandy feet.

The novel feature for the summer of 1901 was the "Floating Casino"—in reality, the ill-fated *Silver Gate* ferry, moored in Glorietta Bay. With a fairy-like bower of flowers and palms, it had electric lights, and music supplied by a regular orchestra. On deck, one could enjoy an ice cream

The Rew-Sharp Mansion at 1124 F Avenue, after a storm in the 1920s. (CHA)

parlor, rest and reading rooms, a dance hall and casino, a small stage for theatrics, and church services every Sunday!

Besides the tents, thatched or palm frond roofed cottages were also available. Electricity from Hotel generators provided some power for light bulbs that hung from each ceiling. Stores, restaurants, amusements, and even a pool hall sprang up as the summertime resort grew.

New recreational facilities such as Tent City, along with the general growth of the island population, required fresh water in increasing amounts. On August 24th, the Southern California Mountain Water Company decided to extend its water mains by way of the head of the bay, to connect with Coronado. By September 1900, the first grading camp line had been established in order to get the work moving as rapidly as possible. In Coronado, a number of taps for customers were installed with more going in each day.

The Board of Trustees received a letter from E.S. Babcock in 1901, recommending formation of a Board of Health, and suggesting Dr. W.A. Edwards, Charles Nordhoff, A.S. Childs, A.L. Reed and Andrew Ervast be appointed to serve. This group may have been, according to City Record Book No. 2, instrumental in establishing the "Dr. Edwards' Hospital." He and Dr. Raffaele Lorini were classmates at the University of Pennsylvania and members of the Class of 1881. Dr. Edwards married Francis Louise Taft, daughter of Alphonso and Louisa Torrey Taft, which made him a brother-in-law of President William Howard Taft, who became President in 1908.

In 1901, Louis C. Bandel became Superintendent of Parks. He would be responsible for much of the landscaping and beautiful, large trees Coronadans enjoy today. Water was an expensive commodity and the town parks often suffered due to the lack of it. Trees and shrubs got a drink periodically when Mike Quinlan, who sprinkled the dirt streets with the city water wagon, would give the greenery a spraying. Bandel, who was also fire chief, worked out an arrangement whereby the volunteer fire department could have their weekly fire drills in the parks, using water in the fire drills to help keep the grass growing.

Within the community, areas such as the center of the Glorietta section were used for farming, with windmills pumping water to farm houses. A white Victorian cottage built about 1889 still stands today at the corner of San Luis Rey and Guadalupe. Around the few houses was the wildlife:

doves, quail, horned toads, gophers, and lizards. Out on the "flats," which were low, sandy and marshy, everything was overgrown with vegetation common to salt water beaches. The shore was littered with driftwood. The bay, particularly at low tide, brought a salty smell which permeated "the flats" and drifted across the Glorietta section.

The football team of 1900 was composed of boys from the school, and some "ringers" from outside, who played on a nice, hard pan field on the west side of "E" Avenue between Sixth and Seventh Streets. Miss Caroline M. Balch, former Coronado student and elementary school teacher said, "I best remember the football heroes and the girls who took them out for a 'nice cold drink' during the intermission [halftime]. I was one of the girls."

Churchill-Pratt House, built 1898, was designed by architect Irving J. Gill. Originally located at 1300 Orange Avenue, it was moved to Pomona Avenue and later to 1106 4th Street. (CHA)

According to Art Mathewson, school children always listened to, and remembered their teachers. Mathewson said his German teacher was Miss Adele Meyer (Outcault)."

> The class was small and we were sent to one of the little upstairs rooms to do our studying—trusted to do it without supervision! We did it the shortest way possible, dividing the lesson into parts, each one taking a part. This saved a lot of time for other activities, but it sometimes proved most disastrous if the whole class made the same mistake in translation.

Mathewson also remembered a physics class taught by Mr. Baldwin. "James Brown Herreshoff, who lived at 654 Adella Avenue, was one of the pupils. I remember the long, long discussions he and Mr. Baldwin used to have about 'perpetual motion'. Jim kept thinking that he had discovered the secret." As the Coronado School Board would find over the years, a great many Coronado High School graduates, like James Herreshoff, would achieve national and even international acclaim as architects, yacht builders, and designers of automobiles.

C.B. Daggett resigned his post as a City Trustee, and George Holmes, Purchasing Agent for the Spreckels Company took his place. Holmes would serve on the Board for over twenty-five years and was Mayor during the period July 1902 to April 15, 1912. In March 1902, Graham E. Babcock, Elisha's son, was on the Board, giving the Hotel faction more leverage. Mary Cossitt, wife of the Episcopal minister, was appointed to serve on the Coronado Library Board of Trustees, while Mrs. C.M. Crandall became the first city librarian at the salary of $30 per month, serving in that job until

April 1903. Adaline Bailhace succeeded her until June 1905, when Mary E. Balch took over until February 1908.

J.W. Waller was appointed Deputy Marshal for the Coronado Fire Department. Repairs were ordered for the portable city jail, a small shed-like structure with bars on the door, which could be towed from one place to another as needed. Then, as now, the Trustees had minutiae to deal with. The City Marshal was directed to "scrape a path" on Isabella to serve as a bicycle path; (he had to have ordinances printed and posted on the door of the City Hall meeting place) and before 1902 was over, the Trustees had established a tax of 75 cents per $100 valuation as a levy on property. They issued an ordinance establishing the grade of the circular space around Star Park and that area was paved at that time. There was a question as to the cost of maintenance of the fountain in Star Park. One trustee suggested using salt water, while another suggested filling in the pond and just maintaining the fountain.

> When General Mendal Churchill unexpectedly passed away in Coronado in 1902, he left a lasting legacy in the city. A Union general in the Civil War, Churchill built a considerable fortune in railroads, iron, and banking. He chose Coronado as his perfect retirement setting, bought the triangular Block 10 across from the Hotel Del, engaged noted architect Irving Gill, and built one of the most distinguished homes on the Island. This home would later be moved to 819 Pomona Avenue, becoming a boarding school, and then to the corner of Orange Avenue and Fourth Street to serve as a nine-unit apartment within the Home Use Program of World War II. It was further remodeled and restored in 2015. Shortly after his passing, the City formally changed the name Bachelor Row to Churchill Place in his honor

The paving of "C" Avenue was completed during the year, while additional landscaping was done at Tent City. Efforts of the Trustees and the Beach Company complemented each other in upgrading the town. Sewer lines connecting to the public toilet facilities were also installed at Tent City. By the time of the opening in June, everything was ready for the new season. Henry Ohlmeyer and his orchestra provided a program on the floating casino that received raves in papers up and down the coast. New amusements and amenities promised lovely diversions for the visitor.

The Diamond Carriage and Livery Company took people riding. Hattie Johnson Stout, as official reader, conducted the palmistry parlor, and Mr. Burnell held forth at his curio stand. John E. Slocum became official photographer for Tent City, and P.M. Burge barbered. Mr. Ammon opened his restaurant and lunch counter, while Charles Hardy had his deli, fish store and meat market. Mathius F. Heller opened a grocery store, Herman Tewkes managed the ice cream parlor, and Mr. Stout provided a news stand so people could keep up-to-date with the latest newspapers and magazines.

Joseph V. Montijo, born in Coronado in 1901 at 831 Adella Avenue, was delivered by Dr. Sara Braithwaite Fleming, Coronado's first female physician. His father, previously the first butcher in Ensenada and in Tecate, was a carpenter at the Hotel del Coronado. Joseph remembered crossing the north beach to get to the Bight, where he fished and saw the golfers on the course.

J. Bartlett Richards was a wealthy Nebraska cattleman and banker. He brought his family to Coronado for the first time in 1900, to vacation at the Hotel del Coronado. The family bought four lots on Ocean Boulevard, and spun plans in 1901 to build a winter residence. Richards graduated from Phillips Academy, and as a cattleman of note, was voted into the National Cowboy Hall of Fame and the Western Heritage Center in 1970. He is the subject of a full biography, "Bartlett Richards, Nebraska Sandhills Cattleman," whose life spanned nearly all the periods of the open range in the Trans Mississippi West. He witnessed the rise of the Wyoming and Nebraska cattle industry, and took part in the struggle with unrealistic land laws. When fencing infringed on the business of cattlemen, the "law" set out to enforce an 1885 legislative action, which had forbid fencing the public domain. Richards and other cattlemen disobeyed the law and were forced to remove fences which enclosed 212,000 acres of grassland. Angered by a light prison sentence handed out, President Roosevelt ordered government agents to make an example of Richards, and in March 1907 Richards was fined and sentenced to a federal prison, where he died.

Earlier, while in Coronado, Bartlett and Inez Richards met architect Irving John Gill and William Sterling Hebbard, who designed their Coronado home. Inez Richards signed the Notice of Completion on their Ocean Boulevard residence on November 17, 1902, for the residence at 1015 Ocean Boulevard. After the death of Bartlett, his family stayed in Coronado until July 28, 1913, when Inez sold the home and property to Walter Hamlin and Florence Kennett Dupee, and took the family to Nebraska.

In March 1903, the Coronado Board of Trustees adopted a new system of house numbering for Coronado, as reported in the San Diego Union of April 9, 1903. Residents were asked to place the proper numbers on their houses.

Houses are numbered from north to south, and from west to east. On streets running from north to south, there are 50 numbers in each block, or one number to every ten feet. Commencing on the southwest corner of First and Orange Avenue, the first number on Orange Avenue is 100. The last number on that block would be 198, even numbers on the west side and odd numbers on the east. The numbers at the street crossings are First Street, 100;

Second, 200; Third, 300; Fourth, 400; Fifth, 500; Sixth, 600; Seventh, 700; Eighth, 800; Ninth, 900; Tenth, 1000; Tolita avenue, 1100.

> On the streets running from west to east, ten feet are given to each number, the even numbers being on the south side. The numbers at the street crossings are Boulevard 100; Alameda Avenue 200; K 300, J 400, I 500, H 600, G 700, F 800, E 900, D 1000, Orange 1100, C 1200, B 1300, A 1400. Adella and Pomona

> 1500. All irregular streets are numbered from north to south and west to east, taking the block number from the corresponding regular block. Numbers can be obtained at the office of the city clerk from the map on herein.

Meanwhile, sand dunes along the Strand had been leveled and more sand was dredged up from the bay to continue the building of Tent City. The Orange Avenue electric line was extended from the Hotel terminal down, the hill to a junction with the Belt Line running through the middle of Tent City.

In 1903, the ferry boat *Ramona* was built by the Risdon Iron Works at Oakland and acquired by the San Diego and Coronado Ferry Company. Powered by steam, with side paddle wheels and a wooden hull, it had a two cylinder engine—700 horsepower. This vessel served until 1931 when it was dismantled. She was anchored in San Diego Bay, and used as a night club until she went down in a storm. Raised, and without superstructure, she cruised the bay for a few more years as a scow.

The world-famous Scripps Institute of Oceanography in La Jolla had its start in 1903, but surprisingly not in La Jolla, rather in Coronado. Only the Marine Biological Laboratory in Woods Hole, Massachusetts has a longer history in American ocean sciences. On August 1, 1903, the *San Diego Union* carried a headline that Professor William Emerson Ritter, a biologist, had revealed some remarkable discoveries, particularly that Glorietta Bay had great biological diversity. San Diego Bay was also so rich that the possibilities for marine investigations were worthy of starting a permanent marine station. As early as 1891, Ritter, who taught in the Department of Zoology at the University of California at Berkeley, recommended a biological survey along the slope of the Pacific.

Ferryboat RAMONA in 1910. Built in 1903 in Oakland, she was 118 feet long, powered by steam with side paddle wheels. (CHA)

For several summers, he and his colleagues made collections, all the while keeping an eye out for a site suitable for their proposed station.

In San Diego, he met Fred Baker, M.D., whose avocation was collecting shells. He indicated he would try to raise funds locally to support such a facility. University of California President Benjamin Wheeler and E. S. Babcock had met while Wheeler was staying at the Hotel; Babcock quickly offered the Hotel's Coronado Boathouse in Glorietta Bay for the summer study. He threw in the Hotel launch as an additional incentive.

In June 1903, Ritter and several marine investigators arrived in Coronado. They collected specimens of plankton, corals, copepods, and other marine life in their nets from the schooner *Laura*. A number of prominent San Diegans and their guests came to visit Ritter. In this way, he developed patrons and benefactors, particularly newspaper publisher Edwin Wyllis Scripps and his sisters Ellen Browning and Virginia, who would own the *San Diego Sun*. With the summer coming to an end, the Marine Biological Association of San Diego was formed with the help of Scripps, Baker, and the San Diego Chamber of Commerce. Out of this meeting and other sessions, prominent San Diegans associated themselves with Ritter and his work, with the goal of providing a permanent laboratory in the area. Ritter continued to provide reports on his investigations, intriguing men like George W. Marston and John D. Spreckels. The biologists returned to the Coronado Hotel Boathouse in the summer of 1904, but before long they had a permanent home in La Jolla, which came to be known as the Scripps Institution of Oceanography, a part of the University of California, San Diego.

> *[The Coronado Beach Company agreed to improvements to the Boathouse during the second summer session of 1904, including the addition of an extra room and strengthening of pilings, but it became evident that the Boathouse could never hold the expanding laboratory (including plans for an aquarium). Yet ... Coronado stands as the site of the second oceanographic laboratory established in the United States.—ed.]*

Kneedler House on Ocean Boulevard, after 1905 storm. (CPL)

A maintenance railroad was planned in Coronado, along Seventh Street between Pomona and "B" Avenue. Alarmed citizens protested the proposed railway, including Anson P. Stephens, who owned the home at the southeast corner of Seventh and "A" (later known as the Stephens-Terry residence). The City Board of Trustees vetoed the project after hearing the outcry from so many vocal citizens.

The first electric carriage, made to order for E.S. Babcock, arrived in Coronado in July 1900. Built by the Waverly Manufacturing Company of Indianapolis, it weighed 1,400 pounds with a storage charge that would permit it to run 30 miles at 15 miles an hour. Complaints were registered about automobile speed limits, until they were set at four miles per hour in 1904. (By 1912, a comprehensive speed law went into effect for both autos and motorcycles, which points out the desperate chances motorists were taking, operating their machines at more than 15 miles an hour.)

On Christmas Eve 1904, the lighting of the large tree at the entrance to the Hotel del Coronado took place. The first officially-lighted, outdoor Christmas tree, that same Norfolk Island pine (still standing today), was lit every year, except during World War II, and in 1973, during an energy crisis. Due to the tree's size, this tradition was eventually ended, and the ceremony transferred to the lighting of the large pine at Rotary Circle on Orange and Isabella Avenues.

Coronado's own ostrich farm boasted the arrival of another course of young chicks, sustained in incubators in 1901. The farm had 39 animals, and as plucking time drew near, W. Harvey Bentley looked forward to the harvest of plumage. He kept in touch with similar farms all over the United States, and bred only superior birds.

The Sunday, January 1, 1905, edition of the *San Diego Union* featured a two-page spread on "Beautiful Coronado Homes," accenting growth of the city across the bay, and noting that many attractive cottages had been built during the year. Photos of residences of Graham Babcock, Giles Kellogg, Bartlett Richards, Frazer-Robinson and Mrs. Syms were spread across the page. Mentioned were cottages owned by William Roach and Grace Health. The Israel brothers bought and remodeled one of Orange Avenue's smaller cottages, and J.W. Wines built a five-room cottage on "F." The article emphasized that the city was growing in favor with Easterners, who were keeping architects busy.

Spreckels, meanwhile, continued to make improvements, especially at the Hotel and at Tent City. The beauty of the resort was its isolation, yet it offered many conveniences and reasonable costs. Added in 1905, were: a new club house for the Woman's Club; a public library and reading room; the Japanese Tea Garden (not to be confused with the one at the end of Ocean Boulevard); and a new German Garden, "as thoroughly foreign as though it existed beside the Rhine, instead of on the shores of the Pacific". Along the shore of Glorietta Bay, from the boathouse to the floating casino, a row of Australian salt bush was put down – green foliage that required little water.

In the Village, some of the main streets were graded and paved during 1904. Much more foliage had been planted, and during school vacation, painters and carpenters had been tidying up the public school.

Spreckels Companies are worth noting (even though their general offices were headquartered in the Union Building in San Diego), showing how, in less than a decade, John D. Spreckels had become a major economic force of the region.

> **Spreckels Companies 1905**
> Coronado Beach Company
> Hotel del Coronado
> Coronado Tent City
> Coronado Plumbing Company
> San Diego Electric Railway Company
> Coronado Water Company
> Southern California Mountain Water Company
> San Diego and Coronado Ferry Company
> San Diego and Coronado Transfer Company
> United Light, Fuel and Power Company
> San Diego and South Eastern Railway Company
> San Diego and Arizona Railway Company

Officers of the Spreckels Companies were: John D. Spreckels, President; W. Clayton, Vice President and Managing Director; H.L. Titus, General Counsel; Claus Spreckels, Secretary/Treasurer. Others included: B.M. Warner, General Superintendent; A.H. Kayser, General Auditor; George Holmes, Purchasing Agent.

Until 1905, the Home Telephone Company housed its exchanges in the Coronado Beach Company offices. But on April 17, 1905, Charles E. Sumner made an application, on behalf of the Home Telephone Company, to construct, erect, maintain and operate telephone and telegraph lines in Coronado by means of conduits and poles, with wires attached, over and along the public highway and alleys, for the purpose of a telegraph and telephone company. The Board of Trustees approved Sumner's plan by Ordinance 131 dated May 22, 1905. The mile of connecting wire, shipped from New York, was dropped into the bay near the foot of "H" Street in San Diego to the end of "E" Street in Coronado. On the reel, the cable weighed fourteen tons. The telephone exchange was set up in the real estate office of H.S. Stocking at the southeast corner of Orange and Loma Avenues. Within the year, the directory listed 65 subscribers, both individuals and businesses.

Major disasters hit the community during the year. On January 4 and February 18, 1905, severe storms struck, doing great damage both north and south of the Hotel del Coronado. Winds and ocean waves played havoc with Ocean Boulevard, beating it with such tremendous force that the entire street was undermined. Water came up to the big homes on the Boulevard, and inundated front yards. There was no beach along Ocean Boulevard and, therefore, no protection from wave damage. Breakers were so high that they splashed against the verandas of the Hotel del Coronado. Two-hundred-pound sandbags, 30,000 of them, were piled along Ocean Boulevard and in front of the Hotel after the storm subsided, in order to erect a barricade in case another storm followed. March storms continued to cause serious wave erosion; ultimately 110 feet of land was removed along Ocean Boulevard.

After the storms, two large residences on the Boulevard were moved "inland," by their distraught owners. The George S. Gay house at Loma was moved to a point of land at Isabella and "E" Avenue, and Dr. William L. Kneedler's home, the personal physician to President Howard Taft, moved his home to 1000 Adella, where it remains today. The old Hotel fishing pier had withstood the assault of the ocean for some years, but finally, it too was destroyed by the 1905 storms. Another pier was soon built, this time of wood. It had a landing platform at the end for the convenience of small boat passengers, primarily U.S. Navy shore boats.

The storm also ruined the Japanese Tea Garden at the north end of Ocean Boulevard. Subsequently, an agreement was signed by Messrs. Spreckels and Marsh to build a new Tea Garden on a large part of Spreckels' property bordered on three sides by Clarita Row, Ynez, and Adella. The lovely garden on Spreckels' leased grounds remained open for some thirty years until Colonel Ira C. Copley, who purchased the Spreckels estate, acquired the garden for private use. This second Japanese Tea Garden, tremendously popular for private parties, wedding receptions, and birthday celebrations, was right out of an old pictorial book.

In 1905, after an epic storm washed away most of Ocean Boulevard. (CHA)

On July 21, 1905, an explosion aboard the USS *Bennington* (Steel Gunboat No. 4) caused one of the major peacetime disasters in the Navy's history. Broeck Newton Oder, a Coronadan, tells the story. While berthed in the San Diego harbor, a boiler suddenly blew up, killing one officer and 61 men, injuring 46 others. Helpless, scalded men struggled in the waters and scores of boats raced to their aid. Coronado's ferry *Ramona* was one such vessel. The San Diego community pulled its unprepared resources together and did what it could as far as offering food, shelter and comfort for the stricken survivors. Funeral services were held, and a mass burial for 47 of the dead was conducted on Sunday, July 23, 1905, in the post cemetery at Fort Rosecrans. Three years later, a 64-foot granite monument, paid for by public subscription, was unveiled in honor of the USS *Bennington*'s dead.

[*Coronado jeweler Joseph Jessop, as a boy of seven years, recalls being almost blown from his feet, while standing on the sand at the Coronado ferry landing. Boatswain's Mate William S. Cronan was awarded a Medal of Honor for extraordinary heroism while helping to save three of his fellow shipmates aboard Bennington. He is recognized today with the naming of Cronan Park at Pomona Avenue and Sixth Street in Coronado. —ed.*]

Coronado's Ocean Boulevard seawall was built in 1906-1907, after the ravages of the 1905 storms. Spreckels had gained the Belt Line Railroad as a subsidiary company, and used it to bring rocks to make a foundation in front of the Hotel del Coronado, in order to lay additional railroad tracks. When completed, the Belt Line train then hauled rocks for the seawall over those tracks from the Sweetwater Valley. Some 67 tons of rock were piled on flat cars, driven to the boulevard, and rolled into place. In addition to the rails in front of the Hotel, the Belt Line also used tracks formerly placed on Olive Avenue, as well as those used during construction of the Zuñiga jetty. This enormous undertaking was all possible because property owners along the Boulevard voted a bond issue of $145,000 to finance it. The huge boulders did not totally stop the ravages of Mother Nature. In future storms, the rocks themselves would be hurled on to the boulevard.

Rocks being hauled for seawall after 1905 storm. Track ran down Olive Avenue to Ocean Boulevard. (CHA)

By January 1906, the Hotel was described as "the finest seaside resort in the world," after many improvements and changes. Furnishings had been replaced, rich, new red carpets laid, old electric light fixtures taken out and new ones substituted. A great deal of money was expended on the ballroom, reading room, billiard room, and bowling alleys. A large amount of work was invested in re-turfing the grounds, planting new trees and flowers, and installing an electric fountain.

That same year, Spreckels added to Coronado's reputation as a playground for the wealthy, when he built a polo field near the Spanish Bight. The field included four city blocks from Fourth to Eighth Streets, along the west side of the golf course, running parallel to Alameda. In later years, when polo ceased, the National Horse Show would be held in the same location.

As polo became popular, the streetcar line carried crowds to the Coronado Country Club, for the enjoyment of both golf and polo. After the 1905 storm, the Clubhouse building was moved from Ocean Boulevard to a site between Fifth and Sixth Streets, just off Alameda. It was a large two-story redwood building with enclosed glass balconies, though it was not posh. In fact, the club was very plain and practical, but with a feeling of warmth and friendliness. Members and guests enjoyed amenities such as luncheon rooms, reading rooms, and dressing rooms.

During this era, assumptions have been made that the town was without a newspaper. *The San Diego Union* of April 27, 1906 reported however, that its offices had received a copy of the *Coronado News* published by Neyenesch and Reed on Orange Avenue. The illustrated paper was to be a weekly and, "people with axes to grind ... will be discouraged, and politics tabooed." No copies of this paper are known to exist.

The Los Angeles Times on January 13, 1906 reported that the Hotel Del Coronado was headquarters for the daring Los Angeles-San Diego Motor Car Endurance Run. A hazardous, inland route was chosen from Los Angeles to such points as Corona, Elsinore and Temecula, up and over the Agua Tibia Mountains, and down to Pala. It took the drivers two days to complete the 180-mile journey and the maximum speed limit was set at twenty miles an hour. After the grade to Escondido, cars went to the Bernardo country store, along the stage road to Poway Pass, and down into Mission Valley to the ferry. Twenty-two of the original thirty cars moved up Pomona Avenue for their destination the Hotel del Coronado. The race ended in a dispute with no winner, but not long afterward, the Southern California Automobile Club asked the Board of Supervisors of San Diego County to begin construction of a more direct highway connection with Los Angeles.

Coronadans had been ever alert to the danger of fires, especially with so many tent and frame homes on the island. The City Board of Trustees had already given consent to purchasing two chemical engines. Chemical engine carts, like the hose carts, were pulled by the firemen. Precincts were set up by Fire Brigade Chief Waller and the precincts then further divided into twelve districts, each led by a volunteer assistant chief, usually a resident of his own district. Fire drills and contests were held regularly to train the men and to keep them physically fit, in addition to providing a feeling of comradeship.

Besides the main firehouse at 124 Orange Avenue, the fire brigade rented an engine house for $5 a week for company No. 2 near the Hotel del Coronado. Still, the inherent danger of fires at Tent City and the number of visitors to the island caused the fire insurance underwriters' inspectors to warn the city fathers that other towns this size employed paid firemen instead of utilizing volunteers. Fire rates could soar if a change were not made. Largely with the help of the Spreckels Company, more carts and hoses were bought.

On May 21, 1906, Fire Chief Waller asked the City Board of Trustees for space in Engine House No. I, where a volunteer fireman could live permanently. At the same time, he asked that a central fire station equipped with a bell tower be built. Waller, an extremely perceptive chief, sought a number of improvements, all meant to provide safety, and the Board approved them. Quarters for a permanent caretaker were completed at 124 Orange Avenue and C.E. Brown took over as resident volunteer.

In 1906-1907, the central fire department was built on Sixth Street facing West Plaza – the same site as today. Within a pleasing architectural design, stucco with protruding decorative beams near the roofline, the new fire station included living quarters. A year later, A.B. Shaw established an adequate electrical fire alarm system with alarm boxes fastened to the poles of the Gas and Electric Company.

> In 1909, a 70-foot tall steel-frame bell tower was erected in the West Plaza behind the Library. An old steel locomotive wheel rim formally used as an alarm was raised to the top and connected to a mechanical striking system like a grandfather's clock. It struck once each hour. If a fire broke out, it struck a number corresponding to a certain alarm box pull station.

By 1912, the department had a new four-cylinder, Knox-motor drive engine with a two-bucket seat, right-hand drive and windshield. The up-to-date fire engine was Coronado's pride and joy, kept in perfect mechanical condition. In 1913, it rushed to a blaze at the Orange Avenue Hotel on the northeast corner of Orange and Third; the Coronado landmark, however, was consumed by the flames. In 1914, silver badges were presented to the "fire boys," and in 1915, Spreckels bought a Cadillac to be kept at the firehouse at 1011 Sixth St and had it converted to a well-equipped ambulance for the city.

Volunteer Fire Department pictured in front of their firehouse, c. 1912. Firehouse was built in 1906-7 on Orange between First and Second Streets. (CHA)

1907 had to have been one of John D. Spreckels' most productive years for the town of Coronado. In August, the *Union* carried architect Harrison Albright's rendering of Spreckel's "beach cottage" at 1043 Ocean Blvd. Albright, a native of Shoemakertown, Pennsylvania, was one of the early, successful designers who worked in steel reinforced concrete construction. It may have been his expertise in this medium which resulted in a fire and earthquake-proof building that led Spreckels to commission Albright for so many of his projects. Spreckels had suffered through the 1906 San Francisco fire and seen the total devastation caused by wooden buildings. Among the major buildings designed in San Diego at Spreckels behest by Albright were the Golden West Hotel, the Spreckels Theatre, the Timken Building, and the Spreckels Organ Pavilion in Balboa Park.

In 1908, the Library Trustees authorized Charles T. Hinde to ask Spreckels to make a gift of a new library building, contingent upon proper maintenance by the City. After some discussion as to location, Spreckels suggested the West Plaza (which he also donated for library use), and contracted with Harrison Albright to build the library at a cost of $10,000, built of course, of reinforced concrete with a storage basement. The building, typical of the period, was small, with Grecian columns at either side of the entrance and similar columns supporting the ceiling inside. Interior and exterior friezes would bear the names of great literary forefathers. It was one of the first California buildings built of reinforced concrete and was planned to hold 5,000 books. Indeed, perhaps more than any other signal of his endeavors, one can see the hand of Coronado's Spreckels in this building, for its construction reflects his strength, and the elements suggest the heart of the man.

The handsome, little library presented to the people of Coronado by Spreckels in March, 1909 became a source of great pride to the city. Charles S. Robinson was the first librarian in the new building. His resignation was accepted in October 1910, but he continued to serve on the Board of Trustees, and later from 1912 to 1914 became the acting Secretary. Two librarians, Mrs. Mary G. Balentine and Miss Anna H. Allsebrook, served five and three years respectively until Miss Gabrielle Morton was appointed to the position of librarian on October 1, 1918. She remained a beloved figure, known to all Coronadans until her death in 1951.

Also during this period, Albright was kept busy building three other Coronado residences: two for John D. Spreckels and one for Harry L. Titus, attorney for the Spreckels' interests. In addition to his "beach cottage," Spreckels commissioned a main residence for his family to overlook Glorietta

Bay and to occupy an entire block. The magnificent marble and brass staircase and the 1914 music room built to house Spreckels' forty-rank Aeolian organ are part of the mansion that still exist today as the Glorietta Bay Inn. By May 1908, reporters looking over the island said that Coronado was enjoying an unprecedented building boom, with costs for homes averaging from $3000 to $5000 for attractive residences.

For some years, the people of Coronado had received their water from the Otay wells. The water was pumped through a pipeline to Coronado, then distributed through the city's mains. While the supply was adequate, it was not the pure, mountain water which the city's citizens would soon have. At a cost of $150,000, plans were made and completed whereby the water of the Otay reservoir was diverted and brought directly to Coronado. A water main was laid from the San Diego main at Otay down to Nestor, through which the water for Coronado was brought. There, it was purified by means of an immense aerating table which had a maximum capacity of three million gallons every twenty-four hours. From there the water was brought to Coronado through the old mains. This was regarded as the major project of the town during the year.

From the City Book of Records comes the information that the Board of Trustees considered putting up the bandstand in the Plaza for sale. In need of repair and apparently not used, the original bandstand was sold to C.W. Houts, a building contractor. The Trustees felt that the Tent City bandstand was sufficient, and if Mr. Spreckels was to build the library in the Plaza, then that was no place for the bandstand.

Yet other history was being made in the city, more quietly. At Fourth and "J," a vivacious lady of Castilian parentage, aged seventy-three, had come to live with her relatives, the Israels of Point Loma Lighthouse fame. The step-daughter of Thomas Wrightington and Juana Machado Alípaz de Wrightington, Maria Arcadia had known San Diego and Old Town from the days of the War with Mexico in 1846-1848. Robert Decatur Israel had married Maria when she was but sixteen. They would have three sons, Henry Clay, Joseph Perry and Robert Lincoln, all descended from the Machados who had come with the first settlers to found the Spanish Royal Presidio in San Diego.

> The largest spectacle in Coronado history up to that time and one of the most impressive of all time, began at the crack of dawn on April 14, 1908. Sixteen pristine, brilliantly white, powerful American dreadnaughts of the Great White Fleet appeared over the horizon and crisply anchored in ordered rows of divisions – right off the Hotel del Coronado in Coronado Roads. Twenty thousand people lined Coronado beach to witness the arrival. Streetcars and ferries were jammed and everyone was in a festive mood. Spectacular weather continued for a weekend of parades, speeches, balls, sporting events, and intense tourism. J. S. Hammond, manager of Tent City, released a brochure that said: "The Only Place from which to view the Fleet in its Entirety. Palm Tent Houses and Cottages will be open for the accommodation of visitors. The Lunch Counter will also be open during the visit of the Fleet." The Hotel Del was said to have had its largest house count to date during the visit – 1,000 names on the register.
>
> The fleet had been ordered by President Teddy Roosevelt to circumnavigate the world, demonstrating to all the expanding power of the American navy. San Diego and Coronado represented the fleet's first port of call along the U.S. West Coast after leaving Hampton Roads and rounding Cape Horn. It was a dazzling event and resulted in a terrific outpouring of public good will toward the Navy that would set the tone for decades as the Navy expanded their bases into Southern California. As important, many of the officers of the fleet and decision makers in the Navy would never forget their warm welcome and that would later set the stage for many decisions involving Navy basing in Coronado and San Diego.

Teddy Roosevelt's Great White Fleet of 16 front-line battleships, anchored in Coronado Roads off the Hotel del Coronado in April 1908. Making an unprecedented round-the-world cruise, thousands flocked to Coronado to view them. Their impact on Coronado and San Diego was immense, directly influencing later decisions to establish bases around San Diego Bay. (CHA)

The San Diego Union of Friday, January 1, 1909, summed up the state of the town in its headlines that in large bold type reported "Coronado has water system equal of any in the country." The emphasis of the newsprint lay on the many handsome homes erected during 1908, and the fact that the town was able to keep up with the public services required for those homes. The cheap transportation rate between San Diego and the city across the bay suggested that Coronado was becoming a home for "thousands."

In 1909 the Coronado Beach Company planted 40,000 eucalyptus trees on North Island to cover a strip bordering on the bay front and to enhance the barren appearance of the island as seen from San Diego.

The planting started at a point 1,000 feet west of the Marine Ways, followed the shore line east and along the bank overlooking Spanish Bight to the ocean front, where it could be seen from the Hotel del Coronado, almost two miles away. With the idea of future development, North Island had been platted out in city blocks and streets, and a number of men worked to clean the brush off the thoroughfares which were soon to be graded. The Coronado Beach Company set aside an area of fifteen acres for park purposes along the bay shoreline.

As for South Island, the Trustees passed an ordinance to ensure free postal delivery. A decision had been made on how streets and houses would be numbered, and now the Trustees passed an ordinance requiring all property owners to put numbers upon buildings owned by them, such figures to be not less than two inches high and visible from the street, to be done within thirty days.

The Trustees acted upon the sewage question by having city staff prepare a list of all houses not connected with the city sewer lines. Forty thousand dollars had been voted for the purpose of enlarging and providing the improved sewer system. To begin in 1910/1911, the changes provided for sewers in the alleys of every block of the city and for the extension of the sewer outfall in the bay as far as the main channel, thereby eliminating any possibility of contamination.

The City Attorney was asked to give an answer to the question as to whether Orange Avenue had ever been formally accepted by the city; for it had remained as part of the street car right-of-way under the ownership of the Coronado Beach Company and the Spreckels Company. He replied in the negative, but stated that the city could legally go ahead and pave the street out of the general fund or by voting bonds. The Trustees, however, showed little disposition to inaugurate any paving project for the main street at this time, but fifteen miles of guttering and curbing were laid, and paving of twenty miles of cement sidewalk took place elsewhere on the island. Also, one hundred and eighty electric lights were installed during the year, which placed one on almost every street corner of the city.

Every morning at 5 a.m. joggers met at the end of Tent City near the Hotel del Coronado, limbered up with muscle-bending antics, and made their way about the island. Thirty men and women ran down Orange Avenue, past the park and library and then back to Glorietta Bay where they rested awhile, swam a mile, and then ran another mile. Apparently they did this throughout the year, regardless of the weather.

At the onset of the year 1910, Coronado's population had increased again, officially at 1,477 persons. San Diego's Mayor had declared a half-holiday on Monday, January 23rd, so that everyone could have a chance to cross the bay over the weekend. The attraction was a spectacular air show to be held at the grandstand of the Coronado Polo Field January 23-25, when people could see the miraculous "flying machine" soar to the heavens. In front of a grandstand packed with excited spectators, Charles K. Hamilton flew a Curtiss "pusher" from the field to make the first powered flight in San Diego County, on January 23, 1910. The young pilot started the engine and the bi-plane went bouncing down the rough turf for a hundred feet, and jumped into the sky. The plane flew

Beginning in 1910, the Navy's Pacific Squadron began basing their Destroyer and Submarine squadrons in Coronado, with many crew members living in Coronado—the beginning of a residential influence that would span a century. (CHA)

along Point Loma, over Fort Rosecrans, down the Strand to the Hotel del Coronado, and back to the Coronado Country Club where it circled the Polo Field and landed. Those watching knew an incredible feat had taken place. Two other flights were made by Hamilton that day, and on Monday, January 24, he flew to Tijuana and back, the first aviator to fly across the international border. The following day, Hamilton flew a Curtiss "pusher" from the Coronado Polo Grounds and made an emergency landing in the sand dunes on North Island – the first airplane ever to land on North Island.

In 1948, William S. Doty, who had moved to Pittsburgh, Pennsylvania, reminisced that in 1910, telephones and automobiles were becoming an everyday affair. "We even flocked to Coronado to see Hamilton demonstrate a weird bailing-wire-and bamboo thing called an aeroplane." According to him, "North Island was then a large, flat expanse of sagebrush, cactus, sand and jackrabbits. The Spreckels' Marine Ways, at the corner of North Island, reared empty skeleton-ribs against the sky. Occasionally the thing could be rolled down a track and into the water and pick up a very small vessel to be hauled out for repairs."

The USS 'Grampus' and USS 'Pike,' the first submarines in the Pacific Squadron were based in Coronado during 1910-11, sharing piers near the Ferry Landing with a Navy destroyer division. More advanced submarines followed them to be likewise based in Coronado. (CHA)

Bank of Commerce and Trust, c.1910, at the corner of Park Place and Orange Avenue, current home of the Coronado Historical Association. The storefront offered ice cream and the door at the left was the Post Office. (CPL)

At Tent City in 1910, a huge dance pavilion and a nice, wide boardwalk were completed at the resort. The pavilion, the largest on the Pacific Coast during its heyday, became a bowling alley and skating rink. It was one of the last buildings torn down when Tent City was demolished in 1939, and its roof exists today as the roof of the theatre building at North Island. A number of contracts also were issued to vendors for concessions at Tent City. Jim Pandel was allowed to sell peanuts and popcorn at the monkey cage; a barbershop was constructed; and a card room added to the growing list of businesses.

About half way down the Strand from Tent City, away from everything and everyone, were several coves where small palm shacks had been built for overnight camping or for a day's picnicking. Sometimes people took small boats into the coves for outings.

In the wake of the visit of the Great White Fleet in 1908, the Navy ordered two divisions of torpedo boats to be based in San Diego Bay. By 1910, the small torpedo boats and their support tender *Iris* had arrived and were moored at two piers in Coronado, near the ferry slips – Coronado's first naval base. That same year, two of the Navy's first experimental submarines (USS *Grampus* and USS *Pike*) were also ordered to Coronado to operate with the torpedo boats. Although a tiny 63 feet in length, they could dive to 60 feet and make a top speed of 8 knots. Colorfully named "demon divers" in the press, their test dives in San Diego Bay attracted much attention from Coronadans, including one episode when the ferry *Ramona* had to swerve to avoid what startled passengers described as a dark, foreboding shape of what looked to be a whale rising wet and gleaming close aboard. The subs returned to the Mare Island naval base in 1911 after receiving some maintenance at the Spreckels' Marine Ways at North Island. Within a year, the Navy dispatched newer classes of submarines to Coronado and San Diego and established the Navy's first formal submarine training school, named Camp Richardson, on the bayside of Coronado's First Street, near D Avenue.

During the year 1910, over $200,000 had been invested in Coronado as more and more San Diego business and professional men saw the merits of Coronado and its beautiful assets The city was quickly growing into a prime residential, tourist and business location. Providing financing for many of these various business ventures was the first bank in Coronado—the Bank of Commerce and Trust–begun in a small storefront at the corner of Tenth and Orange Avenues, while a new building to house it was constructed. The bank was headed by G. Aubrey Davidson, a former railroad executive, who founded the Southern Bank of Commerce and Trust in San Diego in 1907.

Davidson, a 24-year resident of the Hotel del Coronado, helped shape the future of San Diego and Coronado in many key ways. He is called the "Father of the Panama-California Exposition" for suggesting the idea and leading the group which organized, financed, and implemented the 1915-16 Exposition in Balboa Park, greatly spurring development of San Diego, and putting the small city with big ambitions on the world map. Davidson was also instrumental in helping bring the U.S. Navy to San Diego, transforming the city.

The landmark building at 1100 Orange we admire today was designed by two San Francisco architects, Kenneth MacDonald, Jr., and George A. Applegarth. They both trained at the Ecole des Beaux-Arts in Paris, and collaborated on over 30 residences in San Francisco, including the palatial home of Adolph Spreckels. Applegarth later designed the California Palace of the Legion of Honor, which Alma and Adolph Spreckels donated to the city of San Francisco as a European Arts museum. Many classical Beaux-Arts elements—rigid symmetry, perfect proportions, columned entries and coffered ceilings—were employed in the design of the new Coronado bank, which was estimated to cost $160,925. A local contracting firm, Gallaher Construction, was the builder. Construction began December 15, 1910, and the new building opened for business on June 17, 1911.

G. Aubrey Davidson, who lived at the Hotel del Coronado for 24 years, founded the Bank of Commerce and Trust which now houses CHA and the Coronado Visitor Center. Well known in San Diego as the President of the San Diego Chamber of Commerce and the visionary behind the 1915 Panama-California Exposition in Balboa Park. (Balboa Park, Committee of 100)

In 1999, 1100 Orange Avenue became the Coronado Historical Association's headquarters when Don and Leslie Budinger gifted the historic building to CHA, allowing it to move from 1126 Loma Avenue to a location in the heart of downtown Coronado. CHA's move would not have been possible without the visionary and philanthropic assistance of Mr. and Mrs. Budinger, which continues to this day.

J.H. Eskridge, realtor, had the honor of being the first depositor. Stockholders were Julius Wangenheim President, B.W. McKenzie, John D. Spreckels, A.B. Daniels, Captain C.T. Hinde, Nelson E. Barker, Frank Von Tesmar and Mrs. Syms, all residents of Coronado. The bank building would become the longest, continuously utilized commercial building in Coronado history, and would later become home to Coronado's City Hall, the Coronado Post Office, Central Drug Store, Bank of America, various offices, Marco's Italian restaurant, and the Coronado Historical Association.

More and more San Diego business and professional men, as well as the wealthy class of retired merchants, were investing in property in Coronado. Homes had been finished for Arthur Dewar, G.O. Tutt, F.C. Winchester, William.E. Ingelow, H.B. Hakes and Captain J.S. Sedam. All were pictured in the *San Diego Union* of January 2, 1911.

Class in front of Coronado's first real schoolhouse, c.1900. (CHA)

Aside from a few family squabbles and occasional gun fights, Coronado was virtually free from crime. In June 1911, the city hall was moved to upstairs quarters of the Bank of Commerce and Trust, at the corner of Orange and Park Place, where the police force could be in closer touch with city management. Local government occupied those quarters until March 1918. The police force, small as it was, found itself spread pretty thin, its jurisdiction running from the south end of the Strand to North Island. Heavy concentration was needed on the Tent City area. Also, in the summer months, many easterners and middle westerners rented Coronado homes, which placed an extra burden on the small force.

With growth, increased pressure was put on the City Board of Trustees for civic improvements and citizen needs. The increase in student numbers had overtaxed the school accommodations and the School Board Trustees recommended an addition to the existing building.

Private enterprise also flourished. During 1911, Dr. Tel Bergren opened his health place, Halsohem, a musical Swedish word signifying health and home, the prime ingredients of human happiness, on Glorietta Boulevard. The clinic, much like the modern health, diet and exercise clinics, was limited to certain types of illnesses. At that time, one of the Wegeforth doctors tried to lease a frame house at 935 "D" Avenue for a maternity hospital, but neighbors objected and the location was not zoned for hospital use. Mr. F. H. C. Furnald established a drugstore on Orange Avenue known as the Central Drug Store. Although his business had been good at the Hotel del Coronado, the site on the main thoroughfare was felt to be more convenient for the general public.

Of great interest to the community was the announcement, accompanied by photographs, that Frank A. Hyatt, inventor, scout and terror of outlaws who had won fame as a gun fighter and detective, had at last been conquered by Cupid. He and his bride, married on September 13, 1910, resided at 131 Orange Avenue, in their house called "The Alamosa." The noted Indian fighter, former

Sheriff of Conejos County, and Marshall of Alamosa, Colorado married Mrs. Jennie M. Bazier. He was sixty-eight and she was sixty-two. They had a quiet wedding.

By 1911, a need had come for the public scavenger, (city worker with a garbage cart) to move trash a bit further from Coronado Beach. In that year, Henry and Rudolph Riis lived on a spit of land that became known as the "Hog Ranch." They leased this farmland four miles south of Tent City from Spreckels Company specifically for raising hogs near a source of edible garbage. The Hotel Del and Tent City provided enough to help feed Jacob Riis' pigs. Riis, who marketed the hogs and had a good income from the farm, had 200 acres, measuring southward from Brickyard Cove (now Crown Cove) along the bay to Imperial Beach. In addition to pigs, he and his brother raised horses, cows, and chickens. When North Island operations accelerated beginning in 1914, the Riis brothers acquired feed from North Island. The experiment would remain short-lived, however, for when the Otay Dam disaster occurred in 1916, the bay waters rose and virtually inundated the ranch, forcing the family to move to San Diego.

Fertile topsoil was cleared off the Hog Ranch site and hauled to the Coronado Country Club golf course by the Hotel del Coronado crews after the Riis family left. In the meantime, however, Coronadans adopted the practice of dumping their trash in any convenient nearby vacant lot since the city trash collection was not adequate. While the city had a legitimate dump area near the bay on the northeast corner of town, it simply was easier to carry the garbage anywhere one would not be seen dumping. In 1912, the City Marshal enforced the law prohibiting dumping of trash and so the City Engineer provided plans for an incinerator. When the city did not have funds on hand, Spreckels' Coronado Beach Company flew to the rescue one more time and provided a site down the Strand, two miles southeast of the Hotel del Coronado. A two-unit, W.H. McGuire patented sanitary oil furnace, with all driveways, water, light, sewer connections, fuel storage and other necessary appliances for proper operation of the plant was located on a site of 1.24 acres.

The city, however, would have to lease both site and plant with the idea that they someday, would become owner of the incinerator plant. Cost of the incinerator was $9116.20, of which 10% was to be paid each year with an interest rate of 6% for 10 years.

The Hotel announced in 1911 that the management would change hands on August 1st. Some 250 applications for the $9,000 a year position were received. H.W. Wills was selected for the job, but on July 12, 1912, when he inherited an estate, he resigned and returned to England. Succeeding him was J.J. Hernan, who had been the assistant manager for a number of years. He had moved on to manage the Palace Hotel in San Francisco, the Baltimore Hotel in Kansas City, and the Brown Hotel in Denver. He returned in August to take the enviable position, and was described as having a great understanding of human nature, as well as being friendly, considerate, kind, and adored by young people.

Up to this time, the use of the harbor and North Island by the armed forces was under an amicable arrangement with the city. Lloyd Harmon, former mayor of Coronado, and a member of the crew of the armored cruiser *Maryland* when Admiral Uriel Sebree (later a Coronado City Councilman) commanded the Pacific Squadron, told of Sebree sailing his flagship, the armored cruiser *Califomia*, into the narrow and winding channel which opened into San Diego's harbor. Harmon explained that this was of the greatest import to San Diego because it pointed out that ships of that size, which had never before come inside the bay, could easily enter and berth there. San Diego had at last become a liberty port, and North Island was used for the fleet's landing parties.

To win a Navy contract for new aircraft, Curtiss had to prove he could take off and land on both water and land. He did so in 1911, with a famous flight from the Spanish Bight to the beach by the Hotel Del and back. (CHA)

In 1910, development and change would begin to come to North Island, the result of a newfangled contraption that flew through the air. Inventor and entrepreneur Glenn Curtiss of Hammondsport, New York who once held the world record in motorcycle racing was looking for a winter location for his fledgling aeroplane company for both experimentation and pilot training. In Curtiss' eyes, North Island was the perfect location for his operations with warm winters, inviting weather, near perfect winds (vital for early low-powered aircraft who needed the lift from winds), and a degree of isolation where he could experiment without large crowds. The San Diego Aero Club helped arrange a rent free lease for three years and Curtiss moved his crews to a North Island site on Spanish Bight near the Marine Ways where he built several clapboard work shops and hangars in late 1910.

Glenn Hammond Curtiss' specialty was seaplanes or flying boats or, as he labeled them, "hydroaeroplanes." As an entrepreneur, he attempted to sell his idea to the Navy for a unique aircraft that could operate from water (partly to avoid the Wright Brothers all-encompassing patent on aircraft inventions) and to sweeten his offer, he arranged to train a naval officer in flying for free.

In January 1911, LT Theodore "Spuds" Ellyson, a former naval submariner, began flight training at the Curtiss Aviation School on North Island and later in the year was designated as Naval Aviator #1. On January 26, 1911 Curtiss attracted international attention by flying the world's first seaplane from the waters of Spanish Bight. Shortly afterwards, challenged by the Navy to invent an aircraft that could operate from both water and land, he built the A-1 "Triad" with the world's first retractable landing gear and test flew it from Spanish Bight to the beach just south of the Hotel del Coronado and back. By July 1911, Curtiss had sold his "Triad", as the first aircraft purchased by the Navy. These accomplishments forever marked North Island as "The Birthplace of Naval Aviation." Curtiss would return for two additional winters to operate his Flying School for some of the military's first pilots as well as many civilians and foreigners and at least one woman flyer and two married couples.

The military however, did not dominate the Curtiss Class of 1911/1912. A number of civilians attended classes including several VIPs from foreign countries. The "Bird Girl" Julia Clark enrolled, along with two married couples. William and Lillian Atwater purchased their own hydroplane from Curtiss and eventually went off to China and Japan. Julia qualified as a licensed aviatrix in April 1912, and continued to fly, joining the Curtiss Exhibition Company. During a performance in June 1912, her plane hit a tree and she was killed. The Curtiss School, renamed the San Diego School of Aviation continued until the lease expired in 1913. The landing field was named for Lt. Lewis C. Rockwell, a pioneer Army aviator who was killed in a test flight in 1912. The U.S. Government took over the hangars in 1917

Ellyson's Naval Aviation Detachment returned to North Island for the winter of 1911-12 calling their center of operations "Camp Trouble," a reflection on difficulties inherent with early aircraft. They soon departed for the East and Gulf coasts, not to return. By mid-1913, the Army Signal Corps, acting within the bounds of the original Curtiss lease, established a military aviation camp rent-free and, in December 1913, the Signal Corps Aviation School was formally established with twenty officers assigned. Army operations expanded rapidly including the establishment of the First Aero Squadron. The Army attempted to buy North Island outright from the Coronado Beach Company but was bluntly refused.

Curtiss and his wife bought property on Alameda Boulevard between Third and Fourth Streets by May 1912. The Curtiss home, a two-story redwood arts and crafts style-dwelling, had an office, a laboratory, solarium, and other features costing about $7,000.

[Curtiss' home had a delightful view of Spanish Bight and North Island. As important for an avid golfer, it sat directly across the street from one of Coronado's golfing greens. Curtiss' mother purchased the land next door on Alameda and lived longer in Coronado than Curtiss himself.—ed.]

The Coronado Strand of November 8, 1912 announced that during the winter, a large colony of Army officials would arrive for flight training. More machines were to be shipped to North Island

LT Theodore Ellyson was sent to Coronado by the Navy in January 1911, to become the first service member trained as a pilot. He is shown here, perhaps on his first day in the Curtiss aircraft (still in uniform), at a public air show held at the Coronado Polo Field. (CPL)

and three new hangars erected to house them. The camp was located on the northeast corner of North Island along the bay. So by 1913, when Curtiss' lease expired, there was quite a military encampment on North Island, all rent free.

> The Army's presence at North Island was rapidly growing during 1914 and 1915, of great concern to the Coronado Beach Company. In addition to the Army, the Marines had established Camp Thomas on North Island overlooking Spanish Bight in 1911 and then a larger Camp Howard in 1914 and 1915 (led by Colonel Joseph Pendleton). The Coronado Beach Company finally ordered the Army to vacate "as soon after March 1916 as is possible," so that the Spreckels Company could continue to develop North Island as "a high-class" residential property.
>
> With the coming of World War I, the Army and Navy jointly condemned all of North Island and assumed control by executive order on August 7, 1917 with compensation to be finalized after the war. Arguments and litigation continued until December 30, 1921. The Spreckels Company held out for a price of $5,000,000 – a figure confirmed by an independent jury. When final agreement was rendered and title to North Island transferred to the US Government, the end value paid to Spreckels was $6,098,330.33 including interest. Interestingly, the final agreement for North Island averaged $2400 per acre; but the Coronado Beach Company had originally offered all of North Island to the government in 1891 for the bargain price of about $300 per acre, including extra provisions for water and ferry services.

Coronado itself reaped praise as a thriving little town full of beautiful homes and exquisite gardens. Within two years it had expended more than $400,000 for new buildings and some $50,000 for improvements. The Coronado Beach Company leased their nursery to Albert Lenk on Blocks 141 and 154, in 1912, as the Company moved to divest itself of some of its minor responsibilities.

In fact, private enterprise flourished and building permits doubled during 1912 over the previous year. The Coronado real estate market was booming, led by the Hakes Investment Company of San Diego which had negotiated not only a number of home sales, but also offered developable land. In October, the Mission Apartments, "without a doubt the largest and most pretentious structure being built at the present time [was] the magnificent apartment house at 1015 "A" Avenue. The two-story, 16-apartment structure with a center courtyard cost $25,000." It served as temporary home for many military families throughout the years and still graces the site today.

Frank B. Moson, a prominent cattleman of Hereford, Arizona erected the first large business building in Coronado on the north side of Orange Avenue at "B" Street. It was of reinforced concrete, a one-story structure with arches over the store fronts. Over the years the building had many shops such as the Klass and Parisienne Cafe; it was the birthplace of the *Coronado Journal*, first issued under the name of the *Coronado Strand* begun in 1912. The building continued in use until 1983 when it was demolished to make way for the Bank of America building.

Away from the downtown district, A.B. Shaw finished construction of the Coronado Motor Car agency for Baker Electrics at Third and "F" Avenue. The fireproof and concrete building was to open in January 1913 to repair electric automobiles.

The Western Salt Company operation came into the hands of E.S. Babcock Jr., in 1911, after he bought land along the south end of San Diego Bay from the Spreckels Companies, the South San Diego Investment Company and the Santa Fe Lands Company. He built levees and expanded the firm to shipping by boat to the Pacific Northwest. In July 1914, Babcock reincorporated the Western Salt Company. These La Punta Salt beds were the source of salt from the earliest days, not the kind found at the table, but that used for cattle feed in the meat packing business and San Diego fishing industry. By 1922, Henry G. Fenton would acquire and manage the Western Salt Company which became one of his many contributions to regional business.

The City Board of Trustees was kept busy putting out local 'fires.' By 1912, a massive sinking of the seawall occurred requiring another bond issue of $75,000. Again rocks were brought from the Sweetwater Valley – the job supervised by Andrew Ervast.

School board members Nelson E. Brown, Herbert R. Fitch and Armand Jessop saw the need for a fireproof building sufficiently large to care for the likely increased enrollment in coming years. The approval of school bonds allowed the start of the reinforced concrete school, designed by the San Diego-based architectural firm of the Quayle Brothers and Cressey. During the same year, the Coronado Parent-Teachers Association was established with Mrs. Herbert R. Fitch (Nellie S.) as first president.

Preliminary steps were taken by the City Trustees to improve all of the unpaved streets west of Orange and north of Tenth Street (on a 10-year payment plan). The intent was to establish an assessment district. Orange Avenue would remain the principal business street, having a total width from curb to curb of 100 feet, a double boulevard, with an electric railway in the middle between rows of palms. The main street had not been paved earlier because the Coronado Beach Company was struggling with its accumulated debts during that time and property owners were reticent to pay any assessments. In 1912, Fairchilds-Gilmore and Wilton Company were awarded a contract for asphalt concrete paving of Orange Avenue at a cost of $80,000. Alameda was paved in 1913; Ocean Boulevard in 1914. To complement all the paving going on in 1912, a movement arose to form an Orange Avenue Improvement Club, an East Side Improvement Club and a West Side Improvement Club all for the purpose of beautifying the parkway strip between the sidewalk and the curb.

In 1912, Peter Harry Vondenberg was appointed City Marshall. Born in Holland in 1878, the son of a Dutch mayor, he had been an officer in the Dutch Navy and then arrived in San Diego about 1900. When named chief, he appointed six Deputy Marshals: Charles S. Robinson, Samuel

This postcard, circa 1903, shows great detail of the Hotel del Coronado and the Coronado Public Library and Free Reading Room in the foreground next to the trolley station. (CPL/LCC)

Pedlar, C.D. Mackey, H.W. Wells, James W. Waller and Louis C. Bandel. One of their major duties became clamping down on reckless drivers. There were no driver's tests required, no stop signs, brakes did not always work, and rights-of-way were unheard of, so Coronado's streets became the site of numerous accidents.

On December 15, 1912, Marshal Vondenberg and Detective William Gabrielson raided a house at 951 "G" Street, where they seized a complete wire tapping plant and confidence men's outfit. The outfit consisted of telegraph and telephone instruments, bookmakers' board, bogus money, bank checks, office furnishings and wire tappers. A victim who had been fleeced of $1,530 led the police to the gang's headquarters.

Polo had taken a firm grip on Coronado's elite, and ponies were being shipped to Coronado from various parts of the world. One string of the Honolulu team arrived by steamer with the owners being Walter Francis Dillingham, Frank F. Baldwin, Arthur Rice and Harold K. Castle. Still another string of ponies came from Kansas City, the property of S.H. Velie. The stables of Walter H. Dupee and those of Major Colin G. Ross were already at the Country Club awaiting the coming winter season when for three months all society would revolve around the matches and the millionaires and movie stars who played in them.

Walter Dupee was a businessman and a Chicago stockbroker, a partner in the brokerage firm of Charles G. Gates and Company. He had wintered in Coronado, and in 1907, he moved here. He had married Agnes Florence Kennett of Chicago in 1900, and they spent their honeymoon at the Hotel Del Coronado. Dupee was a trained horseman and one of the top breeders of polo ponies in the U.S. He joined the Coronado Beach Country Club and the Coronado Beach Polo Club. In 1909 he was one of the organizers of the Coronado Country Club Four, made up of Dupee, Lord Innes-Kerr and Lord Tweedmouth of England (who lived at 547 "A" Avenue), and Major Colin G. Ross, Retired Commander of the Canadian Mounted Police.

Dupee was instrumental in the promotion and growth of the sport throughout the U.S., Canada, Australia and England. He was responsible for the Coronado Polo Grounds and innumerable horse shows. He owned forty polo ponies and a large ranch of 55,000 acres in Loma, twenty-four miles from Tijuana, which he turned into a game preserve.

Sports writers began to call the Coronado Country Club the "Meadowbrook of the West" (after the famous Meadowbrook Polo Club in Jericho, New York), because of the significant teams who came to play polo. Dupee bought a dairy farm at Santee and changed it to a fancy pony farm. Ponies would be brought to "Edgemoor" and trained for each season in Coronado. Among the facilities he had built was a large pony barn to accommodate twenty-two horses. In time, Dupee would sell that ranch and concentrate on being a member of the Agua Caliente Racing Board.

Meanwhile, the sport of water polo attracted Major Colin G. Ross who encouraged the start of a water polo season in 1912 as a tourist attraction. Contests were at Tent City, arranged with teams from Venice, Long Beach, Redondo, Santa Monica and other towns.

In 1912, the golf course across from Alameda was completely renovated; a number of the fairways and greens were changed. Varieties of trees, including pines and eucalyptus groves were planted. The golf greens along the waterfront furnished a lovely view, especially those across Fourth Street on the San Diego Bay side. In the early days, the course had one very tricky hole which golfers found quite a challenge. The player had to walk out on a wharf over the waters of the Spanish Bight, near the Fourth Street trestle, and drive back over the marshland toward the green. This was a terrific mental hazard so the Bight was well filled with golf balls. Many a good score was ruined on that water hole as it was on 580-yard, number six, referred to as "the long hole." The fairway was hard clay (evidently the same kind found at the Brick Company on the Strand.) Although hundreds

Recreation and tourism were growing rapidly in the first few years of the 20th Century. Shown here, a regatta is taking place, probably on a weekend morning, from the Coronado Boathouse. (CHA)

of dollars were spent trying to grow grass, it refused to respond. Many a wooden shaft was shattered and a good disposition wrecked on hole number six, when just at the golfer's darkest moment, a cheery horseback rider dared to trot along the bridle path on the edge of Spanish Bight.

On May 24, 1912, the *Coronado Strand*, a 12 page weekly tabloid with flashy illustrations brought the newspaper business back to Coronado. H.W. Crooks from Los Angeles headed the firm, installing complete printing facilities in the Moson Building. The Strand was purchased by Mrs. Lola Burks Hattich.

Only a brief announcement, however, noted the opening of The Star, Coronado's first movie theater, at 1009 Orange Avenue, near the corner of 10th Street. G.I. Wark took a five-year lease on the property to build a theater, 20 x 110 feet. The fireproof structure seating 250 people, opened its doors on Thanksgiving Day, 1912 with a brand new player piano. The Star's only competitor was the picture house at Tent City that showed free movies during June, July, and August so The Star shut down during those months.

One of the earliest stories in the new paper described F.E. Boggeln's Ivy Hotel Cafe, and how it was entirely made over and refitted. The lot in the rear containing shade trees and shrubs was being converted into an ice cream parlor and a Tea Garden, "delightful, cool, and attractive," became Ivy's Tea Garden.

The paper also described a flower shop constructed in the patio of the Hotel del Coronado, a cottage built of bark-covered split logs, as very rustic, with ornamental grape vines creeping over it. The building was leased out in 1916 to Miss A. M. Rainford, a niece of the well-known horticulturist Miss Kate Sessions, who continued her flower sales there for some time.

1912 had been an important year for Coronado, now twenty-five years old. Its reputation as a resort town and residential community was becoming known across the country. The Hotel

The central building of Coronado School held an auditorium, offices, and several classrooms in its three stories. (CHA)

del Coronado was famous, and so was Tent City. The polo games attracted the wealthy and the playboys; the climate was perfect and even L. Frank Baum, author of the *Wizard of Oz*, had written a poem about its beauty. It lay in good hands. Wilmot Griffiss was President of the Board of Trustees; George Holmes; A.B. Cunningham; L.B. Hakes, and Earl Cameron were Trustees. W. Tilden Clark as City Clerk; H. Vonderberg, City Marshall and Tax Collector; H.C. Hizer, City Attorney; W.E. Ingelow, City Treasurer; and Andrew Ervast, City Engineer had the town under control.

Between January 1 and March 31, 1913, building permits in Coronado increased 160% with homes going up in every section. The first home in the Glorietta area. built on the point in 1913, was the Rogan residence at 928 Glorietta Boulevard, followed by the Dent Hayes Robert house at 1000 Glorietta, in 1916, designed by architect William Templeton Johnson.

Singularly important in 1913 was the opening of nine bids for the construction of the Coronado school building, utilizing the drawings of the Quayle Brothers and Cressey architects of San Diego. The Brothers had designed hundreds of commercial and residential structures across the country (including some which are on the National Register of Historic Buildings in 1987), and which included the Police Station at the foot of Market Street in San Diego, the North Park Theatre and the Old Balboa Stadium. The contracting Wurster Construction Company had likewise built a number of significant buildings in the region including the Balboa Theatre.

Coronado's first major multi-building school complex, and perhaps Coronado's most exceptional school ever, was finished in late 1913. The San Diego Union issues of March 30, June 4 and November 23, 1913 carried the architect's renderings and photographs of the magnificent Spanish Renaissance buildings to occupy blocks bound by 6th and 7th, "E" and "F", and later 6th and 7th, and "D" and "E." The newspaper descriptions are glowing and range from detailed information about the kindergarten to the movie theatre and the cooking department. Coronado authorized an election on the formation of a high school district and the Board of Education consisted of President, Neal Brown; Clerk, Herbert B. Fitch; Clerk Armand Jessop and Ivan Desch, School Superintendent.

Named simply "Coronado School" it was a marvel, called "the most perfect structure of its kind," by one reporter. Built entirely of fireproof concrete and steel and featuring high transom windows and full-length French doors for fresh air and light; it had specialty rooms for kindergarten, typing, woodworking, and home economics. High-tech touches included a fully-automated bell system, telephones in every classroom and one of the first motion-picture systems for a California school.

Coronado School was originally designed for all grades K-12 but the school population grew so much in two years from design to opening that it was decided to keep the high school in the old Sixth Street building, using only the new school's specialty classrooms such as home economics. The Coronado High School Class of 1916 was its first formal graduating class with Coronado diplomas and its own high school district (not that of San Diego County). Five graduates were awarded; four girls and one boy: Samuel Sherman (president of the class), Francis Malmgren (born in Coronado, her father was a deckhand on J. D. Spreckels' yacht, *Venetia*), Mary Meza (emigrated from Mexico, her father was a fireman at the Hotel Del), Gladys Jones, and Margaret Snyder (became a noted pianist and music teacher in Coronado).

Coronadans had every reason to be proud of one of the most beautiful series of school buildings in the southwest.

In this era Janet Owers, wife of judge Frank W. Owers, established in 1910, a small school in her Coronado home. Several years later, probably in 1913, she signed a contract with the Hotel del Coronado to operate a school on the Hotel's beach. Under a lease, the Spreckels' Companies built one or two buildings, part frame, part canvas, for the facility known as The Beach School. The school accommodated boys and girls of all ages. Mrs. Nellie Wattawa taught there as did Caroline Balch. This was one of the first to use the Montessori system of teaching. Students learned French, art, cooking and carpentry, which the public schools did not offer at this time. Mrs. Peddicord taught the students dancing and put on a number of parties for special Valentine's or May Day celebrations. The school educated visiting children at the Hotel del Coronado as well as many of the children in the town who opted for it over the public school. The school remained until 1941, when the largest of the three buildings became a war ration stamp center, and later an Arthur Murray dance studio, and in the 1950s it was refurbished as a cottage for Harry Jacobs, Trustee of the Goodman Estate, former owner of the Hotel Del Coronado.

Coronado School (later Central School) in 1913. (CPL)

The historic Tent City carousel was special-ordered for Tent City by H.D. "Harry" Simpson (working for the Spreckels Company) and made by the Herschell Spillman Company of North Tonawanda, NY. Since 1913, this Carousel has been enjoyed by generations of children, first in Tent City, and later in Balboa Park, where it still operates today near the Zoo entrance. (CHA)

The Methodist Church opened its handsome new grammar school on Block 90. In order to make space for the school expansion the Methodist Church had to be moved to the corner of 7th, "D" and Olive. Thus the church site at 7th and "E" was exchanged and the building was moved to the new location in late 1916. At the time the church was called St. Paul's United Methodist Church.

In 1913, the Coronado Yacht Club was founded with the Coronado Boathouse as its headquarters. Hotel manager J.J. Hernan served as the club's first commodore from 1913 to 1916. Previously, in 1910, the San Diego Yacht Club had purchased the old ferry *Silver Gate* – that had been in use at Tent City as a ballroom, casino, and a space for locker rooms – and moved her to the San Diego side of the bay where she became the headquarters for the club. The San Diego Yacht Club relocated *Silver Gate* back to Coronado in 1914, mooring her to a short pier near the foot of E Avenue at First Street. In 1916, the San Diego Yacht Club and Coronado Yacht Club merged into a single combined club with headquarters aboard *Silver Gate*.

The combined yacht clubs fell on hard times with the advent of World War I – with many small craft appropriated by the government and club members joining the reserves. Worse, beloved clubhouse *Silver Gate* finally met her demise, salvaged and broken up for war materials in 1918. San Diego and Coronado Yacht Clubs looked to revitalize following the war. John D. Spreckels donated land for new San Diego Yacht Club headquarters on Glorietta Bay, near where the current boat ramp and the City's Club Room and Boathouse are located. The San Diego Yacht Club boathouse, complete with a small pier and floats and including many Coronado members, opened on August 18, 1923. The San Diego Yacht Club ultimately relocated its new clubhouse to its current Shelter Island site in the early 1930s.

The City Board of Trustees appointed an assistant for the City Marshal at $10 a month and installed a telephone so that persons calling could find someone available to whom they could tell their troubles. They ordered the installation of some street lights, including those at Third and "H" and at Sixth and Pomona. Lights were to be installed only for those streets already paved. A new speed limit ordinance was passed restricting travel to 25 miles an hour. Marshal Vondenberg, using fines as the lever, increased the city coffers for a variety of offenses, particularly for those who had been speeding.

The Home telephone company moved its quarters in 1913 from the real estate office to a cottage on Orange Avenue. Sunset Company, which also now served Coronadans and the Home Company, would continue to serve the subscribers until 1915 when Pacific Telephone bought both companies and combined them. This proved to be a relief to customers as Home and Sunset lines were not interconnected. The subscriber of the Home telephone could not call anyone on a Sunset line and vice versa. Some offices and families had subscribed to both telephone companies for convenience with two telephones in their establishments, one from each company.

The click of the moving picture camera had been mingling with the roar of the aeroplane motors for several years as the Ammex Motion Picture Company, stationed in National City, had been taking photos of the Curtiss School. Among those who flew for the camera was Dr. Frank Bell, a red- headed "daredevil" who flew so close to the camera that the camera man began to get green around the gills. Mr. Nakamura, the Japanese pupil at Curtiss Aviation School, broke his own record when he flew one hundred yards at an altitude of ten feet on a perfectly even keel; the event was not captured on film.

As for visitors, Lucile Ramsey Baker, known to many as Becky Sharp of literary fame, passed away March 8th while staying with a friend in Coronado. The sensational British novelist Elinor Glyn, companion of Marian Davies, William Randolph Hearst and others, came to Coronado from London. Her novel, "Three Weeks," only recently published, had been considered "shocking" and teenage girls were forbidden to read it (by their mothers and fathers).

Tent City bustled with vacationers flocking to the beach and the sea in the summer, the bay dotted with yachts and rowboats. Exercise-minded people played tennis while others "rested" in the palm thatched structures. Concerts in the evenings, dancing, and songfests kept folks entertained.

> H.D. "Harry" Simpson and his wife, Muriel, moved from Bangkok, Siam, to San Diego in 1910, to be closer to his parents, who lived in Coronado at 300 First St. and his young daughter, a student at the Bishop's School in La Jolla. Simpson soon went to work for the Spreckels Company, as Superintendent and Inspector of Buildings at Tent City. While on vacation in San Francisco, he observed a beautiful carousel in Golden Gate Park, saw that it was a money-maker, and inquired about purchasing one for Tent City. He subsequently did

Ferry 'Silver Gate' was both one of the most "unfortunate" and "luckiest" ferries in the Coronado Ferry system. "Unfortunate" since she had trouble stopping (a good attribute for ferries), and "lucky" because she enjoyed a long retirement moored and anchored, serving first as a Tent City dancehall, then as a clubhouse for the San Diego Yacht Club. (CHA)

purchase one through a Los Angeles dealer for the Herschell Spillman Company of North Tonawanda, New York. The new carousel was then custom made by the New York company, shipped to San Diego, and assembled in Tent City–just in time for the 1913 summer season.

The magnificent Tent City carousel, with its beautiful horses, frogs, zebras, ostriches, roosters, cats, dragons, a rocking boat and brass ring game, was temporarily moved across the bay to Balboa Park for the 1915 Exposition. Thereafter, it moved back and forth several times, before finally finding a permanent home in Balboa Park in the 1920s. Today the historic Tent City carousel is located near the Zoo entrance on Park Blvd.

The opening of Tent City in 1914 broke all previous records. More than 10,000 people passed through the turnstiles and there were hundreds of autos parked on the grounds. More than $100,000 was spent on Tent City in 1914-1915, largely in preparation for the San Diego Exposition crowds. A new bandstand was built and the old one demolished. A newly- constructed bathing float 92 x 14 feet and supported by six pontoons was placed in Glorietta Bay. The bathhouse was remodeled to provide 235 changing rooms. Streets were fixed, and shrubs, trees, and flowers were planted along the entire length of the palm cottages.

Gloria L. Esterbloom published a booklet titled "I Share with You the Years," in which she wrote at some length about Tent City. According to some sources she was the "first child born in the Coronado Boathouse," the daughter of James R. Dunne, caretaker of the boathouse. An Irishman, Dunne had married the children's governess of the John D. Spreckels household, Lina Rudolph, brought from Germany by the Spreckels family. The Dunne's new baby was named for the nearby bay, Glorietta. Lina turned the upper part of the boathouse into a comfortable home and would give birth to Rudolph, May and James Rudolph there.

When Tent City opened in 1914, the announcement came that band conductor Henry Ohlmeyer's contract had not been renewed after nine summers. The charge for his services had now become too high. While the band was excellent and in the off season toured the finest hotels in the country, Spreckels kept a close tab on all his operations and felt the cost too much even though the band played Strauss waltzes, John Phillip Sousa's marches, and semi-classical music. Frank

A rare photo showing a working day at the ferry landing, with ferry 'Ramona' circa 1910. (CHA)

Palma, the original director of the Floradora Company, announced in December the organization of the Tent City Band which would begin playing during the summer of 1915. He had thirty-three musicians, fifteen recruited from the country's leading soloists.

Ironically the salaries ranged higher for his performers than had those of Ohlmeyers.

At the Hotel Del Coronado, I. Magnin and Company leased several rooms at a cost of $2,000 per year to be used as shops for the sale of ladies' wearing apparel. The exclusive dress shop attracted clients from all over southern California.

L. Frank Baum, famed author of the "Wizard of Oz" book series. Baum vacationed in Coronado for years, first staying at the Hotel, later renting a home on Star Park. He wrote some of the six books in the Oz series during his time in Coronado. (Wikimedia Commons)

Visitors throughout the year returned to Coronado, some reserving the same room or suite at the Hotel del Coronado; others renting the same residences in town, bringing their own servants, or taking over the owner's servants and the family car along with the house.

General C. Reeve, returned to his winter home at 953 Adella (also called the Mayor Coleman Gray home) and he always encouraged other Minneapolis families to come to Coronado. The Pillsbury's stayed in the Major Colin Ross' home. Other visitors included Howard Baker who stayed at his home at 519 Ocean Boulevard; the Dummer family who owned 1005 Adella; the F.S. Shermans who wintered and ended up by building the home at 708 "A" Avenue, and the Anson P. Stephens who built the original part of the Terry mansion at 711 "A" Avenue.

Among the winter visitors over a period of time were Mrs. Cyrus McCormick (Nancy), whose husband had made a fortune in manufacturing farm implements; L. Frank Baum, who worked on six of his Oz books here; and three opera singers who owned homes in the city: Chevalier Scovel, Madame Ernestine Schumann Heink, and Miss Inga Orner. Other persons captured by the town included Charlie Chaplin's family and W.W. Driscoll, one of the wealthiest cattlemen in the country.

In 1913, Walter Hamlin Dupee purchased the Richards residence at 1015 Ocean Boulevard. It underwent a transformation in 1914, when Frederick Louis Roehrig an architect-graduate of Cornell University School of Architecture, who had been in practice in Pasadena and Los Angeles, was asked to make changes in the home. Roehrig had designed the Hotel Green in Pasadena for the patent medicine magnate, Colonel George Gill Green. Roehrig designed the addition to the mansion which made it the most impressive home on the boulevard by making major changes in the kitchen area and adding two wings to the residence, bringing it to its present 20,000 square feet with 17 bedrooms and 13 bathrooms. Dupee wanted these rooms added to house the famous polo team players and to entertain them in style. Morris Trepte & Sons was one of the contractors on the additions and ran afoul of F.G. Peacock, the gardener at the Charles L. Tutt residence next door. Peacock went on trial, charged with assault and battery on Mr. Trepte because Peacock claimed that Trepte's workmen trampled the gardener's lawn and plants and used vile language. Peacock said he could not possibly have been drunk because he allowed himself but three pints of claret a day. He was found guilty and fined $15.

In 1915 the Dupees divorced; Walter worked as a steward at the Agua Caliente Jockey Club, maintaining his extensive racing stable known as the Golden West Stable. He lived at the El Cortez Hotel in San Diego, and in May 1933, died in Hollywood.

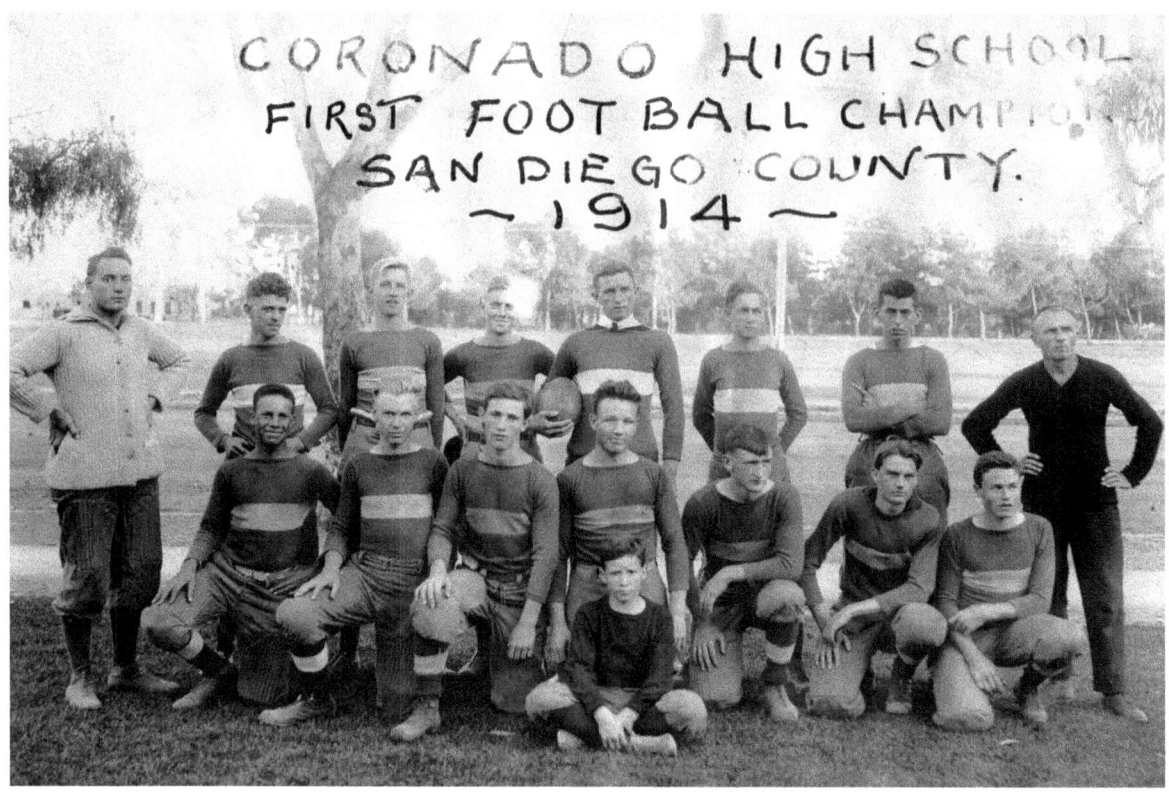

The Coronado High School football team won the County championship even before the high school had graduates. In fact, they won it three years in a row, earning permanent ownership of the large silver trophy that resides today in the school's athletic trophy case. (CHA)

Activity in the town included some new ordinances by the City Board of Trustees and Dr. Lorini, City Health Officer, recommended the limits wherein cows could be kept: from the north side of Ninth to the ferry and from the east side of "I" to Glorietta Boulevard. This came about because owners keeping their cows in the rear of 360 "C" Avenue brought flies and made neighbors' lives miserable. Steps were taken to have stray horses, mules and burros banished from the island. The dog muzzling ordinance was enacted due to the prevalence of rabies.

Major Colin Ross, now managing the Country Club, solved the problem of keeping down the weeds and grass on the Polo field. He acquired 29 guinea pigs which kept his lawn in trim at his Isabella Avenue home and he simply turned them loose in the polo grounds.

A difference of opinion arose regarding the name of the park dubbed "Bologna Park" on Pomona Avenue. How this name came about is not clear: "Bologna" rhymed with "Pomona"; the land was bologna-shaped, and City Engineer Andrew Ervast on one occasion said "baloney" when told the contour of the park should be changed. Ervast provided the Trustees with a map showing how it would look when enlarged. Trustee H.B. Hakes said the map was nice, but he had not yet closed the deal with owners of the lots. Pondering what to do, the Trustees chose to wait until they could announce that it would be necessary to close a number of streets. María Place was closed, and part of Adella Avenue now received the name "María Place." They now agreed Pomona would be a better name. In 1953, the Pomona Park was renamed to honor longtime Coronado City Clerk Arthur A. "Art" Mathewson.

During 1914, $3,300 was spent on improvement of the seawall. Fortunately, the City Trustees had created a "Seawall Fund," which came from a levy of 10 cents on each $100 of property valuation, making possible any annually-needed repairs.

The population of Coronado Beach nearly doubled between 1912 and 1914, creating an urgent need for a high school. The new grammar school opened on June 20, 1913, the most beautiful school that the city could want; its great dome could be seen from afar. With that beginning, the old Victorian schoolhouse became the high school.

Still worried, the School Board, via a quick election organized a high school district, and meetings were held late in 1914 to discuss how to issue and sell bonds in the sum of $65,000 to purchase lots and build a high school. The school bonds did not carry since people said that too much money was being expended. Thoughts turned to the acquisition of the Josephine Hotel, which had been turned into a military academy. Mr. Harold Swan thought his manual training class could undertake the remodeling. Trustees thought the cost too great, however. The idea was given up, and the Hotel Josephine was demolished. High school students would, for the time being, march in place in the old building until someone with imagination could contrive a way to build a new high school. While the students waited for new quarters the principal was W.A. Pratt; Vice Principal of the grammar school was Miss May Murphy. The Grammar School teachers were: Misses Hazel Avery, Esther W. Pease, Anna Sletto, Helen Dula, Sara Graves, Fay Chalmers, Caroline Balch, Josephine Drewisch, Jeannette Anderson, Helen Toews and Helen H. Bird.

On July 3, 1914, Colonel Joseph H. Pendleton, U.S.M.C. established an outpost on the flat, windswept North Island. This was the start of what ultimately grew into the present Marine Corps Depot at San Diego. The 4th Regiment of Marines assembled in April at Bremerton, Washington, and at Mare Island, California and embarked aboard three U.S. Navy vessels: the USS *South Dakota*, USS *West Virginia*, and the USS *Jupiter*. Not long after the vessels dropped anchor, Colonel Joseph Pendleton, (who would later become a Coronadan, building a home on the island), Captain C.H. Lyman and a crew of ten men went ashore at North Island to select and stake out a camp site. The only occupant of the island at this time was the U.S. Army Signal Corps, which was trying to establish a solid base for aviation. On July 22, 1914, leases were drawn up for the use of the land as a camp for the U.S. Marines, and for the U.S. Signal Corps to erect temporary buildings.

Pendleton chose an area along the Spanish Bight, and the next day men began to clear the land and erect the camp. At the start, the entire regiment of over 1,100 officers and men were on North Island; this outpost gradually dwindled, until by 1916 only two men remained.

In September 1914, the First Army Aero Squadron was organized on North Island. This early flying unit would be the first from America to reach France in World War I.

The era leading up to 1915 was one of the most glittering times that Coronadans would know. Yet along with the Strauss waltz, the polo matches, the champagne dinners and the sun-filled days on the beach, dark war clouds had already begun to form in several parts of the world.

The establishment of the army and navy installations on North Island had been no mere whim at the time, for the United States military had long focused its eye on the port of San Diego. The world was about to change, and Coronado would find itself caught up in the maelstrom.

13575 HOTEL DEL CORONADO, CORONADO BEACH, CALIF.

Chapter 6

1915-1929 World War I and the Roaring Twenties

SPONSORED BY DEE SABEY IN MEMORY OF DR. ANDREW SABEY

THE OPENING OF THE PANAMA CANAL in 1915 was very important to San Diego and the West Coast, because of the number of passengers and amount of cargo that would be transiting the canal every year. Politically, a great deal of work was done to focus attention on San Diego as the first U.S. port north of the canal on the West Coast, mainly through national and international promotion of a world's fair in Balboa Park in 1915, celebrating the canal's opening.

> Fundraising and preparations for the Panama-California Exposition began as early as 1909, with several prominent Coronadans deeply involved, including, among others, G. Aubrey Davidson and John D. Spreckels. Much demolition of older San Diego neighborhoods occurred, and whole business sections were revitalized with Mission Revival, Spanish Colonial, or even Panamanian architecture to tie into the theme of the Exposition. Celebrations meant people, and visitors translated into dollars. But the fair, held over for a second year in 1916, as the Panama-California International Exposition, had a far greater impact on the entire region than the organizers ever imagined, as it also drew attention to San Diego as an ideal location for homeporting navy vessels and large military training facilities.

(Image above: CPL/LCC)

Resentment arose for a moment in 1915, when *The East San Diego Press* announced that San Diego would again attempt to annex nearby cities; Coronado citizens decried the absurdity of such a suggestion, and dismissed the rumor out of hand. The people of the resort city had too much going on to be bothered with such nonsense!

C. Emil Johnson had traded his concertina for a motorcycle. John D. Spreckels was raising a flock of young ducks on his lawn to make short work of any trespassing bugs. Esther Cleveland, daughter of the late President Grover Cleveland, had to be rescued in the surf at Coronado Beach by John Kyle, swimming instructor of the Coronado Bath House. The Maharajah of Kapurthala, with his retinue and one of his wives, was a guest at the Hotel del Coronado. Haircuts were 25 cents. Trustee Wilmot Griffiss was asked to expand the "cow limits." The ordinance was amended so that no cows could be kept south of Third, between Orange and Pomona, and none south of Sixth and west of Orange Avenue.

Rumors of a Tent City romance "gone bad" were heard when Anita Loos, a Hollywood screen writer, left Los Angeles for New York to obtain a divorce. Miss Loos, daughter of R. Beers Loos of San Diego, and editor of the *Tent City News*, had married Frank Palma Jr., son of the bandmaster at Tent City in 1915. The match lasted just two days. Miss Loos would go on to capitalize on romance by writing "Gentlemen Prefer Blondes."

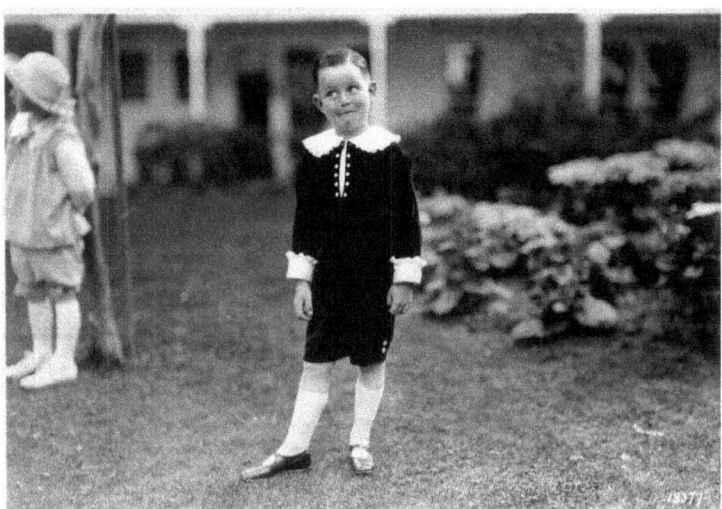

Walter Fitch III grew up in a wealthy Coronado family in the Howard Baker - Fitch house, a majestic home still located at 519 Ocean Boulevard. (CHA)

At one Trustee meeting in 1915, an ordinance was introduced prohibiting the wearing of bathing suits on the streets in the vicinity of the Hotel del Coronado. For any person over 12, a fine of $25 was to be imposed. Dr. Keshava Deva Shastri of Benares, India, the "Sacred City," was another visitor. He was regarded as a brilliant Sanskrit scholar, who was spending time in Coronado to study the merits of our social, economic and educational systems. He met Diamond Jim Brady, who was also enjoying a few days on the island. Upton Sinclair, author of "The Jungle," and other social works of the era, rented a house at 862 "J" Avenue for the winter.

On April 15, 1915, the Spanish American War Veterans, Coronado Camp No. 59, was organized under District Commander R.H. Harris. The organization sought legislation and a variety of benefits for Spanish-American War veterans, but met annually for social events as well. Twenty-two veterans of the War with Spain signed the Charter, including Thomas Frosio, Robert E. Sherwood, William S. Millen, Herbert W. Chittenden, Henry Clay Israel, and M.G. Robbins.

Also during 1915, a beautiful Loving Cup was awarded at the Panama-California Exposition to the Coronado P.T.A., for its activities. The First Church of Christ Science Coronado was incorporated under a charter granted by the State. When the Mitchell Art Gallery opened in the mid-1920s, many church services were conducted there until 1928, when noted architect Irving Gill designed the present church at Eighth and "C." Costing approximately $30,000, it was completely paid for at the time of its dedication, as was the custom of Christian Science churches – no dedication without ownership. The lofty and gracefully curved arches reflect the simplistic style of Gill architecture. On June 6th, the cornerstone was laid; by December 2, 1928, the first services were held in the new church building.

The Christian Science building was designed by Irving J. Gill in 1928. It still stands at 1123 Eighth Street. (CHA)

Activities of the 19th century Women's Christian Temperance Union had died down, probably due to lack of a local newspaper to give the organization an outlet for publicity. Their campaigns had gone way beyond what some temperance enthusiasts wanted: "Flatten the tight dresses, peek-a-boo waists, bow shoes, and silk stockings with a steam roller ... and to the ash can with eyebrow pencils and short skirts." Exhibitions such as these were a willful lure to men, claimed the Coronado Branch of the W.C.T.U., which disbanded on June 26, 1915.

The Coronado Chapter of the Woman's Section of the Navy League was organized November 19th at the Hotel del Coronado. The motto of the Chapter was "Patriotic Homes, the Safety of the State." Names of the charter members included nearly all the well-known ladies in the City at that time, such as Mrs. Alexander Sharp, Mrs. Uriel Sebree (Annie B.), Miss Margaret E. Erle, and Mrs. F.A. Lloyd.

Architects like Walter S. Keller began to discover Coronado. He designed a "group system" of housing, in which occupants would share a common area. Keller's project, consisting of eight houses (or apartments) sat at the southwest corner of Ninth and "D." It had central heating and a hot water system, and is still there today.

Looking down Ocean Boulevard toward the Hotel Del Coronado, c. 1920. (CPL)

Glorietta Boulevard was paved in 1915-16 at a cost of $60,000. John Engebretson, an associate of Henry G. Fenton's was in charge of making improvements all over town. (Engebretson achieved fame as the Dean of Foreign Consuls on the Pacific Coast, and was recipient of many honors for long and faithful service rendered to the Norwegian government.) The unpaved road along the bayside was formerly called "Bay Boulevard," but after paving was completed, the road was renamed "Glorietta Boulevard"--as it led around Glorietta Bay.

The storm of 1915 affected a number of property owners, especially along Ocean Boulevard. Waves broke over the seawall and vast quantities of water ran down the new Ocean Boulevard pavement. George Sturges captured three big lobsters on his property and numerous fish. Pat Ingle Dowden remembered lobsters clinging to bushes in the gardens. All the spectators agreed, nonetheless, that the seawall had done an excellent job protecting Boulevard property.

One major event of 1915 that really impressed Coronado residents, was the arrival of motion picture giant Siegmund Lubin. Lubin was not, however, the first moviemaker to showcase the charms of Coronado on celluloid.

In 1901, the Edison Moving Picture Company had filmed surf, bathers, the children's pool, and Tent City. A Mr. Ramsey also photographed the ferryboat entering the Coronado slip. In 1912, Allan Dwan, whose life was chronicled by Peter Bogdanovich, and who made a large number of films in the San Diego area, shot several documentaries, including, "Winter Sports and Pastimes at Coronado," and "Curtiss' School of Aviation." But it was the European Lubin who, for a while, became the "King of the Motion Picture" and built studios in the village.

In 1915, Lubin secured a five-year lease from the Spreckels Beach Company for property between the ferry landing and First Street at $1 per year, intending to erect various buildings to be used in making pictures. The main Lubin studio stood on Orange Avenue and First Street, next to the offices of the Beach Company (and about where the Southern Baptist Church is today). The corporation spent about $10,000 for improvements, including a studio, film plant, and an enclosing stonewall around the properties, all of which were of a highly ornamental design. The theatre structure had a 60 x 100 foot stage, with adjoining dressing rooms. All sorts of garages, storage rooms, and repair shops were built nearby.

By late summer 1915, the walls of the open-air stage could be seen, and photographs in the *San Diego Union* gave a complete view of the Lubin Moving Picture Studio at work in Coronado. Activities connected with the studio generated work for the community, as Spreckels' lease with Lubin Studios required that every member of the company be a resident of Coronado. City Marshal R.L. Chew hoped to supply needed horses, and City father Sam Pedler wanted to be an actor and play the part of a villain. The *Coronado Strand* threw a damper on the motion picture company when it editorialized:

> ... they [the young Coronado men] had no chance at all with the fair maidens of this village between the ocean and the bay, for no sooner do the handsome aviators, with their dare-devil stunts and regular pay checks, leave for other parts, than a bunch of 'movie pitcher actors,' descends and captures maidens fancies.

In October a reception and dance opened the studio with many prominent San Diego and Coronado people attending. A tent-like pavilion, lavishly decorated, was set up. Japanese lanterns furnished the soft lighting and suits of armor, spears, and other ancient war materials served as dramatic decor. A buffet supper was served and a special platform was built for the orchestra and dance floor. After the reception, the first film made at the studio was shown, a two-act play called "Retribution," which included many scenes of Coronado. Less than a year later, May 27, 1916, the studio shut its doors and workers were told the company had failed. Lubin's Coronado studio may have made as many as 20 films, including some short documentaries.

Edward Sloman, an actor with Lubin, and later a prominent director, acted in his first picture in Coronado. In "Saved From the Harem," Sloman sailed a real battleship, and the company discharged a full complement of sailors in white battle dress, who charged up the beach with rifles at the ready. Although Lubin would be the island's first—and only—motion picture studio, from then on the beach city would get its share of movie fame and serve as the setting for scores of films which took advantage of the Hotel del Coronado, the U.S. Navy, and the general beauty and climate of the famous seaside resort. Other Lubin Studio films made in Coronado included "The Power of Salim Bey" (1915), and "Billy Joins the Navy" (1915).

The opening headlines of papers for the year 1916 signaled that Europe was at war. Major Henry "Hap" Arnold, twice Commanding Officer of Rockwell Field, and ultimately the 5-star general who led U. S. Air Forces in World War II wrote:

> Real pioneers of the air, they were, those Rockwell Field birdmen of the early years who braved the unknown regions of the skies. Some of the records made by the army fliers, particularly during the period 1913-1917, seem of little importance now. Yet they marked the foundations upon which later day army air records were built.

The "great" altitude of 11,690 feet reached over Rockwell Field in 1915, by Lieutenants J.E. Joseph Eugene Carberry and R.E. Christy, amazed Coronadans. That same year, Lieutenant B.Q. Jones remained aloft for eight hours and 50 minutes. A record was broken a few months later when Lieutenant Walter.R. Taliaferro established an endurance flight mark of nine hours and 48 minutes. The first bomb dropping experiments to be carried out in the world were safely conducted at Rockwell Field in 1914, and two years later Lieutenant C.C. Culver conducted the first successful radio test by plane.

Throughout 1916, citizens on South Island watched test flights and experiments in the air, perhaps without full realization that war lay on the horizon. The Philip D. Armours III of Chicago honeymooned at the Hotel del Coronado. Eleanor Randolph Sears, noted American athlete, bagged the most rabbits on a North Island chase, and also won a polo pony in a dice game. The Christensen School of Music, located at 540 "D" Avenue, taught Ragtime piano in 20 lessons, while Madame Ernestine Schumann-Heink, one of the world's greatest contraltos, sang at the Panama-California Exposition across the bay. Dick Jessop married Katherine Weiss; Edna Furnald came home from a young ladies school in Berkeley for the summer; and Dr. Lorini vacationed in Brookline, Massachusetts. Those were the events reported on the social scene during the year.

Eugene M. Estoppey opened his Marathonia, an open air gymnasium, in January, 1916. A Tent City lifeguard, he was also a famous trainer, athlete, and masseur. He held several world's records in distance running and competed in the marathon race held at the first set of Olympic Games under the Knickerbocker Athletic Club of New York in 1896. He won the first marathon race held in California, running 1,000 miles in 1,000 hours. The Marathonia was located at 624-630 "J," and listed in the City directory as "Palmhurst." It had a baseball diamond, handball court, tennis courts, running track, a miniature golf course, and a bathhouse.

Polo had not lost its appeal in 1916; four important competitions were held during the three weeks of the annual tournament. Among the classics of the polo world to be decided at Coronado field were: The Pacific Coast All American Trophy; the California Challenge Trophy; the Coronado Junior Championship; and the Hotel del Coronado Handicap Cup.

The annual tennis tournament for men and women was held at the Coronado Country Club, while Club Cup matches were played every weekend during January, February, and March. Basketball began to also gain prominence in local athletic programs, with a fine practice court at the club house.

In 1916, the Coronado branch of the Boy Scouts of America came into being. Among those citizens who promoted the first Boy Scout Troop were the Reverend Charles Edward Spalding, John D. Spreckels, James D. MacMullen, George Holmes, W.A. Pratt, W. C. Harland, Alonzo Jessop,

Clarke Rude, Dr. John C. Yates, Nat Rogan, H.A. Collins, B.W. McKenzie, and Harold A. Swan who served as Scout Master.

The *Coronado Strand* had a new owner in 1916, W. A. Cassell, who soon sold his share to Dick Henderson and Harold Brand. Henderson kept the paper going, but unfortunately wrote scathing editorials against the Spreckels' faction, which helped keep the village divided over various issues.

As 1916 came to a close, San Diego newspapers featured positive reviews of Coronado's improvements during the year, especially those making the city more clean and beautiful. Its system of public parks was regarded as one of the best of any city in the county; its parking systems were praised; high marks were also given for the extensive system of tree planting that was planned and followed; and the fact that "no slums, no poorer sections, and no saloons are to be found there."

Adding a picturesque touch to Coronado's social life from the ranks of the Army and Navy, were officers and their wives from the army post, naval officers from aboard ships, and aviators from North Island, who all joined in local social activities, adding to the gaiety.

All types of activity, from fishing to polo, from Tent City to the school system, were explained in the *Tent City News*. However, in 1916, John Spreckels, threatened to close Tent City due to an unfortunate disagreement with the City Board of Trustees. In March, he wrote in the *Coronado Strand* that Coronadans for 15 years had enjoyed Tent City, with its free band concerts, dance pavilion, and other amusements that he felt were being taken for granted. Yet, the Trustees showed open hostility toward Spreckels over the matter of a liquor license. Mr. Gandy, a Trustee, had shown much anger, while Griffiss absented himself when the vote came up to grant or deny the license.

The Trustees saw no reason why the Hotel and the Royal Inn of Tent City should be allowed to serve alcoholic beverages, while no other businesses in Coronado were allowed to do so, although package stores were permitted by this time. After much bickering, inflamed by the newspapers, Spreckels won. Coronado could not afford to bite the hand which fed it.

This Tent City program, 1923. (CHA)

That matter resolved, the J.D. and A.B. Spreckels Securities Company undertook construction of a large commercial building that formally opened on July 20, 1917. Designed by Harrison Albright, and located at the intersection of Orange Avenue and Loma, this graceful new structure followed the curve of the streets, fronting 372 feet on Orange Avenue and 211 feet on Loma. In addition to Spreckels' Bank of Coronado, it contained 14 stores and 12 office suites, with apartments on the upper floors. The Silver Strand Motion Picture Theatre in the building had 800 seats on the main floor, and 200 in the balcony, and was Coronado's premier movie house for many years. Over the decades, this magnificently designed building has served as a cornerstone for many local and long-established businesses, as well as countless residents. Acquired in 1944 by the prominent San Diego Schulman-Neumann family, the "Spreckels Building" has been maintained in pristine condition, and today remains one of Coronado's favorite landmarks.

More building progress was made by a number of architects, contractors, and builders. Sidney D. Chapin compiled a record by having built more than 200 Coronado homes, drawing his own plans, but incorporating owners' ideas. Chapin came to Coronado from Michigan in 1898, and was himself an extensive property owner on the island. Chapin's houses resembled English cottages, with attractive sloping roofs, decorative exposed beams, and leaded-glass window panes, as seen today in homes at 590 "A" Avenue or 1109 "F" Avenue.

Harrison Albright (1866-1932), Architect for the Spreckels Mansion and Beach House, the Coronado Library, the Bank of Coronado building, Spreckels Theater and other prominent buildings in Coronado and San Diego. Known for reinforced concrete construction. (Marshall University Library)

After each bout of rough weather, piers constructed years before began to need more repairs. The Board of Trustees had to decide whether to demolish the structures or repair them again. Not able to decide, they appointed a committee, and discovered in the case of one major pier, the cost was going be $1,500 to fix it; so, instead the Board decided to burn it down—which ended up costing $2,300! The committee overlooked the fact that a fireboat had to be hired to do the job. Meanwhile, the pier at First Street was washed away by the 1916 flood, and interest in its replacement became a community affair. Some contributed money, while others volunteered labor. The pier had a handrail, with piles driven outside the wharf to which to tie small boats. This pier, which stood until the ferry building was demolished, proved to be of great service to Coronadans, as well as to naval personnel.

The flood of January 1916 caused the bay waters to rise severely, and broke the lower Otay dam, destroying Babcock's entire salt plant in the South Bay. The Merchants National Bank, which had just refinanced the Salt Works prior to the flood, had to help rebuild the plant to recoup their loss. Babcock suffered considerably from the flood because many of his investments, such as the La Jolla railway, were also damaged.

Coronado Heights had likewise fallen on hard times. In 1916, the Spreckels Company files show leases for hog, pigeon, and chicken ranches at the Heights. Allen's Sand Pit operated there, as did several companies gathering kelp. Another portion of the Strand became a trash dump run by various rubbish companies. Over a period of time, as development continued along the Silver Strand, these various operations ceased to exist.

By 1917, Coronado's population was 4,000, sometimes swelling to more than 5,000 during the winter tourist season, and 6,000 during Tent City summers.

On April 6, 1917, the United States entered the war against Germany. A month later, a joint Army-Navy Board recommended North Island be obtained for use by both the Army and Navy Air Services.

Consequently, on July 27, 1917, Congress passed a Condemnation Act, acquiring the 1,232-acre island as a permanent site for a military aviation school and base. The U. S. government occupied the island, even though it remained in litigation as the Spreckels Company held out for the value of $5 million, a sum assessed by a jury. However, by the time actual payment was made on December 30, 1921, records show the value had increased to $6,098,330.33 (including interest).

Nicely annotated view of North Island showing the relationship of both the Army and Navy sides. In 1922, North Island was much smaller than it is today. Dredging of the bay eventually rounded out the edges. (CPL/LCC)

On August 11, 1917, the commanding officer of Rockwell Field was directed by the War Department to assume control of all of North Island. A week later, joint tenancy agreements were reached between the Army and the Navy, with each branch allowed to occupy roughly half the island.

> The Navy claimed the bay side of the island to enable use of harbor piers and access to ships at anchor in the bay; the Army's Rockwell Field stretched along the ocean side of North Island including harbor entry defenses at Zuniga Point. Rockwell Field was the largest of six Army aviation training schools in the country, primarily used for the training of rookie pilots, and also became a central base for fighters and bombers. Lieutenant Jimmy Doolittle reported to Rockwell Field for initial flight training, and stayed as a flight instructor.
>
> Curiously, the venerable military "dog-tag" may have been invented in Coronado in September 1917. Following a midair collision over North Island that claimed the lives of two Army cadets (leaving their bodies almost unrecognizable), Colonel Alexander Dade required all fliers to wear aluminum identification tags around their necks, inside their shirts. These tags were stamped with name and squadron, and by 1918 were required of all American servicemen.
>
> The official date for the beginning of the U.S. Naval Air Station was November 8, 1917, when Lieutenant Earl Winfield Spencer, arrived as the base's first commanding officer. The Secretary of the Navy had big plans for North Island, calling it "undoubtedly, the largest and most important naval aviation station on the west coast," referred to as San Diego Naval Air Station. Spencer and his wife, Wallis Warfield Spencer, took up residence for a time at the Hotel del Coronado.
>
> Army and naval personnel poured into Coronado from all over the country. As the Navy reestablished itself on North Island, a flight school for student pilots was established, as well as a school for aviation mechanics, and a coast patrol department for aerial patrols of California waters. Before massive construction efforts were begun late in 1917, some of the first personnel

Army training aircraft crammed Rockwell Field during World War I, 1918. (CHA)

were quartered in hangars and sheds left over from the Curtiss Aviation School, while others were sent to now-vacant buildings from the Panama-California Exposition in Balboa Park.

With the outbreak of war, many Coronado yachtsmen volunteered for reserve service or provided their craft for national service. Several Coronado yachts were commandeered for national service, including several which routinely patrolled the harbor entrance. John D. Spreckels' imposing steam yacht, *Venetia* (a frequent visitor to Coronado), was turned over to the Navy at the beginning of the war, and, it was said, famously attacked German submarine U-39.

The Board of Trustees—now referred to as the City Council—was regarded as well-organized and composed of practical, progressive and wide-awake businessmen. The 1917-assessed valuation of property in the City was $3,700,000, with a City tax rate of $1.87 per $100. W.C. Harland, president of the City Council, served with Council members George Holmes, H.A. Collins, S.A. Johnson and I.S. Chamberlain. Council committees included Finance, Fire, Water and Sewer, Parks and Trees, Police, Health and Morals, and Streets. The Board of Health consisted of Dr. Raffele Lorini, James H. Dean, H.A. Kuehmsted, Scott Watson, and John S. Herlihy. The Justice Court occupied part of the Spreckels Building in the 1100 block of Loma Avenue, and would continue to do so until 1918, when they moved to larger quarters in the same complex.

With the coming of the war and growth of North Island, Coronado's law enforcement problems became more complicated. Local police and governmental agencies cooperated during that crucial period. The war also put a strain upon the telephone system, since San Diego and North Island had become the nucleus of various military facilities. The Pacific Telephone Company was pressed to provide many more telephones, opening a new office in 1917 at 778 Orange Avenue, at the corner of Eighth Street where it is still located.

Concerning the postal service, by the turn of the century, there were a number of notoriously underpaid postmasters, with the post office located in several different places. In 1912, Postmaster R.E. Robbins urged citizens to put house numbers on their residences to ensure prompt delivery, with the recommendation that numbers be purchased at Troxel's Variety Store.

A squadron of long-range Curtiss H-class flying boats over Coronado offer a great view of the Spanish Bight and North Island in 1922. (CPL/LCC)

By 1914, Robbins' assistants, W.J. Rice and William Chadwick, delivered mail by horse and cart. W.H. Meadows, a carrier who preferred to walk his route, completed the colorful cast of characters. Chadwick's dark-green "chariot" became well known, because the mare was so familiar with the route she could have made it blindfolded. The horse followed him from house to house as he walked the block. In 1919, he bought a motorcycle and tried that for six months, but gave it up to walk until 1939, when he retired. Later, carriers came to use bicycles.

In June 1917, a grand patriotic parade was held in Coronado, winding along Orange Avenue and ending in Tent City, where California Governor William D. Stephens spoke on the need to buy war bonds. Police Chief Louis C. Bandel rode in a decorated auto. Boy Scouts, veterans from the Spanish American War, and service personnel also rode or walked the route.

On June 1, 1918, an Army-Navy causeway was completed from Coronado to North Island. The 3,050-foot wooden bridge began at Fourth Street in Coronado, and ended one block south of the dividing line between the Army and Navy property. The small, two-room guard house built in 1918 to preserve security for the bases, is still present at the corner of Wright Avenue and McCain Boulevard.

Officers and men who were temporarily quartered in San Diego's Balboa Park, moved to North Island. In October, the Army and Navy staged a flyover of 115 airplanes to promote the sale of Liberty Bonds. The Curtiss, Thomas Morse, and other aircraft, varied in speed from 70 to 100 miles per hour. They left North Island in battle formation, with the main groups sailing across the sky. Pursuit pilots, in fast, scout machines, looped, dove, and twisted in every stunt known to the aviators.

Coronadans took part in the action overseas. Tom Frosio, a Spanish-American War veteran, was one of the first Coronado men to go to Canada to enlist. He returned suffering from a shell wound to his thigh. Captain John Wheaton left his job on the ferryboat *Ramona* to take care of the

A weekend event — watching the polo matches. (CHA)

army tug, *General de Russy*, while George D. Sturges drove an ambulance in France. The English polo players, Lords Tweedmouth and Innes-Kerr, returned to their country to join their regiments, and Major Colin Ross returned to Canada to join his. In fact, one collapse in Coronado's social scene came at the war's end, because most of Coronado's wealthy polo playboys, including Walter Hamlin Dupee, had moved away from the town. Although an attempt was made to bring polo back, the effort was never as successful as it was before.

Local women pitched in by knitting warm garments for the soldiers and rolling thousands of bandages. Social and civic leaders helped, particularly with war bond sales drives, the Red Cross, and area hospital work. Madame Ernestine Schumann-Heink sang at Tent City, delivering a message to young ladies in the audience, urging them to go to France as nurses, since there was a desperate shortage. Schumann-Heink suffered from the war more than most. She lost two sons, one on the German side and one on the American.

The Silver Strand Theater showed war movies; the U.S. Government displayed exhibits of war equipment in the Plaza to keep people informed. In September, Herbert Hoover, head of the "Commission For Relief" in Belgium, called for clothing for the people of that country, who had suffered because of the German devastation there.

In 1918, a terrible influenza epidemic raged through a great part of the world, killing 20 million people, including 45,000 in the American armed forces. Little was known about the dread illness that struck all ages. Reports filtered into Coronado about what people saw in other cities, where the influenza had spread like wildfire. While the wearing of masks was compulsory in San Diego, City fathers in Coronado made no such requirement, because Dr. Lorini stated that the masks did not help much. In December, however, the Coronado movie theater was closed due to an epidemic scare. By 1919, the large number of deaths diminished, and gradually the spread of the disease fell away.

> In 1918, Gabrielle Morton became Head Librarian of the public library, where she would stay for 33 years. By the late 1920s, the library was already overcrowded, so the Library Trustees had architect Richard Requa draw up expansion plans that would be the basis of a bond measure. The measure failed in 1929; the two wings were not added on either side of the original "Spreckels" building until 1935.

In 1918, Coronado bought a new fire engine, a beautiful white Seagrave, with gold trim and inflated rubber tires, at a cost of $8,700. This was the City's first pumper. That year, the fireman's pay was raised to $49 per month. Adolph Johnson became head of the department in 1919, though only on a half-time basis.

On November 11, 1918, when the war was declared over, Coronadans went wild with joy. Every other light on Ocean Boulevard, dark since the war, was relit. The Naval Air Station had trained 892 mechanics, and 206 aviators. To prove the base was equally valuable in peacetime, between December 4, 1918, and January 15, 1919, transcontinental mapping flights from Rockwell Field were carried out by the Army.

> On November 27, 1918, to commemorate the achievement of American aviators during the Great War," 212 military planes (141 Army and 71 Navy) staged a dramatic flight over Coronado and San Diego. Under a canopy of gray skies, viewing was perfect, and thousands stopped to look skyward at what the *San Diego Union* described as the "sight of a lifetime." Other mass flyovers had occurred during the war to promote the sale of Liberty Bonds, but everyone agreed that none equaled the spectacle on November 27th.

During the Mexican Revolution (1910-1916), troops at Imperial Beach effected security along the Mexican border. Troop "A," 10th U.S. Cavalry, was based at Camp Hearn near the end of San Diego Bay, along a winding road through the sand dunes, later called Silver Strand Boulevard. Dances were held on weekends for the entertainment of the military there. During World War I, riders from the camp occasionally played polo games in Coronado.

For about 10 years after the war, the U.S. Government leased land west of Orange Avenue, along the bay front at First Street, to be used as a hydroaeroplane station. Spreckels agreed to the lease, but refused to sell. Coronado boat owners along the beach had to relocate their boats. From then until more recent times that strip of land along San Diego Bay, from Orange Avenue to North Island, was vacant and provided magnificent views of the harbor. In hindsight, and with so much of our bay shore now in the hands of private developers, it's apparent that steps should have been taken to acquire the land as a town park. At the time, the bay view and its beauty were simply taken for granted.

At the beginning of 1918, the U.S. Congress ratified the 18th Amendment to the Constitution, prohibiting the manufacture, sale, or transportation of intoxicating liquors within the United States. The National Prohibition Act (informally called the Volstead Act), was passed by Congress in October 1919, but vetoed by President Woodrow Wilson; however, Congress then overrode the veto. The legislation went into effect on January 17, 1920. Prohibition proved to be a failure, since only bootleggers, racketeers, and gangsters thrived. Seaport cities did not "suffer" as much since there were rum-runners operating off-shore, who could move into ports at night or anchor beyond the three-mile limit. For Coronadans, Tijuana was close by, and bootleggers were busy there. Although Prohibition was not repealed until December 5, 1933, Coronadans managed to find alcohol, or even make their own in small stills and crocks at home.

In September 1919, an ordinance created the office of City Manager, and prescribed duties and compensation. Prior to this time, the City Engineer had fulfilled those functions, but without any actual authority to do so.

A number of buildings owned by the Coronado Beach Company, which were utilized by branches of the military, were returned. Regarding other structures, the Council had placed the acquisition of property for the building of a new high school on hold during the war, although it was badly needed. On August 17, 1918, the School Board resolved to purchase Block 90, between Sixth and Seventh, and "D" and "E" Avenues for the school, and set aside $12,000, with a sum of $27,000 already being on hand in the school fund. Still the year 1919 went by with no school construction.

Famed New York architect Bertram Grosvenor Goodhue, working with Navy planners, mapped out the primary buildings that were to be built on the Navy side of North Island. Goodhue's Spanish Colonial Revival designs for the Balboa Park Exposition buildings and the Marine Base (today's Marine Corps Recruit Depot) were enormously popular, and the Navy took unusual care in the North Island designs to ensure they "fit in" well with other Southern California architecture. The principal buildings were organized into a quadrangle, with arcaded blocks of barracks and offices, as well as a soaring, "signature" administrative building and control tower. The buildings were made of concrete and hollow terracotta, with red tile roofs and

United States Department of the Interior, Geological Survey, California (San Diego County) San Diego Quadrangle. Edition of June 1904, reprinted 1941. (CPL)

Early Navy pilots and parachute jumpers in 1928. (CPL/LCC)

tile and hardwood floors. The Navy also had other ambitious construction projects, including hangars and repair buildings. North Island's largest structure was a towering dirigible hangar, 250 feet long, finished in April 1919, ready to host North Island's first airship later that year.

At the same time, noted industrial architect Albert Kahn orchestrated the Army's plans for permanent buildings for Rockwell Field. His design was primarily Mission Revival and Spanish Colonial Revival, and included officer and enlisted quarters, hangars, clubs, administrative offices and repair sites, all within a tight coordinated plan. North Island is listed on the National Register of Historic Places, due, in part, to the significance of its historical architecture.

After World War I, North Island became a station that thrived on training aviators and on breaking records. Station commanders also dreamed of making North Island a center of lighter-than-air operations on the West Coast, which is why a large building for blimps and balloons was constructed. A nice, Coronado-style reception was held on April 13, 1919, to formally open the impressive hangar, with silent screen stars Mary Pickford, Lillian Russell, and Marjorie Rambeau attending.

A real sense of pride in the importance of North Island showed with the sight in the harbor of forty-five naval craft of all types, the largest number of warships and fleet auxiliaries in the history of the port.

Unfortunately for Coronadans, the Spreckels Railroad Company showed another loss of about $500 during 1919, from operating the streetcars running on Fifth Street from Orange Avenue. Too many people thought the streetcar was in use only to take patrons to the Coronado Country Club.

While citizens were warned a year earlier that lack of use would warrant closing the line, this fell on deaf ears, and in June 1919, the streetcar made its farewell trip. Now those going to North Island either had to use an auto or go by "shank's mare."

With more and more automobiles in town, the police department added two motorcycle policemen. Big, rosy-cheeked Pete Glynn was one and Manuel Meza the other. Pete had just come out of the Army, having served as a sergeant in the Medical Corps at Rockwell Field Hospital. These two officers spent most of their time chasing speeders on the narrow Strand Road, but helped the community with such events as leading the annual Fourth of July parade.

The Tent City season opened for its 19th year in early June 1919, but with much grief. Several drunken soldiers fought with a Navy officer; another soldier had a fit on the dance hall floor and was "out" for the rest of the night. The evening was totally ruined with the decapitation of a soldier by a streetcar in front of the Coronado Saddle Stables. Ironically, some of these disturbing events took place while the Secretary of the Navy, Josephus Daniels, was staying at the Hotel del Coronado.

Early in the history of the Hotel del Coronado, Mrs. E.S. Babcock Jr., began children's Christmas parties, a custom later revived by Manager J.J. Hernan, who loved people, especially children. The custom continued long after he left the town. Coronado children arrived dressed in their best clothes, escorted by their mothers. In the ballroom, they saw a large decorated tree. Rows of wicker chairs were set up for the show, consisting of a movie based on the poem "Night Before Christmas," followed by favorite cartoons.

Then, Santa Claus made his entrance and distributed candies to the children. Everyone moved to tables where ice cream, decorated French pastries, and other good things to eat were given to the children. John D. Spreckels was always the invisible host and must have known, under his red and white costume, how much the parties meant to the children. Even now, with the tradition long since discontinued it remains a favorite memory of old-time Coronadans.

> Soon after the end of World War I, the Navy established separate Atlantic and Pacific Fleets and rebalanced its forces. Navy ships by the dozens and aircraft by the hundreds were transferred to the West Coast, including many smaller destroyers and cruisers to San Diego. The Navy established a new Naval Base, San Diego (later to be called the Eleventh Naval District) to be commanded by Rear Admiral Roger Welles, who established his administrative headquarters at North Island.
>
> Commander, Air Detachment, U.S. Pacific Fleet became established at North Island to lead all naval aircraft in the Pacific, originally Captain J. Harvey Tomb and then Captain Henry Mustin. Float planes seemed to be everywhere, anchored off hangars, and scooting like water bugs around the bay. The concentration of both Army and Navy aircraft at North Island resulted in a host of flying records set for speed, distance and altitude, as well as new experimental breakthroughs such as radio communication from the air, aerial refueling, and aerial weapons. In September 1922, Army Lieutenant Jimmy Doolittle set the transcontinental record for a flight from Jacksonville Beach, Florida, to Rockwell Field in 21 hours 19 minutes (with one refueling stop); less than a year later, two Army aviators flew nonstop from Roosevelt Field, Long Island, to Rockwell Field in 26 hours 50 minutes.

In 1920, Coronado had about 3,300 residents. *El Patio*, a slick, society-oriented, 20-page weekly newspaper appeared on August 21, 1920, for a price of $3 per year. It stressed Coronado as a city of wealthy playboys and rich tourists. That approach, without "news," didn't attract the necessary circulation and the publication ceased after a year. Nonetheless, it is priceless today for its portrayal of society at the time, and the work of local artists and photographers it featured

Aerial view of Star Park and Orange Ave businesses, c. 1920. (CPL)

The Realty Board, disbanded for the duration of the war, was reactivated in 1920, and identified itself exclusively with members of the local, state and National Association of Realtors. The intent was to provide the public with a good image of the real estate industry, and so a San Diegan, Charles E. Arnold created what would become the nation's first Real Estate Act. By October 1922, the San Diego Realty Board strongly supported by Coronadans, forced the passage of a law requiring applicants for real estate licenses to pass a thorough examination. The test, which included real estate law, enabled the industry to divest itself of the "sharks," as much as possible

In March 1920, Coronado put into force a "Planning Effect," which purposefully divided the town into a number of districts: business, semi-business, apartment houses, and private residences. The aim was to create some restrictions to prevent the village from becoming a hodge-podge of buildings in the wrong places (an early form of zoning). Property owners met on October 20th at the Silver Strand Theatre to seek a "zoning" law. Nat Rogan, president of the City Planning Commission, explained how the Commission did its work, stating that there were about 4,800 lots in Coronado.

When polled by mail, 1,697 non-resident owners (93% of them), were in favor of a zoning law. Well-prepared to illustrate what the Commission desired to do, Rogan flashed a number of pictures on a screen showing Coronado's beauty spots and its blemishes. Rogan then put up a map showing the zones proposed. H. Austin Adams, who lived at 756 "E" Avenue, explained that Orange Avenue was the logical place for business, which should be restricted to that district. City Attorney Alfred Jack Morganstern assured the audience that there was no invasion of personal rights in the ordinance. The proposed zoning ordinance, however, as outlined by the Planning Commission, was blamed for a radical increase in property values. Three lots on Orange Avenue between Ninth and Tenth and between First and Second jumped in price when the plan was announced. Some lots on Orange Avenue were offered for as much as $600 each in the 900 block!

In September 1920, *El Patio* warned Coronadans to "Wake Up!" Coronado, the editor said, was one of the finest places of residence in the world." Yet the census noted a population of only 3,200, when the town had room for 25,000 people. He blamed a lack of community spirit; investments by a large portion of permanent residents made elsewhere; and a town with a large percentage of idle rich (30 millionaires living on the island). "We are a playground, and never hope or wish to be anything else. On that point," he said, "the community is united!" The editor pled with residents to do something, to look upon Coronado as more than a hotel, to give the village an identity, for as a town it had never done anything. Perhaps the editor at that time had a point. Babcock and Spreckels had done it all. The idea seemed to be that, particularly with the selection of San Diego as the main base for the destroyer fleet of the Pacific Coast, a marine base, a naval training base, and a repair base, all of which called for permanent investments of government and personal income, investors should get busy and "reap the golden harvest." What was being proposed was, of course, the beginning of private development for profit.

In March 1920, a school bond issue passed 14 to one. Block 90, just west of the present library, was bought for $20,000. Now, the School Board could move ahead with its plans for the much-needed high school, and would soon arrange for the land clearance. Architectural plans were to be drawn by Theodore C. Kistner, who, it seemed at the time, was designing every school between Santa Barbara and Coronado.

The City fathers again talked, argued, and mulled over the need, cost, and location of a police station. Coronado already had a fire station, but it was outmoded and in need of repair. Tent City, the growth of North Island, and increasing tourism all contributed to the need for new stations.

Newspapers of the 1920s reported great numbers of highway accidents, because suddenly the automobile was no longer a luxury, but a necessity. Fords and other cheaper cars were being manufactured in large numbers. While traffic multiplied, there were no stop signs or traffic lights in Coronado, and few driving rules. People drove instinctively; cars had little pick-up and no signal system. Roads were poor and many were unpaved. When Prohibition came in, drinking the "illegal stuff" added to the driving problems. Autos rammed into each other and the streetcars. They knocked down lamp posts, shrubbery, and trees. At least two dangerous curves caused a number of deaths, "Dead Man's Curve" around the Hotel laundry, and the "S" curve at Coronado Heights. In order to discourage speeding and reckless driving, the City inflicted stiff fines on errant motorists, but not until 1922 did the village get organized to deal with the auto problem. The streetlights were "sorry," as one reporter called them, and so poorly arranged that street signs could not be read.

In 1920, the *Morena*, a new ferryboat, was built by Rolph & Chandler of Wilmington, California at a cost of $200,000. It was steam-engine powered, side-paddle wheeled, with a wooden hull: she remained in service until 1938.

With the coming of the *Morena*, a new building with another slip large enough to accommodate her, was needed, so one was built just west of the existing slip in front of the (rail) car barn. The car barn, constructed in the 1920s, was sold for salvage, and completely demolished in 1949, when streetcars were replaced by buses. This second Ferry House, a cement and plaster building in Spanish architectural style, had a large central waiting room containing benches, toilet facilities, and a newsstand.

Herbert E. Fears signed a newsstand concession contract with the Spreckels Companies on December 30, 1920, and sold newspapers, magazines, and candies, with punchboards available. The railroad tracks were looped to the south of the Ferry House to allow passengers to get on and off the streetcar. A small park was built with a sprinkling system.

Among the social highlights of 1920, was the marriage of Dr. Paul Wegeforth, a native of Baltimore and graduate of Johns Hopkins Medical School, to Mrs. Lillie Spreckels Holbrook, daughter of John D. Spreckels. They lived in a beautiful home at 831 Adella, which Mrs. Holbrook had just built. An important visitor to Coronado in January 1920, was General John J. Pershing, Commander of the American Expeditionary Force, who was making a tour of the United States. His auto made its way along Orange Avenue, a large flag flying from the front fender, acknowledging the enthusiasm of the onlookers.

It must be admitted, however, that all other social happenings of 1920 were eclipsed by one single event that, even today, lingers full of nostalgia and romance – the visit of Edward, Prince of Wales. For over a week before his arrival on April 7, headlines heralded his coming. The Governors of California, Arizona, and Utah, as well as society people, civic leaders, military officials, and other VIPs, were invited to meet the 26-year-old Prince and his cousin, Lord Mountbatten, at a reception aboard H.M.S. *Reknown*.

Coronado attracted the wealthy and famous. In this picture, two familiar faces pose with their friends. From L to R: Mrs. Emory Sands, Mrs. Wallis Simpson, Charlie Chaplin, Miss Rhoda Fullam in 1926. (CPL)

Three days later, a grand dinner and ball was given in His Majesty's honor in the Crown Room at the Hotel del Coronado. It was then, and is still, considered by many to be the most dazzling evening ever seen there. As part of the elaborate preparations, special gold embossed china was ordered, a few pieces of which remain in existence today. Efforts to secure a place on the guest list were fierce, and the unenviable task of controlling it was given to a committee headed by Mrs. Claus Spreckels Jr., who was also to act as the Prince's dinner partner.

On the day of the banquet, Edward, Prince of Wales, asked if he might call on Mrs. Spreckels, saying it was customary to make oneself known before escorting the lady for the evening. The Prince arrived at 1043 Ocean Boulevard at 5:30 p.m. with his official bodyguard. From there, they attended the ball to which over 1,000 guests were invited. Hosted by Mayor and Mrs. Louis J. Wilde (Francis) of San Diego, the affair also served as a coming out party for Miss Lucile Wilde, who danced with His Royal Highness. Bands from the USS *New Mexico* and the Hotel del Coronado performed during the evening. *El Patio* reported the evening in detail, including the interminable handshaking. At some point during the festivities, the Prince bowed to his partner, asked to be excused and left the party. After all, he could go to many other parties, but this was his only chance to visit Tijuana!

Over the years, there has been much speculation and research about whether or not the Prince met his future Duchess, Wallis Warfield Spencer, then wife of North Island's Commanding Officer, during that April 1920 visit. She could have been presented to him at either the reception on board his yacht or at the ball in the Hotel's Crown Room, but no specific documentation proving that theory has been located. If it is true, however, it did not result in the beginning of the famous relationship. That would come years later, when, as the wife of an American businessman, Ernest Aldrich Simpson, she met the Prince in Europe, and began the love affair for which he would give up the throne of England, in 1936.

Polo attracted the wealthy to Coronado, and polo season energized the crowds. (CHA)

William Boyd lived in Coronado in 1919, and was known as "Coronado's handsomest chauffeur." By 1921, he had become a film star. By the '30s, he became better known as "Hopalong" Cassidy. Mrs. Cornelius Vanderbilt, Jr., and her Spitz dog, ChouChou, stayed at the Hotel del Coronado, as did the famous dancer, Ruth St. Denis. Mrs. Frank Hall Moon, mother of Mrs. Claus Spreckels Jr., entertained the distinguished British writer, Charlotte Cameron, who was enroute to the South Sea Islands to soak up some native culture, while writing about the islanders. The Duchess of Manchester, about to shed her husband, the Duke, was in Coronado prior to returning to London, where she hoped to achieve success as a singer.

The George P. Fullers owned a string of pure bred horses and were racing them at Tijuana; they stayed at the Hotel. Elaborate preparations were always made for entertaining. Mrs. Luther Kennett (Isabelle), who resided at 1105 Alameda, was a prime mover behind a February masquerade party at the Coronado Country Club, with the Navy contingent largely represented. Mrs. Rufus Choate, in a pretty frock of black satin with a handsome Roman sash, was hostess at a bridge tea in her cozy home at Seventh and "C." The Hotel del Coronado made preparations in January 1921, for the first of a series of elaborate costume balls, this one to be a Bal des Quarte Saisons, which inspired the planning of many original costumes to impersonate the different elements.

Society was caught up in the opening of the polo season on January 22, 1921, starting off at the Country Club with the Major Colin Ross tea, where everyone would say "hello" to the visiting polo players. One of the outstanding 1921 polo teams was that of Major Ross, Arthur Perkins, Carleton Burke, and Max Fleischmann, the latter of the Fleischmann yeast fortune. During the year, Welford Beaton played polo with Charlie Chaplin, having already bested the actor at golf and bowling. After several hours of two-man polo, the match was declared a draw, with no goals scored by either man. During the season, Chaplain and his wife rented a gabled house at Tenth and Olive on the northeast side of the street. So did Will Rogers, and the suave, handsome Hollywood actor Jack Holt (born Charles John Holt). In 1921, sadly, Spreckels stopped financing the games. For all the glamour associated with this sport, it was not a moneymaker.

The war and bad seasons had financially checked the progress of the game. In its place, the newspaper reported, would be a golf course. "Golf will take the place of polo," Beaton wrote, "though golf alone will not draw anyone to Coronado. All the Spreckels' money cannot supply Coronado with a course like Pebble Beach, or those courses around Los Angeles and Pasadena." Even though there were no local polo teams in Coronado after this time, the games continued for several years. Such teams as "The Hawaiians," the Honolulu cavalry teams, the Riversides; the Denvers; and the Midwicks all played, and through the Coronado Merchant's Association, a fund was established so that Major Colin Ross could occasionally get a team together. Spreckels decision was correct, however; polo was too expensive and in ensuing years, annual Horse Shows took its place.

In 1921, the polo colony, nevertheless, started a new fad. Julius Fleischmann and Earle Hopping each brought three Scootamotors with them, and as a result, a whole flock of orders were sent out over the wires to New York. These little vehicles were simple to operate, and could carry a person 60 miles on a gallon of gas. Even Charlie Chaplin had one while he was in Coronado. Owners called it "Scootamoting." For those who preferred more sedate travel, two well-known car rental services also existed in Coronado. Tanner's and the Pioneer Garage, at 1027 Orange Avenue, provided vehicles for rent, including Pierce Arrows, Cadillac Eights, Hudsons, and Twin-six Packard busses, which took people on tours. Tanners had enough cars at the Hotel to take care of all the patronage.

By 1921, Tent City had its own police force and fire department. One of the palm cottages was fitted as headquarters for the combined services, with officer Pete Boisserie in charge. Police and fire signals were established all over Tent City. On April 30, in preparation for the June opening, over a hundred workmen were busy making improvements. Tent City had expanded; no less than 17 families moved in on one day. A new restaurant provided a floor for dancing to the best Hawaiian band that Hotel general manager William A. Turquand could procure. For diners in a hurry, a lunch counter was made available.

During the 1920s, some home-grown Coronado men and women made their way into the motion picture business. George J. Lewis, president of the Coronado High School student body, and captain of the basketball team, went to Hollywood after Clara Bell Cutler discovered his dramatic talent. Within a few years, Johnny Downs, also from Coronado, would be a motion picture star.

Although social life of Coronado revolved heavily around the Hotel and the Country Club, a new place opened that struck everyone's fancy. A restaurant called the Blue Lantern Cafe, and later the Blue Lantern Inn, opened in 1920 in a small rented house owned by Nellie Madden. Mesdames Mariani and Esrey leased the restaurant in the first half of the 1920s, and their fine culinary art made the place so popular it gave the Hotel del Coronado and the Country Club much competition. They took a vacant lot next door and transformed it into a patio garden with colored lights and tables shaded by bright umbrellas. In 1921, they held dinner dances, and later, bridge luncheons and teas with diners both in and outside the house. The Rotary Club was founded during a meeting there and, for a time, held luncheons there. In 1926, Mrs. Madden sold the building to Mr. and Mrs. Alex Rutherford, who moved it to Block 33 (between Ninth and Tenth, "G" and "H") where it was redesigned as their home. A three-story brick and stucco hotel, called the Blue Lantern Inn, was then erected on the original site by W. S. Stephens (some documents show it was designed by Wayne Douglas McAllister). Over the years, the Inn had several different owners and names, including the Ritz, the Biltmore and the Village Inn. Today it is called Hotel Marisol Coronado.

El Patio recounted Coronado's activities for part of the year 1921, before another paper, *The Sun Dial,* was issued from October 1, 1921 to February 18, 1922. That paper seemed to stress the idea that, except for the regular military stationed there, those who had poured into North Island during the war had folded their tents and gone home. Coronado Beach seemed deflated. To unload

This aerial photo by Harold Taylor shows Coronado before beach was formed. Also, note the Beach School at the Hotel del Coronado and the pier that extended from Tent City, c.1922. (CPL/LCC)

some of Coronado's empty business and residential lots, land auctions were held. A.G. Ruce, who lived at 1127 Sixth Avenue, was a nationally known auctioneer, and he was selected to sell whatever he could. The *Coronado Strand* advertised that land was being sold cheaper than when it was auctioned in 1887. Despite the hard sell, because of taxes few prospective buyers took advantage of the lots that came up for sale. Therefore much of the land continued to remain vacant.

The Spreckels Companies had their own troubles during the year. On November 6, 1921, at four in the morning, the ferry landing caught fire as a result of burning oil spread along the waterfront. Reacting quickly, Mate Wells Davis was able to get aboard the *Ramona*, yelling to the captain of the Spreckels' yacht *Venetia* to tow the old ferryboat to safety out in the bay. In the meantime, Captain Bill Kertner arrived with his fireboat and poured salt water on the blaze. The Coronado and North Island Fire Departments joined in on the shore side, and were able to salvage the ferry building, although the dock was a crumbling mass of charred wood.

The Company continued to buy new streetcars and, by 1922, owned four open street cars just for the Orange Avenue lines. The older cars were made available at $150 each for anyone who wanted them; George Holmes, purchasing agent for the Spreckels Companies, noted they could be made into substantial homes.

The employees of the San Diego and Coronado Ferry Company began to get testy in early 1921, seeking one day off per week from their jobs. The request was denied, but they did get a raise. Captains made 65 cents per hour or $175 a month; the mate 52 cents an hour or $140.40 a month; the purser, 40 cents an hour or $121.50 a month, and deck hands, 40 cents an hour or $108.08 a month. The Company could not see its way clear to grant a day off a week because of their large investment and operating expenses.

Construction in Coronado continued at a fast pace during the year 1922. Coronado High School plans were redrawn by the Quayle Brothers, allowing for more than 500 students, but construction costs rose to $125,000. The *San Diego Union* of February 21, 1921, carried a photograph of the location, and noted that the cornerstone was to be laid with impressive ceremonies conducted by the Masons. Other fine homes were being built, like that for E.E. Summers at 970 "I" Avenue in a sort of Colonial Pueblo architectural style. Other persons bought homes for $9,000, "on the ridiculous terms of $1,000 cash and $100 per month including all interest."

The first issue of the *San Diego Union* in January 1923, called Coronado "without equal as a place of residence; the attractive city can boast of every advantage" and noted "the refined people, perfect climate, and beautiful homes." Some buildings were also demolished during the year. The paper reported, "…the ancient Beach Company building that has stood for thirty-nine years will be razed…" because she had fallen into a state of disrepair.

Telephone history was made in October 1922, when new telephone numbers were provided Coronadans. That same year, telephone subscribers were listed separately in the San Diego telephone directory under the heading, "Coronado."

Recreation probably attracted more attention in the bay town than any other activity. A Coronado Cycle Club was organized by Mr. W.E. Holland of Holland's Bicycle Shop. The Club equipped a race track on the grounds south of Tent City, and organized the "greatest bicycle parade in Southern California on May 6, 1922, with the line of march on Ocean Boulevard and Orange Avenue." More than 60 members, sponsored by various civic and merchant's groups, paraded. Holland arranged to have a carload of antique bicycles brought down from Los Angeles to take part in the parade, which was judged by Harold A. Taylor, General J.H. Pendleton, Harry Chrimse, Lt. Comdr. W.A. Richardson, W.A. Turquand, Manager of the Hotel del Coronado, William Kettner, and H.R. Moore.

This was also the year that Harold A. Taylor, an outstanding local photographer, proposed a community Flower Show, although a number of people pointed out that Coronado did not have enough flowers, and that no one would come to see them since that was the case. He went ahead anyway, and formed a group to set up the first Coronado Flower Show. This premier event, held in the East Plaza, took place on May 13, 1922, and proved to be a huge success. Taylor went to the Commandant of North Island and borrowed a canvas airplane tent to house the exhibit. Boy Scouts set up camp in the park during the flower show weekend, to guard against fire, theft, or vandalism. The Flower Show continues to this day, and remains one of the village's best-loved traditions.

Other recreation included a Spreckels Golf Tournament for Women, with a very special cup for the winner. The tournament has been held every year, except between 1942 and 1958, when there was no golf course on the island.

Coronado's newspapers continued to evolve. The *Coronado Saturday Night* started in April 1922, merging with the *Coronado Strand*, and was published weekly every Saturday, with Harry Chrimse as managing editor. The *Coronado Strand* and the *La Jolla Journal*, including all the furniture and fixtures, were both purchased by the Coronado Publishing Company, whose stockholders were Harry Chrimse, J.D. Ashton, Albert H. Foret and Harry Titus. Another paper, called the *Sun Dial*, which was a continuation of *El Patio*, moved to San Diego on March 4, 1922.

The social status of Coronadans seemed foremost in the minds of many people in the 1920s. Everyone wanted to see his or her names in print as having attended an intimate party or a night at the Hotel. Major dinners, luncheons, teas, and suppers were given for the slightest excuse. A golf or tennis championship match, in which participants clothing was described in detail, grabbed more attention than did the match. "Katherine Richards was most effective in her all white sweater, hat, and skirt. Her scarf of Belgian blue, lent the proper color tone. Mrs. Claus Spreckels and Mrs. Roy Pickford (Gertrude) always could be relied upon to bring to Coronado the last word in what to wear.

Coronado High School, dedicated in 1923. (CHA)

Roy Pickford looked very 'golf-y' in his blue knickerbockers, which brought out the burnished gold of his red hair most effectively," wrote one columnist, while another noted, "Commander George Murray in toupee, spats and hat to match, not forgetting his virtuous white carnation, is running a race with himself in and out of uniform."

Such a town deserved its own flag, and 1922 was the year it got one. As the result of a contest, Louis de Ryk Millen, who was still a schoolboy, created the winning design, green and white, with a gold crown in the center. Still the official Coronado flag, it is flown along Orange Avenue during major holidays and visits by VIPs.

In the year 1922, the City had its plusses and minuses. A pseudo-vigilante committee was organized (or was self-appointed) to do something about violations of traffic ordinances. Twenty-five "deputy marshals" were appointed to report infractions. Their names were not known, even to each other, to avoid enmity among neighbors. However, after the vigilantes began to report on one another by happenstance, the whole plan soon fell apart.

Violations of traffic ordinances still had to be grappled with. Dick Klass, Coronado's hamburger king, made a trip to Long Beach, averaging 27 miles per hour. He reported that stop signs were the key to prevent speeding. Only a short time later, Cornelius Vanderbilt, while visiting in Coronado, sped up Orange Avenue to catch the ferry *Ramona*, and was fined $15.00.

> The new Coronado High School was dedicated and opened in 1923, after an impressive cornerstone-laying celebration by the Masons, on February 22, 1922. The dedication speaker called Coronado High, "...an enduring center of culture for Coronado. Think of the concerts, lectures, and plays that can be given right here in this school theatre – a real post-graduate course for all the grown-ups – an opportunity to benefit the mind and to build up a community center that will be one of the greatest assets the city has."
>
> The new Coronado High School dominated the block between Sixth and Seventh Streets, D and E Avenues, and would become one of the finest buildings in Coronado history. It featured superb architectural bones ... solid, reassuring, prominent ... its two-story graceful, columned entry represented classic Midwest and East Coast educational themes, brought westward to a rapidly expanding California.

The grand Mitchell Estate sat at the corner of Flora and Ocean Boulevard, extending down to the Spreckels Mansion. John Mitchell left an extensive art collection in a large gallery on the property when he passed away. Remodeled in 1924, and demolished in 1935. (CHA)

The *Coronado Saturday Night* and the *Coronado Strand* provided islanders with local news until September 1, 1923, when the newspaper became the *Coronado Journal*, published out of offices at 943 Orange Avenue. While much of the news was local, the national scene often made headlines.

Three divisions of Navy destroyers met with disaster in dense fog on Saturday night, September 8, 1923, at Point Honda near Point Arguello. George Olsen, lighthouse keeper, recorded that nine U.S. destroyers ran aground due to high seas and heavy fog. Distinguished naval officers commanded the ships. One eyewitness, Coronadan Thomas F. Carlin, a young ensign, wrote about the tragedy in a letter to his mother. "I have just been through one of the greatest [peace time] disasters that ever happened in the United States Navy." He described in detail how the destroyers piled on the rocky point. Twenty-three men died in the wreckage at the place mariners had long called, the "Devil's Jaw." The rescue of the survivors, the search for the dead, and recovery of the equipment, required moving up and down rocks and cliffs. Some 10,000 navy men and civilians attended memorial services at North Island for the 23 men lost. The disaster and the aftermath of courts-martials came as shocks to Coronadans, since a number of the men involved were residents of the island.

In Tent City, the thatched roofed cottages were stripped of their palm leaf toupees and given permanent roofs. Wooden sides on the houses were built three quarters of the way up with canvas drops which could be rolled up or down. The intent was to provide for a permanent winter population. When the Tent City Fire Department torched the brush and dead palms, no one had told the Coronado Fire Department. They rushed past the Hotel del Coronado thinking Tent City was going up in flames.

On February 17th, *Coronado Saturday Night* reported the fire station at Sixth and Palm had been sold by the City to L.C. Bandel who moved it in sections to be used as houses at Third and "B," Palm and "G," and on "C" between Third and Fourth. By July 1st, a new fire station had replaced the old ramshackle structure, while the police department was still headquartered at City Hall.

Fire Chief George Sanven in front of the Public Library, c.1923. (CPL)

In 1923 the subject of a combination firehouse and police station to be located at Sixth and Orange came up again, having been defeated by voters the prior year. The noted architectural firm of Requa (Richard S.) and Jackson (Herbert) was hired, and Al Laing was awarded the building contract. The total price for land and improvements was $27,415.90 and paid to the Spreckels Securities Company in 1933. The handsome new building was to form the nucleus of a proposed civic center that would eventually include City Hall. This plan, however, was never carried out and the police and fire station stood alone.

In 1922, noted art collector John W. Mitchell moved from Los Angeles to buy the Alvin B. Daniels' estate, at the southeast end of Ocean Boulevard and Flora Avenue. The house, built in the 1890s, was originally owned by Graham Babcock, son of Elisha S. Babcock, Jr. The Mitchells, using the architectural talent of Louis John Gill, completely remodeled the redwood home, removing the roof, adding wings, stucco and tile, and converting it into a Moorish arcade. Mitchell built the castle of his dreams as a combined gallery and library, a magnificent repository for his works of art. His library contained 8,000 volumes, and the home held treasures from all over the world. When he passed away in June 1925, he requested that his widow, Adina, keep the gallery open on regular occasions for the public. She also encouraged musicals in the auditorium. The Mitchells had intended to donate the gallery and its contents as a foundation for a school of art. At Mrs. Mitchell's death, the property was offered to the Christian Science Church, which turned it down for financial reasons. Subsequently, the art museum with a debt of back taxes, was offered to the City of Coronado in the midst of the Depression.

A San Diego bank foreclosed, and the City of Coronado refused the building. After relatives took possession of what they wanted from the estate, the remainder was put up for sale at auction in 1933. Gone were such represented painters as Thomas Gainsborough, Bartolome Esteban Murillo, Stuart, Francisco de Goya, and Childe Hassam. As it stood idle, the landscape died. The home and art gallery were razed in the late 1930s, having stood only twelve years! The City, afraid to risk the financial burden, missed another golden opportunity to acquire private property for the public good, a failure that sadly appears endemic to Coronado thinking, and would be repeated many more times.

Architect Ray Alderson received the contract to design the Winchester apartment and business building at the corner of Orange and Loma Avenues for Fred C. Winchester. Constructed by J.E. Alcaraz, the land and building cost $165,000 for the seven apartments on the second floor, and four large and commodious rooms for stores on the ground level.

At about the same time, Dr. Arthur B. Wegeforth realizing the necessity for a hospital on the island, offered his suite of rooms upstairs in the Spreckels Building, Orange Avenue at Loma, to City officials. Those were to be used by Coronado residents in case of any acute illness, accident or obstetrics, with the privilege of calling any physician desired. City officials accepted the four private rooms, a well-equipped surgery room, laboratory, diet kitchen, x-ray room, consultation and examination rooms. The generous offer of Dr. Wegeforth lasted but two years, at which time the hospital had to close because of financial reasons. After this, Doctors Arthur and Harry Milton Wegeforth set up offices across the street at 1111 Orange Avenue, in the building formerly known as the Coronado Court Apartments, and later the BayBerry Tree Gift Shop. Renovations were done under the supervision of architect Louis J. Gill; however, these changes were not made for a hospital, but rather for doctors' offices.

Golf was played at the Coronado Country Club, on land surrounding the Polo Grounds next to the Spanish Bight. (CHA)

The City Council still did nothing about a hospital, and the Wegeforths had simply gotten out of the hospital business. Officials were confronted with a lesser, but nonetheless time-consuming matter, as the Planning Commission wanted to change street names again. Primarily, the Commission tried to push through an ordinance changing the name of Orange Avenue to Coronado Avenue. But the ordinance did not receive Council approval–failing as did the attempt to change Orange Avenue to Roosevelt Avenue a few years earlier.

Late in the year, the County Board of Supervisors contracted to have 4.61 miles of the Coronado Strand paved with Portland cement, creating a highway 18 feet wide and five inches thick. John D. Spreckels said he would pave the adjoining 3,000-foot section of the Strand Highway at the end of Tent City at his own expense.

Mostly, Coronado indulged itself in living the "Roaring Twenties" to the hilt. A miniature golf course was established, bordered by Dana Place just west of the Hotel del Coronado, supervised by golf pro Charles Detrick. The real golf course along Alameda had various changes made during the years leading up to World War II. In 1923, the sand greens were converted to grass as were the driving tees. More golf tournaments were scheduled for both men and women, and handsome trophies were awarded, including the beautiful A.B. Spreckels Cup. But that much-used golf course, so meticulously manicured by the Spreckels' gardeners, including Joseph Peters, was gone before the outbreak of World War II.

Art lovers founded The Franklin Club in 1923 in honor of Miss Mary E. Franklin, a direct descendant, it was said, of Benjamin Franklin. Meetings were held at her home and later at the Mitchell Art Gallery. By 1938, the club met in the studio of artist Dayton Reginald Eugene Brown (the stable of the old Balch house at 725 Adella) where Mr. Brown spoke to the club on oil painting and etching. The club continued after the death of Miss Franklin, and remained in existence for about 20 years.

Enthusiasts held their first annual Dog Show at Tent City in 1922, with Mrs. Claus Spreckels as Chairperson. Major interest came in April 1923, when the second show attracted newspaper coverage all over the country because of the distinguished judges and careful selection of breeds. No shows were held after that time, however, because the ferry trip frightened many of the animals, making the San Diego side of the bay preferable for such an event!

Tennis would become a very important sport in Coronado, and over a period of time produce nationally known players. The first public tennis court was located in the West Plaza, where it is today, near Sixth Street, and officially opening on March 31, 1923. A second court was added in 1940; others, including those on Glorietta Boulevard, were added later.

The major sporting event of 1924 was the Gymkhana, which involved more than 40 entries from all over the state; it was hosted by the San Diego American Legion Post at the Coronado Country Club in July. Major Colin Ross chaired the events committee, and scores of horsemen and horsewomen attended. Exhibitions, trick riding by the 11th Cavalry from Camp Hearn, Pony Express races, rescue races, jumping contests, and a polo game or two made up events, which more than 5,000 people attended. The proceeds were used by the American Legion for the care of indigent servicemen and their families, while some of the funds went to the Balboa Park Memorial Fund.

Not until April 1927, however, was there any effort to help the Coronado Hospital Building Fund. A Gymkhana was held by the Coronado Riding Club, inspired by Raymund V. Morris, Percival Thompson, Arthur J. Scully, Frank W. Von Tesmar, Claus Spreckels, Luther M. Kennett, Nat Rogan, and Marcellino Molino. That Gymkhana spawned the First Annual Horse Show on April 14, 1928; in nine years, the show donated over $11,000 to charity, including the Hospital Building Fund, the Resthaven preventorium, Coronado Community Chest, and other organizations. The *San Diego Union* of March 4, 1928, carried a photograph of a group of Coronado children who would ride in the first annual Horse Show, and included a long list of Coronado luminaries who would be participating. Those annual shows, held at the stables located at Fourth and Alameda, ended abruptly at the onset of World War II.

Even though interest in polo was beginning to wane, riding continued to be a favorite activity. Riding parties were planned and conducted by instructors from local stables, and bridle paths fit well into the landscape. The best known stables were those of the Coronado Riding Club, and the Hotel. A popular one located at 231 Alameda Boulevard, a two- story barn later converted into a very attractive residence, had a smaller building on the front of the lot, both painted "barn red."

Shenandoah (ZR-1), the first zeppelin-sized airship ever seen on the West Coast, arrived at North Island in October 1924, for training with Navy units. (CHA)

Manager Mel S. Wright said that Hotel Del reservations were the heaviest in the history of the property, and that as a result, much more had to be offered to keep people busy. Dances were held two nights a week in the ballroom, and every night in the Casino and Silver Grill.

Aquaplaning, a sport combining water skiing with flying, as well as innumerable sightseeing trips, were arranged for those who wanted to exercise or see Tijuana or the back country. Golf tournaments were provided, as were Sunday night concerts. The Coronado scene continued to be a veritable whirlwind of social and recreational activities. Mah-jongg, a Western version of a Chinese game played with tiles, became such a rage that the Hotel organized games.

> Coronado was the national focus of another aviation breakthrough on October 10, 1924, when the massive *Shenandoah* (ZR-1), the first zeppelin-sized airship built in America and the first rigid airship ever seen on the West Coast, reached North Island after a transcontinental trip. She arrived over North Island after dark, looming as large as a battleship in the field's floodlights, with loud droning engines that could be heard all over town. During her stay, Navy dignitaries, press, politicians, and thousands of lucky Coronadans were able to stand beneath the huge dirigible, where she was moored to a large stationary mast at the far end of the field. After six days, *Shenandoah* cast off on a cool, marine-layer morning (as everyone stopped and stared at the imposing airship) and flew out around Pt. Loma, and then northwards to operate with the fleet.

Aviation breakthroughs continued with regularity. In August 1924, the flying Marines moved to the Naval Air Station from Santo Domingo, marking the start of Marine Corps activity in aviation on North Island. Also, the first night catapult launch from a battleship, USS *California*, was accomplished by Lieutenant Dixie Kiefer off the Coronado shore. On Coronado itself, another aviation first took place when W.A. Koehler applied for a permit to use the strip of land described as "north of Glorietta Bay and south of Glorietta Boulevard" for use as a commercial aviation field. However, residents near the proposed landing field brought a petition before the City, which denied the application.

> On November 29, 1924, Coronado's destiny changed forever with the arrival of what the press referred to as, "The Deadliest Ship Afloat." The arrival of the Navy's first aircraft carrier, USS *Langley* (CV-1) would mark the beginning of Coronado's strong link with carrier aviation, and would bring hundreds of thousands of carrier aviators and their families to Coronado, which, in no small measure, transformed the City. Carriers would become the most powerful ships in America's Navy. And, during nearly 100 years of operations, over 100 different carriers would come to Coronado.
>
> *Langley* had been converted from the large collier Jupiter, largely as an experiment. In the years from 1924 to the early 1930s, though, *Langley* would generate an amazing number of "firsts." All the processes of running a complex ship, and inventing complicated routines and tactics, were tested and honed during busy operations off the coast, many times in view of Coronadans looking seaward from the beach. All the advances in aircraft, weapons, training, carrier design and tactics that would later prevail across the Pacific during World War II, were effectively perfected in local waters by aircraft carriers and aviators centered on Coronado. Even today, thousands in Coronado wake up every morning and go to work aboard carriers or indirectly support carrier aviation from worksites at North Island. Many thousands more drive through our community daily to reach North Island to join in this carrier-centric activity. All this began in November 1924.
>
> In mid-1924, the Navy suggested that a "landing base" be established on the ocean beach near the Hotel del Coronado so that launches could be used to ferry officers and men ashore from battleships anchored in Coronado Roads, rather than sending launches on lengthy trips

Aerial view of the "Harborette" Boat Landing Harbor at the Hotel Del Coronado. (CPL)

around North Island. Sensing the economic benefits of thousands of sailors coming ashore, San Diego and Coronado split the construction costs of $150,000 for a C-shaped harbor with two breakwater arms of rocks and cement, right in front of the Hotel and the nearby trolley stop leading to the ferry. In September 1924, Coronado voters approved a tax levy for the project.

On December 23, 1924, the *Coronado Journal* noted that the construction of a rock jetty to be used as a "Battle Ship Boat Landing Harbor" by the Hotel could be completed by the summer of 1925. The Hotel owners believed that this would be a marvelous way to provide easier access for officers to go to the Hotel, and enlisted men to Tent City. Even Rear Admiral Ashley H. Robertson said that "the operating part of the fleet goes where adequate facilities are provided, and where natural conditions are most favorable." In other words, San Diego and Coronado could get the fleet away from San Pedro or San Francisco by providing a landing facility of this kind. The City Council moved rapidly into action, and at a special meeting proposed a $75,000 bond issue for the project. G. Aubrey Davidson, known for his ability to rally men and money for civic projects, said the other $75,000 could be raised by San Diego men and donated to Coronado. Merchants and most of the citizens raved about the idea of a harborette.

By March 1925, the fleet anchored in Coronado Roads and the partially completed "harborette" was tested successfully, but then San Diego funding dried up and the work "temporarily" ceased. Beginning just before New Year's of 1926, three consecutive Pacific storms battered Coronado beaches. Waves pounded the harborette's concrete walls. Damage mounted, but calls to San Diego for repair funds fell on deaf ears. Protective pilings were washed away and sand rushed into the dredged portion of the ocean shore. To save homes, Coronado focused its emergency efforts toward Ocean Avenue's protective rock breakwater, and ignored the harbor.

Babcock Court - Heilman Villas, 706-720 Orange Avenue & 1060-1090 Seventh Street. Demolished in November 1993. (Library of Congress)

> The repair costs or the expense to dismantle the unusable harbor now exceeded any affordable estimate, leaving a huge scar on Coronado's pristine beach. The 1925 harborette slowly disintegrated over the years but parts of it (breakwater rocks and few portions of cement walls) still remain visible for the confused tourist asking the question: "Why are there rocks on the Hotel Del beach?"

On January 1, 1924, the San Diego Union provided photos of Coronado's completed fire station, High School, the Motor Courts (later called Babcock Courts), the Bank of Coronado, and the Southern Trust and Commerce Bank. A home on Tolita for Roy Pickford was under construction at a cost of $12,000. Later the Pickfords would buy the Arthur J. Scully home on Loma, designed by the distinguished La Jolla architect Edgar V. Ullrich. A home on Tenth Street, owned by Commander James S. Woods, was valued at $15,000, while a residence being completed for Mark Vilim at 1022 Olive was worth $11,000.

On a philanthropic note, the White Elephant Shop at 953 Orange Avenue was opened by Mrs. Frank Hall Moon, Mrs. Paul Wegeforth (Lillie), Mrs. Andrew Wessels (Hulda), and Miss Harriet Holbrook (Hamilton). Donated goods sold in the shop provided monies to help the Children's Rest Haven Home in Chollas Valley.

The Coronado Beach Company still eventually hoped to develop Coronado Heights, especially with the new Strand road opening June 29, 1924. Watchmen had to be employed to make sure no one tried to use it before the date of its official opening, since it took two weeks for the cement to harden. Since the race track in Tijuana had just reopened, ministers in Coronado declared from the pulpit that this "driveway was the road to hell," while Coronado citizens cried out that the road would get them to Mexico much quicker.

During the early 1920's, the Board of Trustees began to look seriously at making changes to Coronado's regular grid of residential streets, alphabetical north and south, numerical east and west. Many considered this arrangement to be uninspired or "pedestrian." Several schemes were suggested such as renaming lettered streets with Spanish names beginning with that letter (A Avenue might become Alicia for instance, with numbered streets taking on a Spanish equivalent (Octava for 8th Street for example). On January 7, 1924 the Board of Trustees took its first action passing a resolution to rename First Street as "Cabrillo Esplanade." This exciting development only lasted three years when public opinion revolted when it was too hard to pronounce and when you couldn't find First Street any more.

In June 1924, Major General Joseph H. Pendleton, USMC arranged for the donation of a brass, muzzle-loading gun captured by United States Marines from the fortifications of Santo Domingo, Dominican Republic in 1916. Pendleton had been in command of the Fourth Regiment of Marines stationed at North Island, when he received orders to serve as Military Governor in Santo Domingo. The Board of Trustees accepted Pendleton's gift and directed that it be placed in the East Plaza (Spreckels Park). The gun ultimately found its way to Star Park, joining another gun also donated by Pendleton. The second gun of Star Park is a French (not Belgian, as indicated on its brass plaque) Mitrailleuse, an early machine gun, or Gatling gun, with the nickname "Grapeshooter" for its small "Grape Shot" pellets fired by a hand crank. It was almost certainly manufactured about 1875, or later.

During the "Roaring Twenties," Coronado had acquired a reputation primarily as a resort community. One newspaper called Coronado "the ideal residential center and seaside holiday resort," noting further that, "to discriminating men and women of refined tastes who yearn for congenial surroundings with a mildly tempered climate unsurpassed anywhere in the whole world, where all the good things of life are everywhere at hand, Coronado, the residential paradise, holds out an urgent appeal." In November, the City passed an ordinance meant to keep Coronado a quiet place, in which people could get their sleep. The fire chief was instructed to sound a warning of three loud blasts for all children under the age of 16 to be off the streets and inside their homes after 9:15 p.m.

As quiet as Coronado appeared, there were always interesting tales of derring-do that seemed to follow North Island aviators like frosty contrails. In 1925, Lieutenant Daniel Tomlinson was flying a Hispano Jenny over Coronado at 1,500 feet, when his engine suddenly quit. Too far to make it to the North Island field, Tomlinson aimed for a wide, straight street in Coronado for an emergency landing. Diving under telephone wires, he flared with the last ounce of lift, and touched down. "When I came to an intersection there came a milk truck. I was going pretty fast, really charging down Olive Avenue. I just hopped over the milk truck and landed again on the other side." He finally came to a stop at the corner of Olive and Tenth Street to the astonished stares of several residents.

At 10 a.m. on March 12, 1925, for as far as the eye could see, a parade of warships appeared from the haze, and within an hour, the battle fleet and light cruiser divisions of the scouting fleets could be seen. Miles astern were the eastern destroyer and submarine squadrons and their tenders. More than 16,000 passengers and 4,000 cars ferried the bay to Coronado on that Sunday. Between 11 a.m. and 3 p.m., an uninterrupted procession of 167 U.S. naval vessels passed into Coronado Roads and the harbor of San Diego led by Admiral Robert E. Coontz.

Even though the Lubin Motion Picture Company had folded almost a decade earlier, the beauty and glamour of Coronado continued to attract Hollywood stars, and actors and actresses were familiar figures on Coronado's streets. In 1924, the great German actor Eric von Stroheim

Aerial view of Coronado Schools in the mid-1920s. Note the intersection of Seventh Street, D Avenue and Olive Avenue at the bottom left of the photo. The Methodist church sits at the corner. (CHA)

spent much time in town, as did the director Hal Roach, who played polo. In 1925, Warner Brothers made a movie near the ferry landing. The studio chartered the ferry *Ramona*, and several hundred locals served as extras in mob scenes.

In 1926, Pola Negri and Charlie Chaplin stayed at the Hotel del Coronado, taking part in a talking movie with the Famous Players Lasky Company. A seven-reel film feature, "Good and Naughty" was also being made in Coronado, directed by Malcolm St. Clair and Ted Camp. Cast members included 150 Coronado extras. The excitement of a film in progress took a tragic turn with the death of Paul Humphreys, age 24, of 1321 Pomona Avenue. Humphreys was part owner, and director, of Humphreys-Gunn Production Company. He was killed almost instantly when a 10-pound stick of dynamite on a raft in the water, near the Coronado boat landing, exploded and hurled him into the air.

Clara Bell Cutler, well-known head of the drama department at Coronado High School, would, over a long period of time, be responsible for a number of young people making their way into the film industry. Her husband, J. Leslie Cutler, who also spent many years in Coronado's school system, served as principal of the high school. During this time, several Coronadans were fairly well-known stars, and a film titled, "Love My Dog," an Our Gang comedy produced by the Hal Roach Company, may have been made in Coronado. This was one of Coronadan Johnny Downs' first films; the only extant copy is in the British Film Institute in London.

Dramatic aerial photo emphasizing the Fleet's close association with the Coronado. One of several Fleet-wide exercises of the late 1920s. (CPL/LCC)

Gertrude Ederle, the first woman to swim the English Channel from France to England, visited Coronado in 1926. Captain W.B. Perkins brought his familiar launch, *Glorietta*, to the boathouse because Gertrude was going to learn to aquaplane. Fox movie cameras shot film of the action for the Fox Movietone News, a weekly part of all movie house programs.

In 1926, the future direction of Coronado would take a drastic turn. John D. Spreckels died that year. Funeral services were held at his mansion in his arched, flower-banked music room. People from all walks of life came to pay their respects. Spreckels' body was escorted on the ferry *Ramona* for his last trip across the bay. His grand yacht, *Venetia*, lay moored alongside, with her flag at half-mast and her proud double stars of gold reflecting in the afternoon sunlight. When the *Venetia* was later sold to James Playfair for $60,000, she still had the gold stars on the funnel, earned for her World War I service.

At the time of Spreckels' death, his companies obtained a franchise from the County, and applied to the War Department for a permit to construct a bridge from Market Street in San Diego to First and Alameda in Coronado. The proposed drawbridge, designed by John Lyle Harrington, was to be 2,700 feet long with a width of 55 feet for pedestrian, vehicular, and streetcar traffic. The Army Corps of Engineers recommended the project despite the objections of the Navy Department, which, although not rejecting the application, suggested certain changes in the design of the bridge before granting a permit. For reasons never made public, the Spreckels Company made no move to amend the plans, and waited until 1929 before abandoning the project. The plans never advanced.

On July 29, 1926, representatives of Spreckels' San Diego interests filed articles of incorporation in Sacramento with the Secretary of State, for three new companies: the Claus Spreckels Company, the Spreckels Commercial Company, and the Spreckels Company, with respective capitalization of $25,000, $100,400, and $300,000. John D. Spreckels' son, Claus Spreckels, headed the directorate of all three companies. At the same time, an announcement was made that the principal office of the company would be maintained in San Diego, instead of San Francisco. From this point in time, Donald E. Hansen was appointed to oversee disposition of a number of Spreckels' enterprises. The Southern California Water Company was transferred to the City of San Diego at cost. The fabulous, multi-million dollar Mission Beach Amusement Center was donated to the State of California in 1934, and in turn transferred to the City of San Diego. In 1928, Spreckels' two newspapers, the *San Diego Union* and *Evening Tribune* were sold to Ira Clifton Copley. In 1933, shares in the

Fishing in front of Holland's store on Orange Avenue, after 1926 storm. (CHA)

largest Spreckels project, the San Diego and Arizona Railway Company, were sold to the Southern Pacific Company. Thus, the distribution process went forward. In the end, only a few places would bear Spreckels' name: the Spreckels Organ Pavilion in Balboa Park, and the Spreckels Theatre – a rather sad commentary on his once vast holdings, since not even a boulevard commemorates his enormous contributions.

A recall election in 1926 threatened to split up many Coronado friendships. Dr. Humphrey J. Stewart was president of the Board of Trustees; Mrs. Margaret F. MacMullen, George Holmes, J.E. Alcaraz, and Fellows Jones served as the other Trustees. The City had just hired its first manager, T.H. Messer, who came highly recommended, having held managerial positions in various cities.

The Police Department, headed by Marshal J.E. Meyers, and the Fire Department, headed by Chief George Sanven, were placed under Messer, who had different ideas about how to operate these departments. When the chiefs refused to cooperate, Messer fired them. The matter came to the Trustees who, in a split vote, apparently agreed with the City Manager. However, one of the Trustees was out of town at the time of the vote. In the interim, the City had to pay the fired chiefs, while also paying the salaries of two new chiefs. Citizens and taxpayers, upset about the wasted money, blew off steam all over the village. The Board chambers, upstairs at City Hall (1125 Loma) were packed at each acrimonious hearing, with disgruntled citizens quickly concluding that a recall would solve the controversy. While the matter dragged on, and was appealed to higher courts for decisions, Coronado did not have the funds to carry out a recall election. The small town political storm blew over, but everyone involved lost.

There were other more important matters to be solved by the Trustees during the year, however. A four-day storm, which tattered a thousand miles of coastline, did considerable damage to the sea wall, making it unsafe. The cost to repair the wall, which stretched all the way from the Hotel del Coronado grounds to North Beach, near the government-owned Naval Air Station property, amounted to $31,000.

During the year, the part of the town known as "the Flats," the Glorietta Section, was being developed with new sewer lines and streets, which were graded, curbed, and paved. A Safeway store at First and Orange opened, making commercial history in the village, as the first "class" store. It included Merritt's Fruit Store and Storm's Consumer Meat Market.

In 1927, Drs. Arthur and Harry Wegeforth moved their medical practice to San Diego, leaving Coronado once again without a hospital. At that moment, Mrs. Maude Carson Lancaster, a widowed, registered nurse visiting Coronado, liked what she saw of the village. She and her doctor-husband had operated a small hospital in their Nebraska hometown, so she bought a two-story house at 803 Alameda, and started a convalescent hospital. Needing more space, and learning that the Wegeforth building on Orange Avenue was available, she rented and set about furnishing and equipping the hospital. The new Coronado Emergency Hospital opened on January 1, 1927.

The hospital eventually became so crowded, that with the help of the Community Chest, it was enlarged. Fully accredited as a "Class A" hospital by the State Medical Society of California, a staff of doctors, dentists, and nurses provided around the clock care. Mrs. Lancaster kept Coronado's only hospital going until her health failed in 1941. Others stepped in to take over her accounts, finally closing it with no outstanding "bills payable."

In 1927, the 477th Photo Section began training at Rockwell Field, composed entirely of Coronado "boys." The section included Major Harry A. Erickson, Air Service Reserve, who lived at 329 "G" Avenue, Sergeants Robert McLain, and Maurice Rogers. The Section was very active taking photographs both from air and ground, producing aerial maps and land pictures. Erickson was already known as one of the most skillful photo-aviators in the service.

The event of the year 1927 involved a tall, handsome, and rather shy young airmail pilot who became America's hero of the century—Charles Augustus Lindbergh. In 1925, T. Claude Ryan, a San Diego flyer, rented an old fish cannery on the San Diego waterfront, where he built his own planes. In 1927, his company built the *Spirit of St. Louis* for Lindbergh.

Aerial view of Coronado, showing location of the polo field, 1925. (CPL)

> *[Lindbergh's links to Coronado were strong. As the plane was being built, he worked closely with naval aviators from North Island to learn long-distance navigation and dead reckoning, especially over water. While testing his aircraft, Lindbergh also used the Navy's three-kilometer speed range marked by buoys along the Silver Strand. —ed.]*

Lindbergh was ready to depart for his now-historic transcontinental flight on May 10, 1927, a planned flight with three legs: Coronado to St. Louis, St. Louis to New York, and New York to Paris – flying solo all the way from Coronado to Paris. His first leg would carry a heavy fuel load, and so Lindbergh selected North Island as his departure point to avoid the many telephone wires in San Diego. He set his takeoff time as 4 pm. At the appointed time, he easily took off, and in a wide sweeping turn to the left, circled over Coronado once to gain altitude, then departed eastward.

On July 15, 1927, Mayor of San Diego Harry C. Clark received a telegram stating that on his return, Lindbergh would undertake an air tour of the country to promote aeronautics. Would the mayor head a reception committee for the idol of two continents?

Since Lindbergh had resided in San Diego for two months while his plane was assembled by the Ryan Aircraft Corporation, it was as though a native son was coming home. On September 21st, he flew the Spirit of St. Louis above Balboa Stadium, where 60,000 admirers awaited him. He was honored at the Hotel del Coronado, where Will Rogers suggested that if San Diego ever had an airport, it should be named for Lindbergh. (Will Rogers and his wife Betty stayed in room numbers 180/181 for the night, at a cost of $30.)

> *[Lindbergh was driven up Orange Avenue in a motorcade, with hundreds of Coronadans lining the street for a glimpse of the famous aviator, on his way to the celebratory banquet at the Hotel Del. —ed.]*

One other aspect of Coronado received much attention during 1927– construction. Money was still easy to come by; therefore the "Roaring Twenties" continued bringing people of wealth to retire or build homes on the "Enchanted Island." Mark W. Vilim, a Coronado realtor, built a Spanish-style residence at 727 Alameda; General and Mrs. Marshall Orlando Terry completed restoration and additions to their home at 711 "A," designed by architects Richard Requa and Frank Mead at a cost of $80,000, while Paul Wegeforth's home at 831 Adella was featured in the *San Diego Union* of August 21, 1927. Under construction was "Las Placitas" for Mr. and Mrs. Arthur Scully (Luella) at 1015 Loma; Ivan H. Snell's home at 1054 Glorietta Boulevard; and for Mrs. Evelow Mann (Lena E.), a beautiful home at 1045 Loma.

Early in the year, the City Council was busy on a number of matters. Captain T.H. Messer declared he had submitted his resignation to the Council, although the Council insisted they had removed him from his office. The Coronado Planning Commission, mandated by a new state law, added a new commissioner, W. C. Harland. Actions taken by the Commission allowed construction of a number of new buildings, including a $25,000 steam-heated bungalow court at Third and Palm streets. The Council named Paul Valle as Coronado City Engineer, without pay. He was to be paid the usual fee of 5% for the engineering he provided in the paving of certain Coronado streets, but the decision whether to pay him for any other work was referred to a special committee to study the matter. At the same time, the Council boosted other salaries. The *San Diego Union* of January 4, 1928, announced, "…the City gardener is a better job than the City clerk in Coronado." The gardener made $25 a month more than the clerk, and by action taken on that date the gardener received a title as well: "Superintendent of Parks and Boulevards."

The Army's Rockwell Field seen along the beach side of North Island, with the Navy's air station on the bay side. Aircraft carrier 'Langley' is moored at the carrier pier. Note the causeway to Coronado at the left, and the carrier practice landing pad in the center of the field (1927). (CHA)

The Council also considered the matter of charges for cleaning up vacant lots in Coronado. Coronado had an ordinance requiring owners to keep vacant lots cleared of weeds and trash. When a property owner failed to do so, the City, after giving notice, would hire workers to clean, burn and carry off materials. The owner was then billed for the costs. In 1928, the Council, led by City Attorney C.J. Hizar, agreed with some property owners that Mr. Messer had charged them for services above and beyond that required.

In June 1928, Major General Joseph Pendleton, USMC (retired), was elected Coronado's mayor by a vote of the City Council, upon the sudden illness of the incumbent. Pendleton was the single individual most responsible for first bringing Marines in large numbers to San Diego and Coronado, establishing their enduring footprint. In early 1916, Pendleton and his wife, Mary Helen, bought an undeveloped lot at 745 A Avenue and moved a house to the property. He added a large veranda or piazza to the home in 1922, after a costly house fire, and gave the home the name "Penhaven."

When Pendleton retired in 1924, he returned to Penhaven and became active in Coronado community affairs, including serving on the School Board and as president of the Coronado Civic Club (a then-powerful voice in City politics). Major General Pendleton died quietly at Penhaven in February 1942 at age 81. Fondly remembered for his easy-going but proper manner, the City Council authorized the naming of Pendleton Road in

Aerial view of an NY-1 trainer and utility aircraft; here conducting aerographic flight over Silver Strand, 1928. Note Tent City below. (CPL)

the General's remembrance. The Marine Corps would later name their huge base north of San Diego, Camp Pendleton.

For the first time, in the summer of 1928, the new aircraft carrier USS *Lexington* was seen off San Diego, joined by her sister ship *Saratoga* a year later. These carriers were massive in comparison with the *Langley*, carrying air wings two or three times bigger. Too large to enter San Diego Bay at first, *Lexington* and *Saratoga* frequently anchored in Coronado Roads to be close to their North Island squadrons, and were an impressive seaward sight for Hotel Del visitors.

In August 1928, the station and battle fleet aircraft staged an aerial exhibition as part of the dedication of Lindbergh Field, marking the 25th year of powered flight. Dr. José A. Perez of the Marine Medical Corps, who lived at 737 Orange Avenue, had for sometime been assigned to the expeditionary force of Brigadier General Smedley D. Butler, Commanding Third Brigade of Marines. But that year he was on detached duty, joining the American Museum of Natural History's explorer, Dr. Roy Chapman Andrews. He was venturing into the distant desert wastes of Inner Mongolia, as leader of the 1928 Central Asiatic Expedition of the American Museum of Natural History. They were headed for the Gobi Desert in search of the "Dawn Man," and would find the first dinosaur eggs, to the astonishment of the world.

Anita Evelyn Pomares, whose movie name was Anita Page, with her parents, Mr. and Mrs. Mararino L. Pomares, brother Marino Pomares, Jr., and maid, used the house at 866 "B" Avenue as headquarters, while Anita was working with Ramón Novarro in the elaborate filming in Coronado and at North Island of the great Navy picture, "Golden Braid." The screenplay for the film was written by Lieutenant Commander Frank ("Spig") Wead of 868 "J" Avenue.

Shooting a crash scene on the ocean for the movie, 'Flying Fleet' in 1929. (CHA)

Construction moved along in 1928, as though there was an abundance of space and money. The *San Diego Union* of August 19, 1928, carried photos of the Van Sickle residence at 1133 "F" Avenue; the Campbell residence at 815 Alameda Boulevard; the A. F. Healey home at 1200 Glorietta Boulevard; the Mitchell residence at 1063 Ocean Boulevard; the Walter B. Neill home at 1313 Tenth Avenue; and the Moon residence at Seventh and Orange Avenues.

The high school followed its path of excellence in education and produced athletes who excelled academically and in their sports. In 1927, Coronado High School also had a high-powered girls basketball team; in 1928 the football team won the regional championship, with stars Malcolm Wright, Merle Corrin, Tody Greene, Joe Israel, Tom Kenney, Glover Nichol, Dave Jessop, Bud Webb,

Girls Basketball Team at Coronado High School in 1924. (CHA)

Sailing on Glorietta Bay, with the Tent City Dance Pavilion seen in the background. (CHA)

Cy Perkins, Dudley Wright, and Captain Johnny Lyons. Amos E. Schaefer coached the team that won the San Diego County League. The team also included William Skinner, Bill Raaka, A. Albeck, G. Nichell, D. Young, R. MiIna, N. Mathewson and D. Mathewson on the squad.

> William A. Gunn, who listed himself as a "capitalist," told a Coronado newspaper reporter that "Coronado will continue to be a marooned sandbar, unless adequate ferry service is provided." At almost the same moment in 1929, the first of the diesel-electric ferries, the *Coronado*, was built by the Moore Drydock Company of Oakland. Her sister ferry, the *San Diego*, was also built by Moore in 1931. Both ferries were designed and built specifically for service with the San Diego-Coronado Ferry Company. Nearly everyone who knew about the ferries *Coronado* and *San Diego* will tell you they were identical, but that is not true. The *San Diego* was 191 feet in length and 556 tons to *Coronado's* 178 feet in length and 502 tons. The *San Diego* also had 3 engines to *Coronado's* 2 engines, but *Coronado's* engines were rated for more horsepower.

In February, articles appeared in the newspapers about potential ways to open up the island: a bridge, a tube, and the ferries. The February 13, 1929 issue of the *San Diego Union* reported that Coronado and San Diego would eventually be linked by a tube.

Around the same time, John E. Blackman of Ocean Boulevard announced that he had purchased San Diego Chamber of Commerce industrial building lands, comprising 600 yards at the southern end of San Diego Bay near Chula Vista. The purchase, according to Blackman in the Chula Vista Star, was so he and his associates could develop their bay frontage, and cut a channel through the Strand to permit ocean-going vessels to enter and leave from the lower end of the bay. At last, there would be wharves, docks, and warehouses near Chula Vista. Coronadans reacted with horror at rumors of a charge to cross a second channel to travel southward to Tijuana. A 1929 film depicted the emotions of Coronadans seeking to encourage Californians to save Coronado Heights and the Silver Strand as a State Park. When costs soared out of sight, the issue of a second bay opening ultimately died.

The question of a tunnel or subway was partly resolved when results of a test, conducted by the California Bridge and Tunnel Company, informed the City Council that 40 feet below the surface, Coronado rested on a bed of sandstone of questionable solidity. However, the question of whether a bridge or a tube spanning the bay from Coronado to San Diego was feasible at that time, was never really settled since voters rejected both ideas at the ballot box.

Miss Ruth Alexander, a 24-year-old aviatrix who resided at 915 "E," easily passed the rigid tests required by the Federal Aeronautical Internationale, and was therefore qualified to try for any world aviation record for women.

In athletics, Coronado's new baseball park opened on May 26th, with a game between the San Diego Gas and Electric Company and the Coronado All Stars. The new grandstand had a large seating capacity; the team and diamond were supported by Coronado businesses. The high school football team won the County Championship in 1929, again beating Point Loma, by a score of 55 to zero.

> Interesting baseball trivia: Coronado also had a professional baseball team in 1929, the Coronado Arabs. The Arabs were a Class-D team that played in the California State League against teams from Bakersfield, Santa Monica, San Diego, and elsewhere. The team compiled a 16-14 record under manager Jess Orndorf, with several players batting over .300. Trouble was, the team never played in Coronado, but played at Navy Field in San Diego. Apparently, there

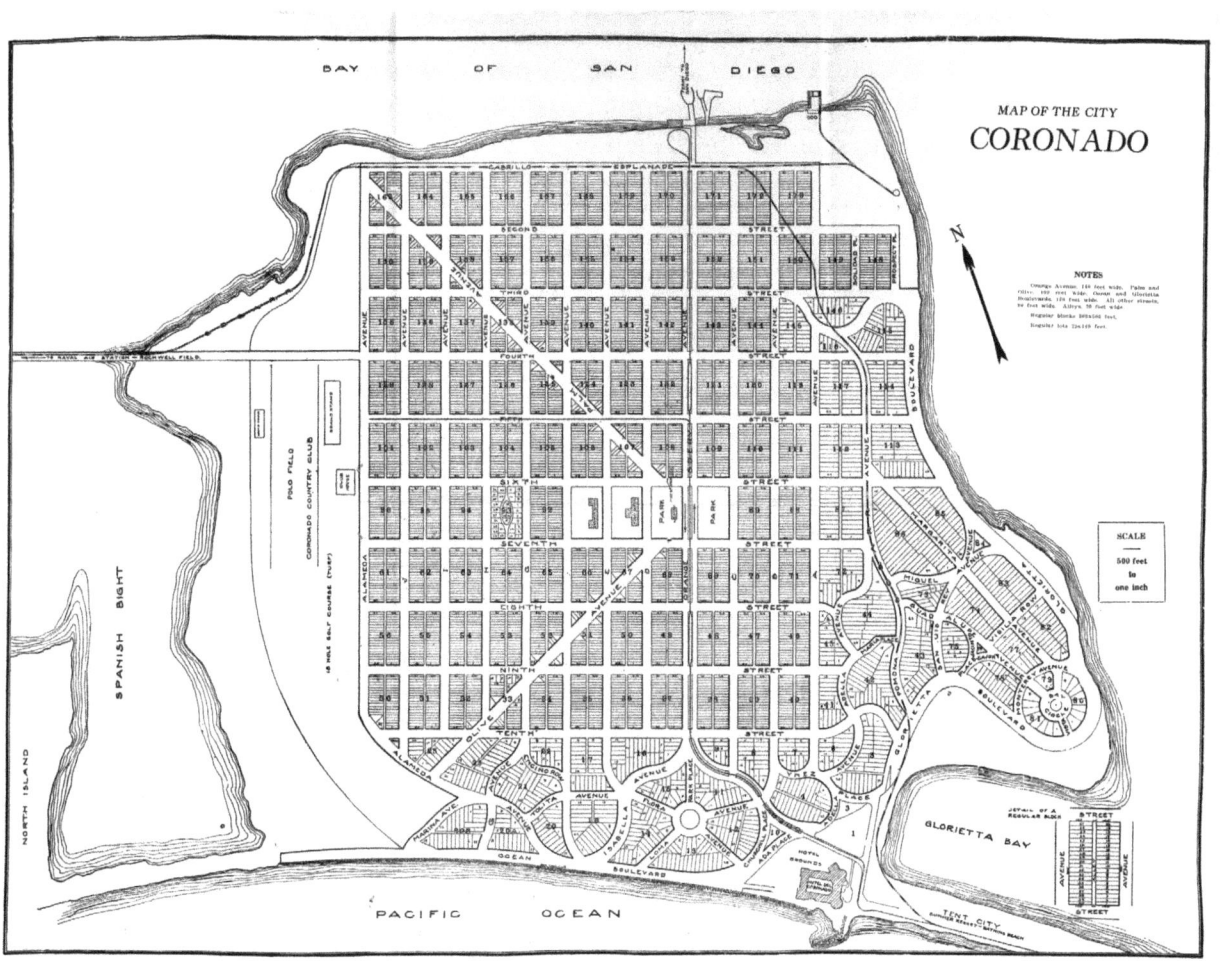

Street map of Coronado, c.1923, shows the city blocks by number and gives descriptive dimensions. (CPL)

was a stigma attached to any effort to have two different teams in the same city and, so, when the Arabs moved to San Diego – a city that already had a ball team – another team name had to be found … á la "Coronado."

Another Coronado landmark was born in 1929, when Thomas H. Pickford, a hotel owner from Washington, D.C., bought the property on Orange Avenue, near the Hotel del Coronado and built El Cordova Apartment Hotel. Incorporated within the new building was the original Elisha S. Babcock, Jr. home, still part of the complex visible today.

The dedication page for the Coronado High School 1929 Yearbook, "The Poppy," helped capture a sense of the community at the time: "Unique among all high schools is Coronado … overhead, the roar of motors echoes all the day … aviation history has passed before our eyes like scenes in a gigantic pageant." Scenes for "The Flying Fleet" were filmed at North Island. Starring Ramón Novarro, Ralph Graves, and Anita Page, the story was a melodrama of naval air exploits. One of the best films of the year, "Jazz Mad," starred George Lewis, a CHS graduate.

Without a doubt, the "Roaring Twenties" were Coronado's most glamorous years. Society-especially the "new" society–had gone wild over such pleasures as good food, extravagant clothes, big cars, luxurious yachts, and frequent trips to Paris, mostly to purchase gowns and exquisite hats. Society columns were filled not only with what society did, but also what society wore. It was as though everyone was making up for time lost while World War I was being fought, and was obsessed with the joy of living.

The economists, however, failed to heed the clues and hints of the previous several years and put them together. Tourist travel had begun to drop off, real estate prices were on the upswing, and too many buildings were being constructed in the San Diego region. The worst sufferers were the owners of office buildings, where "For Rent" signs appeared everywhere.

What is surprising is that during the year, not a word appeared in Coronado newspapers about the Wall Street crash! It was as though the Depression hadn't begun. Coronadans, so far removed from Wall Street, had not yet heard the thunder of fallen banks and businesses.

(US Navy)

Chapter 7

1930-1944 The Depression and World War II

SPONSORED BY JACQUELYN A. McCOY AND JAMES H. LARE

IN 1930, CORONADO HAD A POPULATION OF 5,424, including servicemen and their families who lived on North Island. They had begun to feel the effects of the Great Depression. Those landlords who rented houses, when they could find occupants, were charging $35 a month for a fair-sized home. A five-room house sold for $3,000, with 10% down. When the fleet was out, many families went home or away to visit, so times became difficult for landlords. Rentals were a big part of Coronado's business. The town became so cluttered with "For Rent" signs that the Coronado Realty Board held a special meeting and decided to remove them all, concluding that the signs were unsightly, and could also give an impression that Coronado was not a very good place in which to live! Merchants, hotels, restaurants, amusement centers, and transportation systems suffered.

The Spreckels Companies helped by advertising that all of its properties, including Tent City, were purchasing whatever goods they needed from local firms. Coronadans bought in Coronado, and the store owners knew everyone. Especially between 1929, and prior to World War II, credit became a necessity. The stores needed to offer credit in order to stay open, and the townspeople needed credit in order to survive, particularly just prior to each payday. Service personnel were in some instances better off than civilians, because they had regular paychecks.

(Image above: CPL / LCC)

Due to the collapse of the bond market in 1929, several projects proposing alternate transportation across the bay were doomed before they got off the ground. Most of them involved a bridge of one form or another, an idea constantly opposed by the military as being hazardous to ship and seaplane operations.

With the New Deal and creation of the U.S. Public Works Agency (PWA), rumors once again hit town about modernizing transportation across the bay. The Coronado City Council strongly favored an underwater tube. Joseph Strauss, who built the Golden Gate Bridge, came to Coronado, took soundings, and prepared plans and estimates. He had designed the Arlington Memorial Bridge across the Potomac River at Washington, D.C., and the bridge over the Neva, built for the late Czar of Russia.

He designed a two-way traffic tube that would cost upwards of six-and-one-half million dollars. Negotiations with the PWA provided for a grant of 45% of the cost of the under-bay project. The balance would be financed through revenue bonds. Coronado City Attorney Shelley J. Higgins, went to Washington to meet the Secretary of the Navy, who assured him the Navy would benefit from such ready access to North Island. The Secretary promised he would bring his influence to bear on the project.

Encouraged, Higgins waited for word of final grant approval from the PWA, when suddenly a new bureaucratic roadblock arose. By virtue of an earlier California Supreme Court decision, a city of the sixth class, such as Coronado, could not issue revenue bonds. Higgins, searching for a solution to the unexpected problem, told the City Council that under the State constitution, any city having more than 3,500 people could adopt a freehold charter by vote of the people, and in this way assume the right to issue revenue bonds. Freeholders were elected, and Higgins helped them draw up a charter to be submitted to Coronadans for their vote.

Almost at once, "opposition which had been hiding all this while, showed its head." A group organized to defeat the charter pointed out that hidden in it was language that could be construed as opening the way for the city to establish and operate a cemetery! The charter and the tube were defeated by a margin of 35 disgruntled cemetery haters. Twenty-five years later, the State legislature would appropriate $200,000 to survey feasibility of a vehicular tunnel under San Diego Bay.

The City Council had its hands full during the early years of the 30s. The 1932 City budget was down $12,000 from 1931. Some representative budget lines included: City Manager (3/4 time) $3,600; Automobile Upkeep -0-; Chief of Police $2,700; Fire Chief $1,650; Park Superintendent $2,250; Library Expenses $8,097.56.

Council agendas were loaded with problems such as traffic congestion at the ferry landing, the matter of cleaning lots, and an accumulation of wrecked automobiles at Seventh and Eighth Streets between "G" and "H" Avenues. The City Planning Department involved itself with a proposal to change street names to Spanish names, and regulation of billboards.

Other Council issues had to do with disposition of the outdated 1888 water storage tank. The storage tank was 55 feet in diameter and 26 feet high, occupied the center of the "high" block between Third and Fourth Streets, "D" and "E" Avenues, and had a capacity of 500,000 gallons.

Until the summer of 1930, keeping Coronado's beaches cleared of smelly kelp was the job of one man with a rake and a wheelbarrow. A complaint was made to the Council that this fellow was caught raking the kelp toward the water so that each successive tide returned the refuse. The city fathers took this under long and careful deliberation but concluded the city (1) lacked authority; (2) lacked funds; and (3) that the State had jurisdiction over the beach between mean low water and mean high water. Thus, the City abdicated its responsibility for a distasteful problem and did nothing.

Famous aviator Roscoe Turner at Coronado Beach in 1930. (CHA)

In 1930, the State Park Commission and the Coronado City Council resolved the question of how much each governmental body would advance to purchase the park site on the Silver Strand from the U.S. Government. Based on appraisals of other County properties being considered for State Parks, a figure was calculated and the matter appeared to be resolved. But the question of what to do about beach squatters' shacks had to be addressed. The *Coronado Journal* reported that a dozen unsightly buildings made of a few old boards and pieces of driftwood piled against sand dunes marred the ocean and bay view. Representatives of the State Parks Commission served notice on owners of these homes that they would have to vacate or be prosecuted. The beach people left, and voters approved a State Parks bond issue of $435,000, which included Coronado's share of the Silver Strand State Park.

Chris A. Cosgrove completed the Monterey Apartments on "D" Avenue, between Eighth and Ninth Streets in 1930. Kate Sessions oversaw the landscaping. Lieutenant Commander Ben H. Wyatt, who owned three homes in Coronado, was gone for three years on a Naval Mission to Peru. He held the Distinguished Service Cross for his role in the first aerial survey party in Alaska conducted in 1926. He and his family occupied "Villa Illahee" at 1110 Isabella Avenue.

H. Austin Adams, Coronado playwright and author, who had written the biography of John D. Spreckels ("The Man, John D. Spreckels") in 1924, released the Spreckels estate from monies due him at the rate of $250 per month. This had been provided for in the late financier's will, but Adams felt John D. Spreckels had already done more than enough for him.

The Blue Lantern Inn, now known as Hotel Marisol Coronado, still stands on Park Place, next to Coronado Historical Association. (CHA)

The papers often carried news of Constance Halverstadt Cummings, who was making her way in the film industry. A native of Seattle, she was the daughter of Dallas Vernon Halverstadt and Kate Logan Cummings, whose home was at 846 "A" Avenue. Inga B. Orner, the internationally known soprano was back home at 1025 "E" after her European tour.

Eugene M. Estoppey made athletic news once again. The 60-year old American Indian arrived at Kezar Stadium in San Francisco at the conclusion of a 198-mile marathon he had run from Fresno to San Francisco in 86 hours.

In 1930, work was begun on the installation of a new private telephone branch in the Hotel del Coronado to provide facilities for more than 540 telephones. The exchange was to be a combined manual and dial service.

The *New Republic Magazine* featured the Hotel del Coronado at the end of the year 1931, still described in lofty and lavish phrases:

> The Coronado Beach Hotel must present the ultimate satisfaction of the dreams of the architects of the eighties. It is the most magnificent example extant, of the American seaside hotel as it flourished in that era on both coasts; and it still has its beauty as well as its magnificence. White and ornate as a wedding cake, clean, polished and trim as a ship, it makes a monument not unworthy to dominate the last blue concave dent in the shoreline before the United States stops and the Mexican Republic begins... at the top a tall white flagpole flies an American flag.

East of the Mississippi River, the Depression following the 1929 Stock Market Crash hit rock-bottom in 1932/1933. Southern California had little industry of consequence; the economy, therefore, simply drifted. Even at the height of the country's economic and financial plight, Coronado residents suffered less than most. Sound practices continued the excellent education of young people. Governmental municipal work programs, the presence of the military dollar, and a variety of recreational activities were factors that helped ease the town through the lean years.

Individual initiative was seen when Albert Bram came to Coronado in 1929, bringing his wife, daughter and $125. He bought a lot for $5,000 on the corner of Orange and "B", took out a $10,000 loan from the Bank of America, hired architect Walter Vestal, and built La Avenida Restaurant. Bram persuaded the Mexican artist Alfredo Ramos Martínez, colleague of Diego Rivera, to paint murals within the restaurant. In May 1930, Thomas Henry Pickford, a Washington, D.C. hotel owner, with the help of his brother Percy, opened the El Cordova, a modern apartment hotel designed by noted architect Frank L. Hope, of San Diego. Today this hotel, with its courtyard, shops and outdoor cafe, forms one of Coronado's most frequented and charming sites.

During the Depression the Federal government struggled to find ways to help people without jobs. Through the Federal Emergency Relief Administration, created May 12, 1933, loans were made available to the states for relief. The law permitted local authorities to provide either work relief or an outright dole. Coronado projects included a purchase of concrete by the city to be used in connection with unemployment work: making gutters and cutting back street corners as examples. The pay would be 30 cents an hour for unskilled labor and 35 cents an hour for skilled. Mr. and Mrs. Thomas E. Sharp gave $4,000 toward a fund to help the City provide more employment for citizens.

Silver Strand Theater in the Spreckels Building. Lamb's Players Theater began entertaining in the theater space after the building was refurbished in 1994. (CHA)

The Coronado Community Chest continued to turn over sums of money for unemployment relief. Madame Ernestine Schumann Heink toured the country raising funds, exhausting herself in the process; she finally returned to her home at 800 Orange Avenue for some rest. The Coronado Branch of the American Red Cross held drives for clothes, and the Coronado Theatre with R.E. Archibald, owner, gave a percentage of box office receipts for the cause of helping those down and out.

On January 11, 1933, the bay/tube question arose again when the announcement was made that the Reconstruction Finance Corporation (RFC) would finance a traffic tube, and advance a loan of $3,000,000, if the California Bridge and Tunnel Company raised a matching sum. Plans were prepared by an expert, "Drydock Smith." Optimism grew with rumors of a new promise of five million from the RFC. But, once again, the transbay crossing fell through the cracks somehow.

The matter of Glorietta Bay development arose one more time, and proponents ran full-page ads in a push to get "yes" votes for the project to dredge the channel and anchorage southwest of Coronado in an August 29th election. The project, expected to cost $350,000, was passed by a large majority. The Council approved plans for dredging with a minimum wage scale of 45 cents per hour for common labor, up to 75 cents per hour for dredge operators.

Above: The Oxford Hotel was first built in the 100 block of Orange Avenue as housing for Hotel del Coronado employees, relocated to Ynez Avenue for many years, and moved to its final destination at the Hotel del Coronado in 1983 to serve as administrative offices. This photo was taken in the 1930s. (CHA) - Below: The War Salvage Committee held a scrap metal drive during WWII, at the corner of D and Palm Avenues. (CHA)

The Council was continually confronted with problems, not the least of which was the location proposed for another City Dump. Fred W. Kohl, a gardener, was given the contract to haul rubbish to the new dump, located at the foot of Second Street.

The very young still found work by becoming bounty hunters; setting traps and collecting ten cents a head for gophers, which continued to overrun the island even destroying trees. Businesses managed to keep their doors open. Davy's Super Service Station, at Orange and "C", did a good business, but then, the town only had a couple of gas and service stations. Omar's (Henry M. Omar) Coronado Dry Goods Company, at 1033 Orange Avenue, held "nine cent sales" occasionally, like ones advertising a china cup and saucer; a pound of salted peanuts; aluminum pans; men's fancy hose; and tumblers "that won't shatter."

The Ritz Hotel, formerly the Blue Lantern Inn, at 1017 Park Place, where Mrs. Earl Robison was proprietor, advertised Club lunches for 35 cents, and dinners for 50 and 65 cents. Clarence T. Anderson and Sons Bakery, at 956 Orange Avenue, had in the window:

> Parker House Rolls, 15 cents a dozen
> Poppy Seed Rolls, 20 cents a dozen
> Bread, 12 cents a loaf

The Humpty Dumpty Market, at 925 Orange Avenue, advertised:
> Butter, at 23 cents a pound
> Number 2 can of corn, for 10 cents
> MJB Coffee, 3 lbs., with a 2 lb. package of MJB Rice for 90 cents.

At the El Cordova Apartment Hotel:
> Housekeeping apartments (with daily maid service), $70 a month.
> Single Rooms, $2 a day or $12 a week
> Lunch, 50 cents and dinner 75

Menn's Chocolate Shop, with Katherine Douglas managing, offered
> T-Bone Steak and French Fries for 75 cents

The Continental Grocery Store, at 957 Orange Avenue, sold:
> Sugar, 10 lbs. for 48 cents
> Coffee, 1 lb. for 37 cents
> Apples, 7 lbs. for 25 cents
> Juice Oranges, 7 lbs. for 23 cents
> Steer Chuck Pot Roast for 18 cents a pound
> Veal Chops for 25 cents a pound

John R. and Bessie D. Lamb, parents of singer/performer Bernard Lamb, kept their Mom and Pop grocery, "Lamb's Market" (established in 1928), open at all hours at Fourth and Palm for anyone who needed help. Often on the verge of closing because of the innumerable tabs they carried, they were almost always paid off on paydays. The building remains at its original location today.

One bright spot during the Depression was knowledge that some of the banks, with local branches, remained open. The Bank of America and the First National Bank held firm. They gave 3% interest on deposits, thus encouraging many people to leave what money could be spared in savings. Banks regularly sent cardboard tellers windows to the schools and handed out small metal impossible-to-break-open "piggy banks" with keys, to encourage youngsters to learn to save.

By 1932-1933, Tent City had established itself as a year-round resort with continuous occupancy by local residents and visitors.

Coronado circa 1934. Note the Hotel Del's new swimming pool, the expansive grounds, the remains of the rocks on the beach and how much open space still existed in the city. (CPL/LCC)

1933 marked the 32nd summer season. Swimming remained the most popular island sport, but "pitch and putt" miniature golf also came into vogue. At 1029 "B" Avenue, G.D. Brown leased the spot and opened a small course with a food stand for refreshments. Later, Kenny MacArthur and M. Smith opened a golf course that could be played under flood lights: called the Petite Golf Course at 1300 Orange Avenue, enthusiasts played amid the shrubs, flowers, windmills, and water holes. In addition, a miniature golf course was located for a number of years on the triangular lot behind the Hotel del Coronado bounded by Churchill Place and Ocean Boulevard. Putt-Putt golf took not only Coronado, but the entire country by storm, until it began to fade during World War II.

Yachting, which seemed custom-made for the beautiful water surrounding Coronado, continued to grow in popularity. Six yachtsmen leased a portion of the first floor of the Coronado Boathouse, and formally reestablished the Coronado Yacht Club on April 23, 1932, after many lapsed years. The years 1932-1935 were under the able Commodoreships of Henry G. Weston and Major U.S.A. (Ret.) Ivan B. Snell, whose home at 1504 Glorietta Boulevard overlooked the Boat House. Club members and volunteers built the first three slips for the club connecting them to the Boathouse. Members also spearheaded efforts to continue dredging Glorietta Bay. A five-year dredging program ended in 1937-1938, when the thin channel leading from San Diego Bay to the Boathouse was expanded to allow yachting across the entire breadth of Glorietta Bay. Now with much deeper water the Yacht Club added a series of improvements including the addition of fifteen new slips. This spread Coronado yachting out along the northwest edge of Glorietta Bay, giving it a true "marina" feel for the first time.

The Strand Theatre did its best to keep townspeople's minds off of daily problems by offering movies such as "That's Romance", first of the all talking dramas of the North Woods, featuring George O'Brien, Helen Chandler, and Antonio Moreno. In addition, customers got to see Chapter No. 4 of "The Lone Defender," the talking serial, with Rin-Tin-Tin, and a rabbit cartoon to complete the bill.

Coronado newspapers continued to keep readers informed about bridge parties, team polo luncheons, the comings and goings of socialites in the East or Europe, and new residents arriving in Coronado and North Island. "Hometowners" were important too. Johnny Lyons, former Coronado High School and Tulsa University grid star, had been playing professional baseball for two years and came home to visit his parents Mr. and Mrs. Benjamin H. Lyons.

Students of high-school teachers Claude Webster and Clara Bell Cutler went on to make headlines in New York and Hollywood, including Virgil Simons, George J. Lewis, John Clearman, Ward Beachley, and Peter Cookson.

Coronado High School continued to receive praise from the State of California Department of Education in Sacramento for the outstanding teachers and students they produced. The principals had focused on bringing distinguished professors to the high school such as Dr. Ernest Charles Watson, professor of physics at the California Institute of Technology. Grammar, literature, writing and foreign languages were emphasized.

> A private school reopened in 1931, after a few years at its previous location, 819 Pomona Avenue. La Escuela de Coronado, was a boarding and day school for children ages two through ten. The schoolhouse was originally built by Irving Gill as the home of General Mendal Churchill on Block 10, but moved from Orange to Pomona in 1928. The school "offered a real home atmosphere for the child, as well as thorough training in school work and character building." It is also remembered for its interesting fire escapes, which were long metal slides from its higher floors to the ground.

Coronado High School, c. 1928. (CHA)

From 1929-1933, Henry O. Temple, a local landscaper by trade and a sports enthusiast by avocation, organized a baseball team composed of Coronadans who played no less than once a week. They beat the "Colored Giants" and the "All Star Team" on the Coronado field. By 1933, Temple felt the total weekly gate receipts of $3.75 showed Coronadans wouldn't support a team, even a fine one. The cost to run a ball club each Sunday was $22. Henry invited any Coronadan to take over the club, and when none did, the team disbanded. The Coronado Tennis Association kept going, however, and the Coronado Country Club continued to sponsor golf tournaments. Coronado's Boy Scout Troops 35 and 75 made their summer treks and camp-outs to Barroll Anderson's back country ranch.

The Coronado girls basketball team of the Telephone Company made it to the State finals with Long Beach, Pomona, Santa Ana and Glendale. Coronado members active in the San Diego Pigeon Racing Club included Luther M. Kennett, William Ball, E. Davy, F. Garty and Bradford Gladding. This sport began some ten years earlier, and consisted of training pigeons to "home" — to race back to their lofts in Coronado after being taken to distant points and turned loose. Pigeon racing flourished in Coronado until World War II.

Coronado Public Library, c. 1935. (CPL)

The Coronado Colts football team beat Hoover, El Centro, Sweetwater, and Escondido, only to lose the title to Grossmont by an extra point, 7 to 6. Among the players were Raaka, Hewitt, Wegeforth, Needham and quarterback Jimmy Blaisdell. Malcolm and Dudley Wright, twin sons of Mel S. Wright, Manager of the Hotel del Coronado, were by then playing for Cornell University's football team. They sent their best wishes to the Colts, as they had played for CHS when the team won the State High School championships in 1928 and 1929.

A Filipino Sporting Club was organized by young men of that nationality, most of whom were employed by the Hotel del Coronado or were in the U.S. Navy. They leased a building at 1015 "C" Avenue which had been built as a studio about 23 years earlier by the Irish artist Henry Joneas Thaddeus. The club was meant for recreational and social entertainment.

During 1933, the police department had its hands full with a variety of cases. A number of speeders got tickets including Claus Spreckels Jr. Bad check passers were about town, especially at the El Cordova Hotel which seemed particularly susceptible to taking phony paper. The Ivy Pool Hall at 1319 Orange Avenue was raided, and the police recovered much evidence of gambling.

Cliff May was a great-great-grandson of Miguel Estudillo, who built the Estudillo house at Old Town. At the age of 15, Cliff had a dance orchestra, and by age 17, furnished dance music for the Hotel del Coronado. He took up architecture in college and designed a number of residences in San

Diego and in Los Angeles. When contacted about homes he had designed in Coronado, he said that there were four, all especially designed for men he called "adventurers," men who had traveled and experienced unusual adventures. All four homes are still standing as built for Lt. Morton Seligman at 777 "G" Avenue; Lt. Nicolas Frank at 266 "I" Avenue; Commander H.E. Knauss at 633 Alameda Boulevard; and for Roy Pickford at 1033-1039 Loma.

On Thursday, June 22, 1933, Johnson A. Mathewson retired after 47 years of community civic and business ventures. He locked up his store at 1309 Orange Avenue, still having the first telephone, numbered "1", in Coronado. In his recollections, he said, "Girls here can't fool me as to their age. I have been here a long time and know them all, and remember when they were born." Coronado lost a soldier, poet, author, musician and businessman when Joseph Troxel died at the age of 87. He and his son opened Troxel's Variety Store after their arrival in 1911.

In 1933, President Franklin Delano Roosevelt celebrated his 52nd birthday and thanked the nation in a fireside chat. Huge plans for the President's Ball on January 30th were made at the Hotel del Coronado to raise funds for the Warm Springs Foundation, established to fight infantile paralysis.

To help provide some relief from the Depression, Merle Corrin and Jessie Kelly were employed to organize summer activities for youngsters, a number of whom took part learning boating at Glorietta Bay. Softball teams with twilight leagues and recreational activities were held at the grammar school and at Cutler Field every day.

Such activities tended to give people mental relief from the difficult times. At Tent City, despite a huge warehouse fire, the Airdome theater showed "Movies Under the Stars," costing 15 cents for adults and a dime for children. Shows started as soon as it became dark with a change of programs each night. A local horse show and gymkhana were held at the Coronado Saddle Stables near Fourth and Alameda, opening on July 23. Outstanding entries were Bud Jensen, Peggy Holloway, Mildred Kennett, Bill Alexander, Tookie Spreckels, and Mr. and Mrs. F.G. Belcher.

The Coronado Merchants organized a baseball team made up of Coronado High School graduates who played each Sunday at Cutler Field. Among the stars were Don E. Needham, catcher; Ray Fifield, second base; Jimmy Blaisdell, first base, and Bill Raaka, center field. Colonel Harry H. Bissell organized the Coronado Rod and Reel Club, a local organization meant to attract fishermen to the Coronado region.

By the end of the year 1934, one-sixth of the population of San Diego County was on relief. Each community had a quota of men who could be hired under government programs. With 128 Coronadans unemployed, 40 men were employed at the Marine and Border fields; another twenty-eight painted the local schools, police and fire stations. A few kept busy at the Civil Works Administration offices in San Diego, while others worked in the Coronado Library. Mrs. Luther M. Kennett (Isabelle) and Mr. and Mrs. Tom Sharp helped financially at every turn. Navy personnel, whose pay remained skimpy but steady, also contributed to the Community Chest.

To encourage attendance, the Federal Emergency Relief Administration (FERA) began part-time employment for college and high school students. Seventy-six Civilian Conservation Camps (CCC) were opened in the West, and some Coronadans chose to opt for that kind of mountain or desert work receiving food, clothing, medical care, and some education.

Coronado youngsters spoke out about the Depression that they felt had gone on for too many years. Every person in Coronado felt some loss, great or small. High school graduates found difficulty in getting employment when just out of school.

The west end of Ocean Blvd in 1939, with the sand spit beyond leading to North Island. (CHA)

Many people went on relief, but with the US. Navy spending $1,400,000 on construction projects and the U.S. Army about $1,800,000, most of it at Rockwell Field, this region fared better than most. Some people turned to Bolshevism and some to crime, but the one lesson learned well was that work is a blessing. A building surge during April brought a dose of optimism as contractors C.M. Anderson, R.E. Erwin, Charles Martin, Al Laing, Fifield and Son, Chris A. Cosgrove, J.M. Beasley, and A.L. and A.E. Dennstedt all signed building contracts.

> The community of Coronado was particularly attuned to the tempo of Navy life in the 1930s. Many young naval aviators or fleet officers shared trim rental flats or established family homes in order to commute either to North Island or to ships at anchor. "You can board a ferryboat, cross the bay between hurrying destroyers and cruisers, and drive out into the little town of Coronado," read one account of the day. "More than seven-tenths of this quiet little resort is taken up with the homes of naval officers who have only to drive across Spanish Bight in order to be on base. Here, along palm-bordered streets, Navy wives stop to chat and discuss the affairs of Navy life, as only Navy wives can. Along the sand beaches and on the tennis courts, Navy juniors romp amid the roar of 'daddy's squadron coming up the Strand.'"

The year 1934 brought events that rocked the globe. Two European kings were killed. Nevada, Utah, and California were shaken by earthquakes. Henry Ford restored a $5-a-day minimum to 47,000 of his workers. Maximillian A. ("Max") Baer knocked out Primo Carnera to win the world's heavyweight championship. Texas "bad man" Clyde C. Barrow and his cigar-smoking sweetheart, Bonnie E. Parker, were killed in a gun battle, while the Japanese denounced the Washington Naval Treaties of 1922.

Newspapers noted that Johnny Lyons and Frank "Toady" Greene had signed contracts with the Chicago Cardinals professional football team. Greene and Lyons, both Coronado High grads, had gone to Tulsa University, and Greene gave up his law school program at the University of Chicago to play pro football. He would return to Coronado to become a policeman and be involved in one of Coronado's most tragic events.

The Hotel del Coronado demolished the old hotel bathhouse known as The Plunge, in 1934. The famous swimming pool had been in service for forty years. In May, the Hotel public relations people announced that the hostelry would undergo renovations of major proportions, extending from the tower to the basement on most of the west or ocean front with a general overhauling of guest rooms, new fixtures and glassed-in porches. Mrs. Lillie Spreckels Wegeforth laid the cornerstone for the outdoor pool at the Hotel del Coronado on June 12th, 1934.

Despite the difficult times, the Hollywood crowd made headlines in Coronado during 1934. Mae West brought an entourage, had lunch, and sailed in the bay. Other vacationers included Mr. and Mrs. Eddie Cantor with three of their six daughters, and Mr. and Mrs. Al Jolson (Ruby Keeler). John Barrymore, Dolores Costello and two of her children, stayed at the Hotel in April, (with her mother Mrs. Hawthorne, and niece Miss Peggy Hawthorne). Alberto. M. Campione, who had been appointed resident Manager of the Hotel in that year, hosted most of the celebrities, topping out the season with arrival of the yacht Jobyna R, owned by Richard Arlen, with guests Gary Cooper and Jack Oakie.

As evidence of the island's small town charm, City Clerk Arthur A. Mathewson made a practice of sending the following interesting note to the home of each infant arrival:

> Dear Baby: Believing that a Certificate of Birth is an important document in one's life, we hand you a true record of that event with the compliments of the City of Coronado and its best wishes for a long and happy life.
> Yours very truly,
> A.A. Mathewson, City Clerk
> The Local Registrar of Vital Statistics

A vivid portrait of the Coronado of the future, as it could be orchestrated through careful planning, was presented in 1935 at a Rotary Club meeting by two members of the Planning Commission, Harold A. Taylor and Colonel Walter W. Crosby. Both speakers agreed Glorietta Bay was Coronado's greatest asset, from which all other developments would radiate. They urged development of plans that would ensure a community in which residents could live in pleasure and comfort. No longer, they said, should the town permit the crowding of dwellings. There should

The Navy's first aircraft carrier 'Langley' (CV-1) arrived in Coronado in 1924, and tied up at the Carrier Pier. This was the start of Coronado's association with aircraft carriers that extends to today. (CPL)

The aircraft squadrons from carriers 'Saratoga,' 'Lexington,' 'Ranger,' and 'Yorktown' were all based at North Island during the 1930s making it a busy place for operations. (CHA)

be ample park and playground facilities, supervised planning of construction in the business district, well-lighted streets and boulevards, removal of telephone and power-line poles, and the beautification of the city's waterways. The impression that became indelible, however, was the necessity for a real civic center!

A heavy downpour of rain hit Coronado on January 5, 1935. The drains at Tenth and Orange Avenue, didn't carry off the flood waters and considerable damage was done to merchandise and property. Every building on the east side of Orange, and on the east side of Tenth, had a foot of water. Several boys quickly launched a duck boat and ferried people across Orange Avenue for a three-cent fare. And, as if that weren't enough, a violent windstorm struck on January 18th, blowing down dozens of trees.

Storms of varying strengths and the constant action of the ocean continued to erode the beach. By 1935, original construction and on-going maintenance costs of the seawall had run over $450,000. In March, an effort was made to hold the Federal government responsible for the maintenance. The City claimed it had constructed the seawall because the government built the Zuñiga jetty at the harbor entrance. The jetty diverted the ocean currents in such manner that making a seawall was necessary to prevent damage to property. City officials sought an examination of the situation by army engineers.

From Washington, D.C. came the announcement that $1,800,000 had been made available for the immediate dredging of the channel in San Diego Bay, extending from Zuñiga jetty to the Naval Air Station pier. This assured accommodation of the deep-draft aircraft carriers *Saratoga*, *Lexington*, *Ranger*, *Enterprise* and *Yorktown* It also meant another 580 acres of land on North Island were added by dumping the fill onto the shoreline.

World events were beginning to shape the future of our nation as Italian troops with cannons and rifles attacked Ethiopian warriors who threw themselves at the invaders with spears, and bows and arrows in the Danakil Desert. Premier Benito Mussolini announced national mobilization of 20 million soldiers. The U.S. adopted a policy of strict neutrality. In the Saar Territory, a plebiscite on the future of that region, voted to return to Germany. And at Nuremberg, a Nazi Party gathering ended with a show of military strength as 100,000 men, heavy tanks, artillery, and 100 planes joined to destroy a sham town. President Franklin Delano Roosevelt signed the Neutrality Act requiring all American arms-makers to register with the government. Persia became Iran.

Hartmann's Beauty Shop at 878 Orange Avenue advertised ParcoOil for permanent waves at $2.50, and haircuts for 50 cents. A brand-new, fully-equipped Studebaker could be purchased for $889, while a standard Chevrolet Coupe was priced at $599; a used car, such as a 1932 V-8 Ford Cabrolet, was listed for $498. A 1931 Chevrolet Sport Sedan priced at $364, and a 1934 Sport Chevrolet Sedan for $584, were sold at Guarantee Garage at 931 Orange Avenue.

In September 1935, "Going to Coronado" was filmed by Paramount studios using the Hotel del Coronado, Tent City and the Hotel Boat House as backdrops. Stars were Johnny Downs, and Betty Burgess, Alice White, Leon Errol, Andy Devine, and Jack Haley.

> The first U. S. aircraft carrier built as such from the keel up, Ranger (CV-4), arrived in Coronado on April 15, 1935, and remained based in North Island until 1939. Although smaller than other U. S. carriers, she radiated a distinguished air when tied up to the carrier pier. "Her great length was what you saw first," recalled retired Vice Admiral Lloyd Mustin. "Hundreds of portholes dotted her sides, she was quite a sight."

On September 5, 1935, worn out headlines in a San Diego newspaper read, "Bay Bridge Now a Possibility." Action taken by the Coronado City Council consisted of adoption of a resolution authorizing an application for WPA funds. The cost of the bridge was tentatively estimated at $5 million, which would require a deferral grant of about $2 million. Plans called for a 40-foot roadway, enough for four traffic lanes, with a six foot wide pedestrian lane on either side

In addition to a grant from the government, it would be necessary to have the sanction of the War Department before the bridge could be constructed. Someone pointed out that both the Oakland and the Golden Gate Bridges in San Francisco brought bitter opposition from citizens when they were proposed, but equally strong influence won their approval by the War Department. The Council authorized the Mayor to sign a contract to develop the plans with private or government agencies. On November 4th, City Manager Edwin A. Ingham presented Coronado's application for the bridge to the War Department. Once again, however, the Navy's objection to possible obstruction of water traffic was the primary reason that bridge plan did not become a reality.

Rumors circulated that because of the increasingly crowded condition, the Navy wanted the Army off of North Island, and was prepared to swap them the Sunnyvale lighter-than-air base in Northern California. The Army, not surprisingly, was resistant to the move and suggested the Navy abandon their portion of the island instead. The argument was soon settled by a presidential visit.

> On October 1, 1935, President and Mrs. Franklin D. Roosevelt came to Coronado, arriving late in the evening by train from the East Coast via Los Angeles. He became the third U.S. President to stay at the Hotel del Coronado, staying in a two-room suite on the northern corner of the building facing the beach; his four-star presidential flag flew from the Del's highest turret. The next morning, Coronado school children were dismissed early from school, and joined thousands of other Coronadans who lined Orange Avenue and Fourth Street waving American flags as the president crossed the causeway to North Island, received a 21-gun salute, and reviewed aircraft of both Rockwell Field and the Naval Air Station. He then traveled across the bay by ferry, escorted by junior sailboats of the boys and girls Rainbow Fleet, and visited the California Pacific Exposition in Balboa Park. Later that afternoon, Roosevelt boarded the cruiser USS *Houston* and sailed offshore to review the Pacific Fleet, 129 ships and over 450 aircraft, before continuing southward for the Panama Canal and the Caribbean (and days of blue water fishing).

By Presidential Executive Order in October 1935, a coordinated land swap occurred between the flying services of both Army and Navy. Shared aviation bases at North Island, Ford Island in Hawaii and Terminal Island in Long Beach were formally shifted to the Navy, while

President Franklin Delano Roosevelt on the ferry heading over to the California Pacific International Exposition in Balboa Park, after leaving the Hotel del Coronado, October 2, 1935. (CPL)

the Army received the land at Naval Air Station Sunnyvale (today's Moffett Field, south of San Francisco Bay). At noon on October 25, 1935, Captain John Towers formally took possession of all of North Island for the Navy, at a ceremony punctuated by the landing of 28 *Langley* planes on the Army-built circular paved mat.

The Coronado Parent Teachers Association was organized, with Mrs. Davenport Browne (Katherine) elected president. Committees of all sorts were set up to undertake activities for the year. The idea of self-help had taken hold.

In an edition of the *Coronado Journal*, charter members Clarence Anderson, Amos E. Schaefer, and James P. Vernetti pointed out that 50 years had gone by since a group of community leaders had joined forces to form an organization to promote the interests of Coronado and lure tourists. Though the idea began to foment in 1935, the Chamber did not formally organize until 1936.

WPA projects reduced youth delinquency in Coronado according to talks given by Hal Neidermeyer, coach at the high school, as he urged the town to be more creative in sports and recreation for youngsters after school hours, on weekends, and in the summer. He pointed out that the summer camps such as those of the San Diego YMCA and the Marston Camp were very important, and that the idea of taking youngsters to them during the summer had a salutary effect on their growth.

On August 20, 1936, the War Department approved the application from the City of Coronado for consideration of a vehicular tunnel under the bay. Once again a feasibility study was undertaken.

In 1936, rumors that fan dancer Sally Rand, appearing at the California Pacific Exposition in San Diego, would speak to the Coronado Rotary Club and make an appearance at a church benefit, rocked the community. The published statement that "Miss Rand would appear," said the Reverend Harry O. Nash of Christ's Church, "was unauthorized and incorrect. This is no reflection upon the abilities or intentions of the dancer. It merely happens that there was no basis for the report." Sally did appear before the Rotary Club and spoke about the theatre as an institution.

Madame Schumann-Heink sold her expansive residence at 800 Orange Avenue to Thomas H. Pickford for over $40,000. Built in 1907, by John D. Spreckels as a home for Harry L. Titus, the Spreckels Company's attorney, Madame Schumann-Heink, had resided in the Harrison Albright designed home since April 1923. The great diva passed away on November 17, 1936, in Hollywood.

A steady increase in building of residences and apartment houses began, in what can be seen with hindsight as pre-war stimulants to the economy. In large part this was a private housing boom as a direct result of the influx of Naval personnel to be stationed at North Island. The newspaper coverage of happenings about Naval and Marine Corps families increased as well, especially on the society pages where photographs by Lou Goodale Bigelow filled out the stories.

Mrs. William Ball (Annie) of 468 F Avenue, was winner of a studio bungalow given away at the Exposition in San Diego. Unfortunately for her, the City Council determined its construction did not conform to requirements of the city building codes so it could not be erected in Coronado. The building was sold to another party and is still located in La Mesa.

In 1936, the movie industry did its best to call attention to Coronado's amenities. Stan Laurel brought his Ruth L, a 56-foot motor cruiser, to the Yacht Club, and from there his party enjoyed fishing off the Coronado Islands. In May, Paramount studios made "Yours for the Asking," starring George Raft, Dolores Costello Barrymore, James Gleason, Reginald Owen, and Ida Lupino. Most of the shooting was done around the Hotel del Coronado and the Coronado Flowerland — a flower shop. In that same month, Hal Roach filmed "Mr. Cinderella" featuring Jack Haley and Betty Furness. Shooting went on during the days and well into the late evenings at the Coronado Yacht Club and the Copley Home on Glorietta Boulevard.

To everyone's surprise, in June 1936, the Spreckels Company spoke of abandoning Tent City as a resort and straightening out the State Highway. Hotel patrons were concerned that another of their favorite recreational activities would be lost. President Lazaro Cárdenas of Mexico had prohibited casino gambling since 1934, precipitating the closure of the Agua Caliente Club in Tijuana. For a century, however, Mexico had permitted betting on horse races. The closing of Caliente caused labor problems in Lower California and Mexican citizens began to cross the border to find badly needed work in a region just beginning to regain its own economic strength.

At Christmastime in 1936, at the corner of Orange and Isabella a star pine tree was dedicated by Mrs. Emily T. Thompson as a memorial to her husband, Charles. The tree was transplanted from the grounds of the Thompson home, 848 Glorietta Boulevard. The movement of such a mature tree was a very difficult business and often resulted in failure. People who knew him said Louis C. Bandel was the only seasoned horticulturist who could have successfully managed the replanting.

New Year's 1936/37 opened with high winds and rough seas that caused the gambling ship, Monte Carlo, anchored three miles off the Coronado coast to break her mooring and come hurtling toward the shore. Floating gambling vessels such as the Monte Carlo were quite a draw in this era of Prohibition. Small boats ferried partygoers to the festive ships where they could gamble and drink without fear of the law. Sometime after midnight on January 1st, 1937, after the crowds had gone ashore and leaving only the two man crew aboard, the party ship lost her anchor. She began her helpless drift toward shore, finally settling just south of the Hotel del Coronado. Coronadans by the

The gambling ship Monte Carlo grounded on the Silver Strand, January 1, 1937. (CHA)

hundreds flocked to the scene, grabbing gambling tables, roulette wheels, silverware and liquor that washed ashore as the vessel lay pounded by the surf. Although the two crew members managed to get to shore, one sailor swam out to claim salvage and drowned.

Because the Monte Carlo was technically illegal once she was beached inside the three-mile limit, no one wished to claim ownership and slowly her wooden superstructure began to break up without any private party or body of government laying claim to her. Because of this, the concrete hull lies today, exposed at low tide, in front of the most southern Coronado Shores condominium, south of the Hotel Del Coronado. Various agencies including the U.S. Navy, U.S. Coast Guard, and City of Coronado are still in dispute as to whose responsibility and liability lies with the wreck.

A Civilian Conservation Corps unit moved into the Silver Strand State Park to install shelters, latrines and parking areas. By July 1936, initial improvements on eight acres on the bay side were completed. During the year, records for commercial and residential construction were broken as the Dennstedt Company, Walter Vestal, Chris Cosgrove, Al Laing, and Paul Hathaway designed and built their particular styles of buildings.

Colonel Walter W. Crosby, a member of the Planning Commission, explained in a public meeting a proposal for a land swap with the Spreckels Company. In short, if the citizens would vote to permit closing the road along the ocean side of Tent City, and a short strip of street then exiting through the Hotel del Coronado and garage, the Spreckels interests would deed to the City eight separate pieces of property comprising more than 40 acres. This would permit Orange Avenue to be straightened and became the main artery directly down to Coronado Heights. In return, the town would gain lands between the public highway and the Bay, from Third Street and Glorietta Boulevard, and allow development of the waterfront for public use. Coronado would also obtain title to North Beach, with contiguous land for ample parking. Other elements in the proposed swap included the retention by the town of the dance pavilion, the children's pool, the bath house, and several other buildings in Tent City. Voters approved the plan without much controversy and in the process the fate of Tent City became sealed.

In March, the U.S. Beach Erosion Commission was approached with a request that a cooperative study be made of the area in front of the seawall then known as Center Beach. Coronado contended that the Government's act of erecting the Zuñiga jetty, caused the erosion that destroyed Ocean

Boulevard during the 1905 storm. Coronado asked the Federal Government for reimbursement of the cost of the seawall, a request that was quickly refused. Russell W. Rink, City Manager, said the only encouraging aspect of the situation was the possibility that thousands of tons of sand from the dredging of San Diego Bay being deposited on the ocean side of the Silver Strand (south of the city limits) might eventually be carried by ocean currents and deposited in front of the seawall. This is exactly what happened. In time, a new beach formed, remarkably wider than the original one.

In June 1937, Warner Brothers came from Hollywood to film "Submarine D-1" starring Pat O'Brien, George Brent, Wayne Morris and Frank McHugh. The performers stayed at the Hotel del Coronado and El Cordova Hotel.

Sports remained a major part of the Coronado lifestyle. Roy Pickford became President of the Coronado Sports and Recreation Association, organized in April 1937, by more than 100 of the City's civic and sports leaders. Interest had been stimulated by Bob Carrothers, who at 15 years of age at the time, had become the U.S. National Tennis Champion in his age group, winning in both the singles and doubles competitions. During the same year Alice Marble played a match with Chilean Anita Lizana, U.S. National Champion, at the Hotel del Coronado. Later, other famous players including the Wightman Cup Team, were entertained at the home of Mr. and Mrs. George Burnham (Florence) at 1015 Ocean Boulevard. The Coronado Sports and Recreation Association became very active promoting Coronado as a sportman's paradise and publicizing outstanding athletes such as polo great Major Colin Ross, and dancer Jean Jurad.

From February 18-22, festivities marking the half-century anniversary of the hotel were held throughout Coronado. Sponsored by the Coronado Chamber of Commerce, a huge celebration was staged which included a carnival, street dance, barbecue, a WPA concert, and fireworks. Townsmen

James Cagney and Pat O'Brien in Devil Dogs of the Air, a Warner Brothers film made locally in 1935. (CHA)

formed a "Whiskers Club," and NBC radio broadcast the celebration to an estimated three million people. James W. Reid, Architect of the Hotel, even attended a dinner there, reminiscing about the hostelry's construction.

Building permits soared in Coronado as the population reached an all time high of 8,000 due to the influx of U.S. Naval personnel. Rentals also began to reflect the rise in prosperity. Strand Realty advertised a furnished three-bedroom house with bath for $65 per month; and a four bedroom with two baths for $75. E.A. Johnson of Chicago bought a mansion at 1127 "F" Avenue for $75,000.

On May 18th, the Silver Strand State Park was dedicated. Fourth Street between Orange and Alameda was finally declared an arterial boulevard carrying Coronado's heaviest traffic load at all hours. Chief J.W. Jordan declared that the street should have reflector or blinker stop signs, and the Council finally granted approval.

Mayor Henry G.S. Wallace presented to the City Council the plans drawn by Herbert L. Jackson and Samuel Hamill for a proposed new civic center — a two-story structure in Mission Revival style, facing Orange Avenue at Sixth. The *Coronado Journal* printed the Jackson/Hamill architectural renderings of City Hall, and of a proposed gymnasium and library for Coronado High School, all in proximity to one another. Late in the year, the California Public Works Administration allotted a grant of $146,454 for the school additions. The new construction was of reinforced concrete, earthquake proof, and built by C.L. Heskins, contractor.

> In 1938, the city bought "Little Mac," a 750 gpm pumper fire truck. It remained in use until 1976, when it was sold. In 1998 the pumper was found abandoned in a field. It was brought back to Coronado and restored by Bill Gise and volunteers from the Fire Department. Today it is frequently seen in parades.

In December 1938, residents waged bitter arguments against dumping dredged material to create approximately 200 acres of barren ground for a golf course, along the east waterfront of Glorietta Bay. The basic objection, from residents living along Glorietta Boulevard, was that they would find themselves a considerable distance from the bay. Instead, they found a tenderly-cared for golf course at their front doors. The dredging of Glorietta Bay brought a five-year Yacht Harbor Development to its conclusion.

The Vinson Naval Act of 1938 authorized expansion of a "Two Ocean Navy," a fact not missed by very many people who saw war on the horizon. Most Coronadans knew that a buildup of ships and crews was occurring on North Island. Yet there were those who persisted in the belief that a conflict could be averted by ongoing discussions with German or Italian diplomats. Speakers at local business clubs advocated continued isolationism, while others clearly saw the handwriting on the wall. Coronado had benefited from the wisdom of resident naval officers such as Ellis M. Zacharias who had lived in Japan and had seen the result of the disarmament treaties of the 1920s, when our nation had stopped building ships, even going so far as to sink vessels to keep our part of the bargain, while the Japanese continued to build and arm their fleet.

A major rain and windstorm in late February 1938, dampened spirits as a number of trees blew down. Bernard Lamb, at San Diego State College, majoring in business, had the lead in the comic opera "The Bartered Bride." For the regular 4th of July celebration, Central Drug Store advertised fireworks for sale, since one could legally set off Roman candles, sparklers, and pinwheels in those days. The 11th Annual National Horse Show was held in July with Mrs. Frank Von Tesmar (Alice) as chairperson.

Warner Brothers began shooting "Wings Over the Navy" at North Island, starring George Brent, John Wayne, and Olivia de Havilland. This was only one of many films about the armed

Central Drug Store, 1933. Left to right: Carl Hemenway, Que Roy, Lyman Latham, Betty Rand, Arthur Henry. (CHA)

forces that would hit the silver screens before U.S. involvement in World War II began. Quite a few of these were made on both North and South Islands.

In December 1938, before Christmas, a Navy dive-bomber crashed in the alley behind 844 "J" Avenue, killing two fliers attached to the USS *Saratoga*. The crash of an airplane with the loss of life, although uncommon on Coronado itself, was not a rare event. North Island Naval Air Station was an active station, and not only did many planes call the base home, but aircraft from other stations or carriers also landed there. Papers frequently reported the loss of a gallant officer or his crew due to accidents either on the island or at sea.

The threat of war loomed larger during 1939 and 1940. Residents of North and South Islands began to clearly recognize signs of preparation by the Axis for the war in Europe before any formal declarations. In January, Colonel Harold Strauss, commandant of Rockwell Field, turned over the keys to the post to Captain Arthur L. Bristo, Naval Air Station Commander, officially ending the Army's tenure on North Island. Improvements to the base were already underway. New Navy squadrons could now be based on the western side of the island. In May, Coronado welcomed the return of the fleet from maneuvers.

Over 50 ships arrived on one weekend, including aircraft carriers, cruisers, destroyers, and a number of other craft as 15,000 people descended upon Coronado and San Diego. A half-page ad appeared in the *Coronado Journal* urging the U.S. to stay out of war, headlining "Neutrality: An Appeal for America." The reality of world events had still not struck home for some.

During 1939, L. Deming Tilton, a city planning consultant, was asked to assist the Planning Commission in drawing up a master plan for Coronado. A number of factors were to be emphasized not least of which was how much land could be added by dredging. By using land filled by dredging

By 1938, with the addition of sand dredged from the San Diego Channel, the perimeter of North Island had grown much larger. Whaler's Bight, out by the jetty, had also been filled in. Spanish Bight was still intact, but would soon be filled in due to wartime needs. (CHA)

the city would not have to acquire more land by purchase. Included in the study were these proposed projects for filled areas: 1) a public airport location; 2) a recreation harbor; 3) an aquatic park; 4) a site for a new school on the bay; 5) Navy landings and adequate parking; 6) a new waterfront drive and promenade; 7) new recreation areas convenient to North Island; 8) a large area for a new golf course; 9) and a new beach and picnic areas.

By the late 1930s, transportation was becoming a serious problem for workers and residents. To get to North Island, one drove a vehicle around the Silver Strand, rode what was commonly called a "nickel snatcher" — a small vessel from San Diego to North Island–or took one of the ferries on the San Diego-Coronado run. Traffic backed up on Orange Avenue as far as the eye could see, even though at times two of the three ferries, the North Island, San Diego, and Coronado were making the bay crossing.

Coronado schools benefited tremendously from Depression Era construction sponsored by the Works Progress Administration (WPA), including: a new high school library wing and artistic panels along Seventh Street, new Central School classroom buildings, a new gymnasium (Carrothers Gym), and new spectator stands for Cutler Field.

Artwork for the school was (and still is) important, representing the absolute best in public art with clean presentation, mystical subjects, and a renowned creator. Donal Hord was a distinguished sculptor specializing in California, Mexican and oriental themes, but also a sculptor struggling with little work during the Great Depression. He had turned to the Federal Arts Project, a work-relief program where he could earn a regular salary ($75 a month) producing works for public places. An enchanting historical saga arose from Hord's passion–seven grand panels, intricately sculpted in Indiana limestone, telling the sweeping saga of the land called California. The central panel features California and its Amazonian ruler Calafia; the rest of the composition symbolizes different eras or dimensions of California life. The panels were finished in late 1939, and mounted shortly thereafter. During the panel's dedication in February 1941, Coronadans spoke lavishly of Hord's work as having "lasting value to Coronado."

Coronado's Community and Club building in the West Plaza of the Library Park was under construction. Clarence C. Fifield laid the concrete for the general contractor F.E. Young Construction Co. The building served many civic groups after the Mayor dedicated the center on December 17th. Residential construction was at an all time high. In the first nine months of 1938, over $700,000 had been put into new homes. Fifty-five residential permits were issued in eleven months with an average cost of a home in Coronado set at $5,100.

In civic affairs, Paul Corriere was elected as new Chamber of Commerce president. The City Council appointed Ajax Gray Recreational Director with a salary of $100 a month to organize, publicize, and develop community recreational facilities. Gray got right to work and with plenty to publicize. At the Ink Tennis Tournament in San Diego, Bob Carrothers was top-seeded. Other players seeded in their classes were Ezra Parker, Marie Jacks, Mary Ann Bratz, and Jack Carrothers. Marie would achieve national recognition and be elected to the University of Arizona Hall of Fame. The Coronado Yacht Club was called one of the finest on the coast. The *Coronado Journal* of May 25, recounted its history, with a full list of membership naming people from all over the country. The Coronado Riding Ring held its annual Gymkhana and Horse Shows; the 1st Annual Power Boats Race in Glorietta Bay drew over 3,000 spectators to watch the vessels perform. That day was sunny, but during the year Coronado experienced some unusual weather. In September, a serious electrical storm blacked out the town and that same month heavy storms, weekend gales and high seas washed much of the sand away at Center Beach. Boat owners rushed to Glorietta Bay, but found the area very well protected and most vessels held to anchor.

A Halloween celebration brought several thousand revelers to Cutler Field, where the City sponsored boxing matches and a variety of sports and entertainment organized to avoid pranks elsewhere in the city. City fathers called it a huge success as did the police chief.

In February, Mrs. R.E. Archibald (the former Lucia Antonia D'Amico) gave birth to the first twins born in the village since 1928. At Christmastime, the *Coronado Journal* put out its green and red edition with holiday greetings from:

> Shell Korner: Kenny MacArthur, Walter E. Shortt, Bob Sweeney and Floyd Seder
> The Island Café, 1031 Orange Avenue
> The Mill Café, 124 Orange Avenue
> Coronado Sheet Metal Works, 955 Orange Avenue:
> R.F. Buechner and Hilding Weisgerber
> Shay's Gilmore Service Station, 4th and Orange Avenues

Coronado's population had shot up to about 10,000 by 1940, with the impact of "peace-time" war efforts and industries. While the newspaper reported 8,500 people living in town, the hiring of many civilian employees at North Island had substantially increased the number.

When Germany invaded Poland in 1939, Federal government plans had already come into play. By the early fall of 1940, reserve and retired officers who were able to return to active duty, were called upon to do so. Important aircraft companies established themselves in San Diego.

At about the same time, the Federal government asked Park Superintendent K. W. Bandel to make a census of the number of trees on city property in Coronado. He reported between 4,500 and 7,000 trees, with hundreds of varieties.

In Coronado, surplus funds were distributed by the State Relief Administration. Lunch programs for children in low-income families were started, and the Works Progress Administration added education workers to assist in the schools.

In order to provide additional land for military use, more dredging took place. A U.S. Navy Seaplane Basin on the bay side was created some two miles south of Coronado, where the ocean shore line was pushed back about 700 feet by displaced bay sand. The entire dredge, the pumps, and other equipment were brought from a dam construction job in the forests of Nebraska, and assembled in the South Bay area for this project.

At a meeting, on August 19, 1940, the City Council granted the Navy permission to fill the waters separating North and South Islands. The filling of this beautiful bay, or inlet from the Bay of San Diego, known as the Spanish Bight, was not completed until 1944. Coronadans strenuously objected to the filling of the Bight, but the U.S. Government felt an urgency to enlarge North Island and provide more space for construction. In the same year, the War Department began dredging San Diego Bay to create an enlarged basin for Navy ships. The fill was deposited on Coronado's northeast shore (helping form what is today referred to as Tideland's Park) running from 12 to 17 feet above mean low or low water.

The huge electric dredge moved south, placing soil on the point southeast of Glorietta Point (where the Naval Amphibious Base is today), creating a peninsula to be used as a bathing beach, picnic grounds, and recreation center. This area proved to be large enough to accommodate a municipal airport that had been under consideration for some time, and an athletic field. In that way, much of Coronado's tidelands came about through Navy dredging.

Then another proposal was put forward to cut a channel through the Silver Strand, leading from the bay to the ocean. This became the topic of a civic conference. "Studies" by the War Department and other Federal Government officials reflected the need for such a channel since San Diego Bay had only one entrance; in the event of an enemy blockade, vessels could be locked into the harbor.

For the first time in 39 years, 1940 saw the summer begin in Coronado without the opening of Tent City. A way of life and an era had passed quietly into history. As the great dance pavilion was torn down, and the other buildings were dismantled one by one, only a few curiosity seekers came to watch. The famous Coronado campground had fallen victim to modern life. All that remained, in the end, were the memories.

A major controversy of long duration was settled when, following a suit initiated to determine Coronado's rights to the Otay Water System, Superior Court Judge, Lawrence N. Turrentine, ruled that Coronado "has perpetual and inviolable rights to such waters as it may require from the Otay, Morena, Barrett reservoir system. Coronado may derive its entire supply from Otay Reservoir or from Tia Juana Valley reservoir or from both sources as its option."

The war in Europe captured much attention in Coronado. In June, as reserves were being called up, employers were asked by the Chamber of Commerce to protect the jobs of men who enlisted. A garden fête at the home of Mrs. George Burnham (Florence) for the relief of war sufferers of France and England raised a great deal of money, while Red Cross war relief donations began to pour into the headquarters. On October 16, 1940, 564 Coronado men between the age of 21 and 36, registered at 13 precincts for the first peacetime military service draft since the founding of the nation. The first two Coronado names drawn in the national lottery draft were Herbert Henry Herman Webber of 619 "G" Street, and Byron Nicholas McKinney of 932 "H" Avenue. Other Coronado names came up rapidly.

In sports, the high school Class "A" team won the Metropolitan Basketball League Championship, with a number of familiar names on the roster, most of whom would soon go into the armed forces. That same year, the high school football team captured the Metropolitan League title with eight straight wins. In tennis, Bob Carrothers and Marie Jacks won the Senior Boys' and Girls' entries in the Ink Tournament, and in the junior Boy's Division, Jack Carrothers won. In mid-October 1940, the sad news reached Coronado that Bob Carrothers, returning from the University of Southern California, was killed in an automobile accident in Rose Canyon,. Two weeks later the Coronado gymnasium, only recently completed, was dedicated to him.

In April, two swimmers were pulled out to sea by strong currents, near the beached Monte Carlo; Dexter Lanois, a high school lad saved their lives by pulling them up to the edge of the vessel until a U.S. Coast Guard cutter could come from San Diego to rescue them. When it was announced that four Coast Guardsmen would receive medals for rescuing the two people, Coronadans demanded Lanois also get a medal, rather than simply a paper commendation from the City. Lanois, later an aviator, would be killed in a wartime aviation accident.

Coronado was fortunate to have outstanding leadership in J. Leslie Cutler, Superintendent of the Coronado Unified School System; Fred A. Boyer, Assistant Superintendent and Principal of the elementary school; and Amos E. Schaefer, Principal of the high school. But the young men of the graduating classes of 1940 and 1941 looked forward towards draft registration, and an uncertain future.

Orange Avenue, between 8th and 9th Street (looking north), 1940. (CPL)

On September 1, 1939, the prospect of war became real with the invasion of Poland by the Nazis. Following that devastation, Norway, Denmark, the Netherlands, Belgium, and France were overrun. In June 1940, the United States Alien Registration Act was enacted and by August 1st, the first peacetime program of compulsory military services in the United States had begun. Military towns such as Coronado were hard hit, because such a large number of retired servicemen and women were called back to active duty.

An editorial in the *Coronado Journal* insisted, "We Cannot Isolate Ourselves." FDR had condemned the unholy alliance of dictators and avowed program of world domination. Radio commentator Fleetwood Lawton's column spoke of Neville Chamberlain's wasted attempts at appeasement. With the impetus of World War II during 1940-1941, Coronado's population increased to over 15,000. During the peak of the war, the number of residents would soar to 25,000.

Between January and May 1940, only 18 new homes had been added, at an average cost of $5,000. But a new water tower constructed at 1st and "C," at a cost of $80,000, held a half-million gallons to accommodate the increased number of residents.

On June 22, 1941, Germany attacked the Soviet Union, capturing several important cities. As other nations became involved in the struggle, Americans read and heard of the horrors of a war the U.S. was reluctant to enter. All during this period, American relations with Japan were far from ideal; by the spring of 1941, Japan and the United States were plainly on a collision course. Yet the average American did not have a clear picture of what lay ahead.

The Siebrand Brothers Circus and Carnival came to Coronado for four days beginning on February 24th, with a three-ring circus at the north end of Orange Avenue. This was the year coaches Niedermeyer and Thomas A. Callister had "A" and "B" basketball teams, which both won Metropolitan League championships, with the players awarded gold basketballs.

Jean Jurad's Dance Studio at 1015 Isabella, now an apartment complex, offered dance classes. Her studio put on a show at the Hotel del Coronado ballroom, with proceeds going to the Coronado High School athletes. A number of students took part, including a very talented singer and musician Fanchon Acosta, who would later have the lead role in Hemet's annual outdoor drama, "Ramona," alongside movie-star Victory Jory.

Over 200 visiting yachtsmen showed up the last weekend of May to officially open the summer yachting season at the Yacht Club. In August, "Home Run Bing" Crosby did his stuff in the Del Mar/Agua Caliente Jockey vs. City Officials Softball Game at Cutler Field. Coronado residents flocked to see the movie stars staying at the Hotel del Coronado, including Errol Flynn, Fred MacMurray, Ralph Bellamy, and Robert Armstrong, who were all in the movie "Dive Bomber," being filmed at North Island.

In February, ongoing discussions were held concerning Whitie's Commissary on the property to the west of the Coronado Elementary School. Officials felt that if Whitie's could be bought out, and the street closed, then the danger of children crossing to get to the store would be eliminated. The town acquired that block for the school. Whities closed, and owner Mr. F. Oliver Ernst opened another grocery store on Orange Avenue.

Gerry's Restaurant at 957 Orange, served breakfast, lunch and dinner as well as short orders. Coronado's longest-running restaurant advertised "Home-Cooked Food" and was open from 6:30 a.m. to 8:30 p.m. Down the Street, the A & P (Atlantic and Pacific) grocery store advertised:

Cassberries, 3 boxes for 25 cents
Frying Rabbits, 29 cents per lb.. (2 lb. average)
Boiling Beef, 19 cents per lb.
Dry Salt Park, 17 cents per lb.
Borax Soap Chips, large package, 21 cents
Brer Rabbit Molasses, 11/2 lb. can for 8 cents

War relief organizations in Coronado prepared clothing shipments to be sent overseas, and Mrs. Margaret Macauley headed the island units of the British War Relief and of the Red Cross. Efforts began in civilian defense. City officials reported they had a disaster plan and an organization for directing relief and rescue work in the event of a major disaster. The Coronado Defense Unit plan was organized by Dr. William T. Booth, the City Health Officer, whose private practice was at 1012 Isabella Avenue. The Women's Ambulance and Transport Corps of Coronado went into full wartime mobilization at the National Guard Armory in San Diego in December. A benefit was sponsored by the Coronado Red Cross Motor Corps, with proceeds used to equip and maintain a Red Cross station wagon for Coronado.

On December 4, 1941, an extremely enlightened Rear Admiral Charles A. Blakely, U.S. Navy, Commandant of the 11th Naval District, pled for understanding on behalf of citizens of Japanese ancestry:

> The 2nd generation Japanese or Nisei citizen has a definite place in our social structure and we, as Americans, will be derelict in our duty to America, if we fail to acknowledge this position and … to assist these people in their ambition to be true Americans.

His statement was that of a man ahead of his time. He had correctly assessed the attitude of most residents of Coronado that our Japanese-Americans neighbors were loyal Americans.

When the announcement came over the radio just before noon on Sunday morning, December 7, 1941, that the Japanese had attacked our country, some people asked, "Where is Pearl Harbor?" Other families, whose husbands had served there, knew instantly where it was. Rumors spread like wildfire that North Island Naval Air Station was the next target to be attacked by the Japanese. Since it was a large and strategic base, it seemed very logical. Word spread that the Hotel del Coronado would be bombed. It stood out on the beach like a giant sentinel, an ideal target. Guests panicked. They tried to get out of town any way they could, but Coronado was not an easy place from which to escape in the days before the bridge. People jammed the telephone lines, called out all taxis, and crowded the ferries. People out yachting didn't hear the news until hours later. A softball game between the Islanders and Marines was stopped, as the Marines were called back to their bases. Naval officers reported to their stations awaiting orders.

At North Island, the carrier *Saratoga* had just pulled into the pier, arriving at 11:30 a.m. Early that morning personnel assigned to the *Saratoga* air group had been mustered in their hangars, arranging for baggage, administrative files, and spare parts to be readied for loading aboard ship. Over a hundred planes waited to "waddle" in a long line across base to dockside, for hoisting aboard. When word reached the hangars of the attack on Pearl Harbor, *Saratoga*'s fighter squadron refueled and stood station-ready for take-off for the defense of the base.

Captain Reuben Smith, 11th Naval District Plans Officer, and his wife were having a late breakfast in their sunny Coronado home when the phone rang. "I'm going to the office." Smith told his surprised wife a moment later, "Sit by the radio." Shortly afterwards, Smith issued orders to all military personnel to return to their ships or stations, and to wear uniforms at all times. At 3 a.m. the next morning, an exhausted Smith finally returned to Coronado. "How bad was it," his wife asked? "I can't tell you," Smith answered haltingly, then turned away and began to weep.

The events of December 7, 1941, wounded the heart of every proud American. Captain and Mrs. Herbert A. Jones of Coronado felt the pain more than most; their only son, Ensign Herbert Charpiot Jones, serving aboard the USS *California*, made the ultimate sacrifice for his country that morning.

Coronadan Herbert C. Jones, a Pearl Harbor hero. (CHA)

Herb, as he was known by family and friends, was a fun-loving California native who spent summers with friends, sunning by the pool at the Hotel Del, but was prepared to fight for his country, following in his father's footsteps. He enlisted in the US Navy as a reservist in 1935. In 1940, he entered and passed an intensive training program to become an officer. As a young officer, Ensign Jones understood the events unfolding around the world at the time, and, like so many others, proposed to his college sweetheart, Joanne, well aware of the possibility that the United States would be entering the war. They married shortly before the USS *California* weighed anchor for Pearl Harbor.

Herb's ship was one of the first to be hit by Japanese bombs on December 7th, and when her ammunition hoists were badly damaged, he quickly organized an ammunition-passing party. In the midst of the chaos, he was struck by a bomb, but refused rescue, fearing for the safety of those coming to his aid. He stayed aboard the California, doing all he could to fight for the fleet although mortally wounded.

Ensign Jones was posthumously awarded the Medal of Honor for his actions during the attack on Pearl Harbor. Two years later, the U.S. Navy commissioned the USS *Herbert Jones* (DE-137), with his young widow as the sponsor. Ensign Herbert Charpiot Jones' actions and his sacrifice will echo for eternity for his family, and for the townsfolk who will always be proud to call him one of their own.

After the bombing of "Pearl," events in Coronado followed in rapid succession, almost too fast to relate in proper order. Guard stations, or dug-outs, were set up by the Marines on the beach and down the Strand. Red Cross volunteers drove down the dark, narrow peninsula delivering hot coffee and sandwiches to them.

In fear of an air attack by the Japanese, government officials drew up regulations that required owners of houses and business buildings to install thick dark shades or draperies at their windows so no gleam of light could shine through. The City Defense Council, headed by Captain Ivan B. Snell, USA RET, went into action with a substantial advisory committee structure, composed of the Mayor and city officials, including:

The Committee on Survey & Intelligence
Air Raid Wardens
Transportation
Communications
Medical Aid and Sanitation
Registration of Labor
Utilities
Food and Shelter
Rehabilitation Committee

Coronado's blackout ordinance banned lights in cars, homes, and all buildings and provided for punishment of violators. The blackout signal was three short and one long blast, repeated three times from the gas company whistle in San Diego, along with the turning off of all street lights. Casualty shelters were selected in various sections of the village: the high school gymnasium, the public library basement, Hotel del Coronado, Coronado Hospital, and the Catholic Church. Doctors, registered nurses, and two ambulances were allotted to each of the designated stations.

Every citizen was urged to keep handy an adequate supply of blankets, canned goods, water, candles, and a flashlight. Villagers were also requested to wear identification on his/her body either a necklace or a bracelet engraved with name, address, date of birth, blood type, and tetanus shot date.

Eleanor Ring was at the Family Hospital at North Island on the day of the Pearl Harbor attack, recovering from the birth of her third child, Susan. In an all-too-familiar Navy story, husband Stan was not present for the birth, but away leading the aircraft carrier Hornet's new air group in Norfolk. Within days of Pearl Harbor, Jane Keck Reynolds had taken charge of the Ring and Reynolds collective families, and, like many in Coronado who were fearful of attack, decided to move away from the beach, ending up at a home in Alpine. Many who remained in Coronado profited indirectly as real estate values plunged. Captain Frank Van Valkenburg's family was able to obtain a home with an exclusive Star Park address "for a song, because people were afraid to live on the coast and near a military establishment."

Early in 1942, the School Board ordered air raid drills, and air raid wardens were assigned definite sectors. Red Cross Civilian Defense Committees were ready to act, and the Office of Production Management set up a local tire rationing board.

Following the attack on Pearl Harbor, at a City Council meeting, City Clerk Arthur A. Mathewson read a resolution drawn up by Japanese nationals. Local Japanese families urged that it be presented to the Council:

Whereas, we, being resident aliens of the country and community for the greater part of our lives, and being parents of American citizens, do hereby pledge our resources, our children, and our lives toward a victorious conclusion of the war upon the axis nations.

Furthermore we pledge our wholehearted support towards civilian defense, Red Cross, and all city, county, and national agencies devoted to national unity and defense.

Signed:
>Masanori Tom Koba, 962 Margarita
>Ikuyo Takeshita, 685 Guadalupe
>Masaichi Tom Tanaka, 769 "J"
>Zenbei (James) Iwashita, 662 Margarita
>Kunitomo (George) Mayeda, 131 Orange
>Keitara Karamoto, 614 Third Street
>Harry Tateyama, 1156 Isabella
>Sadahiko Takeshita, 1109 1/2 "F"
>Benson Iwata, 2036 Logan Avenue, San Diego
>Iwaguma Tsuneyoshi, 640 "J"
>Mrs. Frances Mayeda, 765 Alameda
>Harusuke Harry Hoi, c/o Hotel del Coronado
>Mrs. Haruyo Hatada, 275 "C"
>Shigeru Sugita, P.O. Box 281, Coronado
>Masahiko Koba, 464 "H"
>K. Katsumata, 534 Island Avenue, San Diego

Coronado residents Ed Chew and his son, Ed Chew Jr., during World War II. (CHA)

Despite the efforts of the local Japanese-Americans to demonstrate their loyalty by actions such as purchasing of war bonds, and eagerly turning in anything that might be construed as contraband, anti-Japanese sentiments grew until they were shipped off to internment camps.

Attorney General Francis Biddle announced new regulations affecting the conduct of German, Italian, and Japanese nationals throughout the continental U.S. A presidential proclamation of January 14, 1942, ordered that those residing in California, Oregon, Washington, Nevada, Arizona, Montana, Utah and Idaho would be required to file information about themselves at the nearest post office.

Dozens of Coronado women joined the American Women's Voluntary Services (AWVS), helping out wherever needed, performing jobs like plane-spotting, driving ambulances or delivering mail among many other tasks. (CHA)

April 2, 1942, the papers reported that the evacuation of all Japanese nationals had begun. Police sergeant Joe Hoppe completed the inventory of Coronado families before their departure to the detention camps. Before very long, several of Coronado's Japanese students had developed into devoted correspondents with their Caucasian friends in Coronado, writing from the Santa Anita processing center, and later from the camp at Manzanar. The letters were discreet, but nostalgic. Fumiko Karamoto and Kuniteru Mayeda, recent high school graduates, were the most active writers. J. Edgar Hoover would say that the internment was a result of politics and hysteria, not a measure of national security.

The town received $30,228 from the Federal government to build grammar school classrooms, badly needed due to the influx of aircraft workers and military families. Garages and store rooms were converted to "guest houses." Many islanders, responding to the need, rented spare rooms in their own homes. Long-time friendships often resulted from "taking in" these roomers. To prevent wartime profiteering by "landlords" who sought exorbitant fees, deposits and rental charges, permits were required that had to be obtained locally from the Office of Price Administration.

People were quickly learning to stand in line for whatever they needed, whether that was personal identification, ration stamps, or gas coupons. Shortages came as industries turned their productions to support the war effort. Simple things became precious. Tin cans and or grease became important and worth saving. Used clothing was needed to ship to war-torn Europe. The *Coronado Journal* suggested:

> Old silk and nylon hosiery collected, or silk and cotton, can be vitally important for use in making gunpowder bags. Silk and nylon are the only materials which burn up completely, leaving no ash which might cause premature explosion upon the next reloading of the gun.

The War Salvage Committee of Coronado completed a collection of materials in 1942. Over 20 tons of metal, rubber, grease, and newspapers were piled at the corner of Sixth and Palm to be converted to war needs.

Hundreds of servicemen wandered around in Coronado and San Diego, and there was no difficulty in finding dates. The Hotel del Coronado's downstairs dance floor was one of the most popular places for socializing. In January 1942, a group organized the Coronado Defense Recreation Council with Lieutenant Commander Henry Guilmette, USN RET, as the first Chairman and through his committee's guidance, the Men's Service Club opened its doors on March 3, 1942, at 937 Orange Avenue. As the club grew, affiliation came with other service clubs in town and on April 12, 1943, became the U.S.O. Club of Coronado.

World War II shortages in manpower and materials made it unwise to continue publication of two newspapers in the town. On March 19th, the announcement was made that the two Coronado newspapers would be consolidated; and the *Citizen* and the *Journal* continued under the name *Coronado Journal*, with the sub-legend *The Coronado Citizen*.

A Coronado policemen's auxiliary unit was organized and trained in first aid. This group took up many of the extra tasks regular officers were finding difficult to keep up with. The auxiliary was also prepared to assist in the event of emergencies. The Parent Teachers Association sponsored distribution of identification tags for children, and the Chamber of Commerce started a committee to stimulate growth of Victory Gardens.

One of the most distinctive and famous aircraft of World War II was the famed PBY Catalina flying boat. In the days before wide use of radar, fleets depended on very long-range patrol aircraft that could search far out to sea to detect the approach of enemy ships or to target others for our own attacks. Patrol aircraft were, literally, the "eyes of the fleet," and PBYs were the best. PBY's played a huge role in the American victory at Midway, a British PBY found the Bismarck, and squadrons of PBYs were based throughout the Pacific.

One of the most famous aircraft of World War II, and the most numerous on North Island, was the PBY Catalina long-range patrol bomber, manufactured across the bay in San Diego at Consolidated Aircraft. (CHA)

The great majority of PBYs manufactured were built at Consolidated Aircraft at the edge of San Diego's Lindbergh Field (beginning in 1936). As each one rolled off the assembly line, it taxied across San Diego Bay to North Island. Hundreds and hundreds of PBYs crammed onto the North Island field, used ramps to enter and leave the water, and took off and landed from watery runways along Coronado and the Silver Strand. They were ubiquitous throughout the war, and easily remembered by Coronadans. The plot of *Wings of the Navy*, a 1939 Warner Brothers film starring Olivia de Havilland and George Brent, concentrated on North Island's Catalinas, bringing the Navy, PBYs, and Coronado nationwide attention.

America's First Lady, Mrs. Franklin Delano Roosevelt, arrived by train on February 20, 1942, to visit her son Ensign John Roosevelt in his Coronado home. On that same day, the men of the town looked at a full page of local draft serial numbers; and on April 23, the City Clerk secured the local draft order numbers. Coronado was covered by Draft Board 163. The lowest number on the Coronado list was Jim L. Estes (10,003). The highest was Richard B. Gowan (13,200) listed as 3,200. Local numbers were between 3 and 3,200.

Sugar rationing began on May 4th. On the 28th, a directive from the 9th Civilian Defense Region, in the Office of Civilian Defense, banned: street lights, auto lights & highway lights; advertising signs, commercial flood lights; display lights and amusement places; lights in residence, commercial and industrial windows; camp fires on beaches.

Coronadans were treated to a surprise in mid-July when the Harry James Orchestra, playing at the Pacific Square ballroom in San Diego, boarded the ferry in the late evening. James and some of his men performed as they traveled across the bay, and then on the streetcar while making their way to the home of Mr. and Mrs. Frank Martin and daughter Peggy Lou, near Star Park, for a visit. The men played there during the night, and the next day went to the races at Agua Caliente. James predicted that Martin's son, Francis, who played trumpet in the CHS band, would have a brilliant future in the music world.

The new Coronado Hospital on Soledad place, 1942. (CHA)

Coronado Homes, Inc., a development corporation, began construction of 28 homes in the area of "G" to "H" and Fourth to Sixth, designed to serve the influx of military personnel. These homes are still in existence.

The names of the first of the Coronado men who gave up their lives, or who were wounded or missing in action in the war, began to appear in the newspapers. Captain Cassin Young, Congressional Medal of Honor awardee, and captain of the heavy cruiser San Francisco, met a heroic end when his ship was struck by a Japanese shell in the Battle of the Solomon Islands, November 13-15, 1942. Another hero, who would later become recognized as one of Coronado's most illustrious servicemen, was Captain Ellis M. Zacharias, whose family lived at Alameda and Tenth. He returned to Coronado for a short time. Later he would write at least two major books about his experiences during the 1920s in Japan, and during the war. Also, at this time, heroes of the Flying Tigers, Ed Overend, Frank Lindsay Lawler, and Harry Edward Fox returned home. Another one of Coronado's earliest casualties was Henry Bramstedt, killed aboard the USS *Hammond*, which was sunk with the USS *Yorktown* in the Battle of Midway on June 6th. The Hammond's commanding officer, upon seeing a submarine launching torpedoes at a cruiser, positioned his vessel to take the brunt of the attack.

A *Saturday Evening Post* article called Coronado the "Port of Navy Wives," noting that 2,000 heroic women, wives of U.S. naval officers lived on Coronado Island. Among those photographed were Ensign James Bryan, Jr., getting a farewell hug from his wife Norma, and Coronadan Jackie Goodhue (Davis) sharing a letter from her husband with other recent brides.

During World War II, bay-side barracks on First Street housed the Navy's first female sailors (WAVES), both officers and enlisted. (CHA)

In November 1942, the U.S. Government announced its intentions to build quarters for 500 WAVE officers and enlisted women along the strip of land north of First Street, bordering San Diego Bay. The property was chosen because of its convenience to the ferry and dock landing, as well as to the Naval Air Station. The building, which cost $370,000 was erected just north of the old car barn, through a lease negotiated with the Spreckels Companies for the duration of the war. While First Street residents complained about the large temporary building blocking their bay view, the real need was understood, and in 1944, additions were made, bringing the number to seven wood frame buildings, with facilities for 58 officers, and 488 enlisted female personnel.

By February 1942, the Federal government also completed another military camp, but this was promised to directly benefit Coronado. The gift was a 135-acre tract of fill being added to City lands just south of the old Tent City property. This reclaimed area, dredged from the bottom of the bay, extended 4,200 feet from the old shoreline, and was 1,500 feet wide. It became the location of the Naval Amphibious Base. The Federal government kept its promise to give the dredged land to the town, but promptly leased it back from Coronado at $1 per year for wartime military purposes. However, that arrangement did not end there, as would be seen in ensuing court cases.

The Amphibious Training Base, Coronado was formally commissioned on January 15, 1944. The building of barracks and Landing Force training buildings continued through 1944 and 1945, assisted by approximately 500 German prisoners of war, who were transported to Coronado and lived in a stockade in the middle of the base. One of the big advantages to the Navy of their new Amphibious Base was that training could readily be conducted in both bay and open-ocean environments. Various specialized training took place at several different sites along the Silver Strand.

In early 1943 the *Coronado Journal* wrote: "Residents Tighten Belts. Housewives Study Ration Book Issue." Ration books were issued with different colored stamps for different types of food, and required standing in line for new books every twelve weeks. Gasoline rationing dropped to two gallons per week. Rubber was so scarce that only retreads were available, and statewide speed limits were reduced to thirty-five miles per hour to save gas. Transportation bogged down; street cars were overloaded. With the need to get workers to night shifts, the ferries and street cars operated around the clock, 24 hours, for the first time ever. The old Belt Line Railroad chugged around the Strand day and night carrying heavy loads of supplies to the Amphibious Base and the Naval Air Station.

In a crash program beginning in 1942, the Navy dredged mud from the bay to establish the Naval Amphibious Base, widening certain parts of the Silver Strand to help with amphibious training of sailors in the bay and along the ocean shore. (CHA)

Television had not yet come into being. War news from the battle fronts was slow and not released by newspaper or radio until after it was censored! Mail too was censored, and a form of envelope/letter called "V-Mail" came into being. Often a letter reached its destination with large sections cut out as censors were permitted to read everything to ensure that servicemen did not accidentally leak information that might help the enemy.

Still, more space was needed. In 1940, at the northeast corner of the island, additional land was created by dredging which was then leased to the U.S. Government. Family housing was erected here for the duration of the war. Terms of the lease were for 12 months, starting September 30, 1943, renewable on a yearly basis.

By January 1944, the units under construction were nearing completion. Eventually there would be 744 living quarters for singles and families. Included in the compound were a cafeteria, a nursery school for 75 children, and a community building, which included a barber shop, a beauty parlor, and a soda fountain.

In November 1943, the Navy contemplated acquisition of property on the west side of Coronado, including areas north of Fourth Street, for warehouses and loading platforms, much to the distress of Coronadans, who would lose their golf course, but even more so to the residents who faced the golf course. A *Coronado Journal* article pessimistically reported that "because of the huge amount of concrete to be used, it is doubtful whether the property will ever be returned." On the south side of Fourth Street, areas would be used for barracks, presumably to be removed at the end of the war. The Spreckels Companies had not approved of the land sale.

Mayor Carl W. Ince appealed directly to President Franklin D. Roosevelt, saying that the people of Coronado asked him to intercede on their behalf to prevent seizure of this land by the Navy Department.

American Women's Voluntary Services (AWVS) sponsored dances at the Hotel del Coronado's Circus Room, during the war. (CHA)

Coronadans, despite their war fervor, regarded the seizure as a "careless destruction of home values of our residents." Ince then suggested proceeding with filling in the Spanish Bight (which was also an error in logic in the long run). By the end of the year 1943, all efforts ceased, due to the President's more pressing matters.

To assist in the war effort Mrs. John Henry Towers (Pierette), wife of Vice Admiral Towers, was put in charge of a local war plant project, a trial balloon for Consolidated Aircraft Corporation. It was placed at 1000 Isabella Avenue in the building that Coronadans knew later as the Free Brothers Market. Here, women who wanted to work part-time during the war, probably making small parts for aircraft, while keeping homes and raising children, could help out for patriotic reasons. The plant operated for about a year.

At the southeastern end of the Silver Strand, the beautiful Coronado Heights site, which had been platted and planted by the Coronado Beach Company as a planned residential subdivision with some streets laid out, now lay fallow, bordered by windblown cypress and pine trees and a section of the old state highway.

> The Navy first came to Coronado Heights on May 20, 1920, when it established a Navy Radio Compass Station on 1.9 acres of land. The site helped ships navigate with accurate radio fixes. In 1939, the Navy began planning for installation of a new high-frequency, direction-finding station on the Coronado Heights site. In October 1941, land for the new station was condemned, and title transferred from the Spreckels Company to the government. By December 1942, the Navy had expanded these operations beyond Direction Finding to include radio intelligence activities. The radio intelligence intercept cell at Coronado Heights was known as Station ITEM (ITEM was the phonetic letter for I). Large numbers of WAVE communications personnel were assigned to the station, beginning in 1944.
>
> Just five weeks after the attack on Pearl Harbor, the Army established Battery Imperial adjacent to the Navy signals station; in October 1942, they took over additional land and designated the site Fort Emory. A huge bunker of reinforced concrete was constructed between 1943 and 1944 to support two 16-inch guns for coastal defense that were never installed. On May 4, 1944, Fort Emory was declared "in standby" by the Army; at the end of the war the complex was transferred to the Navy.
>
> The Navy retained the Fort Emory name, and developed Amphibious Training Base Fort Emory on that portion of the site, beginning in 1944. A variety of buildings were constructed, including 240 Quonset huts, landing craft repair buildings, and a dock. Following the end of the war, the Navy established a radio technician training school with training aimed at cryptologic subjects. During one period, over 1000 technicians were receiving training at the same time.

During the war, the Navy's installations at Coronado Heights included both super-secret radio intelligence collection stations, and an amphibious training base for boat landings, serving as the "front." You can also see both the original main road and the main Belt Line railway to Coronado cutting right through the middle of the base. (CHA)

The October 1943 issue of *The American City* magazine carried an article by Russell W. Rink, Coronado's City Manager, about the foresight of town officials who had constructed a municipal incinerator two years earlier, thereby avoiding the difficulties neighboring communities were having disposing of their waste materials in open dumps.

January 22nd spawned what was called the worst wind and rain storm in the history of the town, sending 70 mph winds ripping across the island. Roofs were lifted off of homes, windows smashed, small craft were blown ashore, some 100 trees were uprooted, and telephone and electric lines downed. And Coronado virtually became an island, as the ocean swept over the Strand into the bay.

Mrs. Walter Cantrell of 952 "C" Avenue had five sons in the service, later a practice forbidden, and a sixth son had been killed. Yet another son was waiting for orders to report. Similarly Mr. and Mrs. James Ludlow had five children in the service. Thaddeus and James in the Navy, George and Paul in the Army, and Nina Ludlow Cassell in the WACS.

At Coronado High School, students made a flag with the names of nearly 200 graduates who had joined various branches of the U.S. Armed Forces. Among them appeared the names of Katsumi Koba, Haruki Koba, Masa Koba and Yo Koba. Throughout the year, letters appeared in the Coronado newspaper from men overseas telling of their experiences, and asking to be remembered to those at home. Some wrote of their participation in campaigns or from prison camps.

When school opened in the fall of 1942 in Coronado, 26 new teachers appeared for their classes; the ranks had been depleted by the war. Gone as well was Fred A. Boyer, Assistant Superintendent of the Coronado Unified School District and supervising Principal of the Grammar School, who had concluded 26 years of continuous service as an educator.

In November Mrs. Enrico Caruso (Dorothy), widow of the late Enrico Caruso, the famous Italian tenor, now Mrs. Dorothy Holder, moved to Hollywood from her home in New York City to supervise the filming of a motion picture on the life of her late husband. As Mrs. Dorothy Holder, she had earlier lived in Coronado on Ocean Boulevard, between Flora and Isabella.

The year 1944 began, not unusually, with a week-long windstorm and high tides. Some damage occurred again in Glorietta Bay, because sizeable "jags of lumber" were carried from the San Diego side of the bay into the channel and Glorietta Bay. Waves slopped over Ocean Boulevard, and in the bay the 60-foot schooner *Mahpe* went aground.

During April, a new street built around the bayside was named Mullinnix Drive, honoring the late Rear Admiral Henry M. Mullinix, who was lost on the USS *Liscombe Bay* in the Battle of the Gilbert Islands. President Roosevelt approved an appropriation in April for a five-classroom school to serve the children in the military housing project located at 235 Prospect Place. The Glorietta School would become part of Coronado's public school system.

By February 1944, the news leaked out that over four and a half million dollars had been allotted for barracks at North Island. A Bachelor Officers Quarters, shops and a 1,500 seat theatre, along with a mess and recreational facilities, were to be built on the Fourth street golf course property, which Rear Admiral David Worth Bagley of the 11th Naval District said "was a temporary Navy occupation." The Navy held a lease from the Spreckels Company, and still insisted that once the war ended, the property would be returned to its owners. By March 9th, the golfing green at the Coronado Country Club had been cut in half for the duration. The Navy project would cover 82 acres, on which 5,000 enlisted personnel, and 500 officers would be quartered for housing or administrative functions.

North Island as seen from Banker's Hill, c. 1942. (CHA)

In January 1944, Palmer-Built Homes Inc., started construction of 154 single-family dwellings in Coronado. Permits were granted for five-and-a-half entire city blocks in different locations. The cost was projected to be $616,000, at an average cost of $4,000 per house. In accordance with requirements of the Federal government, houses were rented to civilian war workers and their families. The reputation of Palmer-Built Homes was that they were extremely well-constructed. These three-bedroom dwellings, finished in stucco with composition shingle roofing, as required by the Federal government, sold for about $6,000. In 1976, these same houses were selling for about $60,000!

The Hakes Investment Company also built 39 new homes in the price range of $5,600 to $6,000. A large home, near Ocean Boulevard could still be purchased for $23,000.

In early 1944, the ocean-front estate of Mr. and Mrs. Thomas E. Sharp was donated to the Coronado Chapter of the American National Red Cross, in memory of their only son Donald, killed in the war. Occupying an entire block, the estate featured a grand mansion at 1100 "F" Avenue, which the Red Cross used as its headquarters for one-and-a-half years.

Tidelands areas in Coronado were in the spotlight in 1944. Earlier, through condemnation proceedings, the Federal government had sought to acquire a leasehold right, but now they wanted permanent ownership. Clarence Anderson, selected Mayor on April 20, 1944 (the first change of Mayor in six years, as Carl Ince stepped down) was notified in June 1944 of the leasehold condemnation action, involving the area at the northeast corner of the City, where civilian housing units were being built. The government had offered to pay rent for use of the land, but when the City Council refused, a notice of condemnation was predicted as a probable Federal action.

The second tidelands issue involved the controversy over the Spanish Bight and adjacent properties. The City Council received mixed signals–on the one hand a promise to return properties after the war, and on the other to acquire permanent title to this area. While the City Attorney indicated the exact location of Coronado's western boundary, the eastern boundary of North Island remained had not yet been determined. In other words, did the eastern boundary of North Island include the Spanish Bight?

To encourage women to work for the war effort, the U.S. Government also condemned park land property at Sixth and "D," for a nursery school where mothers could safely leave their young children. An $18,000 school building, said to be the first of its kind in California built and operated under a national public works program, was completed. Miss Pearl H. Braithwaite managed volunteers, many of them naval officers' wives, who helped care for the little ones. After the war, it became a children's library.

> Wartime expansion on North Island inevitably brought more traffic; therefore in 1944, the Navy pressed the San Diego and Coronado Ferry Company to add a fourth ferry to their system. The ferry company resisted, hoping perhaps for some financial assistance. The Navy countered by threatening to establish their own Navy-owned ferries. Its bluff called, the ferry company begrudgingly agreed to purchase a fourth ferry (aided by a Navy certification as "essential for the war effort"), that they named the *Silver Strand*. *Silver Strand* (formerly, the *Elwha*) had been built in 1927, providing service in San Francisco Bay and Puget Sound. She would continue in Coronado service until 1969.

At one point in 1944, the Coronado Theatre showed the movie "Corvette," with Randolph Scott and Ella Raines, and at the Saturday children's matinee, "Hi'ya Sailor" with Donald Woods and Elyse Knox.

Bowman's City Market at 960 Orange Avenue advertised:
Flour,   25 lbs.. for $1.33
Soup, 3 cans for 25 cents
Bisquick for 30 cents
Camay Soap, 3 bars for 25 cents

The A & P Market at 844 Orange Avenue offered:
Potatoes, 10 lbs.. for 33 cents
Lettuce, large head, 7 cents
Navy Beans, 1 lb.. for 12 cents
Tuna, No. 1/2 can for 23 cents
Rice Puffs for 9 cents a box

J.R. Townsend, Inc., at 718 Third and 1027 Orange Avenue, announced it was taking deposits for new cars with delivery priority. He also carried a list of new Studebakers that would be available when deliveries were possible.

Yet the war was ever-present. The Southern California Telephone Company sought applications by people to help see the war needs through. Robert B. Ferris had come home after 50 missions with the Army Air Force in Europe, and Captain Ellis Zacharias and his family were again at home at 1000 "G". He addressed the high school students on the meaning of freedom, for those who might have forgotten.

Thomas M. Rice wrote an essay that was published in the *Coronado Journal* about his jump as a paratrooper at Normandy on D-Day, Jack Carroll of 658 "B" Avenue told of his escape from the Germans, after his B-26 bomber was shot down, and Fred Boggeln Jr., wrote to his mother about the war in the Pacific.

The City Planning Commission began to plan post-war projects, estimated to cost about $200,000, including: City Hall and furnishings; harbor improvement; swimming pool, bath house and cabanas; Community Center building and furnishings; and an addition to Police Department.

As a final footnote to the enormous military presence that existed in Coronado throughout the war years, permission was finally granted by the U.S. government to fill in the Spanish Bight. The 11th Naval District awarded a bid of nearly two million dollars to accomplish the task of joining North and South Islands forever. A significant change had taken place, and the people of the Enchanted Island would feel its effects from then on.

Katherine Eitzen Carlin, author of **Coronado, The Enchanted Island**, *1st edition. (CPL)*

Naval aviator mans his plane aboard an aircraft carrier during training operations off North Island. (US Navy)

Chapter 8

1945-1959: The Post War Years & A Growing Village

SPONSORED BY FLAGSHIP PROPERTIES, CARRIE AND JOHN O'BRIEN

AT THE BEGINNING OF 1945, Coronado's population numbered 25,382 men, women and children, many of whom were military families. In five years, the population had soared from 6,932 people, who, prior to World War II, had known one another for the most part. Many young military wives came with reservations about their future, but the "veteran navy wives" gave reassurance that all would turn out well. The American Women Volunteer Services organization heard an early postwar speech by Mrs. Stanhope Nixon. The Business and Professional Women's Club heard a similar talk by Mrs. Bregitta Wilson, who said that the community had to continue with its wartime role, yet not forget that planning ahead was also important.

To boost the morale of those working to help the war effort, a Red Cross Blood Donor Rally was held in mid-January. Hollywood and Broadway stars, who were active members of the military, provided entertainment. Carnivals were held at Cutler Field to raise funds for a Coronado Youth Club. Prize fights, dancing, food, and fortune-telling provided a distraction from other daily pressing matters.

(Image above: CPL/LCC)

St Paul's Methodist Church, at the corner of D Avenue and Seventh Street. (CPL/LCC)

Mrs. Fred T. Berry, of 534 "B" Avenue, and widow of Commander F.T. Berry, christened a naval vessel named in his honor, the USS *Fred T. Berry*. Berry was lost in April, 1933, when the USS *Akron* dirigible went down off the New Jersey coast. A number of Coronadans were awarded the Air Medal, the Purple Heart, the Navy Cross, or the Legion of Merit, and, as the war in Europe neared an end, bronze and silver stars. Recent Coronado High School graduate, Yo Koba, wrote from Camp Blanding, Florida to thank the Journal for the article about his brother Masafumi. During the period of war-time Japanese internment at various camps, their father was interned at Camp Poston, Arizona. Their sister worked as a secretary at the camp.

Coronado was quiet on V-E Day (Victory in Europe), May 8, 1945. Many families still had relatives in the Pacific, and a number of persons were still in prison camps or missing in action. Churches held services commemorating the historic date and remembering those who had given their lives for the war effort. The end of the European conflict meant a semblance of return to pre-war days. The nation would never go back to its previous way of life; the scarcity of goods had created a natural inflation. A few advertisements for cars appealed to buyers: a 1938 Chrysler, 4-door sedan for $955.00, a 1939 Mercury sedan $1,112.50, a 1935 Chevrolet Town sedan $ 455.00.

The First National Bank offered 5% home loans. By May 31st, Coronado had the first supervised citywide recreation program in its history--a program submitted to the Council, which they approved without a whimper. The proposal was presented by Mrs. Hester Ann Hickey, the recreation director, after approval by the recreation committee. The purchase of between five and six hundred dual parking meters was approved at a cost of $60 each. The War Production Board announced that the "Brownout Order" was to be cancelled at 6 a.m. on Tuesday, May 8th, meaning it was now possible to use electricity for outdoor activities.

A new open air theatre called the "Palms" opened at 145 "C" Avenue with R.E. Archibald, Manager. The slogan was "Movies Under the Stars," which was just what it was – warm summer air, long wooden seats, a popcorn and soft drink stand. The town began to come to life again, with all sorts of other activities. Although the Coronado Yacht Club had reduced the number of events during the war years, that summer they kicked off the season with a variety of races and trips to military areas that had been off limits for some time. Bing Crosby, Pat O'Brien, and the Del Mar jockeys played benefit softball games, while riding donkeys (donkey softball) at Cutler Field.

Naval Air Station North Island had been a city within a city, having a population of 33,000 military and civilian personnel. Many of its servicemen had been lost in the war or taken prisoner. When VJ (Victory in Japan) Day took place on August 15, 1945, further thanks were given that the global war had finally come to an end. Word arrived through North Island of the release of U.S. prisoners. In October, Marine Major Paul A. Putnam, Commanding Officer of Wake Island, who had been a Japanese prisoner for 1,359 days, was released. Lt. Colonel Donald Spicer, taken at Guam, and Commander Campbell Keene, along with civilians Spencer Hewitt and Ray Roberts, captured at Wake Island, were all released and returned home to Coronado.

> During the latter years of the war, North Island's intense expansion added a potpourri of buildings, warehouses, hangars, repair facilities, piers and quays, recreational facilities and – of course – runways. All of these were added by necessity, but for decades afterwards, any Coronadan could easily recognize most of these wartime improvements. The most visible improvements involved reclamation of the Spanish Bight and the new construction in that area, as well as the establishment of the aircraft carrier quay wall, which could hold three carriers. Beginning immediately in 1945 and extending into the early 1950s, hundreds, if not thousands of naval aircraft were arrayed in tight rows along the western side of the base, awaiting ultimate disposal.

The City Council worked on its master plan, proposed land purchases, and attempted to pass an ordinance which would outlaw pinball machines. The Council also considered the length of time jobs needed to be held for men and women returning from the war.

The year 1946 began auspiciously with a small earthquake. On January 1st, at 4 p.m., many revelers still celebrating were jolted by the tremor. There was no damage, but the ground rumbled, causing people to rush from their houses.

Despite the happiness Coronadans felt now that the war had ended, all of the major decisions that had been put off until peacetime, came back to confront the town of Coronado. Space had become a premium, particularly in light of the close proximity of the Naval Air Station and the Amphibious Base and the loss of some major land areas, such as that along the Spanish Bight. There was no doubt that monumental problems placed on the back burner, would now have to be addressed.

The old-timers, including many retired military personnel, wanted Coronado to return to its pre-war days, with just a little bit of traffic, vacant lots, and few houses. While to islanders it seemed logical that Coronado would return to a pre-war quiet, those thoughts had little to do with reality. The reality was that Coronado had changed, in some cases irreversibly, and to gain something, one had to give up something. A great deal of compromising began. Traffic had become unbearable. Long lines of vehicles lined up from the ferry landing to Tenth Street every day, and cars circled the island on their way to the Strand from North Island. Eyes began to look toward a bridge or tube once again.

Rush hour traffic, lining up for the ferry on Orange Avenue at 6th Street, 1946. (CPL)

Early in the year, Coronado's first destructive business fire in 32 years destroyed the Island Bar and Cafe at 1031 Orange Avenue. The last fire in the business district had occurred on January 10, 1914, when a combination pool hall and tailor shop, at the approximate site of the present El Cordova Hotel, was lost.

Local businesses at the war's end had to adjust to the times, based on what became available for sale. Full-page newspaper ads included: The Yarn Mart (1136 Loma), Perkins Flowers (1114 Orange), Town & Country Shop (1118 Orange), Andre Grimaud, Landscaping, Arthur L. Cohen, Real Estate (861 Orange), Coronado Furniture (1009 Orange), Gordon Skinner, Photography (1202 Orange).

The Free Brothers opened a market at the corner of 10th, Orange, and Isabella. The Colony, at 1107 Orange Avenue, had Sunday dinners which included an appetizer, soup, salad, two vegetables, dessert, a drink, and entree: Lobster Newburg ($1.75); Prime Rib au jus ($1.50); Baked Meat Loaf ($1); or a choice from seven other entrees. Crown Shops was a new distinctive shopping center, which opened May 15th on "C" Avenue, between 10th and Orange, and included Oscar's Drivein Cafe, the Coronado Upholstery & Drapery Shop, Coronado Sport and Hobby Shop, The Deb Shop, Laing's Appliances, Higgs Jewelers, White's Shoes, and Elva's Beauty Shop.

The Mexican Village had an informal opening on July 1st, 1946. Jim and Polly Calvert, who also owned the Island Cafe, Jim Burtron, and Carl Betts owned the popular restaurant. The Calverts sponsored Coronado's former athletes on a team in the San Diego Basketball League, which won the championship. Team members were paid off with a house specialty drink named, "The Islander."

Bowling at the Strand Bowling Alleys, 952 Orange Avenue, c. 1946. (CPL)

The team included forwards Art Blaisdell, Fred Gurney, Ray Brandes, and Herbert Hakes; centers Bud Ingle, Art Dewar, and Bill Johns; guards Herman Reidlinger, Stanley Gurney, Buddy Hakes, Roy Farmer, Walter Lowe, and Allan Galpin; Stan Norris was coach and manager.

In October 1946, a former four-bed ward was converted to a children's clinic at Coronado Hospital. An $8,000 gift from the Coronado Branch of the American Women's Volunteer Services made this possible.

To bring the news to Coronadans, the *Coronado Compass* and the *Coronado Shopping News*, a small eight-page tabloid with very little editorial content, made its first appearance. The paper was edited by Richard M. Riddell, a former U.S. Marine Corps officer. Though the Compass proclaimed in its masthead that it was 100% Coronado-owned and operated, the publisher remained anonymous for the first few issues. Finally, to quell the spate of rumors, Louis de Ryk Millen, a 35-year resident of Coronado, revealed he was the owner of the paper. Millen was vice-president of Strand Realty Company and president of the Coronado Realty Board. The *Coronado Compass* expanded its editorial content to a six-page broadsheet, requiring a paid subscription, causing no end of consternation to rival *Coronado Journal*. The Compass claimed a circulation of 6,500, before it was sold in 1952.

Aviation-minded Coronadans had their sights set on a dredged strip of land on the Amphibious Base, which extended into the bay on the Strand side, as the perfect place for an airport. The new site was to be called the Silver Strand Skyport. Former pilots, encouraged by the Veteran's Administration educational benefits program, promoted the idea. The plan, spearheaded by Bradley Woolman Jr., received approval from the Federal Aviation Administration, but with obvious Navy objections. The plan was rejected by the County Board of Supervisors. Most Coronado residents felt the skies were already too full of planes and noise.

Early in January 1946, the Chamber of Commerce began a serious campaign for rebuilding, after lagging throughout the war years. It played a role, along with governmental affairs officials in the City, in facilitating the building of a new U.S. Post Office on "B" Street, between Ynez Place and Orange Avenue. The Coronado Youth Club, a recreation center near Cutler Field, dedicated March 30th, was the first of its kind in the United States built entirely with citizen support, at a cost of $25,000.

The March 26, 1946, edition of the *Coronado Journal* included a map showing the architectural renderings and locations of City Hall, the library and the police department around Spreckels Park, and proposing the Amphibious Base area for an anticipated Silver Strand Skyport, and a recreation area. The master plan adopted by the City Council on May 11, 1942, was to be voted on during City elections on April 9, 1946. A proposed bond issue of $131,800 would finance the municipal buildings. When voting day came, however, for financially conservative reasons, voters rejected the bond issues. In hindsight, the failure to approve the monies needed cost Coronado taxpayers much more in dollars and services in the long run.

With overwhelming demand around the country for veterans' housing, and with wartime production quickly converting to peacetime industries, the U.S. government banned certain types of construction. Most construction projects set to begin after a March 26th deadline (declared by the government) were forbidden, unless they had to do with building veterans' housing. A proposed theater building in the 800 block of Orange Avenue, and two stores for Coronado Homes, Inc., were approved. John Washington, contractor for those buildings and the new post office had filed the appropriate paperwork prior to the March 26th deadline. But the Sacred Heart Parish School project was put on hold, because the contractor did not complete his paperwork on time. The school had to wait.

The coming of buses on June 1, 1947 brought removal of street car tracks from the center of Orange Avenue. Buses, filled with passengers, boarded the ferries and made regular stops in Coronado. While much citizen opposition had been raised to the introduction of buses, the compelling reason to allow them seemed to be the need for faster transportation and fewer cars.

The U.S.O. on the Strand, located about one-quarter mile south of the Hotel del Coronado, had opened in a government-constructed building in November 1944. Since its opening, it was operated by a Citizens Committee for about two years. The club, about to close, had been heavily used during the war, when thousands of people from Coronado and nearby cities had helped make wartime away from home bearable for servicemen and women. Just prior to the New Year 1946, square dances took place, and Christmas and New Year's Eve programs were held, but everyone knew these were the last parties to be presented in the building. It closed on February 23, 1947, after hosting and entertaining half a million military personnel there.

The U.S. Government wanted to sell the U.S.O. building to any organization that would buy it, despite its deteriorating condition. The price of $17,000, plus $1,800 for the furniture, attracted no takers. Then Federal housing authorities said, "If it is not bought, it will be locked up." They "locked it up." The building became an armory for the National Guard, and was used for various purposes until May 8, 1976, when it was turned over to the City of Coronado.

Residents on Glorietta Boulevard held community meetings to object to the planned street lighting of this boulevard, protesting that there was enough reflection from other sources. Without further prompting, City planners took the funds allocated and placed lights on other streets.

This aerial photo shows the area formerly occupied by Tent City. Note the USO building in the foreground, and the growing Naval Amphibious Base, c. late 1940s. (CPL/LCC)

World War II would never be forgotten. Many Coronado residents would remember honors awarded and deep friendships made; others would cherish memories of lost loved ones. Captain Henry T. Stanley, 300 "B" Street, became a Chevalier of the Legion of Honor. He was awarded the Croix de Guerre, with a palm, for services performed in France. Fred E. Boggeln, 822 "C" Street, was featured in an article in the Journal on April 11, 1946, and photographed in uniform.

Major A.E. Shaefer, who left the school system during the war to serve in the intelligence service, came home about the same time that Captain John C. Waters returned to practice dentistry. Malissa A. Carlsson, a former WAVE, was the first woman admitted to Legion Membership in Coronado Post 450. H.W. Reed had been senior military governor of Coblenz, Germany. He was a recipient of a Purple Heart, four battle stars, and Belgium's Order of Leopold. Reed turned down offers to return as City Manager at a salary of $3,600 a year. It was the same salary he had received in pre-war days, which, in his view, was tantamount to a decrease, considering the increase in the cost of living.

De-regulation might have been the best way to describe some of the early events of the year 1947. The Office of Price Administration's regulations governing daily rates of rooms in hotels and motor courts were abolished on February 15th. The Sacred Heart Parish School project was finally given approval to be built (by the Golden Construction Company) at a cost of $100,000.

The Coronado Woman's Club was organized on March 5, 1947, by a group of 10 women, under the leadership of Mrs. Merle R. Francis, and incorporated in 1948. Members took part in seven activities: Garden, Music, Sewing, Spanish, Speak Easy, Book, and Home Decoration. The founders included Mesdames Merle R. Francis, Clarence T. Anderson, Elwin T. Anderson, Robert A. Bradt, Merrill H. Duncan, Charles C. Latham, Lyman H. Latham, Hubert L. Rose, Huge M. Rush and Martin Wicarius. Not until April 1958, did the organization find a suitable location for a clubhouse; they later broke ground for an $80,000 building on land leased from the City on Glorietta Bay.

After the death of John D. Spreckels, the Spreckels' lands were offered for sale to Coronado and purchase recommended by the City Planning Commission on May 26, 1947. R.S. Regal, Spreckels representative, met with the City Council to discuss the lands that would cost about $729,000. The areas included: 1) 13 acres along First Street where the WAVE Barracks had been; 2) all of the ground which had been the 18-hole golf course (between First and Tenth, west of Alameda); 3) an additional 26 acres that had been filled along Alameda; 4) the "Hog Ranch" on the Strand; and 5) an additional 40-odd acres. Discussions over the Spanish Bight did not occur because it had been filled with sand. Talks and negotiations continued throughout the year.

Vacant land to the east of the fire station was purchased by the City for $16,800; the grand jury had long condemned the jail and the rented City Hall headquarters. The City asked the Federal government its intention regarding the lease or purchase of the Naval Amphibious Base land. All of this, however, represented little more than talk.

The Coronado Yacht Club secured a lease on its present property on Glorietta Bay in 1946 and started to develop the area. A government surplus building, which had once been the mess hall and the galley of the WAVE's quarters on the bay side of First Street, was moved in 1947 onto the Yacht Club property. The building was cut into sections, loaded on barges, and shipped around the bay. It was unloaded at the new site and remodeled into a 5,000-sq. ft. clubhouse, which opened with great fanfare in June 1947.

Coronado Yacht Club, c. 1959. (CPL/LCC)

At the high school, students received a memorial plaque for Coronado High alumni who died during World War II: Henry Bramstedt, Kenneth Brown, Ronald Hutchinson, LaVerne Jones, Paul Lowthian, Lane Miller, Seymour Owens, Richard Pierce, Donald Sharp, Phillip Weems, and Bernard Wilson.

After 43 years as a Coronado teacher, Miss Josephine Drewisch, 815 "D" Avenue, retired. She had been an exceptional teacher and there were few people in Coronado she did not know. She taught several second generation pupils, and in one instance the third generation.

The year 1948 can be characterized by three main areas of effort. The first involved the sale of the Hotel del Coronado. Rumors regarding a proposed sale were heard around City Hall about the time the Spreckels interests were discussing transfer of properties with the City. A syndicate, headed by Robert A. Nordblom, a socially prominent financier and hotel operator in New York and Boston, completed the acquisition of the Hotel del Coronado on January 22, 1948.

Then suddenly came the startling headline, "Hotel Changes Hands Twice in 24 Hours." Mr. Barney Goodman of Tucson, Arizona became the new owner. Nordblom may have been simply brought in because he met the requirements contained in the Spreckels acquisition presentation, indicating he would continue his plans to develop other parcels of land purchased in Coronado. Goodman, in addition acquired other properties formerly belonging to the Coronado Beach Company, including the Oxford Hotel and the Hotel Annex on Ynez Place.

La Avenida restaurant was a longtime, popular restaurant that served celebrities and local families. The famous interior murals created by Mexican painter Alfredo Ramos Martinez were salvaged and restored. Two of them hang in the Coronado Public Library. (CPL)

An immediate change in policy occurred on September 8, 1948, when longtime permanent residents of the Hotel were informed they would have to pay as much as other guests or move. These year-round residents had been granted special rates by the Spreckels Company, but Goodman termed them "display guests." Some of these guests had fled from abroad during and after World War I. Others were victims of the Great Depression of the 1930s. Most had very little money, just their pride, which Mr. Spreckels encouraged them to retain. They lived at the Hotel in style--giving it some distinction and atmosphere. In a sense, they lent an Old World grandeur to the Hotel del Coronado, but Goodman saw matters through different eyes.

Located on the Strand, about four miles southwest of the Hotel, was a hilly piece of sandy land with windswept rolling dunes, ending in a plateau on the bayside. Across the road was a broad expanse of ocean beach, with some 280 acres in the two parcels. The Spreckels Companies had acquired the land when they bought out the Beach Company and leased it to the Riis family who raised hogs. They had a contract to feed the Hotel's garbage to the animals. Eventually people began to haul their trash and junk to the farm. Everyone used it, with the *Coronado Journal* reporting that "the Navy never disposed of anything smaller than a used battleship there." Coronado had tried hauling its trash to Otay, but this proved too costly.

In April, Councilman Archibald D. Abel, and representatives of Nordblom, discussed a contract with the City to dump garbage on the Hog Ranch, but the new owners of the Hotel would not consider a lease option to buy the Hog Ranch. Optimistically, Mayor George F. Neal said another place could be found, perhaps more distant. So, while seeking an alternative, the town sanitation department extended the municipal trash dump area, from the present-day grocery store parking lot on B Avenue, towards the bay front.

Hotel del Coronado owner Goodman and his partners then divulged plans, estimated to cost $3,500,000, to develop the golf course property at the west end of Ocean Boulevard. Included were a 170-room resort hotel; but the developers did not anticipate the sentiments at City Hall. Councilmen and planners, unhappy over the Hog Ranch deal, refused to change zoning regulations to allow construction. The Navy openly expressed its opposition to a hotel, since this was right in the flight pattern of its airstrip plans. Citizens were infuriated at the thought of a development at North Beach, and railed against it during a number of hearings at City Hall. The Council voted to approve a zoning exception for the Hotel, but with nine major conditions, which could not possibly have been met by the developers.

In August, the Planning Commission granted zoning exceptions for a proposed subdivision along the west side of Alameda Boulevard: 107 lots, one-and-a-half blocks in depth from the site of the new proposed hotel, to be within 480 feet of Fourth Street.

In March, the Spreckels interests sold the San Diego Electric Railway Company and the San Diego and Coronado Ferry to a company that operated transit lines in several other western cities. Owner Jesse L. Haugh of Oakland announced that the new name of the company, purchased for $5,500,000, would be the San Diego Transit System. Some of the old cars were converted into homes; others were moved to Mission Valley for aircraft workers; some were simply hauled to the waterfront and burned, while some found their way to Madrid, Buenos Aires, and to cities in Portugal and Italy.

> The City had sold the ocean side of the "Hog Ranch" to the California State Parks, leaving 231 acres of the original 280 acres of the ranch. A bond election for $175,000 was held in 1948 to purchase the Hog Ranch property (also known as Brickyard Cove, as it was used by the Coronado Beach Company as the site of an old brick kiln for hotel and other uses). The bond was initially defeated, but was rewritten, reintroduced, and passed later in 1948, thanks, in part, to some clever spin the City applied to the argument. First, the Hog Ranch received an official name--Rancho Carrillo--perhaps to provide some class to a garbage dump. The City was also careful to point out that not all of the Hog Ranch would be used for rubbish; a portion of it would be saved for "recreational purposes." What they didn't mention was that this goal would not be realized for another two decades. Finally, the City stated that annual fees the town received from the Navy for leasing Naval Amphibious Base property would be used to retire the bond – correct, but this represented a minor amount.

Then came plans revealed by the Coronado Development company, headed by M. Bert Fisher and Herman Miller, for a multimillion dollar development along the bayside of First Street. Their plans included a commercial hotel, apartment houses, yacht basin, a beach, and a tennis and racquet club. Preliminary plans also called for construction of two streets running parallel to Alameda Boulevard, comprising multiple and single residential units. As expected, these proposals upset the residents on First Street. Nonetheless, the City Council approved preliminary plans for subdividing the property on the bay for a tract of residential homes. The Coronado Development Company hoped to sell the lots (the minimum size would be 8,000 square feet), where the WAVES' barracks had once existed.

Several committees appointed by acting Mayor E.G. Stanley studied questions raised by neighborhood residents about the development. Benson Scott, a former Planning Commission Chairman, stated that, in his opinion, it would be mutually beneficial to the property owners and the City for an outer drive to be planned along the bayside waterfront area. Colonel James MacMullen and others argued the idea, the first time the concept of a loop road had been brought forward.

Other areas of the town began to deteriorate. G.K. Williams, who owned the *Coronado Journal*, wrote that not too many years before, over 300 yachts had come to "Opening Day" at Glorietta Bay. But during the last celebration, only 14 yachts came, and two of those had run aground. Commodore Wyatt called for the bay to be properly dredged, in order to build a reputation for a fabulous yacht harbor. Roland C. Hoyt, landscape architect, brought out his plan to improve the center strip on Orange Avenue at a cost of $13,800. The improvements included a sprinkling system to irrigate a variety of trees, plants and shrubs. However, funding for the landscaping was not approved and the plans were abandoned.

Nordblom's interests had purchased the golf course, but four local men who feared the loss of the links leased the land. Adam Messek, E.F. Kohl, E.R. Demetrion and Paul Davy wanted to preserve the golf course, that would have been wiped out when housing was constructed in the golf course area. In a very short time, the Coronado Country Club proved to be a success as over 1,000 golfers regularly used the golf course. They made the course pay, and became heroes in the eyes of their golfing friends. The land was eventually subdivided into building lots in the 1950s, becoming the Country Club Estates.

The last of the vast Spreckels holdings once owned in Coronado was sold to Clara N. Parker, J.W. Rodes, and Mark Beauchamp, Jr. near the end of 1948. The property involved two blocks in the northeastern corner of Coronado, then occupied by the Federal Housing Project. The group's idea was to create a long-term investment. The Federal government still held the lease for another six months, so no immediate plans were made to develop the property.

The old Spreckels' estate, now the James S. Copley residence and the "Marsh Tea Gardens," was made available to Coronado for use as a civic center, but was turned down as unsuitable. Thus, a chance for a "showplace" City Hall, with adequate space for future additions and developments, was shoved aside. The U.S.O. building issue still haunted the townspeople. A hearing was set on May 21, 1949, to again consider its purchase for use as a City Hall. The price was set "as is" at $10,000. When the Council could not agree, the purchase was shelved, pending voter approval.

In late 1949, the Spreckels-Copley grounds and mansion, rejected by the town, were purchased by Louis de Ryk Millen and Allen J. Sutherland of the San Diego Trust & Savings Bank as co-owners. Plans were announced a year later to convert the mansion to a commercial property. The plans were to construct a hotel/motel with cottages to be added sometime later. The surrounding grounds were to be subdivided into 17 lots for apartment and residential sites. A local realtor bought several lots on the former site of the famous Marsh Japanese Tea Gardens. He built a home for himself on the corner of Ynez and Adella, and later resold the remaining land.

> Beginning in March 1949, and extending to January 1951, the Coronado City Council passed at least four different resolutions addressing different parcels of Silver Strand land for annexation. The impetus of these actions was undoubtedly triggered by concerns around the Hog Ranch, but the land at the southern end of the Silver Strand was either unincorporated or federally owned, and there was some concern that if Coronado did not annex, then someone else would. The mayor provided the City's public position on these annexations in early 1951: "The City is a congested residential community in which a large part of the land has already been devoted to dwelling users. There is need for additional areas for future residential, recreational, and commercial expansion."
>
> The mechanism the City used to annex lands on the Silver Strand was a state law allowing communities to expand through annexation of adjacent "uninhabited land." The San Diego and Arizona Railroad, that owned the right of way up the Strand for its tracks, initially opposed the effort. This had the effect of delaying any potential City of Coronado action from 1948 into 1949. Annexation efforts spurred rumors in unincorporated Imperial Beach that Coronado wanted to extend even further to the south, rumors that were adamantly denied by Coronado. Annexation actions not only included the physical land involved, but also clarified title to the attendant bay and ocean areas. All were ultimately approved by the State in April 1950 and March 1951. In December 1951, a surveyed measurement of the annexation tallied the total as: land area, 1636 acres; water area, 15,458 acres; total 18,194 acres.

Along Orange Avenue, Jno. R. Robertson's Super Chevrolet Service had a special on motor overhauls for $56.95; the Coronado Department Store advertised Gibson Girl Cottons, two pieces, v-tucked and checked bodice dresses for $14.98; Coronado Texaco Service advertised 600 x 16 tires for $12.95 and 700 x 16 tires for $18.30. The Coronado Theatre's marquee advertised a rerun of "Gone with the Wind" in February 1949, and the new Coronado Theatre was to open on September 1st.

Coronado High School football players out at the movies, c. 1948/49. Note Beachcombers next door to the Village Theater. (CHA)

In the school system, A.E. Schaefer, Principal of Coronado High School since 1940, became Superintendent of the School District. Max Forney, Principal of the Junior High and Elementary Schools since 1943, resigned. Howard Duff, the movie actor, congratulated half-back Jim Voit, who was named to the All-Metro football team. In athletics, the high school basketball and football teams had great success. The 1948 VFW Colts football team coached by Tody Greene was made up of former CHS football and local stars who won six of their nine games.

Lingering news from World War II, mingled with reports of a possible conflict in Southeast Asia. Draft registration began Monday, August 30th for all men between the ages of 18 and 26. They were required to register regardless of previous military service, draft standing, marital status or membership in the National Guard or Reserves. Arthur L. Goodale and John G. Hedemann of Coronado were among the 10 first peacetime draftees to report to Fort Ord.

Lane Miller, who had been reported missing in action during the War, received the Czechoslovakian War Cross for his participation in the Slovak National Uprising in 1944. He had parachuted into that country and became involved in the conflict. Mrs. Therese E. Alexander, whose Navy dentist husband was killed in the bombing of Pearl Harbor, began her fight to get her widow's pension raised from $50 to $65 per month. At that time, all widows' pensions were the same, regardless of the husband's rank or how many years he had served. Through her untiring work, she was able to persuade the U.S. Government that military widows deserved a raise. She later took up other causes for the rights of these women, and in 1968, organized the Society of Military Widows. The group began with only 32 members, but later incorporated as a national organization, with over 1,150 service widow members.

In April 1949, the 16 buildings constructed on the Country Club property to house Navy personnel during World War II, were sold for demolition and salvage. Construction of the new golf links, along with water mains and sewer lines for the Country Club Estates began within sixty days. The venerable Coronado car barn, which had occupied a prominent spot at Orange Avenue and First Street for 29 years, was dismantled and sold for salvage.

A Center Beach Pavilion on Ocean Boulevard was proposed by City Manager Howard Fuller in April 1949. A place with a large promenade deck was desired for community gatherings. Plans for band concerts, public rest rooms, dressing facilities, and a life guard station were discussed. Public outcry against the visualized center killed the idea because the center would attract too many vehicles and people to a residential area.

The City Council acted to end wartime rent control in 1949. Voted on before an overflow crowd in August, the new ruling became effective in December. Coronado's annual large storm, which usually came in December or January, arrived a bit early, on October 29th, when gusts of northerly winds seventy miles an hour toppled trees. Rain and hail accompanied the early morning winds.

Thanksgiving and Christmas that year were beautiful and sunny. But, as if to mark the close of the decade, Mother Nature provided a 22-second earthquake on a December 1949 afternoon, during the Christmas weekend shopping rush. The shake gave the store clerks and the shoppers a thrill as they held on to one another while running for the street.

The year 1950 was one in which Coronado got some badly needed changes, due to the upswing in the economy. There were a number of suggestions for use of the Rancho Carrillo property belonging to the City, such as riding stables, a gun club, trailer court, motel, and a golf driving range. The Planning Committee viewed all these possibilities for leases. In February, the City Council approved the map for the First Street Subdivision and development, although a week earlier there had been much skepticism. The plan was "roasted" by the residents facing the bay. Bay View Estates would take all of their view!

The census in 1950 recorded 12,700 people, a considerable drop from 1945. That did not mean, however, lesser hopes and desires for a better community. One vision imagined moratoriums on building construction, and no easy access to the island. Another concept called for environmental control with less noise, fewer visitors and more open space. Developers had different plans in mind. In January 1950, the announcement was made that the Country Club Estates were ready for development.

By March 30th, the Country Club and riding stables, those old familiar landmarks, had been dismantled. With the subdivision map already approved, the developers finished plans to sell the lots. The town had opened itself to a policy of growth, whether the realization had sunk in or not. But why did the City Council permit developers to use so much of the remaining open space for residential purposes? Herein lies a critical turning point in Coronado's history.

A number of landmarks that once made the village a nationally renowned place to live--the golf course, the polo grounds, the Country Club, and the riding ring and stables--all fell to the blows of a wrecking ball. With these buildings went a bit of Curtiss, Spreckels, Dupee, Ross, and even the memory of the original golf course that stretched from bay to ocean.

At a town meeting in February, Howard Murray, a Los Angeles engineer, discussed plans for a "subaqueous" (underwater) tube linking Coronado and San Diego. The matter of a bridge was first mentioned in 1889. People grumbled about the ferry service in 1912. Military activities in World War I pointed up the need for easy access to the two "islands." Vessels could not go under a bridge said some townspeople, while others thought vessels would hit a tube or tunnel. In the 1920s, people were happy with Coronado just the way it was, away from the rest of the world. The seclusion was ideal, and the route to Agua Caliente an easy one. From 1926 until 1949, there were "tube committees," and "no-tube committees."

Still in 1950, the controversy raged. Full-page ads in newspapers and periodicals called for $200,000 to undertake a survey on the feasibility of a tube. In an informal poll, Coronado's residents favored a tube to replace the San Diego ferry. By the end of the year, legislators sought an enabling act, which would permit voters to decide if they wanted an underwater traffic tube connecting Coronado and San Diego.

The matter of inadequate school facilities arose, and engineers reported that the buildings no longer conformed to updated earthquake building codes. A.E. Schaefer said the 1923 high school building had been declared vulnerable to earthquake damage in official reports as early as 1934.

The City's first medical/dental building opened August 11th at 10th and "C," with 46 rooms. A group of Coronadans, led by J. Harold Peterson, put up a fight to get the orange trees re-planted on Orange Avenue. The fight created a stir, so much so that one round was held in the high school

Carrier 'Essex' (CV-9) pulling into the North Island quay in 1951, preparing for a deployment to Korea. Note shoreline along First Street in the background with the Coronado water tower. (CHA)

auditorium to accommodate the large crowd of citizens who had plenty to say. On August 17, the City Council vetoed the proposition to plant orange trees on Orange Avenue. They recalled that the orange trees, for which the Avenue was named, lasted only one season due to jack rabbits eating all the roots.

In the matter of civic improvements, a committee was formed with Rear Admiral Ajax H. Gray, U.S.N. RET as chairman, and developed a list of projects they felt were important to the community. These included sewage disposal, fire and police station buildings, library additions, improvements of Glorietta Bay, and a variety of recreational, educational, vocational and entertainment needs. The timing was bad, however, since the Korean War had begun on June 25, 1950, and would not end until 1953. In many ways, Coronado went through a repetition of World War II, with the military bases crowded, the war plants busy, an influx of people, and the stress of having loved ones gone to an area of the world scarcely known to Americans.

Almost immediately censorship came into effect again so that information about troop and ship movements ceased. Coronado aircraft carriers Philippine Sea, Boxer, Sicily, and Badoeing Strait rushed to the front, with accompanying escorts. Coronado men were reported in Korea within a month. First Lieutenant William T. Wygal was in the action; he had served in World War II. By August 24, lists of Korean War casualties were filtering back. The Coronado Disaster Council prepared instructions for townspeople to be prepared for an atomic bomb attack.

Many residents were recalled to active duty. Police Officer John Jeffers went back into the Army, and F.B. Van Valkenburg returned to the Navy. Not too long before, realtors had been putting up "For Rent" signs. Now there were no signs because there simply were no vacancies. Service families from 14 states moved into Coronado within a short time. Hints on ways to find a house included making the acquaintance of a milkman, laundry truck driver, or listening in on farewells spoken over grocery counters.

Lieutenant Commander William Thomas Amen, of 601 Fifth Street, was reported to have shot down the first enemy jet in combat history. Lieutenant Commander Louis W. Church, a U.S. Naval flier, was wounded when he was shot down 125 miles behind enemy lines in Korea. He was rescued by helicopter. The aircraft carrier USS *Valley Forge* returned from the conflict with many Coronadans aboard.

Reports filtered back about local residents killed or wounded in battle; a number of men received decorations. Lieutenant Robert Hunt, U.S.M.C., of 820 "D" Avenue received the Silver Star for heroism in action. Lieutenant Kenneth Wade, an F9F pilot on the USS *Princeton*, was making forays into Korea, as was Captain Harry T. Galpin of the Air Force. As ships returned home, the scarcity of housing created innumerable problems for families.

A highly visible sight for many Coronadans, where UDT personnel trained with helicopters in San Diego Bay. (CHA)

The specialized force of Navy Underwater Demolition Teams (UDT) had been dramatically reduced with the end of World War II to just two West Coast-based Teams, UDT-1 and UDT-3. These two teams, and their assigned boats, were based in Quonset huts and other buildings on the ocean beach side of the Naval Amphibious Base. Personnel from UDT-1/3 (and UDT-5 that was formed in September 1951, and also based in Coronado) were sent to Korea for combat missions. With their knowledge and experience in clandestine operations and explosives, their missions expanded for the first time in Korea to that of maritime commandos blowing up and attacking targets behind enemy lines. This was the beginning of specialized training, based on Coronado beaches, which in the 1960s would be redefined as that of U. S. Navy SEALs.

Town fathers were still concerned about the condition of municipal facilities. State regulations were being enforced, which were bent on destruction of buildings declared unsafe. This became a very controversial issue, with sides clearly drawn between those who favored demolition, and those who believed that buildings designed by outstanding architects and representatives of a town's heritage were worth preserving. Those words fell on deaf ears. Captain Henry G.S. Wallace attempted to get Governor Earl Warren's attention. He argued that the school buildings were safe in case of an earthquake and could be strengthened. The City was prevented from doing so because Coronadans did not pass outrageous school bonds put before them in May 1950. But, renderings of a proposed new kindergarten/primary school building appeared in the April 19, 1951, issue of the newspaper.

The next important question revolved around what to do about the government housing at the northeast corner of town. Under the Housing Act of 1950, eviction of tenants would commence on March 31, 1951, and work on demolition begin July 1, 1952. Emergency provisions of the Act empowered the Federal government to keep units for housing of service members, Federal, and civil service personnel in areas where it could be proven that a definite need for such facilities existed. The Coronado Apartment/Hotel Owners Association began to fight the Housing Project, saying the so many housing units were hurting their business. The Housing Project may not have been pleasing to look at, but the Navy showed a strong interest in the welfare of its personnel. There was a real need for housing, as evidenced by the fact that a waiting list contained 7,500 names; therefore the housing would remain in place for a time.

Work finally began in August 1951, on the Country Club Estates, with 100 homes to be built on a portion of the old golf course on Alameda Boulevard. These homes were designed to sell for up to $20,000. Lots sold ranged from $4,000 to $6,000, with down payments on homes averaging $6,000. The manager in charge of the company's tract office declared, "This company is the one that developed the bay frontage property along First Street a few years ago, and sold some of the most beautiful homes in Coronado." His was not a statement people wanted to hear. He then predicted that "The Country Club section is the last major real estate development possible on the island. . . ." He added that the company was not entirely new in the construction business on the island, having had a part in building Naval Air Station North Island for the Navy!

Citizens pressured the Council to provide deed restrictions as lot sales were made in the Country Club Estates Annex area of the proposed housing development. Concern focused on drainage and sewage disposal where mosquitos might breed or small children might drown. No provision had been made for school facilities and the project developers were reminded that the City had a tree planting program, which had to be observed. Innumerable questions arose. The City engineer resigned and the Planning Commission returned the matter to Council for action. The map of the Country Club Estates Annex was accepted June 24, 1952, with provisions to create an area compatible with the rest of the town.

New Coronado Country Club Estates Home (Coronado Public Library).

The town dump at the foot of "B" Avenue on the bay was closed without remorse. It had been in use practically since the beginning of the Beach Company's development.

The Coronado Theatre in the "Spreckels Building" was to be given up, and an offer appeared in the newspaper, from the owner to the town, suggesting a 20-year lease at $500 a month to use the auditorium as the City Hall. The real estate agent making the proposal pointed out that the quarters, for which the City was already paying $200 a month, were small and cramped, and without a suitable area for public hearings. Unfortunately, the offer was rebuffed.

The Coronado newspaper reported that Admiral Ellis Zacharias and his wife had returned to Coronado from Washington, D.C., and that his two books, "Secret Mission" and "Behind Closed Doors" were selling extremely well. The *Coronado Journal* would, in late 1952, have two newcomers at the helm: Reuben Plevinsky and George K. Williams. Each was a former newspaperman, tired of retirement; thus they purchased the *Coronado Journal-Compass* in late 1952. They renamed the paper *The Coronado Journal*, and established a graphic format that would last for several more decades. Williams' first editorial column, "High Tide," was printed on December 4, 1952, and established him as a person bent on "progress, strong on big development, and all out for the bay bridge."

In November 1952, 42 small cedar trees were planted down the center of the Orange Avenue medium strip as individual memorials, donated by caring citizens. Mrs. Blanche Hervey, whose idea had taken form, thought a living tree would be a lasting and worthwhile tribute to the memory of her deceased husband Arthur, a pharmacist who for many years had worked at the Central Drug Store.

The original Mexican Village restaurant was a local hangout for Navy officers and celebrities. (CHA)

The trees, first lit in this fashion in December 1953, were dedicated to:

First Street:
       In Memory of Catherine G. Fawler; dedicated by Jane Lesher
       2nd Lieutenant Brian D.S. McGlynn, born in 1928; killed in action 1952;
          dedicated by His Friends
       John Edmund Alcaraz; dedicated by His Family
       Captain George E. Mavix, U.S.N.; dedicated by Eda B. and David M. Mavix

Second Street:
       Mr. and Mrs. John W. Crawford; dedicated by the Family
       George H. Crawford; dedicated by L. M. Crawford, G. G. Crawford & Helen Y. Ingle
       Captain and Mrs. WM. Crose; dedicated by Janet Crose Stanley
          and Catherine C. Crose

Third Street:
       Lieutenant Commander Henry J. Gowan; dedicated by Ida Gowan
       Frederick G. Hostetter; dedicated by Jane Lesher, Donated by Camille P. Wyatt

Fourth Street:
       Lawrence P. Priddy Jr.
       CDR James L. Manion, Medical Corps; dedicated by his wife and daughter
       Mrs. Arthur Hervey; dedicated by the Hervey Family

Fifth Street:
> William and Emily Muirhead; dedicated by the Family
> Mr. and Mrs. D.P. Vernetti; dedicated by James P. Vernetti
> Lieutenant John H. Hampshire, SC, U.S.N.; dedicated by Frances Hampshire

Sixth Street:
> Anna Holliday and George W. Smith; dedicated by I. S. Kennett and L. M. Kennett
> John Preston Clark Jr., dedicated by Mother and Dad
> Miss Jessie Miller; dedicated by Mrs. Thomas T. Beattie

Seventh Street:
> Hilliard W. Koehler and Edward Koehler; dedicated by the Koehler Family
> John E. Hathaway and Annie H. Hathaway; dedicated by the Coronado Woman's Club

Eighth Street:
> Leroy F. Reilley; dedicated by Mary B. Rielly and Jenney E. Chevvy
> Charlie Napolitano; dedicated by the Family
> Louis Gordon Campbell; dedicated by Mrs. John S. Walton, Mother
> William S. Millen and Sarah C. Millen; dedicated by Louis de Ryk Millen

Ninth Street:
> Edith Kirby Walker; dedicated by Mrs. John S. Walton, daughter
> Rear Admiral A. T. Beauregard; dedicated by Countess M. De Chilly, his widow
> William John G. Whiley and Laura E. Whiley; dedicated by Dr. Elena W. Wilson
> In Memory of her Mother; dedicated by Edna M. Wall

Tenth Street:
> Melvin and Eileen Free
> Mm. E. SchumannHeink; dedicated by M. J. Goodbody and Barbara S.H. Goodbody
> Joseph A. Vilim and Elizabeth I. Vilim; dedicated by Mark Vilim

"C" Avenue:
> Rod, Jack, and Annette Worlick; dedicated by Harry L. Perkins, Jr.

"B" Avenue:
> Anne Goodbody, Arthur Lee Bailache and Walter Wilson Crosby

The constant issues that had plagued the City Council after World War II, continued to headline the newspapers. The Council looked for an inexpensive way to ease out of the Coronado Federal (Navy) Housing project on the northeast side of Coronado. In 1953, the City of Coronado petitioned the Federal Administration to turn over all the units occupying the Navy project land. If, and when, the property was turned over by the Federal government, it was projected to net Coronado a tidy sum in leases. A letter from the Commandant of the 11th Naval District informed the Council that the Navy Department in Washington, D.C., had approved the transfer of the housing to the City of Coronado, and the Navy Department released all claims to the two Federal Housing Projects on February 26, 1954.

The *Coronado Journal* was careful to editorialize that the City would only operate the big housing development as long as a need for this kind of accommodation existed. So the arrangement for the apartments, worth an estimated $2,232,000, with an approximate $100,000 yearly profit, was completed. The Council set up a Housing Policy Committee, with George K. Sanford in charge. Skeptics thought the housing would be far from "temporary." And, since many of the buildings were 12-years old and little had been spent on repairs, the project began to become an eyesore.

With both World War II and the Korean War over by late 1953, the Council began to phase out the dwellings. A petition signed by 1,300 tenants of the project requested reconsideration by the City, but this only brought a fast move by a company that proceeded to tear down the first five

Glorietta School (1944 – 1976) stood across the street from Coronado Hospital, serving children of military housing, located where the Marriott Hotel and Tidelands Park are today. (CHA)

buildings in the complex, starting at the corner of Mullinnix Drive and Glorietta Boulevard. The Navy protested because there was no low-cost housing for personnel, and for 1,000 Navy families in need of such housing, the situation became critical.

Councilman Robin Goodenough, who appeared to have a handle on the situation, pointed out two major factors: the money derived from the housing had provided Coronado with funding to maintain a number of facilities planned in the near future, and, arbitrary action by the Council could seriously interfere with negotiations for the future of the land. "If the City had not fulfilled its obligations to the Navy," he said, "then why would any individual or corporation want to do business on the same land?"

Land, space, and tidelands continued to pervade the thinking of those citizens looking ahead. Large areas of vacant land had been used up in a short time. The Amphibious Base had consisted of 139 acres but was later enlarged. The ocean side of the highway was "taken" and used by the Underwater Demolition teams for training and housing.

A 36-acre public beach was granted to Coronado Beach, Inc., in an area formerly used as a public beach. The highrise Coronado Shores condominiums would eventually be built there. Other areas of beach land, the former Spanish Bight, and an area along First Street, were now crunched with housing. Some Coronadans felt these lost land areas should have been utilized more for recreational purposes.

During the Housing Project negotiations, a building known as the Hobby Club, on the Strand overlooking Glorietta Bay (partially a Quonset hut), was offered to the City by the Navy for $14,000.

Coronado City Hall, c. 1959. (CPL/LCC)

The Council voted to buy the building to be used for undetermined purposes. Tentative plans included use as a City Hall and court house. Since the City's lease on the Loma Avenue building was expiring November 20, 1953, a target date of September was set for occupancy of the "new" City Hall.

The new City Hall could house all City offices and provide a Council chamber with seating space. Louis A. Dean was architect of the conversion that would cost approximately $25,000. His plans appeared in the *Coronado Journal* on June 25, 1953. The "new" City Hall was dedicated on December 18, 1953, but at a contract adjustable to $34,757. This was the fifth impermanent location of the City government in the history of Coronado, but the first owned by the municipality during 63 years of official life.

The Korean War had not ended for many Coronadans. Aircraft carrier USS *Essex* returned from the war zone, and more than 350 decorations and awards were presented to her officers and enlisted men. Several Coronado men had been prisoners of war. Ensign Gerald Canaan, whose family resided at 1024 Tenth Street, was released from prison camp in Korea in September 1953. Corporal Arthur Bowditch, U.S.A., was reunited with his Coronado family after being held prisoner by the Chinese Communists for two and one-half years. Lieutenant Commander Maury F. Yerger Jr., a pilot aboard the Essex, was home with his family at 531 Adella Lane, after 11 months in captivity.

As if to capitalize on these events, the Metro Goldwyn Mayer movie company settled in at North Island to film a movie titled "Panther Squadron 8," starring Frank Lovejoy, Van Johnson, Walter Pidgeon, Keenan Wynn, and Louis Calhern. Commander Paul W. Gray served as technical advisor while the filming was done, mainly aboard the USS *Princeton*. The cast and crew stayed at the Coronado Motor Inn and the Shoreland Motor Hotel.

In January 1954, Tom Carlin Jr., then just 16-years old, received a Herds Award, which had been presented nationally only four times in the previous seven years. This was a Red Cross honor for saving the life of Lieutenant Colonel Arthur A. Poindexter. U.S.M.C. Poindexter became tangled in the kelp beds off Coronado Islands while spear fishing, but Carlin, seeing his plight, managed to extricate the officer and bring him to the surface.

In January 1951, the First Baptist Congregation began to hold worship services in the VFW Hall. By January 1954, the First Baptist Church was dedicated at 445 "C" Avenue.

Negotiations had been going on with the U.S. Navy since 1941, bringing about payment of $120,000 for the filled-in Spanish Bight land. The closure of the deal came in March 1955. The City Council, meanwhile, approved Rancho Carrillo, the old Hog Ranch, as a recreation area for golf and other sports. As of April 8th, the area was off-limits for use as a city dump; at the same time, the Navy announced it would not need the area for military purposes.

The Council changed zoning for the Glorietta region from residential to recreational, to prevent housing from being added along the bay. This action immediately reversed its decision on the proposal for a golf course at Rancho Carrillo.

In July 1954, comprehensive development plans for the Strand area between the Amphibious Base and the boat house, which included a marina, civic auditorium, boardwalk, promenade and an enlarged boat harbor were presented to the City Council.

In December 1954, a vote taken by the San Diego and Coronado Councils approved the idea of a tube under the bay. The Coronado Council then voted to hold a special election on February 1, to poll the voters. At the same time, Coronado's newest ferry--and its last--the *Crown City*, constructed in Oakland, arrived in San Diego on May 11th, 1954, ready to carry 500 passengers and 70 cars. A press boat met the ferry off Point Loma and escorted her into her harbor berth.

G.K. Williams, controversial editor of the *Coronado Journal* tried to rouse voters to do something constructive to bring Coronado back to the way it had been. He published a number of pictures in the April 8th edition, criticizing actions of Coronado's past City Councils. Some of his wellfounded barbs included:

1. The refusal by the City to accept the Sharp home on Star Park for a hospital.

2. The Coronado Club at 707 Orange Avenue, was offered to the City for a fraction of its value to be used as a civic center building; the Council turned down the offer.

3. The former home of John D. Spreckels, now Millen Manor, had been offered for a trifle for use as a City Hall; the Council did not accept the proposal.

4. The Mitchell Estate, eventually sold and demolished, would have been a tremendous Ocean Boulevard site for a museum or art gallery, had the City obtained it; the City said "No."

5. The fine homes which lined the bay front along First Street, meant the loss of a remarkable, potential recreational area as the land had been offered to the City for park purposes for free.

In 1954, the Naval Amphibious Base added 15 new concrete piers, and a Jeheemy ramp for launching and dry docking landing craft. A central heating plant and a sewage treatment plant were under construction. What began as a rather modest base had now grown into an area that impacted the island town. The question, now moot, is why the Amphibious Base had been placed on South Island, squeezing an urban area between two service installations? The City and the Federal government working together, with more creativity and forethought, could have sought other areas for that base. A suit, brought by the City against the Federal government, sought payment for the land, which had been leased to the Navy since 1942.

The town was shocked twice during 1954, by the loss of two of its most respected citizens. On January 23, Dr. William Telford Booth was killed in a plane crash not far from San Diego, while taking a patient to the East Coast. Dr. Booth had been involved with Coronado, Mercy, and Paradise Valley

One of the most oft-remembered scenes for anyone crossing on the ferry or walking down First Street during the 1950s or 60s, were the Navy tenders moored to buoys in the bay, many times with multiple ships tied up alongside. (CHA)

hospitals. He had headed the Civilian Defense during World War II, was City Health Officer from 1938-1946, and was active in the Red Cross and many other organizations.

Then, on October 12th, Columbus Day, Police Lieutenant Frank Greene was shot to death in the line of duty at 2 a.m. on Orange Avenue, directly in front of the public library. He and a Navy shore patrolman had stopped a vehicle with three suspicious-looking men. As Greene attempted to interrogate them, one pulled a pistol and fired point-blank, killing Officer Greene instantly, launching one of the most intensive manhunts in the history of the entire region. On such a small island, word of the killing spread rapidly, and citizens were paralyzed by fear. But capture of the suspects was rapid. The trial, which began on January 12, 1955, brought in a verdict of guilty in the killing for two of the men. An angry judge sentenced the three men, and lashed out at the jury that spared the killers from the gas chamber.

In 1955, as in the case of nearly every January, heavy winds and rains played havoc with trees and roofs. At 6:20 on the morning of January 13th, because of the storms, one of the ferryboats was driven into a slip at the San Diego side and traffic was held up for some time.

The high school team won the Avocado League basketball title with an 8-1 record. They lost to Citrus High School in the southern California finals, however, Robin Dean, Charles Jon Crawford, and other team members played an outstanding game.

Headlines in the February 10th paper noted the town had received a check from the U.S. government for $484,423 as partial payment, a result of the condemnation suit for the Amphibious Base, an action then in the courts. The dollars were deemed Tidelands Fund money. But following the jury award to the City of Coronado in the suit, the Federal government was displeased and made motions to seek a new trial. Federal Judge Ben Harrison apparently agreed with the Federal government, saying, "take $100,000 off, or I order a new trial." Attorneys on both sides agreed to a settlement. On May 5, 1955, the entire $814,871.98, covering principal and interest in payment of Coronado's claims against the U.S. (in the matter of the base sale), was finally in hand, having been in the Federal court for many months.

By November 1955, the City dredging project in Glorietta Bay began, at a cost of $450,000; 1,850,000 cubic yards of spoils would come from further deepening of the Bay, and create land for a new 18-hole golf course. Figures vary on just how much soil was in fact dredged, and the real cost, but the result greatly improved boating for Glorietta Bay. The golf course extended from the old Housing Project at Fourth Street, around Glorietta Point to the Coronado Yacht Club grounds--about 137 acres—mainly consisting of new manmade land. The conversion of this raw beach and bay bottom sand to a lush green golf course appeared miraculous. Layer upon layer of top soil was brought in and sown with seed and tons of fertilizer. When tree-planting time came, large old palm trees were transported from the South Bay area.

Building Inspector Robert Staunton reported a considerable building boom, the most concentrated in the town's history. The growth hit Coronado with 30 new houses and two apartments in February alone. Ground was also broken for a new grammar school on Sixth Street, from Cabrillo to the Country Club Estates Annex, and in September, dedication of the new Crown School took place.

Commercially, Albert Bram produced architect Robert Bradt's rendering of the new La Avenida Motel at 1321 Orange Avenue. Unfortunately, in order to put in the new motel, two old and architecturally pleasing ones, the San Carlos and Devon Hotels had to be demolished. The Hotel del Coronado garage, built as a livery stable in 1889, was demolished in preparation for the four-lane highway to Imperial Beach.

Coronado 4th of July Parade in 1955. (CPL)

While some were practicing demolition, groups such as the Coronado section of the American Association of University Women were calling attention to historic buildings. They conducted tours of homes designed by distinguished architects John Washington, Richard G. Wheeler, William Templeton Johnson, and Richard Requa.

On April 21st at 8 p.m., 500 citizens attended an open meeting in the Hotel del Coronado ballroom to hear proposals for the development of Rancho Carrillo, the 236-acre parcel of land that was formerly the Hog Ranch. The proposal made by the Rancho Carrillo Development Group showed a drawing with sites for 600 homes, a parking area, shopping center, and a motel. Other project concepts from other groups would shortly come, as the value of the land for potential development became more and more apparent. Various uses were suggested such as trailer camps, oil drilling fields; an industrial park, scientific laboratory, and a polo field, none of which suited the Council or the people. Unlike other projects which were drawn out for decades, there was no bitter animosity or controversy regarding the Rancho development. The majority of citizens wanted a well-thought out, attractive residential marina.

The matter of connecting Coronado and San Diego remained, as usual, on everyone's agenda, with the issue coming into focus again in December 1956. The worst ferry tie-up in years occurred when a transformer used to operate the ferry ramps on the San Diego side went out of service at 1:20 in the afternoon, causing massive traffic jams on Pacific Highway in San Diego, on Orange Avenue in Coronado, and on the Silver Strand where road construction was under way. Word from the State Division of Engineering was that tunnel plans were "going good." Just before Christmas, state and Federal representatives took borings from the bay to determine where the proposed tunnel would, or could, go. In June, after final passage, a $200,000 tunnel feasibility survey bill was sent to Governor Goodwin Knight for signature.

Even before the Korean War, the Coronado Police Department had been keeping an eye on the Silver Strand. The roadway with two lanes, no lights, and only beach sand for shoulders was long recognized as dangerous. As the population grew, and more workers headed for North Island and the Amphibious Base, a center lane was added. But the highway became overloaded and, after 1950, many deaths occurred because more than 7,000 cars used the road daily. Committees looked at the need. The legislature passed the highway construction bill and allocated the money.

After several false starts, the State Division of Highways announced that the four-lane divided highway construction would begin in mid-January 1955.

As occurred in 1935, a proposal was once again brought before the Council, and then the U.S. Army Corps of Engineers, to construct a deep-draft entrance to lower San Diego Bay from the ocean at a point north of Fort Emory by cutting through the Silver Strand. The idea was rejected as "economically unjustified," with no agencies apparently willing to contribute toward the cost.

For years, the overused Coronado Police Station had been in need of replacement. The Spanish-style station was built in 1922-1923, when the population of the city was 2,500 and had a police force of three men. By 1954, there were over 18 officers. The building, designed by the superb architects Requa and Jackson, was simply worn out by use. A grand jury found the facility "termite-ridden, inadequate, unsafe, and unsanitary." With a condemnation threat by the grand jury of the existing jail and police station, City Manager Wade had to make corrections to conform to the jury's demands. Wade solicited the assistance of all Coronadans who might wish to express their ideas about what was necessary in the new building. "Drawings did not have to be professional looking," he said. "A plain, modern style of architecture of simple design, but in accord with present day practices of penal institutions, is considered desirable."

At the same time, a new location for the larger facility was also sought. A proposal to place it at Second and "A" was denied by the State as being Tidelands property, while another idea of locating it on Glorietta Boulevard caused a hue and cry from the residents. All planning decisions were for naught anyway, because when election time came, a new jail bond issue was defeated. This followed a traditional practice in Coronado. Not a single bond issue for construction of a public building had ever been approved by the voters.

La Avenida Motel, c. 1955. (CPL)

Two days later, Chief Robert Manchester closed the jail and transported prisoners to San Diego, at considerable cost to the City of Coronado. Procrastination, indecision, and delays mark this project as one of the most mishandled in the history of the town. Finally, in April 1955, the State of California approved the plans for a new Coronado police and jail facility, to be located on the same site as the old station, at the corner of 6th and Orange, at a cost of $65,000. The new police building was opened and dedicated on February 18, 1956, as Mrs. Betty Walters, a member of Cincinnati's police department became Coronado's first policewoman.

Throughout all the turmoil and politics, Coronado never lost her glamour. Movie stars were still frequently spotted, and many stayed at the Hotel del Coronado, including Doris Day and her family. Donald O'Connor made his movie "Francis Joins the Navy," with Martha Hyers, using the ferry landing and other island locales. In July, John Lund, William Bendix, and Richard Boone were on board the USS *Princeton* at North Island making the film "Battle Stations."

Looking back, the year 1956 appears to have been one of aggravation. Aside from a few capital improvements, news coverage focused on a sewage quarantine in San Diego Bay, the City's inability

A formation of Navy FJ-4 Fury fighter-bombers in the break over North Island. Good view of Coronado and San Diego of the 1950s. (CHA)

to meet the cost of living wages for employees, and the threat of beach erosion. The Council was aware that the Navy was constructing a seaplane base in South San Diego, and that it would have an effect on Rancho Carrillo. Was it an accident that aircraft were flying low over Rancho Carrillo land? Suspicions ran high!

> And Coronadans were right. Coronado had become the West Coast center for Navy seaplane squadrons during the mid-1950s. Everywhere you looked, stately, gull-winged Martin P5M Marlins flew over Coronado, or landed along the Silver Strand. These giant planes marked the latest in an unbroken line of Navy flying boats based in Coronado, stretching back to Glenn Curtiss' A-1 Triad. Beginning in 1954, the Navy started looking for a site for a South Bay seaplane base, a "seadrome," complete with control towers, hangars, ramps, and concrete aprons --with their first choice the current site of the Coronado Cays, and their second choice near Navy housing located on the Strand, south of the Naval Amphibious Base. Public opposition was remarkably light, when the proposed legislation first surfaced, but by late 1956 it was beginning to build, with the Coronado City Council voting in late 1956 for the Navy to "clarify their plans." In 1957, the Navy, to its enduring credit, abandoned plans for a Coronado seadrome, but for the next ten years Coronadans distinctly remember the large, noisy P5Ms taxiing down the bay along First Street and across ferry lanes to their South Bay runways.

In 1956, a rest home was completed at the Coronado Hospital, designed by architect Louis A. Dean. The Council finally selected a site for a municipal swimming pool on Strand Way, a decision that was a long time in coming. The Coronado Baptist Church (Southern) was organized in 1956, in a small store building on First Street, near the current grocery shopping center. In July 1958, the church bought the property at 111 Orange Avenue where the church and a child care day center are located today.

Coronado had been the center for Navy seaplanes since Glenn Curtiss' hydroaeroplane. In the late 1950s, the Navy wanted to build a huge new base for seaplanes near where the Coronado Cays is today, a plan the City helped torpedo. Here is a P-5M Marlin about 1959. (CHA)

The Coronado High School Basketball "A" team won the Avocado League, and became Champions of the Southern California Interscholastic Federation. Roger Nix was elected Player of the Year. Columbia Studios moved on location from Burbank, and shot some footage along Glorietta Boulevard for the filming of "The Brothers Rico," starring Richard Conte and Paul Gallico.

In August, Coronado lost one of its most distinguished ladies and a person who had given much to the community. Mrs. John Sheafe Douglas, who passed away at the age of 75, had been a strong figure in the creation of Coronado's new hospital. She worked for Christ Episcopal Church and had been with the Girl Scout organization for 35 years.

During 1957, the cost of living rose again. The purchase price of a home, with enough for the demand, looked something like this: 4 bedroom, 50 x 140 lot near golf course $13,000; Neat 2 bedroom cottage $9,750; Spanish-style 2 bedroom, 72 foot frontage $22,750; Country Club Estates, 3 bedroom $28,600. Rentals could be had for: 2 bedroom unfurnished $125; 5 bedroom, 4 bath, ocean view $225; Biltmore Hotel, $21/week; El Cordova Hotel, $65/month

> In 1957, floor space was doubled at the Coronado Library, with an addition in the back that provided a large book stack area, as well as expanded seating and staff work space. In the prior year, nearly 150,000 books were checked out.

The Coronado Planning Department was asked that since the possibility of a new bay crossing existed, how much land was left in Coronado upon which to build? Bob Staunton determined that Coronado had only 167 building sites left, and 74 of those were part of subdivisions such as Coronado Estates, Country Club Annex, and Coronado Villas. A number of these lots had only 25 foot frontage! According to those estimates, fewer than 1,000 additional persons could be accommodated on the island. The City also still had plans to demolish the Federal Housing units, even though the Navy continued to protest due to the shortage of low-income housing for their personnel. The announcement arrived that more of the buildings would be taken down as soon as possible.

If a word could describe decision-making over a tube or a bridge, that word would be vacillation. For some time, the feeling had run high for a tunnel or tube. Now a turn of events brought the bridge back to the forefront. On May 30th, 1957, word came to the Council that approval for possible construction of a bay crossing had been sent to the California Toll Bridge Authority by the State Division of Highways. The first recommendation of the Division of Highways was for a four-lane high level bridge at an estimated cost of $23 million. A two-lane tunnel was feasible at a cost of $25,800,000, but would surely be congested in ten years.

The first photos produced in the paper on June 6, 1957, superimposed how the bridge/or tunnel would look with an entrance at 5th and Glorietta. The U.S. Navy still opposed the bridge, because of the feeling that in the event of a disaster the bridge would block the harbor, but gave tacit approval to the concept.

Headlines in the *Coronado Journal* noted, "Controversy Bogs Tube Action. Realtors for it; People against it." The Residential Association voted in July to send a delegate to Sacramento with petitions and documents supporting their opposition, in order to express their feelings about a bridge. The Association claimed that the *Coronado Journal*, headed by G.K. Williams, was pro bridge. They gave a number of reasons for keeping Coronado isolated, including the thought that a tube or a bridge would destroy the feeling of security from crime. The group felt that it would completely change the complexion of the village. With political elections due shortly in late 1957, Coronado's Mayor, Coleman Gray, declared the decision would be put to a vote on the April 1958 ballot.

During this time, the Navy continued its program of building. At the start of the year, officials announced plans to construct an aircraft carrier wharf on North Island, near the west end of First Street.

A new Olympic-size community swimming pool, approved in 1956, was underway, and scheduled to be opened in September.

> On December 19, 1957, the new Coronado golf course along Glorietta Boulevard formally opened, after a construction period of two years. The million-dollar project that began with deposit of dredge material from Glorietta Bay, was designed by golf architect Jack Daray. The par 72 public links measured 6,578 yards. The Clubhouse was designed by Paderewski, Mitchell and Dean Architects, with Allen L. Fowler as general contractor and Ed W. Campbell, long time Coronadan, landscape gardener. Opening ceremonies featured a professional exhibition by a foursome of Billy Casper, Gene Littler, Paul Runyan, and Don Collett (San Diego County Open champion and head pro at Coronado). Coronado Mayor Coleman Gray hit the first ball down the No. 1 fairway.

Paul Ludlow made international headlines by defeating the great British Champion Harry Bentley in the French International Amateur Golf Tournament. Another Coronadoan made news earlier when the Reverend Doctor W. Don Brown, Rector of Christ Episcopal Church, received a Doctor of Divinity degree. The degree was conferred on him by Occidental College. The honor came as special recognition for contributions he had made in the parish life of the diocese he served.

MGM Studios returned in October 1957, to film "Underwater Warriors" at the Naval Amphibious Base, a movie about the Underwater Demolition Team. Based on Commander Francis D. Fane's book "Naked Warrior," the movie starred Dan Dailey and Claire Kelley.

"New" Junior High School building that opened in 1956. (CHA)

In a survey carried out for the town, the following represents the occupational background of some of the Coronado citizenry: 82 Admirals, 234 Captains,13 Generals, 4 Retired Commodores, 321 Active and Retired Lieutenants, 233 Active and 24 Retired Lieutenant Commanders, 300 Lieutenants, 1,435 Navy Fliers and 307 enlisted men of all services, 72 engineers, 7 architects, 1 landscape architect, 3 artists, 2 writers, 111 teachers, 24 nurses, 11 clergymen, 20 doctors, 14 dentists, 75 real estate agents, 10 bankers, and 13 attorneys.

There were heroes, and there were achievers. Councilman Robin Goodenough saved the life of Johnny Hanson in early October, when the boy was caught in a riptide that pulled him out to sea. Leta Labby celebrated her 82nd birthday on October 24 at the Coronado Hospital, where many friends greeted her. For years, she had operated a dry goods store on Orange Avenue and was very active in civic affairs and Christ Episcopal Church. Nick Reynolds, guitar and ukulele-picking member of the Kingston Trio, was exultant over their current hit, a folk ballad called, "Tom Dooley," which was sweeping the country.

On a sad note, one of the seven men killed in a September 16th crash of an Air Force B-52 bomber was Captain Dexter Lanois. Thirty-six years of age, the former Coronado High School football star had been cited for bravery in 1940 by the City Council.

In late November, a storm struck the area with high winds bringing down a number of trees and hot wires. Water spilled over the seawall onto Ocean Boulevard. This was the year the Hotel del Coronado ended the use of its own generating facilities. The hotel had created its own generating system at the time of its construction in 1888. The change-over to the San Diego Gas and Electric Company involved considerable work, equal to providing service to a city of 1,500 residents.

Another storm, with 65 mph winds, ripped through the City on January 6, 1959, knocking down television antennas, pushing over trees, dropping power lines, and beaching boats at the Yacht Club. Water was also driven into the Coronado Playhouse.

Regarding education, the high school building was called unsafe. State architect Ernie Magg said, "This is the type of construction that came down during the Long Beach earthquake in 1932," noting that it was vulnerable to any ground movement. By September, at the urging of the chief structural engineer for the State of California Division of Architecture, citizens were told the building was too dangerous. The Parent-Teacher Association stopped holding meetings there. On the other hand, the school board voted to stay in the high school, but to abandon the old auditorium. The Public Safety committee of the County Grand Jury then began to investigate conditions at the high school. Architect Robert Bradt told the Board of Education it would be mid1962 before a new school could be built. Building of a new Junior High School preceded the construction of the new High School. The Junior High School opened at the corner of Seventh Street and E Avenue in 1956.

The City Council prepared a new lease draft for the proposed Coronado Luxury Tower apartments to review. These apartments were to be built on City-owned lands north of the present bridge toll gates. The Phillip Yousem Company of Venice, California, offered eight, 14-story, "Y" shaped towers. The construction would take three years and ultimately bring the City $175,000 a year in ground rent, plus taxes. This proposal called for demolition of the older housing area in phases. An initiative petition aimed at preventing the City Council from authorizing construction of 14-story apartments on State-owned tidelands went before the voters, and a suit was brought in Superior Court to block the development. The court held that the City could not use State lands for private use. The SnyderLeow Corporation then looked to the Del Sands property, south of the Hotel del Coronado.

The Crown City Marina, at the foot of "A" Avenue, would open July 4th. The lease negotiated proved to be within the Tidelands Act, which specified such land could be used for commerce, navigation, fisheries, or recreation.

The Coronado Community Theatre also launched a $50,000 mail campaign for the construction of a new 200-seat theatre on the site of the old playhouse on the Strand.

Television producers finally discovered what Coronado had to offer, as Revue Productions brought Rod Cameron to star in the television series "Coronado 9." The local scenes were shot on First Street and at the police station. "Border Patrol," a CBS series, starring Dick Webb, was shot at the Coronado Yacht Club. Serving as Technical Advisor was Commander Arthur Giesser of 900 Alameda. Some of the episodes of "Highway Patrol," with Broderick Crawford, were also shot at various locales in town.

Coronado's Citizen of the Year probably should have been Nabor Felix of 242 "C" Avenue, who celebrated his 100th birthday on July 12th. Nabor was a resident of Coronado for 48 years. His wife, Felicita Felix died at the age of 101, two years earlier. Born in 1859 in Lorenzo, Baja California, he joined the Mexican Navy when he was just 13-years old, and worked for many years as a fisherman. In his backyard, he had an impressive variety of fruit trees, but was also known for his uncanny skill of treating sprains, bruises, and disjointed fingers. Known as a curandero (medicine man), he was probably best known by the fair number of Mexican-Americans he treated in Coronado.

Coronado High School's 1958 Homecoming Queen Marjorie Brown and her escort Dwight Johnson. (CHA)

Coronado had changed dramatically since the time of John Diedrich Spreckels. His vast holdings in Southern California were disposed of by his family, which had rarely shown much interest in the huge investments he had made in the City. The work of a man's lifetime had been sold away, in what seemed like a moment. Gone was the shape he had given to transportation, communication, recreation, and public service. Coronado had come a long way, but in the process, had essentially moved from what was tantamount to benevolent "one-man rule" to open season for development. To make matters worse, no figure appeared on the horizon with his strength of purpose to lead the town.

Chapter 9
The Coming of the Bridge
1960-1969

SPONSORED BY SALLY AND NORMAN REYNOLDS

THE POPULATION IN 1960 was right at 18,000 persons, a jump of 5,300 from 1950. The newcomers were taking an active role, alongside the long-time residents, in making decisions about the direction of their island city. Private enterprise was on the move. The Hotel del Coronado was sold in March for approximately $2,500,000. The buyer was the Coronado Beach, Inc., a subsidiary of Alessio Investment Company, owned by San Diego businessmen John, Angelo, Russell, and Tony Alessio. John Alessio said he hoped to restore the palace to its historic grandeur. In referring to the Alessio brothers' acquisition, one magazine article noted that:

> "In view of their purchase of the Caliente racetrack and its subsequent restoration as a leading attraction in Southern California, their recent purchase elicits memories of the close relationship in the Twenties, between the Coronado Hotel and the 'sensational' spa-casino-racetrack facility south of the border, a relationship that marked the hotel's highest level attained, indicates that the hotel's renown as a center of enjoyment may become even greater."

The creative designer responsible for the expansion and redecoration was Al Goodman, former motion picture art director and industrial engineer. Needless to say, historic preservationists

(Image above: CPL/LCC)

Surfing has been a vibrant feature of culture in Coronado since the 1950s. (Coronado Public Library/Russ Elwell Collection)

were quite uneasy lest a "Hollywood flair" should detract from the staid old Victorian atmosphere that the 1888 hostelry represented--the heritage for which it was famous. After World War II, the Hotel had steadily lost much of its glamour and elegance. Her general condition deteriorated at the same time that the new and convenient motels became the undisputed favorite of the vacationing public. "The Grand Lady by the Sea" was decidedly on her way to becoming a white elephant.

It was rumored that the Alessios invested over $2 million on the modernization program. The handsome lobby with its dark oak paneling remained much the same. The elegant and enormous Crown dining room was kept intact. Fortunately, the great Crown light fixtures remained in place. The spectacular lights were said to have been designed by L. Frank Baum, writer of the "Wizard of Oz" stories. During the rehabilitation, the Hotel staff uncovered "thousands of relics, collected, forgotten, and abandoned during its 72 years." The *San Diego Union* of August 19, 1960, reported that trunks and boxes stored years ago in twelve basement rooms yielded treasures, ranging from yellowing photographs and disintegrating clothing with only sentimental value, to elegant punch bowls, Chinese porcelain, and ornate lamps. Crews led by J.H. Tiedemann, then Assistant Manager in charge of maintenance, found 40-foot lockers deserted by anonymous guests of yesteryears. One footlocker was filled with World War I uniforms. Another contained autographed photos of early pilots. Most of the pictures were inscribed to John J. Hernan, who formerly managed the Hotel.

Millen Manor, the old Spreckels/Copley home across from the Hotel, also underwent extensive renovation. Barney Padway, new owner and managing director, altered the original mansion.

During 1960, the City Council viewed the final masterplan for Rancho Carrillo. Several plans had been presented in April 1955, and one was finally selected. The plan, which included a 500-boat marina, was presented by Albert Gersten, Beverly Hills multi-millionaire resort, residential, and business developer. Robert Sully of Daniel, Mann, Johnson and Mendeshall, regarded as the world's second largest architectural and engineering firm, was selected to develop the project.

Mayor Robin Goodenough felt it was vital for the island to acquire any land possible for growth, and that included the vacant hillside triangle fronting Orange, between Glorietta and Pomona. The land was considered to have potential for parking, widening of Pomona, or as a small municipal park. But when the town began looking at possible acquisition of the property, private ventures took an interest and the value rose. Once again, Coronado voted down an opportunity as too expensive--another short-sighted view it would regret.

The original boundary of Coronado was set in 1893, when Coronado and North Island de-annexed from San Diego. Navy-dredged fill changed the line. In July 1960, Coronado and San Diego worked out a new boundary running along the shore of Coronado, from south of Glorietta Bay to North Island. The agreement was designed to draw a new mean high-tide line along the northeast shore. Attorneys correctly predicted that as fill from channel cutting for new aircraft carriers would probably go into the area south of the rock jetty on the ocean side of Coronado, another boundary shift would have to be agreed to by all parties.

The highlight of 1960 occurred in October, when President Dwight D. Eisenhower toured North Island. The schools were closed so children could have a chance to see their President. Over 7,000 people assembled at the First Street ferry gate caught a glimpse of him as he prepared to cross the bay to San Diego.

Coronado lost two of its most beloved citizens during the year. Arthur A. Mathewson, founder of Coronado's first grocery store, died at the age of 75, having lived in Coronado longer than any resident—for 73 years. Awarded an engineering degree by Stanford University, he returned home to enter his father's grocery business. He served as City Treasurer from 1914-1932, and City Clerk from 1932-1957. Harold A. Taylor, perhaps best-recognized internationally as a photographer, died at the age of 81. In another tragedy, U.S. Navy pilot LTJG Neal L. Nassman of Oklahoma died after

Coronado High School's demolition in 1960 made way for a new school of Mid-Century modern designed. (CHA)

he was pulled from a flaming AD-6 Skyraider that crashed on Coronado's North Beach.

In April, voters passed a $1,225,000 bond issue to finance a new educational facility. The decision to build a combination junior/senior school was influenced by deliberations of a cross-section of Coronado citizens. Questions were asked about whether restoration (not demolition) of the old high school was feasible. Decisions were made based on cost and a fear that an earthquake would demolish the older building. Also, a new complex would provide many needed features that the old one did not have.

Compared to the classy, now-demolished, old high school, its replacement was uninteresting—far below Coronado's normally high architectural standards of beauty. At least it was painted in colors that fit the times, "Mellow Yellow." (CHA)

On December 2, a 40-day reign of ruin began as the 38-year-old Coronado High School building fell under the wrecking ball of John Hansen Materials and House Moving, Inc. In 1922, the building had cost $135,314 to construct. It was demolished for $29,889. Historians are trained never to ask the question, "What if?" But, what if in the decision to demolish many Coronado buildings, feasibility of restoration and preservation had been more actively sought from those already doing this kind of work elsewhere in the country, and indeed in the world? Some of Coronado's most gorgeous buildings, surely would still be standing.

Some residents may recall May 23-24, 1960, when surging waves struck the California coast, Hawaii, and the Far East, bringing a halt to ferry service during the morning. Strong currents and a tide that rose seven feet hit the coastline. At 6:45 a.m. on the 23rd, ferries began experiencing difficulty crossing the bay. The ferry *North Island* drifted south for half a mile around a group of U. S. Navy destroyers, before it could return to its course and make a landing in San Diego. All the while, Coronadans going to work in San Diego wondered whether they might end up in the South Bay!

In 1961, remodeling of the grand ballroom of the Hotel del Coronado was the primary focus of the redecorating efforts. Using the existing shell of the 18,000-square foot room, Goodman created a much more elaborate atmosphere. The most startling change, however, was the lowering of the ceiling for acoustical purposes, accommodating the enormous crystal chandeliers. This lowering hid the widow's walk that encircled the room, which had allowed a marvelous vantage point for onlookers. The famed Circus Room at the Hotel, in an area where the bowling alleys once had been, was also completely renovated. The room featured live performers such as comedians Rowan and Martin, singers Harry Babbitt, Tommy Noon, the DeCastro Sisters, the Lennon Sisters, and Barbara Whiting.

In March, C.A. Larsen signed a contract to build the new Coronado High School at a cost of $945,077. He promised the school would be ready on September 8th when classes began. In June, the cornerstone was laid, with School Board members Leo Hansen, Barbara Schuman-Heink Goodbody, and several high school students taking part in the ceremony. The loss of the former

Oscars Drive-In, a popular hangout of teenagers, was located in the 1000 block of C Avenue. (CPL)

elementary/junior high school complex and high school buildings had been a real sorrow to those who graduated from the schools. The buildings had been monumental structures, giving an appearance of a true educational institution - a place to view with respect. The experience record of its graduates related directly to the educational leadership, teachers, and the buildings themselves. What replaced those buildings was, in the opinion of many, a far inferior design. Yet, to be fair, the new, one-story inexpensive structures must be viewed in light of the architecture of the times. Schools constructed during this period appear as if constructed from generic plans developed for use at multiple sites across the country. They do not, in general, provide the atmosphere one sees in other towns, where the presence of inspiring architecture reflects a town's pride in its roots and unique heritage.

The answer may be found in the times. Rising taxes caused conservative citizens to tighten their belts. Taxpayers sought to slow down any emphasis on growth that meant their wallets would be affected. Coronadans virtually stormed the Recreation Commission budget proposal hearings in 1961-1962. However, their efforts did not deter construction of four new public tennis courts on Glorietta Boulevard that were officially dedicated by the Coronado Tennis Association. In September, the City Council prepared to develop Glorietta Bay as a yachtsmen's mecca. The Council pushed forward a lease on the tidelands and water from the boathouse to the southern boundary of the Women's Club.

Around the same time, the City Council was hoping to resolve two major issues. Decisions regarding the Coronado Towers, which had been under City Council and Hotel del Coronado discussion since at least 1959, were needed. Plans for Rancho Carrillo also had to be finalized. Other problems needing resolution included sewage disposal, and the trans-bay crossing situation. The number one topic lay dormant, although much grousing went on in the community over inaction, and the City Council became angry over delays by Coronado Towers, Inc. That company received

USS 'Kitty Hawk,' the first super carrier to be homeported in Coronado, arrived in September 1961. Over 5000 sailors manned Kitty Hawk, changing an important dynamic in Coronado's relationship with the Navy. (CHA)

a setback when the Council voted against the idea of urban renewal, whereby the city would apply for a Housing and Home Finance Administration loan. Less than happy debate about the Towers continued through the end of the year.

> New harbor dredging, along the channel and throughout the carrier-turning basin off the North Island carrier piers, began in 1958. Two million cubic yards of dredge material helped to form Harbor Island. The dredging project was created to allow the basing of new Navy "supercarriers" in Coronado. The Pacific Fleet was being reordered around the big new "flattops," and in order to stay at the forefront of carrier aviation, North Island berthing had to be significantly improved. The first of these supercarriers, the USS *Kitty Hawk* (81,000 tons and over a 1,000 feet in length), arrived in September 1961. Its arrival opened a new era of carrier homeporting at North Island. Her sister ship, the USS *Constellation*, arrived in North Island the next year. The "Connie" was homeported for over 40 years in Coronado, the longest of any ship ever homeported in Coronado.

The San Diego Regional Water Pollution Control Board ordered Coronado to stop dumping new sewage into San Diego Bay. When the city did not, San Diego's Board had the courts issue a cease and desist order. Coronado had not met the deadlines for the stoppage. In November 1961, the Mayor was authorized to sign a 50-year agreement with San Diego to join the Metro Sewage Disposal System, contingent upon a bond passage. He signed the pact. The Council took up the plan for a tie-in with the Metropolitan system by June 1963.

The tube/tunnel controversy reached the hands of State Senator Hugo Fisher, who introduced a resolution in both houses of the State Legislature to bring up a 1957 tunnel feasibility survey to seek prompt action for construction of such a tube. About the same time, a councilman proposed that the town buy the ferry company. The Council recommended a feasibility study. To assist in the decision whether to seek a tube or a tunnel, a group called, "The Citizens Committee for the Preservation of Coronado," chaired by Rear Admiral Herschel House and Louis de Ryk Millen, spoke of a "second phase" in the development of the project. Their main concern was where the bridge terminal would be located. Shouldn't it be outside the downtown part of Coronado? As preservationists, they forecast traffic conditions that would surely congest the island.

Senator Fisher predicted on November 30, 1961, that preliminary work on some sort of transbay crossing would be started within a year. One force, which had a great deal of influence on the outcome of the tunnel/bridge decision, came through the editorials of G.K. Williams, owner of the *Coronado Journal*, whose interests were clearly pro-bridge. He wanted to bolster the economy of Coronado through tourism and believed the bridge was necessary to accomplish this. In June 1961, he provided a blow-by-blow history of the long struggle to get some sort of crossing to Coronado. He did not take a stand on either a bridge or tunnel as long as one of the two came to pass. The bridge began to be favored, probably because a group of Coronado businessmen decided to get behind the idea and appealed to Governor Edmund G. Brown for help.

> In 1961, a children's wing was built at the Public Library. The Children's Library offered many advantages. These were the peak years for childhood population in Coronado, and the Library was keeping pace with special programs for youth – regular story hours, summer reading clubs, and the after-school crush of students working on assignments. The new Children's Library had its own entrance and its own check-out desk.

The "Birthplace of Naval Aviation," North Island, celebrated its 50th anniversary on August 19th/20th, 1961. Top officers of the Defense Department and experts connected with aviation from all over the United States and abroad attended the sessions and conferences. The public was treated

Beginning after World War II, Navy Underwater Demolition Teams were based and trained in Coronado, forming the basis for what would later become Navy SEAL teams. (CHA)

SEAL Team ONE was established in Coronado on January 1, 1962, with SEAL headquarters and SEAL qualification training conducted on Coronado beaches. (CHA)

to special air shows, and the famed Blue Angels came to San Diego to demonstrate precision flying. Estimates of attendance at the "open house" at North Island ran as high as 200,000 spectators.

A group that called itself the "Coronado Citizen Committee on Survival," met to begin plans for community fallout shelters needed in the event of a nuclear attack. Locations considered for subterranean shelters included areas beneath Cutler Field and Orange Avenues. Information was to be provided on power, heating, ventilation, and water. In the event of an attack, according to the report on the meeting, "older people" would stay topside during the attack to try, if possible, to preserve and guard the town! Rapid response came from the Coronado Towers Inc., which indicated that blueprints for their project included fallout shelters. While the paper carried reports on one or two of the meetings, there is evidence that lack of interest, particularly on the part of the "older people," contributed to the demise of the Committee on Survival.

One idea for putting Coronado in the minds of people everywhere was developed by the Chamber of Commerce, in the form of a plan for establishing a Coronado International Film Festival. Don Larson was appointed Director, and Robert Morey headed special events for the 1961 festival. Larson invited Claudia Cardinale to attend the weeklong affair scheduled for October 8-14. Intended to outdo the Cannes Film Festival, Larson said that the concept was to show new pictures from America and abroad; to have exhibits of motion picture techniques and equipment; and to hold seminars with directors, writers and performers. The appearance of celebrities would provide Coronado with a media blitz.

Such celebrities as Van Heflin, Dennis Hopper, Barbara Eden, Michael Ansara, and Jackie Cooper attended. The Festival was held at the Hotel del Coronado and the Village Theatre, and was deemed to be successful enough to prompt planning for a 1962 event, especially when Pedro Vargas and Richard Harris made appearances. It was Larson's hope (and he had every reason to believe) that the Festival would become an annual tradition.

> Navy Underwater Demolition Teams (UDT) were established in Coronado after World War II, but by the late 1950s, the Navy was exploring how best to establish anti-insurgency or unconventional forces. Two SEAL Teams (Sea, Air, Land) were authorized by the Chief of Naval Operations in December 1961. The SEAL teams were formally established a month later with the mission to conduct unconventional warfare, counter-guerilla warfare, and clandestine operations. SEAL Team ONE stood-up in Coronado at the Naval Amphibious Base, co-located with UDT-11 and UDT-12. SEAL Team TWO was established on the Naval Amphibious Base, Little Creek, VA. Throughout much of the Vietnam War, the existence of these two units was classified. SEAL training was broader than pure UDT training; in addition to the UDT experience, a SEAL Team member underwent SEAL Cadre training at Camp Billy Machen in the Laguna and Cuyamaca Mountains.

In early 1962, the movement for the bridge was gaining momentum. The feeling either for or against some kind of bay crossing was so strong that long-time friends stopped speaking to each other. People crossed to the opposite side of the street to avoid arguing with one another about an extremely testy subject. The clear and understood opposition to the bridge was that it would destroy the small town character. If the decision was made to dissect the island with newly created streets and traffic generated to and from North Island, many people considered that to be a negative effect.

By June 1962, after a hearing, the State Board of Public Works spokesman said, "A four-lane bridge seemed to be the only logical trans-bay crossing." Mayor William Seavey demanded that the citizens have a right to "vote on the November ballot" on whether they wanted any kind of crossing. Robert Bradford, Director of the California Department of Public Works, read a letter from the Commandant of the 11th Naval District opposing any bridge. The Commandant said that 300 Navy ships would be endangered by construction of a bridge because of the possibility that in some crisis, sabotage of the bridge could take place and vessels would be trapped inside the South Bay.

In general, the feeling of the island residents was best stated by the Residential Association President Rear Admiral Leon Huffman, U.S.N. Retired. He commented, "I like Coronado the way it is." But the merchants, at least the majority of them, felt differently, and yearned for the business the bridge would surely bring over. Said a motel owner, "We are slowly dying on the vine." In the October 11th issue of the *Coronado Journal*, an architectural sketch of the bay bridge from an aerial vantage point showed the recommended crossing. Application was filed by the California Toll Bridge Authority to the Army Corps of Engineers for construction.

Yet another matter struck home even more deeply. Until 1962, management of the Port fell under a department of the City of San Diego. The bay and its tidelands, beyond the city limits, remained relatively undeveloped. Awareness had grown in San Diego that, for optimum development throughout San Diego Bay, a single separate agency was essential. This realization led to the establishment of the San Diego Unified Port District. The new district would not have jurisdiction over Coronado. Three-quarter inch headlines in the March 29, 1962, newspaper heralded the opening of a long, hard-fought battle on the town's part to keep its tidelands out of the Port's jurisdiction. The Coronado City Council approved the San Diego Bay Port Authority, but with "home rule" and without taxing powers.

The Port District measure for port jurisdiction, without the home rule and non-taxing power provisions, was to go on the November 6 ballot. The ballot was to be voted upon in two sections: the City of San Diego in one, with the four bay cities of Coronado, Imperial Beach, Chula Vista, and National City tied together as one vote, in another. The bill required that the five cities, upon the establishment of the Port District, convey their tide and submerged lands, together with any facilities thereon, to the district. City Attorney J.R. Goodbody warned of the effects on Coronado since the City had the broadest uses of any in the State for its tidelands, uses granted by the State. Mayor Seavy, also an attorney, was vocally opposed and pointed out how curious it was that the bill was being pushed through with such urgency.

Since the Coronado City Council unanimously opposed the creation of the Port District as set up in Senate Bill 41, the Council filed suit in Superior Court challenging the constitutionality of the Port District Act, and asking that the matter be kept off the November 6 ballot. The City Councils of Chula Vista and Imperial Beach joined the suit initiated by Coronado, claiming the Port District was not only unconstitutional, but "taxes the three cities without proper representation." Ben H. Wyatt reviewed the tideland laws of California back to 1910, and regarded the attempt as "a steal of our tidelands, which have been given to us by the State."

On November 6th, Coronadans voted to oppose creation of the San Diego Unified Port District, but the issue passed in other jurisdictions. Creation of the district was seemingly secured, and it looked as though the Coronado tidelands would be lost to the Port District.

In March 1962, Barney Padway bought an undeveloped piece of bluff land overlooking Glorietta Bay for $90,000 in cash. Previously offered for sale to the city, it lay in front of the former home of John D. Spreckels. The length of the parcel was 505 feet. The depth of the irregular lot was from 70 feet to 146 feet. In late September, Councilman Padway offered to turn over the strip of land for use as a town park on the condition that Coronado raise $40,000, and he would contribute the rest. He saw the bluff land terraced as an outdoor theater surrounded by shrubs and flowers, utilized for concerts or for watching sports events on the bay. The Council referred the matter to a "commission." Councilman Walter Vestal warned that citizens in the past had also offered land and buildings to the town, but prior City Councils had refused their offers. He urged, "Let's not make this same mistake again." An attempt made to raise the $40,000 by public subscription failed. No effort ensued to find funding elsewhere. Padway subsequently built an apartment complex against the bluff.

A fire at the Yacht Club caused about $10,000 damage. The membership pulled together, rebuilt and enlarged the structure. The new club featured an entrance foyer separate from the main clubroom, a dining hall with a glass display case housing the club's trophies, and a veranda on the bayside, which included a place to sit and watch boating activities.

The year 1962 brought numerous 75th anniversary celebrations, including that of Christ Episcopal Church. Ground was broken for a new St. Paul's Methodist Church. The sanctuary would be constructed on the site of the original 1887 wood building. The U.S. Naval Amphibious Force, Pacific Fleet celebrated its 20th anniversary in February.

On April 23rd, the School Board held dedication ceremonies for the new Coronado High School in the 750-seat auditorium. The presentation of the new structure was made by Ben Cohen, School Board President.

> Few felt much appreciation for the modern structure, with many describing its unfortunate color as "Mellow Yellow" in deference to the times. No common nickname stuck, but "The Mustard Monster" was frequently heard. The high school's famed mascot, a stone Tiki enshrined in the school's courtyard, was donated in 1962, a gift of the graduating classes of 1961 and 1962. A CHS grad declared, "The Tiki was an inspired symbol. It implied that people ventured across the great water, maybe not by sail but by ferry boat, to view the land of Oz, drink our magical waters (at the Mexican Village) and scorch their skin on our white sand beaches – while all of us as teenagers tried to figure out how to get off the island so everyone wouldn't know what we were up to. More high school or college mascots should be so creative and fun ... and non-controversial."

Since the early months of World War II, Coronado has been at the center of the Navy's establishment of Amphibious Warfare, with new kinds of ships and unique training. Here an LST (Landing Ship-Tank) practices landing on the Silver Strand. (CHA)

Plans were made well in advance for a second annual Film Festival to be held at the Hotel del Coronado and the Village Theatre on July 8th. Bill Pickford, owner of El Cordova Hotel, kicked off the planning with a check, to get other businessmen interested. A number of Hollywood film stars helped with the event including Angie Dickinson, Adam West, Steve Forrest, Nick Adams, Jayne Mansfield, Mickey Hargitay, and Sabrini. Festival Director Don Larson thought the press coverage was superb, especially since represented countries included Spain, France, Italy, Yugoslavia, Sweden, Japan, and Germany. While the event went over quite well in 1961 and 1962, Coronado did not attempt another film festival for some time. The Hotel was facing hard times financially, and funding in general was becoming increasingly difficult to secure.

Scarcely had the year 1963 begun, when the City Council began to approach, with trepidation, problems it left unfinished the previous year. In hindsight, one can see Coronadans were faced with too many problems related to growth and development all at once. The small residential population, the U.S. Navy, the City Council, the business community, and the *Coronado Journal* hardly agreed on any matter. The resident populace preferred to remain small in numbers and somewhat protected from traffic, overpopulation, and high rises. The business element, prompted by the newspaper and supported by the Navy, which needed more and more land for military purposes and housing, pressed the City leaders to open the island.

One increasingly bad situation was that of jet noise, particularly for those residents near North Island and along the Ocean Boulevard flight pattern. Commander Robert W. Leeman understood the problems very well, but he had a Navy facility with 18,000 men and a $75 million dollar annual budget to manage. Although there were 119,204 takeoffs and landings in 1962, he felt Coronado residents ought to better understand the size and mission of the Naval Air Station.

Prior to 1963, the U.S. had military advisors in Vietnam, a problem which President Lyndon B. Johnson had inherited. Almost unconsciously, a build-up took place. That build-up, as in

A mid-1960s view of a busy afternoon on Orange. Note the Safeway (with its blessing of air-conditioning on Santa Ana days), the Coronado Department Store and the Village Theater. Note also the common courtesy of stopping for pedestrians and bicycles. (CPL)

previous times, was felt by Coronado. The Navy had just broken ground for a 250-unit project of "ranch-style" 3-4 bedroom housing on the Strand at the Naval Amphibious Base, at a cost of $4.75 million dollars. At North Island, a filling station, commissary, and liquor store were built for naval personnel.

As for Rancho Carrillo, none of the various offers made for the many diverse uses seemed to suit the Council or the people, so once again the project was stalled. Some alert citizens pointed out the need to do something, or face possible loss of the valuable land to the Port District, which had the right to annex the tidelands. A Coronado Land Use Committee was organized and chaired by Rear Admiral Ray A. Tarbuck (USN RET), City Attorney J.R. Goodbody, Rear Admiral Herschel A. House, (USN RET), former Mayor Coleman M. Gray, and Rear Admiral Wreford G. Chappel (USN RET). These men began an intensive study of the matter.

When Coronado lost the court battle to stay out of the San Diego Port District in 1963, the City Council went on a tear and refused to renew a long-standing contract of support for the Chamber of Commerce. The Council stated that the Chamber had opposed policies of the Council, particularly over the bridge matter and the Port District affair. Councilmen also turned down a School Board request for $35,000 annually.

Coronado's first "own-your-own-apartments" were ready in early February 1963, overlooking Star Park. To make way for these first condominiums, the elegant old Sharp residence had to be demolished. A new Safeway store at Orange and Ninth was shown off with pride on opening day in March, advertised as "being as spacious as a ball park."

El Cordova Hotel was sold for $400,000 in 1963, having been owned by three generations of Pickfords. Bill Pickford resigned from the City Council, explaining he was spending more time in the East with his business enterprises there.

The Coronado Towers construction project appeared to be dead. The Council, led by Barney Padway, pointed out that the Towers group did not have the money to move ahead with the project. The matter lay dormant throughout the year.

The major news of 1963 had to be the sale of the Hotel del Coronado, and other properties owned by the Alessio Corporation, to the Hotel del Coronado Corporation Land Trends Inc., in August, for a sum in excess of $7 million. In the transaction, the company acquired the 20-acre hotel site, 36 acres of ocean frontage southward along the Silver Strand to the Naval Amphibious Base, and the six-acre-plus Glorietta Bay Yacht Club property, which involved a marina development.

M. Larry Lawrence, of the Hotel del Coronado Corporation, said plans were to construct an additional 30 rooms, with up to $100 million to be spent over five to ten years in a development program. Improvements were to include renovation of over 200 rooms. According to Lawrence, "Land-use studies have been under way for about six months. They include proposed hotel plans, which would add up to 300 rooms, and development of more than 2,000 luxury-type condominium apartments on beachfront sites."

In November, the Hotel held the First Annual Celebrity Tennis Tournament, with such stars as Alex Olmeda, George Montgomery, Robert Wagner, Charlton Heston, Efrem Zimbalist, Raquel Welch, Robert Stack, Lloyd Bridges, David Janssen, Rod Taylor, and Rhonda Fleming.

Hal McCreery, one of Stanford University's football greats, and a member of Stanford's Hall Of Fame, passed away. He was a star on the high school grid teams of 1917-1920. Johnny Lyons, a former professional football player with the Brooklyn team, and also a graduate of Coronado High School, became president of the Local 36 of the Teamsters Union.

When President John F. Kennedy was assassinated in November 1963, Coronado, like the rest of the nation, halted and then sputtered along for the balance of the year. Coronado was notoriously on the side of the G.O.P. at election time, but Kennedy had won over the hearts of the nation. In Coronado, stores closed and streets were deserted as news of his death came over the television and radio. Monsignor John Purcell conducted a solemn requiem mass at Sacred Heart Church. Whatever else happened that year seemed inconsequential, compared to the national tragedy.

According to a survey in January 1964, the State Economic Development Agency reported the bridge would give "the 13,000 upper class residential area an additional $80 million dollars a year…" through new tourism and business. In March, California Governor Edmund G. (Pat) Brown went to the top man in the Defense Department seeking permission to build the bridge. Brown bypassed the Navy, asking Defense Secretary Robert McNamara to pitch in, and have the Navy change its policy and approve construction of the $30 million span.

The controversy raged in bold headlines. The local paper announced on December 10th: "BRIDGE HEARING; BOTH SIDES TOLD." The hearing was held before the Army Corps of Engineers at the Convention Hall in San Diego's Civic Center on December 7, 1964. Representative Bob Wilson opposed the bridge; Rear Admiral Dwight Johnson, and Councilman Joseph Callahan, president of the Coronado Residential Association, likewise opposed it and gave long and emphatic reasons why. Ben Wyatt of the Chamber of Commerce, Representative Lionel Van Deerlin, and several of the City Councilmen supported the bridge, reasoning that it would bring economic viability to the city. A Division of Highways Report added to the economic argument by noting, "If the Coronado Towers are built, they will add about 2,900 residents who will be bridge clients…" and the "Hotel del Coronado is concentrating more and more upon the Conference Trade ... to meet their competition, they badly need a bridge." So there it was. Two sides, each with their own story, covering arguments for and against the span that would make the isolated island accessible. In the end, the side with the most energy, resources and political clout simply won out.

In April 1964, the Planning Commission presented its view of Rancho Carrillo, indicating there were projects and problems that should be digested and resolved before Rancho Carrillo was developed. These included a rapid transit bay crossing; the sewage disposal problem; possible lower bay development and an ocean outlet; high-rise condominiums; and whatever else the Commission felt was necessary. Planning Commissioner Dr. Paul Vetter took a different position, urging a decision on the valuable Strand property be made promptly. Mayor Walter Vestal and City Attorney Goodbody agreed, warning that a policy was needed promptly. Goodbody asked, "Do we do something now or do we have someone do it for us and jam it down our throats?" This brought about the decision that the Strand land would have to be sold, rather than leased and frittered away as had happened with the Amphibious Base. This land had been leased from the City during the war years and then bought by the federal government.

The City of Coronado had waited for two years for a court decision to be made relative to the tideland losses to the Port District. On June 4, 1964, the *Coronado Journal* editorialized:

> The City of Coronado has been in the courts ever since the Port District was organized, claiming its rights were infringed by voting methods; that its tidelands would be taken away illegally and that the citizens of this city should not be made to pay part of the charges for bonds issued on votes of citizens of San Diego.

The Superior Court, in two cases, and the Appellate Court in another, ruled against Coronado. Discouraged, but determined to carry on the fight to keep out of the Port District, Coronado took its case to the California Supreme Court, only to lose again. On September 3, 1964, it was announced that the Coronado City Council, by a vote of 3-2, had decided to plead its case against the Port District to the U.S. Supreme Court. The appeal reached the Supreme Court in October 1964. The Supreme Court ruled that not one grain of sand of the tidelands belong to any town or citizen of California. Coronado lost for the last time. The total cost of the court battles was $18,000.

Coronado's tidelands went to the Port District. This included the portion of First Street along San Diego Bay, west of the ferry slip, all of the old Navy housing area in the northeast corner, the Coronado Golf Course, and the Yacht Club. The Port District laid claim to all monies from these sources from the inception of the District in December 1962.

A building site originally named "Del Coronado Sands" by M. Larry Lawrence of the HDC Corporation was profiled in a colorful brochure, with pictures of proposed one-story cottages. So it was surprising news when the HDC Corporation suddenly applied to the town for a zone change on the property, seeking authorization to construct high-rise condominiums on the site! The request noted that the town would benefit from a broader tax base on the high-rise buildings, and that the economic climate prevented development of anything but a high rise. The zoning change was granted and a plan drawn up for 37 acres of land running south of the Hotel. A portion of the acreage included 2,100 feet on the oceanfront. It was subdivided into lots, trees were planted, and streets paved.

On August 2, 1964, North Vietnamese torpedo boats reputedly attacked American destroyers patrolling the Gulf of Tonkin; counter strike against the torpedo boats was led by Commander James Stockdale, a Coronadan. After these incidents, and the Gulf of Tonkin Resolution in August, the war in Viet Nam began to escalate. Military needs brought a substantial number of families to

Coronado. School statistics reflect the increases in enrollments; rentals were at a premium, and the lack of housing once again became a major issue.

In sports and recreation, Coronado High School won two California Interscholastic Federation Championship titles; the five-man CHS golf team captured a title, and the CHS swimming team captured the CIF San Diego Section swimming championship for the second straight year. The second annual star-studded tennis celebrity tournament was held at the Hotel Del on May 28th. Among those who participated were Efrem Zimbalist, James Franciscus, Ty Hardin, George Montgomery, Lloyd Bridges, Richard Egan, and Peter Brown.

Coronado Masonic Lodge 441 celebrated its 50th anniversary. The cornerstone of the Lodge building was placed May 9, 1913 and the building dedicated on November 15, 1916.

The beaching of the Norwegian freighter *Sandarger* off the Silver Strand brought hundreds of spectators to the shoreline, who watched as the vessel broke out in flames. The fire took ten lives of the 45 crew members and 12 passengers.

An 1888 Coronado landmark was demolished when the Niemeyer home at Sixth and "D" (Palm Avenue triangle) was replaced by town house units. This was the fifth building dating from 1888 (or earlier) torn down during the year. The monetary value of Coronado's land was causing profit to overtake preservation, often playing second fiddle to quality. Great homes were subdivided, even cut in half. Architectural treasures were destroyed without a second thought. The importance of preservation to the overall charm of the village had not yet become a part of the vocabulary or the thinking of the community.

Not around to see these demolitions were two men who contributed mightily to the building of the island's heritage. Paul L. Hathaway, who had built many homes in Coronado, died in Monterey in May. Ernest R. Tiedemann, a native of Hamburg, Germany, twice councilman, and member of the Planning Commission from 1946-1961, had worked for the Hotel del Coronado for forty-seven years. He passed away in December.

Coronado's resident population totaled 19,550 in 1965, about 500 more than in 1960. A growing economy brought rising prices in sales and rentals of housing. This trend was augmented by the limited amount of housing available and a constant shift in numbers of servicemen, which fluctuated depending on peace or wartime. The government built the new Silver Strand Elementary School at Silverado Park, with ground-breaking taking place in in January, 1965. The doors opened for the fall session that same year. The buildings, designed by Paderewski, Dean and Associates, were made to resemble South Sea Island huts, but of more rugged construction.

This was also the year that Coronado celebrated her 75th year--the Diamond Jubilee. One reporter commented, "Coronado has only one traffic signal and it merely blinks. It has no major shopping centers, just an old-fashioned downtown…and a supermarket chain took special pains not to make the building look 'super.'" As Councilwoman Eleanor Ring put it, "Coronado still is basically a family town where mom, dad and kids can ride bicycles on Sunday afternoon!"

This was indeed true, but the "Enchanted Island" did not remain the little village it once was. The 76-year-old landmark hotel had made the island world famous, while nearby naval installations brought increased prosperity, population and change. But one more major change was coming in the form of a graceful concrete and steel span. And nothing would ever be the same again.

Coronado appointed its first Port Commissioner to represent the town. In February 1965, Captain Harry A. Sosnoski, (USN RET) became the seventh member of the Port Board. One of his first "yea" votes was to deepen the water in Glorietta Bay and other areas of the South Bay. The dredging would add fill to the Coronado golf course.

Construction workers guiding a bridge beam into place, 1968. (CHA)

In February 1965, the Council voted to spend an unbudgeted $10,000 to advertise the sale of Rancho Carrillo. A minimum bid was established at $4 million. "This is the first definitive action taken by the Council on the Rancho in more than ten years of intermittent discussion..." wrote the editor of the *Coronado Journal*.

Offers came from the State to buy Rancho Carrillo for use as a park, but Coronado refused to sell since the State did not pay taxes on its park land, and the Rancho, with residential development, would provide a good additional tax base. From all appearances no one wanted the Rancho--at least not for the price asked. Then in early November, American Factors Inc., of Kansas City, Missouri, offered to purchase Rancho Carrillo for $2.3 million cash.

Around the same time, contracts were opened for the Bay Bridge, and construction approved by the U.S. Army Corps of Engineers on January 19, 1965. Differing proposals for the dispersal of traffic as it came off the bridge created difficulties for city planners who were at odds with one another. Another issue they had to deal with was the flow of bridge traffic on streets; various plans were prepared for demolishing housing and redesigning the golf course. The work on the bridge actually started in early April 1965, when soil borings were made in Coronado, San Diego, and in the bay at varying depths, ranging to 300 feet.

In July, a lengthy letter was written by opponents of the bridge to Governor Edmund G. Brown proposing a new bridge vote, naming the many reasons why Coronado should have another chance. Not surprisingly, the Governor answered that he believed the bridge had been given ample study. The City Council, finally abandoning the long fight against the bridge, then turned its sights on the toll plaza offices and ticket gates. The construction of the toll plaza was done on the Coronado side because "experts" pointed out that it was not physically possible for it to be located on the San Diego side.

Officials of the California Transportation Department (CALTRANS) reported that the State of California would buy the ferries from the San Diego-Coronado Ferry Company at a negotiated price, somewhere in the $3 million range. The State had always purchased existing ferry systems when bridges were built, and showed concern for displaced ferry workers. The State also bought the Star and Crescent Ferries, and part of a water taxi service then in operation. These were acquired through the bond sale that financed the bridge. The property alongside the Coronado ferry slips, used for parking, would not be part of the purchase.

Early in 1965, services were held at Fort Rosecrans for Commander Henry T. Stanley, who died on January 11th. Stanley had chosen to stay with a plunging jet trainer plane that he aimed towards a

One of the Navy's top secrets in full view: the "Elephant Cage" of Coronado Heights, used for code-breaking, signals intercept, and listening to the Russians. (CHA)

vacant lot in Fremont, California, preventing it from exploding among hundreds of children walking home from two schools in the area. The Coronado-born officer, who had attended local schools, was flying from the aircraft carrier USS *Midway*. Grateful Fremont citizens named a playground for him and the 39-year-old pilot was awarded the Distinguished Flying Cross posthumously.

> Navy use of its old facilities at Coronado Heights had fallen off by the early 1960s. By 1963, they had demolished nearly all remaining buildings, and in May 1964, began construction of a top secret (top secret in full view, by the way) large Wullenweber Antenna and its attendant Building 1 control site. The finished antenna (completed by September 1965) was massive, 1300 feet wide, and known by almost everyone by the nickname, "Elephant Cage." The Wullenweber was German in origin, invented during World War II to help the Germans intercept and decrypt Allied messages. Coronado's "Wully" was part of a Pacific-wide network of stations that could intercept communications, triangulate signals, and break codes with powerful mainframe computers. Security was extremely high, and the technology represented by the Wullenweber was a significant technological, scientific, computing, and code-breaking achievement of the Cold War. In time, satellite communications and satellite intelligence would make the Wullenweber obsolete. It was finally torn down in 2014, with only a small section of the antenna remaining for historic and commemorative purposes.

In February 1965, the Viet Cong attacked two U.S. Army camps; U.S. and South Vietnamese pilots retaliated. By May, Army and Marine units had landed, and the military escalation could be felt all the way back in Coronado.

In 1966, construction started on the new San Diego-Coronado bridge. Measuring 2.12 miles long, with a 90-degree arc, the bridge cost $48 million to build. (CHA)

Fifty-five thousand people lined Orange Avenue to see the town's annual Fourth of July parade. Coronado's 18th official parade was sparked, as in previous years, by Commander and Mrs. Philip Dennler. Coronado's Diamond Jubilee celebration began officially on December 11th, marking the 75th year since its incorporation. At a Jubilee Ball, where guests wore costumes appropriate to the 1890s, Mayor Walter A. Vestal commented that the ball was attended by nearly 500 Coronado citizens. Everyone wanted to keep the occasion a family affair.

> Following the model of other Navy-sponsored sailing clubs on the East Coast, Joe Quicker and Al Tarantino set out to form the San Diego Naval Sailing Association in 1964, with its official founding in December 1965 – Coronado's second official yacht club. Its first race was held on Glorietta Bay that same month and, a year, later, the club's name was changed to the San Diego Naval Sailing Club. The San Diego Naval Sailing club established its first clubhouse and slips at the edge of the Naval Amphibious Base on Glorietta Bay. The clubhouse was really more of an equipment bin, but the club could boast a sandy beach, a pier, sunshine and barbeques. The San Diego Naval Sailing Club relocated to its present site at Silver Strand's Fiddler's Cove in June 1969. In short order, the club and associated Fiddler's Club Marina could boast an operation with 65 member-owned, and an eye-catching 51 marina-owned boats.

On January 4, 1966, the City Council, by unanimous vote rejected the bid by American Factors, Inc., for Rancho Carrillo at $2,300,000. The sale price was still held firm at $4 million.

Good news came to prospective buyers in February, when the Port District announced it would lease the 140 acres of tidelands adjacent to Rancho Carrillo to any developer who might be successful in buying the land. The terms included no residences on tidelands, and development of the perimeter in part for recreation. This had the effect of a "go-ahead" signal; with the future of a tidelands lease in question, developers had been afraid to purchase the Rancho Carrillo land before.

Construction of the bridge was due to begin in January 1967, with a completion date projected for early 1969. On November 15, 1966, the California Toll Bridge Authority in Sacramento approved a resolution for the sale of $47.6 million in revenue bonds to finance the project. One of the "terms" of the bonds required halting any competing forms of transportation, thus dooming the ferryboats. The Toll Bridge Revenue Bonds, due to mature in the year 2003, included acquisition of the San Diego and Coronado Ferry Company at a cost of $1,960,000, and the Star & Crescent Ferry at $2,597,000.

Bridge architect Robert Mosher advised Coronadans to begin planning development of the community immediately to be ready for the inevitable growth generated by construction of the bridge. Mosher stated, "Coronado could become one of the truly great urban areas of the U.S. I am sympathetic to the feelings of the people of Coronado."

In June 1966, Coronado and the San Diego Port District ended four years of dispute with an agreement covering all major points, including the golf course and Navy housing. No money was to change hands. Coronado would continue to operate both housing and the golf course as a landlord under a lease from the Port District. A yearly sum of $51,230 as ground rent would be transferred to a golf course trust fund, used to defray deficit expenses, with a yearly accounting and transfer of any surplus to the Port District. No rent payment was to be made for the golf course.

Coronado was honored a second time with a Navy vessel named for the town. The first USS *Coronado* was a Tacoma-class patrol frigate (PF-38) that served on escort duty in the Pacific during World War II. The ship was eventually transferred to the Soviet Navy, serving her last days in the 1950s as a frigate in the Japanese Maritime Self-Defense Force. The second USS *Coronado* (LPD-11), a Cleveland-Class Amphibious Transport Dock, was built by the Lockheed Shipbuilding and Construction Company of Seattle, Washington. The ship was launched July 30, 1966, under the sponsorship of Mrs. Eleanor R. Ring of Coronado, widow of Vice Admiral Stanhope C. Ring. Her daughter, Susan Ring, joined the celebration. Commissioning took place on May 23, 1970. In later years, the ship was reconfigured as an Auxiliary Command Ship (AGF-11), serving as flagship for several numbered fleets. In addition, the ship served as the U.S. Navy's Sea-based Battle Lab. Decommissioning took place on May 23, 2006.

Eight hundred people cheered Admiral Richard Harrison Jackson on his 100th birthday celebration at the Hotel del Coronado. This man was born on a farm in the Tennessee Valley, Alabama. He was a battleship sailor, rising to command the Battleship Division of the Battle Fleet and then, as a 4-star admiral, Commander-in-Chief Battle Fleet. An Annapolis graduate who, in his lengthy career, earned the Navy Cross, the French Legion of Honor, and many campaign medals, retiring in 1930. Jackson retired initially in Pearl City, Hawaii, and witnessed the Japanese attack on Pearl Harbor,

Small town politics held everyone's attention in 1966, during a high-tension recall election of School Board members that resulted in many a shouting argument across fence lines. This RECALL flag was flown on many automobile aerials. (CHA)

before moving to Coronado to become one of the island's most familiar and beloved figures. The Coronado Historical Association is preserving his ceremonial fore-and-aft hat, epaulets, and sword belt in their collection of artifacts.

A rival newspaper to the *Coronado Journal* appeared on the scene in 1966, when the *Coronado Reminder,* a free weekly, was delivered every Wednesday. Published in Imperial Beach, the paper was actually the *Imperial Beach News*, with an added Coronado section.

Especially popular was a column called, "Coronado Report Card," by Helen Smith Haralson, summarizing Coronado's school activities, and the actions taken during School Board meetings. Ill feelings ran high concerning management of school business, expenditures, and disciplinary problems. The Vietnam War and drug experimentation by students were serious problems during this trying period. In February, the Superintendent of Schools and other top school officials resigned. They declared the School Board impossible to work with. On March 3rd, the Board met to hear questions from parents. Parents demanded answers to 18 questions, which they wanted stated in a clear, concise, and understandable fashion.

In a 1966 recall election, aimed at replacing Board members disliked by the community, three new members were voted in by the largest recall margin in the County. This was the result of a rash of resignations, followed by weeks of disputes between the three board members recalled, and the school administration. The Coronado High School class of 1941 celebrated their 25th reunion with a beach party and dinner, with various local class members organizing the event led by Betty Gene Henderson Pittman. This loyal class has held a reunion every five years since, inviting other classes to join with them.

In December 1966, structural engineer Fred A. Sanderman, a local high school graduate, presented a structural analysis of the Central School and Auditorium, built in 1913. He said the buildings, including offices, classrooms and the auditorium, should be rehabilitated or replaced entirely. The inspection was called for by the School Board, to be in compliance with the Fields Act that required safety standards for all school structures built before 1933, the year of the big earthquake in Long Beach and Southern California. Sanderman said, "It is our opinion that with the expenditure of sufficient funds, the building complex can be rehabilitated."

In August 1967, the Navy announced plans for a Golden Anniversary Air Show and Open House to celebrate the official founding of North Island Naval Air Station on November 8, 1917. In 1967, 10,000 civilians and an equal number of military personnel and staff were on the island. Also berthed at North Island were four aircraft carriers, two cruisers, and four amphibious vessels.

The failure of President Johnson's policies to induce the Communists to negotiate, prompted him, on March 31, 1968, to order a partial halt to the bombing of North Vietnam. The local papers related information about troop deployments, ship movements, and decorations awarded the nation's heroes. Captain Ward S. Meeler was given the National Order of Vietnam, Fifth Class, and Gallantry Cross with Palm. He was Commanding Officer of the attack aircraft carrier, USS *Ticonderoga*. In Coronado, Commander Thomas F. Carlin U.S.N. (Ret.) died at the age of 65. A graduate of the Naval Academy Class of 1923, he had served during World War II.

On May 25, 1967, the *Coronado Journal* revealed the views of editor Williams, who in front-page pictures and stories, showed how there was "Room for a boom. Lots of Room." He explained the situation. Citing available land along First Street; Fourth and Glorietta; Seventh and Orange; Rancho Carrillo; the second bay entrance; Adella at Ynez; Tenth and "B"; the 370-acre parcel along the ocean owned by Larry Lawrence (worth $12 million); and Ocean Boulevard, he believed Coronado "could rival in miniature, the Copocabana Beach property in Rio, or the Malecon in Mazatlan."

Perhaps the editor was only reflecting the attitude of developers who were wasting little time. The bridge began to take form, and Henry D. Reilich was announced as resident engineer. One of the world's largest derrick barges, with a 300-foot deck and a 265-foot boom, was brought into the

Construction of the bridge is recorded by Mayor Paul Vetter, 1969. (CHA)

harbor to help with the construction. Four old Navy housing buildings were demolished to make way for the bridge. Eighty-four others remained to be rented by the City to Navy-connected families.

Planners estimated the population of Coronado to be 24,700 in January 1967. Unquestionably a result of Coronado's recent growth, the County tax assessor quickly responded, having a field day as he boosted land value in Coronado 20% across the board.

The Coronado newspapers for years had customarily observed the formality of not publishing names of young men or women arrested on various violations. It was seen not to be in the best interest of the youngsters. The matter of narcotics, especially in the schools, had become so serious that editor Williams felt the *Coronado Journal* could, and should, relate such matters and name people. He and the Coronado Police Department worked together; while the police investigated LSD and marijuana users and peddlers in the city, Williams named names and places whenever he could. He was particularly concerned about school children being tempted into the drug scene. In one marijuana raid, the Coronado police jailed 13 people and were looking for more. The paper gave names, ages and addresses. In February, Coronado School Superintendent Dr. Jordan told the School Board of plans to develop a program of education on the problems and dangers of drug use. A week later, 11 juveniles were suspended from the high school as a result of arrests involving narcotics.

The School Board had other troubles. It had set in motion plans to raze the 1913 Central Elementary School complex and replace it as soon as possible. The architects hired to design the replacement school were Des Lauriers and Sigurdson. In late December, the old Central School

Coronado High School pep rally in the 1960s. (CHA)

came down. Bill Wilson, contractor for the demolition, claimed, "I have never seen concrete with so little steel reinforcing ... the most dangerous structure I have wrecked in my long career. . ." Another contractor, who knew the Central School, declared, "It was as strong as the Rock of Gibraltar; it put up a terrific resistance." Coronadans who knew Central School have never ceased wondering about the action of the School Board. Designed by world-renown Quayle Brothers and Cressy architects, it was one of the City's most impressive structures.

The Coronado High School Islanders clinched first place in the Metropolitan Basketball League and a berth in the CIF playoffs. Six seniors were finalists in the National Merit Scholarship Competition, and many students received membership in the high school's Chapter of the California Scholarship Federation.

Ongoing problems facing the Council included trying to phase out the Navy housing. Some people complained that while the City collected rents, it did not maintain the housing in a decent manner. Many teen-age Coronadans learned to drive on the nearly-deserted roads of the housing project on Mullinex Drive.

In 1968, the Atlantic-Richfield Company purchased Rancho Carillo for four million dollars. The development plan named the site "Coronado Cays," and specified 1,500 dwelling units, Marina Park sites, a yacht club, and other facilities. Atlantic-Richfield would put in all improvements and dedicate streets to the city. The upkeep of the streets became the responsibility of the City, which also had to build a police station and fire sub-station. The buyers put up $50,000 to move the city dump and provided four acres for parks, three acres for other uses, and twelve acres for schools.

Looking south from the Hotel Del Coronado, this was the view before the Coronado Shores were built. (CPL)

Prospective market value of the development, after completion in five years, was anticipated to be $75 million.

The Port District agreed to dredging and filling on the tidelands property. There would be a 66-year lease, with Coronado Cays paying for the lease by delivering the newly claimed lands to the District. Escrow closed at the Bank of America on September 12, 1968. That ended a period of over 20 years of indecision over use of the "Hog Ranch."

One other project undertaken by private individuals began in July, as architects began working on a new Coronado Hospital. Expected to be completed by November 1967, John M. Weston served as chairman of the building committee.

One of the heaviest rainfalls in years fell on November 22nd. Alameda Boulevard, near 10th, was inundated. Three homes were flooded, and inestimable damage done, as 3.3 inches poured down in several hours.

By 1968, only three parcels of Coronado land remained undeveloped: the ferry landing property along the San Diego Bay front, owned by Haugh enterprises (although many people assumed it was public land); the dredged land on which the World War II housing stood, and the adjoining tidelands; and a valuable piece of property at Seventh and Orange Avenues, owned by the City of Coronado.

In the early years, Coronado's Board of Trustees, a five-member governing board, all elected and serving without pay, ran the town. It passed the laws, headed by its board president, in a similar manner to the present City Council (by the voting process). If decisions were important, they were put to the vote of the townspeople at election time. In the evolutionary process of politics, the Board of Trustees became the City Council headed by a Mayor. Then it was decided that members of the Council should be paid for their services because the job entailed considerable time, study, and often travel.

In 1968, the City Council contracted with the firm of Victor Gruen Associates, City Planners, to help determine the future direction of the City of Coronado as the coming of the bridge would result in major changes. The experts recommended:

- A downtown commercial mall, to be oriented toward pedestrians, located on Orange Avenue between 7th Street and the Hotel del Coronado. Traffic would be rerouted along 7th into "A", "B", and "C" Avenues;
- Multi-level parking complexes behind the present commercial area, mostly on "D" Avenue;
- Applying for right-of-eminent domain to acquire the property along "D" Avenue; and having merchants pay for this using a parking district fund;
- High-rise parking at the Hotel del Coronado (would be advisable, and maybe necessary);
- Possibilities of a coastal road linking the bridge and the Silver Strand;
- Opposition to an international airport built on land off North Beach;
- Possibility of complete elimination of original Palm and Olive Avenues, increasing real estate;
- A bicycle route around the golf course; studies showed water as being too rough for any sort of marina there;
- A civic center in the area of the Coronado Public Library, adjacent to the mall, and a possible location for the City Hall, Little Theater, Women's Club and other civic buildings;
- Closing of Dana Place, because too many streets were running into Orange Avenue;
- Turning Loma Avenue and Star Park from Orange into an expanded commercial zone.

After their six-month study, Ralph Martin and Victor Gruen told the Advisory Committee, "The survey is 10 years too late already." But Gruen Associates had not understood the concerns of the Coronado populace.

The North Island Association was concerned with the loss of the Star and Crescent ferries, the "nickel snatchers," which carried foot passengers to work at North Island. All attempts failed to have the system started up again. An article in the *New York Times* on April 28, 1968, bemoaned the fact time was running out for the San Diego-Coronado Ferry system, which had created romantic memories for thousands of present and former servicemen.

Even the naming of the bridge became a major problem. Assemblyman F. James Bear introduced a resolution in the Assembly to name the new bay span, the Robert F. Kennedy Memorial Bridge. A bridge inauguration committee was established by the City Council, which sat in "emergency" session. They sought resolution by sending telegrams to assemblymen and senators about naming the structure. To no one's surprise, it became the "San Diego-Coronado Bay Bridge"! (And later ... officially ... the "San Diego-Coronado Bridge," when it was astutely pointed out that there is no such thing as "Coronado Bay.")

This iconic photo captures of an end of an era — the dividing line between 'Coronado Past' and 'Coronado Present.' (CHA)

As late as 1968, Coronado was the only town in the region that did not have a historical society. The San Diego Congress of History listed more than 75 historical organizations, but none from the island. The City Council named a committee, which formed the Coronado Historical Association as a non-profit corporation on March 20, 1969, when a charter was granted by the State of California to the Coronado Historical Association, Inc. A Board of Directors was appointed to oversee the organization.

It is rare in the history of a town, that one particular year marks the pivotal point on which the character of that town turns. Usually, change is gradual, almost imperceptible, and residents have time to slowly assimilate the changes into their lives. Yet, for Coronado Island, 1969 was the year that, without a doubt, marked the end of the small residential village, and the beginning of a bustling resort. The change would be immediate and powerful, and for some, adjusting to it would not be easy. Life, as the islanders knew it, would never be the same.

In 1969, Coronado's assessed valuation rose 18.5% above that of 1968, to a total of $36,226,367, according to County Assessor E.C. Williams. The rise, the highest in San Diego County, was due to some construction, increased values because of the bridge, and the addition of Coronado Cays (Rancho Carrillo) property to tax rolls.

The Coronado Public Works Department provided many municipal services, which, when matched with the tax rate, provided citizens with services not available in other communities. Among the operations maintained were 38 miles of streets; 76 miles of sidewalks, curbs and gutters; 38 miles of sanitary sewers; 12 sewage pumping stations, and storm drains; 11 parks and one bowling green; and five and one-half acres of landscaping on Orange Avenue from First Street to the Amphibious Base; an estimated 7,000 street trees; a weed control program; a fly and rodent control program; public buildings; all city-operated vehicles; and supervision of refuse collection performed by a private collector twice a week.

One day began ominously in February when residents of the Country Club Estates woke up to find unwanted springs erupting from the ground on their property, causing great damage both inside and outside their houses. Coronado's City Building Official Robert G. Odiorne, after

Commuter traffic was not the only thing that would change with the coming of the bridge. Weekly rail transport up the Strand, along Pomona Avenue and First Street, to the Navy's industrial operations on North Island would soon end as well. Note the unfinished loom of the bridge in the background. (CHA)

studying the problem, dug out the old maps and found that huge drainage pipes had been put in the ground when the Spanish Bight was filled during 1943 and 1944. He also discovered that these pipes were never hooked up to the City drainage system; the pipes had been covered over and were now leaking. The Federal government took care of its mistake.

In the spring of 1969, ground-breaking ceremonies took place for a new Presbyterian Church School. The new Coronado Tennis Center, designed by Matteson and Snook, opened. The School Board found itself in the middle of a dress-code fight at the high school. Coronado parents complained that young people had become slovenly in appearance, with dirty clothes, bare feet, and shoulder-length hair. The School Board reached decisions such as banning beards and moustaches, hair below the collar line, and skirts no more than three inches above the knees.

As Coronadans watched the bridge edge toward completion, concern arose over the safety of the low side railings. Experts assured everyone through motion picture films that the railing would keep vehicles from going over the side. The bridge itself was a marvel of engineering and design. Stretching like a great curved ribbon, it reached two and one-quarter miles across the bay and soared over 200 feet at its highest point.

With the dedication ceremony about to take place, G.K. Williams, owner of the *Coronado Journal*, who had pushed so hard for the bridge, declared that one man, above all others, should be at the opening ceremonies--G. Edmund (Pat) Brown. The former Governor and his wife regrettably were going to be in Europe and could not attend. But, as Governor Brown said, "the San Diego-

The final link in the bridge is squeezed into place in 1969. (CPL)

Coronado Bay Bridge is one that I will be proud of until the day I die, and I do hope that I will be able to quietly travel that bridge some early morning because I feel this is my baby."

On what some regard as one of the most momentous dates in Coronado's history, at one second after midnight, on August 3, 1969, the San Diego-Coronado Bay Bridge opened for regular car traffic. An antique car parade, a bicycle race, and finally a jogging event had kicked off the celebration on August 2nd, with pennants bearing the City seals of San Diego and Coronado flying in the air. Mayors Frank Curran and Paul Vetter lifted a toll-gate barrier at the Glorietta Toll Plaza, giving the signal to unite in a volley of fireworks. The Hotel del Coronado boasted on its largest outdoor sign, 'AT LAST.' Just moments before the opening ceremonies, a human tide washed across the bridge as hundreds of runners, joggers, and cyclists flooded all five traffic lanes, and poured over the span in a ceremonial gesture.

Governor Ronald Reagan provided the principal dedicatory address on August 2nd and unveiled a bronze plaque, which was placed at the Plaza Administration Building. The Most Reverend Francis J. Furey, Bishop of the San Diego Catholic Diocese, gave the invocation. Coronado's Mayor, Paul Vetter, served as Master of Ceremonies. He introduced officials and then told the crowd, "Coronado is gone; long live Coronado! We'll never be the same." He said that the population, economy, and size of the community would change. But he expressed hope that the "pleasant, little, comfortable town would not change too much." A wide variety of ceremonies took place that day, including a gathering of 1,200 at the Hotel del Coronado for lunch and a tribute to 50 Vietnam veterans. A flotilla of U.S. Navy ships, small craft, and aircraft took part in the salute to the opening.

> The first toll to be charged was 60 cents in both directions. In 1980, that toll was changed to $1.20, collected for traffic going westbound to Coronado only; in 1988 that was changed to $1.00. Motorcycles, busses, and two-person carpools were free. Commuter booklets sold for $24. That represented a reduced toll of 60 cents. In 2002, the bridge was declared toll-free after the original bridge bond was paid off.

All day on the 2nd of August, thousands rode the ferries for the last time--many with family and friends to experience a vanishing tradition. The bay ferries, San Diego and Coronado, two of the five existing vessels, nosed into their slips at midnight on August 2, 1969. Their skipper signaled the engines to stop for the last time. The end of an era had come. Amid the cheers, tears, and celebration of the last ferry ride, the Navy "nickel snatcher," almost unnoticed, also died quietly at midnight. On August 2, 1969, William A. Peterson wrote, "Let this day be proclaimed as a great day of mourning for the residents of Coronado who now own cars. Their small pleasure and the pursuit of happiness was to pay 10 cents for a delightful ferry boat ride across the bay. A day of mourning, a day of shame, a day of disgust." Now Coronado and San Diego were, in fact, inextricably linked together by an umbilical cord.

The year 1969 held more surprises in store for Coronado residents. In October, the *Coronado Journal* headlined the fact that the "Coronado Towers are on again today!" Construction planned earlier was to proceed. The developers, Snyder-Loews, filed the map for Coronado Shores; details of the plans were provided in the *Coronado Journal-Compass* of October 30, 1969. Coronadans were very much distressed that any buildings would be put on property always considered "beach land." In addition, high-rise buildings would now be towering boldly next to the gables and turrets of the beloved Hotel del Coronado.

A new town lay on the horizon, but what had the great bridge wrought?

The ultimate design of the bridge and its specific location was largely predicated on the Navy's height requirements, allowing its ships to pass underneath. (CHA)

A new way to get home. (CHA)

(Image above: CPL / LCC)

Chapter 10
The Opening of the Second Century

SPONSORED BY MIKE O'KEEFE IN MEMORY OF HIS FATHER ART O'KEEFE

AT 12:01 A.M. ON AUGUST 3, 1969, the spectacular bay bridge opened to traffic. That same year, Coronado installed its first traffic signal lights; and on September 4, 1969, the first phase of Coronado Cays was completed. The City Council approved closing First Street in line with a special use permit for R & B Development Company's construction of the Oakwood Garden Apartments. The 549-unit rental complex opened at 1515 Second Street, a project that cost $11 million dollars and was completed in 1971. The structure occupied 13 acres north of Coronado Hospital and stood three-stories.

At the beginning of 1970, the island's population stood at 20,020. A new school resource center of classrooms, library, and cafeteria shared by the high and middle schools was completed at a cost of $851,555. As a bonus, the new facility was the largest meeting room in Coronado.

Nearly 15 years later, John R. Goodbody was interviewed upon his retirement after his service to the people of Coronado. He arrived in Coronado in 1915 from Arizona, and was a second generation lawyer. His specialty was the "interesting business of municipal law." Goodbody served from 1940 to 1970 as Coronado's City Attorney. He observed:

> "We had so many controversies, one after another--someone in the League of California cities said, [that city is the most New England-type city that I know]… they fight over everything.… People came to the Council, raised the devil publicly because they were interested in the city. Some of it got pretty thick".

At his retirement, Goodbody said:

> "Three topics continue--the bridge, Shores, and Cays--progress has already brought a lot of pain to this town. There has always been a group that has been against anything that has ever been proposed."

As for the Hotel del Coronado, it's in one corner of the island and takes care of its own affairs. I don't see, unless there is a radical reason for doing so, why the City should bother with it. What they do to themselves should be their own business. I don't see why so many people in town take an adversative position against the Del.

Mr. Goodbody, one of Coronado's most respected individuals, distinguished himself as a Judge, and understood Coronado perfectly. He had the pulse of the community. Had he made those statements in 1998, there would have been very little change in the tenor or content.

Patients and personnel moved into Coronado's new hospital at 250 Prospect Place. The hospital was designed by Architect Frank L. Hope, Sr. The new Coronado Fire Station at Sixth and "D" was finished at a cost of $248,000. Development moved forward as the old Mission-style ferry building and nearby ferry docks were demolished. At Second and Orange, one of the City's oldest commercial buildings, which housed the first grocery store on the island, was also razed.

Throughout the year 1970, the *San Diego Union* forecast dramatic changes in Coronado since people could now cross the bridge rapidly to get to the City. And the Bulletin of the Economic Research Bureau of San Diego correctly predicted Coronado business would suffer due to competition with San Diego, as Coronado residents found it easy to get to the stores across the bridge.

The new Coronado Hospital built in 1968. (CHA)

On September 1, 1970, President Richard M. Nixon held a State Dinner at the Hotel del Coronado in honor of Presidente Gustavo Diaz Ordaz of Mexico, with 600 guests attending, including former President Lyndon B. Johnson, and California's Governor Ronald Reagan. A welcoming parade took place on Orange Avenue under strict security, while the nation watched on

Looking across Coronado Golf Course to the Coronado Shores, located on the site of the former Tent City, c. late-1970s. (CHA)

television. This was the year the Hotel became California Historical Landmark Number 844; a year later, the hotel was listed on the National Register of Historic Places.

From the moment the bridge opened, traffic overwhelmed Coronado. The bridge seemed to inspire drivers to use Third and Fourth Avenues as a speedway to get to and from North Island in the shortest time possible. In earlier days, drivers waited forever on Orange Avenue to reach the ferry. Neither system of getting people on and off the island has worked. Stop lights and pedestrian crossings have not slowed the speed with which eager North Island personnel get to work and return home.

Before the time of the bridge, 5,000 military personnel used the pedestrian ferry for the bay crossing, and scarcely traveled the streets of Coronado. By March 1970, an estimated 20,000 vehicles were on the new State Highway to North Island. In a study conducted by CALTRANS in 1987, in one 24-hour period over 54,600 vehicles used the bridge.

A frenzy of development followed. Home prices rose 34% in one year, a factor directly attributable to the coming of the bridge. Some older homes were lifted off their foundations and moved to half of a lot, while a second structure was built on the other half. Poor planning allowed housing on the back half of lots, garages below, apartments above, and became one of Coronado's most unforgivable errors. More residential units meant less open space, more houses, more cars, more people, more traffic, and alleys lined with parked vehicles.

In June 1971, owners of the Coronado Shores Towers celebrated the completion of the first tower, "The Cabrillo." This followed construction of the Shores seawall in 1970, over 2,100 feet long. The editor of the town newspaper wrote, "The Cabrillo represented a big step into future development of the area once known as Tent City." This was the first of ten 15-story condominium towers built throughout the 1970s, as a joint venture of Jerome H. Snyder Company and Loew's Corporation, representing an investment of $125 million when completed on the 35-acre site.

> The first fire station at the Cays opened in May 1971. The total cost was approximately $170,000, and originally included a small police substation that was eventually discontinued.

As the new developments blocked the skyline, the village atmosphere of Coronado decreased. Its keepers had forfeited the concept of a low-rise seacoast resort. Even the grand Hotel del Coronado became eclipsed by the new concrete and steel giants. Yet the high-rises jolted the citizens into realizing that if such development were to continue, Coronado would soon resemble Miami Beach. The result of a determined community effort was a 40-foot building height limit imposed throughout the village, restricting any building to three stories. In the haste to limit height, locations for vehicle parking and land needed for horizontal building were overlooked.

The Belt Line train on the Strand made its last run on March 24, 1971. A symbolic ceremony was held alongside the tracks, near the old Coronado Boathouse, signaling demolition of the 83-year old railroad.

In November, G.K. Williams, editor of the *Coronado Journal*, died at the age of 80. "Nobody was neutral in feelings about G.K.," remarked a writer, "They either liked him or they disliked him." What can be said is that Williams pushed as strongly as anyone to open up Coronado. He provided the forum for those who wanted to make the resort town economically viable.

In April 1972, Coronado elected its mayor directly (rather than the "appointment by Council" method) for the first time. Rolland McNeeley, local real estate broker, edged out Councilman Robin Goodenough to become Mayor by 174 votes. Goodenough had stood twice before as one of Coronado's most steadfast and visionary mayors. Bonds for a gymnasium failed due to lack of a 2/3 majority vote.

In the first years of the 1970s, little progress was made toward ending the war in Vietnam. But President Nixon had reduced the U.S. presence considerably in that country, and by mid-1971, the U.S. had almost completely ended its ground combat role in South Vietnam. Still, in March 1972, the peace talks broke off. On January 28, 1973, a treaty was signed by representatives from the U.S., South Vietnam and North Vietnam. By February 1, Prisoners-of-War came home, including Coronadans Captain James. B. Stockdale, Captain Harry T. Jenkins, Jr., Captain Ernest M. Moore, Jr., Commander Edward H. Martin, Commander William R. Stark, and Commander Brian D. Woods. Years of tragedy and torment for the Coronado military community ended. Those years showed the determination and strength of waiting families as they bound together to focus attention on the plight of the P.O.W.'s. In 1970, Mrs. Sybil Stockdale was coordinator of the National League of Families of American Prisoners in Southeast Asia, and nationally known for her brave efforts to focus attention on the plights of POWs. Captain Stockdale would rise to the rank of Vice Admiral and would be awarded the Medal of Honor, Sybil Stockdale would be recognized with the award of the Navy Distinguished Public Service Medal.

Vice Admiral James Stockdale and his wife, Sybil, at the USS 'Avenger' in 1985. (CHA)

Coronado Public Library in 1974. (CPL)

In 1972, a change occurred on the exterior grounds of the Hotel del Coronado, with the addition of 200 units called Ocean Towers and Grande Hall, a large convention center. Toward the end of the year, the Commodore Condominiums were built at 333 Orange Avenue. Structures that did not complement the historic architecture of the village pointed to the need for stricter and stronger design standards. Before the next two decades ended, a half-dozen cookie-cutter motels lined either side of Orange Avenue between Third and Fifth Streets. It became clear the problem was not just what was coming down, but importantly, what was going up.

Coronado had become a place with two freeways, a major ingress/egress bridge, and high-rises with trends toward condos. The growth yielded few amenities for the town. Architectural jewels that would have reflected heritage and continuity with the past were patently missing. Coronado did not have an accommodating Civic Center, Community Center, Police Station, or High School. Its major public buildings were of the inexpensive 1940s-1960s "crackerbox" style. The Council attempted to acquire the area southeast of the tidelands, adjacent to the old Navy housing, as a public park. Council members wrestled with traffic, but neither problem was resolved despite committee meetings, studies, and discussions. The Council did appropriate $362,500 to purchase a parcel of land and a bungalow court at Seventh and Orange to be temporarily occupied by civic organizations. It was given the name "Babcock Court" in honor of Elisha Babcock, Jr.

> The Library Board got in gear to promote the idea of an entire new library building and the Friends of the Coronado Public Library was formed in 1970. With City Council support, architect Homer Delawie was hired to develop plans that involved maintaining the old "Spreckels" building, but demolishing all the other wings and adding some 23,000 sq. ft. of new space. During construction, library services moved to the recently vacated High School library, which the City leased for the purpose. The new Coronado Public Library opened on June 16, 1974, as the cultural center the City had wanted.

During October 1975, the biggest dredging project in the history of the region deepened San Diego Bay. Coronado, the Silver Strand, and Imperial Beach areas received bay bottom soil to replace the beach land lost by erosion. Thirty million cubic yards of sand were dredged from San Diego Harbor. One million cubic yards of that deposit was made north of the Hotel, with 16 million deposited southward, greatly widening the beach.

For decades, citizens had elected public officials to take care of Coronado's business for them. Coronadans, dedicated to the idea of keeping their village a historic residential seaside resort, jammed the City Council meeting during a public hearing on January 8, 1975. Their objective was to fight for the preservation of Ocean Boulevard's "mansion row." Coronadans opposed the

Planning Commission, and the City Council voted "NO," preventing developers from building a cooperative structure of eight dwellings at 1043 Ocean Boulevard. Over two decades later, this decision preserved one of the island's most unique areas.

In February 1976, an idea to give Coronado a needed facelift was offered by the Chamber of Commerce, which made a restrained statement that the "business district was somewhat seedy." The Council voted for a plan to include shrubbery, planter boxes, and sidewalk ramps in a seven-shop section on Orange Avenue, and gave approval to use allocated federal money. Citizens led such a tirade against the proposal that the Council turned to the voters. Tired of the rhetoric, the Council said "NO" to the project.

Changes took place during the bicentennial year of the nation. The Coronado High School gymnasium was reopened at a remodeling cost of $37,000, and rededicated in memory of Bob Carrothers, arguably Coronado's most renowned athlete who was killed in an automobile accident. In March, 1977, the 1930s "handsome Spanish style-building" on the triangular piece of land between R.H.Dana Place, Churchill Place, and Orange Avenue, which had shops, a restaurant and a miniature golf course, was demolished to make way for the Coronado Plaza, another "handsome Spanish-style building."

Demolition of older buildings continued at a regular pace as Coronado's first sanitarium on Ynez Place, "The Annex," was leveled. Institutions no longer needed were closed, such as the Glorietta School, built in 1944, which was boarded up on June 10th. Older residences were demolished to make way for townhouses and apartments.

During January and February 1978, a series of storms and strong winds brought heavy, rising surf, blowing beach sands, and flooding of the streets, reminiscent of earlier times in this century.

On October 6, 1979, a new Beach and Tennis Club facility, and a 96-room addition were dedicated at the Hotel del Coronado, in time for the arrival of President Jimmy Carter. On February 26, 1983, Great Britain's Queen Elizabeth II, and Prince Phillip, Duke of Edinburgh arrived for a tour and luncheon aboard the carrier USS *Ranger* at North Island. They had arrived on the HMS Britannia for a tour of San Diego.

The Council grappled over which firm should build the co-generation plant for the City. In April 1983, the Council voted to spend $311,000 for the plant, designed to save public and private utility bills $88,000 yearly, a dramatic reduction in the cost of electricity. Four years later, news arrived that the enormously expensive plant would probably increase utility costs.

The May 5, 1983 issue of the *Coronado Journal* presented an excellent "History of Coronado's Golf Courses," by Mayor Pat Callahan. This might have had something to do with an ongoing interest in a second golf course for Coronado's duffers at Coronado Heights.

Coronado shares land with other government agencies. Within its town limits are the Naval Air Station, the Naval Amphibious Base, and the base at Coronado Heights. The ocean and bay frontage of Coronado include several State Tidelands. The U.S. Navy, the State of California, the San Diego Unified Port District and the City of Coronado share parts of the bay shores. Restrictions are clear as to how the Tidelands may be used.

In March 1981, the San Diego Coastal Commission backed plans by Watts Industries of San Diego, Inc., to develop the expanded Coronado Point Condominiums complex where Orange Avenue dead-ends into San Diego Bay. The decision was made by the Commission, whom Coronado residents considered "outsiders". In June 1983, construction of the project began. The design used was a direct response to Coronado's citizens, and the Design Review Commission, which insisted on standards that would reflect the "village atmosphere." The 7.5-acre bay front site cost $73 million

Coronadans were thrilled when locals Robbie Haines, Eddie Trevelyan and Rod Davis sailed to win the Gold Medal in Soling Class at the 1984 Olympics in Los Angeles. (CHA)

dollars. One hundred ninety-eight units were constructed in several phases. The project developers wanted the design to be compatible with the Hotel del Coronado. The units have balconies and dormers, using the Hotel as an inspiration. In November 1984, arsonists destroyed the construction. The developers now aimed for completion in early 1986, after the cleanup was finished.

Coronado mourned the passing of Dr. Paul Vetter. He had been Mayor from 1968-1970, and practiced in Coronado for 30 years. Coronadans named a park in honor of this revered man.

SANDAG (the San Diego County Association of Governments) made a forecast that in the year 2000 the population of Coronado would be 23,200. In 1980, the population stood at 18,900. The report suggested that there had been an attempt to preserve Coronado's small town atmosphere, but for two decades it had been very difficult.

In April 1984, one vote decided the mayoral election. Attorney R.H. Dorman defeated Mary Herron by 2,182 to 2,181. In a recount, Dorman won by eight votes. A group named the Citizens for Improved Types of Environment Standards (CITES) intended to help develop guidelines for the City. Coronadans wanted to return the town to a place where visitors and new residents were welcome. Coronadans realized that the things they loved most about the place they called home were eroding. This renewed awareness increased citizen interest and an insistence that government pay attention to what was taking place. Problems such as traffic and density were approached with a strong eye toward the future, rather than on what had already happened. While the bridge had opened the town, construction for business purposes had contributed heavily to change.

The Le Meridien Hotel appeared as a $48 million dollar, 300-room luxury hotel with recreational facilities, banquet and meeting facilities, dining, entertainment and shops. The site, built on 16 acres, was leased to developers by the Port District. This project, completed within several years, later became the Coronado Island Marriott Hotel.

Another project, generally applauded, was the Old Ferry Landing Development facing downtown San Diego, consisting of 40,000 square feet with shops and restaurants. The San Diego Unified Port District included a ferry pier in the project. The 220-foot pier, at the foot of "C" Avenue, was built at a cost of $645,000. It was used both for ferry-docking and fishing. Ferry service between Coronado and San Diego by the Star and Crescent Boat Company, returned after an absence of eighteen years. The ferries no longer carried cars, but instead passengers and bicycles. It was a vague reminder of life on the island in by-gone days.

In June 1984, he Army Corps of Engineers turned down the move for a second channel on the Strand as economically unfeasible. The second entrance project came up a year later. Both times Coronadans turned a deaf ear to the suggestion.

In September 1984, San Diego rejected Coronado's dogged efforts to annex North Island, the fifth attempt in 20 years. The Coronado City Council had made a bid to annex NAS North Island, but this effort proved unsuccessful. The U.S. Navy politely declined to be annexed by either San Diego or Coronado. If successful, it would have brought Coronado $438,000 in annual State and Federal revenues, and enfranchised about 8,000 sailors as Coronado voters. Two years later, Mayor R.H. Dorman was adamant about the plan for the City to annex North Island, with a feasibility study for use as an airport! He would clash with City of San Diego officials over his plan. In 1987, after waiting for 35 years, Coronadans learned that the Council had approved the peninsular city's annexation of more than 1,658 acres of North Island Naval Air Station, except for 715 acres of land--primarily the shore areas--and 3,384 acres of water that fell under the City of San Diego's jurisdiction. The Local Agency Formation Committee (LAFCO) approved Coronado's request to include North Island within its City's boundaries. The idea had been debated for 35 years. If one word could best express involvement in Coronado affairs, that word would be "persistence."

In October 1984, citizens selected a design for a $3 million dollar, 22-acre "park" located just north of the bridge on tidelands. When completed, Tidelands Park featured bike and exercise paths, playing fields with a playground, a beach on San Diego Bay, and large grassy areas and trees. In January 1985, an ad hoc Transportation Circulation Committee studied the idea of a road around First Street to North Island and one around the Coronado Municipal Golf Course to the Strand. The idea of a road around the island was scuttled before it got to the Council. The City formally dedicated the Coronado Development Agency (CDA) in April 1985, in order to provide a funding source for projects such as a Community Center or credit for backing bond issues.

On November 8, 1984, The Landing condo complex on First Street mysteriously caught fire while still in the framing stage of construction, creating one of the most spectacular blazes in Coronado history. Several theories were advanced about possible perpetrators —from opponents of the condo development to vagrants—but no one was ever brought to trial. (CPL)

Coronado High School's Islanders won the CIF football championship with a 28-6 victory over Mountain Empire. The IA champs placed three Islanders, Chad Carpenter, Bob Breglio, and Brett Smitt on the Mountain-Desert first team.

Bank of America building at Orange Avenue and 9th Street, in the early 1970s. (CHA)

The increased number of vehicles on the freeway to North Island led the Traffic Board to decide the solution should be a three-lane tunnel under Fourth Street. CALTRANS agreed with the idea of a Fourth Street tunnel project and set the price tag at $60 million. That decision brought out the intractable resident viewpoint: "We don't want to go over the freeway, under it, around it, or extend it. No tube, no tunnel, no road." That was the dilemma before the Council, which now sought a feasibility study to link North Island and the bridge. In January 1986, The Traffic Board decided the three-lane tunnel under the street would solve the traffic problem. The concept recalled John D. Spreckels' dream of a tunnel from San Diego to South Island in the late 1920s.

In 1986, a record 399 automobile accidents occurred, charged largely to "out-of-town" vehicles moving to and from work. City employees tabulated a list of "Mean Streets," those considered most dangerous. The Naval Amphibious Gate 2, on the Silver Strand, was ranked the place most likely for one to be involved in a fender-bender. Crime was reported to be up 34% in 1986, and without hesitation attributed to "out-of-town" criminals.

In January 1987, when jet parts were found in the parking lot and on the roof of the Hotel del Coronado, residents complained about "TFOA"--things falling off aircraft--called by some "a common occurrence. A 5-ft., 6-inch, 30-pound aluminum door fell off an SH-3 helicopter into a Cays swimming pool. Panels, flaps, fuel tanks, and antennas were also found, mostly in non-populated areas.

The Ferry Landing commercial development was built in 1986, and was fully opened by 1987. The Il Fornaio Italian Restaurant opened in 1999.

> The USS Coronado returned after a 17 year absence. An amphibious ship, it was converted and sent to the Persian Gulf as the flagship for the Commander of the U.S. Middle East Forces.

Within certain groups, discussion focused on lack of business in Coronado. The Planning Commission listed the number of business turnovers, blaming them on the close proximity of the Navy Exchange and Commissary, where military personnel and retirees obtained goods at better prices. For the benefit of those few who wanted the U.S. Navy elsewhere, the paper pointed out that Coronado "Is the Military," with retired military families, including most of the retailers, the banks and businesses, benefiting. The turnover of military also made for a brisk real estate business.

The Coronado Flower Show is the largest tented flower show in the nation, brightening the City every year in April. City of Coronado's official flower is the Crown of Bohemia Hibiscus. (CHA)

That spring, Coronado was hit by a tremendous hail storm. On March 5, 1987, a waterspout struck the Cays. It left damage in its wake and lifted a 30-foot yacht from the water. The wonderful Annual Coronado Flower Show, held for the 62nd year in Spreckels Park, came off superbly in late April.

During 1987, the Coronado Historical Association provided a "Coronado Living History" of 86 homes to emphasize Coronado's architectural and historical heritage. Preservationists were tested when the City-owned "Babcock Court," located on a prime spot at the corner of Seventh Street and Orange Avenue, was marked for demolition to gain space for a public building. The cost to repair it would have been $200,000.

The Planning Commission was hit with turnovers. A host of committees and commissions saw the need for more business and construction, while other ad hoc groups fought to "Keep Coronado as It Was." One matter that struck deep into the hearts of some individuals was the possibility that someone might dare to convert their home into a "Bed and Breakfast" location. A letter to the editor of the *Coronado Journal* threatened the City Council: "You'd better put it to a vote or we will have to consider going to the people with a petition...." The belief was that a bed and breakfast might bring more people, more cars [parking], more traffic, more noise, and would ruin historic homes. An early test came when Bonnie Marie Kinosian, owner of the Drewisch Sisters historic home, desired a special "B & B" use permit where she already operated a dance studio. The City denied her request, and after a second appeal, she was turned down. The reasons given were increased delivery trucks and "strangers coming day and night." The issue was placed on the November 1987 ballot and categorically lost by a 3-1 margin.

At the same time, the Coronado Historical Association purchased a home on Loma Avenue, with the intent of opening the three-story structure as a "Coronado Museum." A local architect called it "a new concept in town as far as parking requirements go--a walk-in museum." Neighbors called it a "Dagger in the Heart of Star Park." Both arguments seemed valid. The idea of restoring

Locals surfing, Central Beach 1970s. (Steve Ogles)

historic buildings for adaptive reuse had been internationally accepted. Without that possibility, older homes might otherwise be demolished. Mayor Dorman, in support, discussed City purchase of the home.

Mr. Dorman also proposed an elevated roadway and six lanes of traffic for Fourth Street, paid for from revenue funds. Coronadans hadn't forgotten that the bridge and the thrust for more business had led to the first man-made traffic disaster. The sentiment expressed by residents charging boldly forward into the 20th century was "Let's Preserve the Small Village Atmosphere." During 1987, a flood of letters arrived in the newspaper mailbox about the tidal wave of development, expressing dissatisfaction with zoning laws that allowed intensive lot coverage. In 1887, H.L. Story had the right idea when he said, "Small lot development would be a model for other cities." The town was divided into 25' x 150' foot lots with alleys, a model of residential development and the envy of city planners. His solution to congestion had long since been disregarded.

A Downtown Task Force appointed by the Council was to review and make recommendations on matters affecting business owners, residents, and the City Government. In November 1987, Coronado had 9,792 registered voters. A much smaller number actually voted, reflecting apathy among Coronadans. Registered voters did not necessarily reflect the attitudes of property owners attending Council meetings. Renters and non-property owners helped the Council make decisions relative to a city in which they had no proprietary interest--not an uncommon practice in California. The Council turned down a request for construction of a "Circle K," the first of many fast-food businesses rejected. But before long, there were other fast-food places within the City. The Best Western Motel at Third and Orange Avenue began construction to include underground parking. This hotel was the second of such sites along Orange, between Second and Fourth, banking the tourism dollar.

Coronado had its typical January through March storms. In January 1988, high tides and winds gusting to 65 miles per hour combined to blast Coronado with one of the worst storms in years, causing $1.5 million in public and private damage. The beaches were hit hard and Silver Strand Highway was closed. Sixty large trees were uprooted in town, crushing cars and knocking down power cables.

The Hotel del Coronado had been active both internally and externally. M. Larry Lawrence was responsible for preservation and restoration of the Oxford Hotel, moving it to the hotel grounds for conversion to offices. Later, the Windsor Cottage was salvaged at the last moment at the behest of the Coronado Historical Association. The building was moved to the beachfront at the Hotel. A number of special exhibits and events took place in anticipation of the 100th birthday of the Hotel during the week of February 18, 1988. The celebration lasted the entire year, with proceeds going to a dozen civic and cultural non-profit organizations.

Another "commission" was jump-started when Mary Herron led a task force to apply for the California MainStreet Program, meant to revitalize downtown areas while encouraging economic development. The State of California MainStreet Program turned down the local initiative, but City Council subsequently voted to appropriate $50,000 for the program. MainStreet Ltd. limited its role to an area called "downtown," from Eighth Street down to the Hotel del Coronado. The organization handled many social functions designed to attract residents and visitors, as well as commenting on parking needs and traffic studies.

Coronado had official government departments and committees. Citizens formed community associations, organizations, committees, and advisory groups. These groups produced three (and sometimes four) layers of involvement in the recommendation-making processes. Duties and functions substantially overlapped. Names of some individuals appeared on several different committees or boards at the same time.

The Coronado school system received a great deal of press after 1985. Few people questioned the instructional superiority of the schools, especially considering acceptance rates of high school graduates into the military academies and colleges and universities. Strong emphasis was now placed on water sports, in addition to football, basketball, and tennis, which had long been the high school's staple sports. Earlier teams had won major Southern California championships as a member of the major Metropolitan League that included schools with much larger enrollments. A new emphasis on participation of women in sports, with hopefully the same amount of dollars given male sports, along with the addition of many new sports, spread out the available dollars. At the same time, the Coronado Unified School District continued to upgrade its sports facilities through bond issues.

If the CUSD had a black eye, it came from demolition of the original iconic school buildings, as "worn-out landmarks." The lack of sensitivity to the high school's heritage can also be seen in the erasure, or omission, of names of men and women on other local icons. Some of the structures dedicated to graduates of the school, whose achievements are legendary and who contributed immeasurably to our nation's military, professional, and athletic heritage, were lost in the name of progress.

The current Coronado Public Library, shaped around the original Spreckels Library, continues to serve as one of Coronado's finest public resources. Director Librarian Christian Esquevin and his staff are not only knowledgeable and pleasant to be around, but are constantly developing creative and imaginative programs. The Library has become a very active resource center in the community, with volunteers tutoring students who are having a tough time at school, while others use it as a secure haven for research and knowledge.

While good things were taking place, the traffic buildup continued. The Department of Motor Vehicles reported Coronadans owned 33,850 cars. The City Development Division challenged these

At the foot of Orange Avenue at First Street is Centennial Park, dedicated on November 13, 1986, 100 years after the historic land sale on Coronado. An original Coronado ferry ticket booth, a reminder of the old ferry days, sits at the spot where cars used to enter to be loaded onto the ferries. (CHA)

figures, indicating its citizens only had 10,711 cars. Clogging the streets were trucks, motorcycles, buses, trolley-style tourist vehicles (on wheels), and cars. Coronado's traffic dilemma was raised in an issue of a Coronado newspaper on January 14, 1924, when the Merchants Association took on the pressing issue of parking.

In a July 1988 election about the tunnel, 56% of registered voters turned out. Quickly 3,129 voters said "NO," while 2,205 marked "YES." As for a mayoral term, 3,718 voted "YES" for a 4-year term, while 594 voted "NO." In November, Councilwoman Mary Herron defeated incumbent Mayor R.H. Dorman. At this time, the City Council and Mayor received $300 per month, while the City Manager drew a salary of $70,000. The Police Chief's salary could range from $50,000 to $60,000; the Community Development Director about the same; firefighters between $22,000 and $28,000, and maintenance workers from $16,000 to $21,000.

The question was never raised about the pittance paid to councilmembers--individuals who suffered the abuses of disrespectful, abusive, and spiteful council visitors. These public servants spent long hours reading the maze of documents they were expected to interpret and analyze, as well as attending endless civic and committee meetings. When asked why council members should not be paid a full-time salary to take care of the business for which they were elected, one response was, "We don't want political politicians". In essence, the City was benefitting from sincere, dedicated citizens who could afford to serve for a meager sum, but who, likely, did not have the professional experience to move ahead with projects and make firm decisions. In the end, the current system caused a loss of public funds, with the lack of time and strength-of-will to produce decisions resulting in a number of uncompleted projects. Instead, there were endless meetings with countless committees, expensive consultants, and people back to the costly ballot box time and again.

In 1988, four separate committees working on what do about Coronado's economy, reported that the village had been in a state of decline for more than a decade. A number of merchants went out of business because of a number of forces working against downtown Coronado. The Downtown Tax Force (TDTF) pointed to the allure of Horton Plaza, competition from commercial ventures at NAS North Island, the Hotel del Coronado, and the Ferry Landing. The TDTF had a microscopic view of "downtown," and did not look at Coronado as a whole. A frequent critic of Coronado wrote, "The 50s and 60s were the golden age of downtown; in the old days the merchants could rake in the business from tourists during the summer and break even in the winter." Furthermore, she wrote, "Downtown Coronado is in a state of decline... and the other side of the world is gang infested; ... lowered [bridge] tolls will increase traffic, [and the] police force will be more strained, [handling] more beachgoers and joyriders."

The Second Harbor Entrance Plan, or SHEP, arose again, recommending a 500-foot wide, 35-foot deep channel through the Silver Strand at Emory Cove. While that was being discussed, the Council was involved in a meeting to decide whether to accept a donation of white Christmas tree lights from the Chamber of Commerce, to replace the colored lights historically draped on Orange Avenue pines.

In March 1989, Susan Keith defeated Greg Walker for a 20-month term on the City Council. She won by 29 votes. Of the 10,990 registered voters, only 4,437 took the time to vote! Parking woes for residents brought forth a plan to issue decals in congested areas near NAS North Island. Some of the concern centered around noise, litter, and vandalism. The subject needed more study and the idea was shelved.

In April 1989, the San Diego County Narcotics Task Force arrested two former members of the "Coronado Company," a drug-smuggling ring. Both were former CHS students involved in an operation headed by former high school teacher Louis Henry Vilar, who had smuggled more than $96 million in marijuana and hashish from Tijuana. While the Council adopted "new" drug laws, violent crimes were on the rise in town. Despite strongly differing opinions, Police Chief Boyd commented on a supposed Coronado "gang," stating that the "'White Boys' were a gang formed to claim North Beach by force from San Diego and South Bay gangs, who now want it." Called CWBs (Coronado White Boys), the *Coronado Journal* took umbrage with the idea that the young men were a gang, suggesting instead that the Chief was being too dramatic. Of the then 60 gangs in San Diego, 14 of them used North Beach. The Coronado Police were protecting Coronado groups.

The Trolley Tours which moved through Coronado were heavily criticized, with most citizens opposing them traveling on their streets. A self-appointed "Coronado's White Knight" gave advice to the Council: "You are allowing people to sightsee at the expense of those living here." Another person moved to prevent trolley buses from traversing "within a zone of silence" along beach routes; therefore, Isabella Avenue and Ocean Boulevard were eliminated from the routes. Another person called the trolley a "commuter infiltration," cheering an ordinance which restricted tour buses from traveling on residential streets.

The ideas promoted by MainStreet Ltd. included a farmers market, beautification, and education about a "face-lift" for storefronts, alleys, stores, and public signs. Still on unsure legs, MainStreet Ltd. initiated, and then plowed under a Farmers Market they had begun to assist, saying it did not enhance their goals. A week later, it was revived for a time, and then discontinued again, only to be taken up successfully at another location in the north part of Coronado's business area.

When "The Wharf," a proposed restaurant/shopping center complex on First Avenue, received the Port District-certified EIR, Main Street Ltd. took no stand. The organization encouraged the City to support "downtown development," further fingering the long-standing unspoken schism that existed within the City's business areas. While the City Council-proposed master plan workshops for downtown, MainStreet Ltd. opposed them. At year's end, the Wharf had been under three years of constant scrutiny.

In June 1989, The Kingston Trio reunited after 20 years for a packed Spreckels Park concert. The July 4th celebration, with Andy Szymanski and John Laing in charge, involved a masterwork program, including a half marathon run, Art in the Park, an Independence Day Parade, the 31st Annual Rough Water Swim, a Navy Air/Seal Demonstration on Glorietta Bay, and a fireworks display. The City Council wondered what to do about the old Armory building on a parcel of land which lay a few yards south of the Coronado Yacht Club. The building served as the USO during WW II. Acquired by the National Guard in 1949 on a 50-year lease, the structure was declared in violation of Fire and Safety Codes in 1975. The Guard unit moved to Linda Vista and the Armory sat unused for years. The Coronado Playhouse Director expressed interest in the vacant building, but the Council could not decide what to do with it. Forty-year-old blueprints eventually surfaced, with the original plans of the Armory calling for a theatre use.

Mayor Mary Herron gave the annual State of the City address in November 1989. In a marathon homily, she spoke of more than 20 issues the Council needed to address:

1. Needs assessment for a Public Services Yard
2. Environmental Impact Report process
3. Purchase of Seventh and Orange Ave site
4. Getting rid of Babcock Court and the Armory
5. Building underground parking under the entire length of properties on Orange Ave
6. A future Community Center on Glorietta Bay Resource property
7. Demolishing the Playhouse, replacing with new one on Glorietta Bay property
8. Needs assessment for Police Station and City Hall at Seventh and Orange Ave
9. Decision to place Advisory vote for new City Hall on the ballot
10. Self-initiating an official "Main Street" designation for Coronado
11. Training of City Employees
12. Improving the Golf Course
13. Organizing a workshop for Historic Preservation
14. Increasing scope of Youth Recreational Programs
15. Pilot Recycling Program
16. Upgrading irrigation system
17. A Visitor Promotion Plan
18. Unified Transportation Plan
19. Environmental Issues
20. Loop bike path under bridge
21. Radar speed enforcement
22. Shorter City Council meetings.

The agenda for future consideration also included addressing the woeful condition of City Public Facilities, presented by the Community Development Agency, after years of process and debate. The list was comprehensive, and one could speculate that the mayor was attempting to overcome with sensitivity the long-standing schism between the two disparate elements of the City.

All of the major City needs of the 70s still needed to be fulfilled, despite the numerous official and self-appointed groups.

Naval personnel were often seen about town, unheralded and without television or cameras taking photos of their volunteerism. The crew of the USS *Cleveland* helped paint the exterior of the Coronado Middle School. Seabees assigned to NAB Construction Battalion took part at Christmas in an event for the homeless at the San Diego Community Concourse. A number of local Naval and Marine units were involved in helping gather and distribute Christmas food and clothing for the needy.

New matters arose to kindle the flames of local problems. The Navy was asked by Representative Duncan Hunter to fill a North Island void, left by conventional carriers, with nuclear-powered replacements. Plans were readied for upgrading of facilities. In response, someone who feared a catastrophic explosion took out full-page ads in the newspaper, under the heading, "A Concerned Citizen."

Coronado's City budget for 1990-1991 totaled $16.98 million, a 2.3% increase over the previous year. At the same time, CALTRANS was working on five projects within the City limits. A new tract of Navy Housing opened on September 5th. The Spanish-style buildings were located off State Route 75, near Silver Strand Elementary School. The housing provided much-needed quarters for military families. A two-bedroom home in the village was advertised at $300,000; at the Shores, a two-bedroom in El Camino Terrace at $450,000; and at 1015 Alameda, a five-bedroom, five bath house went for $1,150,000.

On July 4, 1990, Coronado welcomed *The Eagle*. Dean and Nancy Eckenroth brought a refreshing newspaper to town. They arrived at a time when Coronadans were trying to find ways to unravel their town projects. The Eckenroths understood the concept of restoration. They lovingly restored their own "newspaper home" by adapting an old bungalow for reuse. Within two years, the paper became a welcome weekly with perceptive editorials.

The Council agreed to spend $40,000 to launch a decal parking permit program in a district adjacent to NAS North Island. Any reader of the "Council Watch" column in one of the newspapers was aware that staff at City Hall could handle many of the items that appeared on Council agendas. The items sometimes took an entire session with the Council and the Mayor. Applications for picnics, amending the curfew time for special events, a Kiwanis Christmas lights walk, a portable restroom at the beach, and a report on water consumption took up an entire weekly session, as a parade of familiar citizens took their time at the microphone.

One long-lived project had to do with North Island. At this time, Coronado had jurisdiction over the inner portion of North Island, the City of San Diego its outer fringe (the addition provided by 1930s dredging). Coronado now proposed annexation of the area north of First Street over to the bridge, including the land and water.

For service members and their families, the Gulf War brought tighter security on the bases. Families dealt with issues brought about by the moves of the husband or wife in the military. Students sparked mini-protests at the High School a la Vietnam (during exam weeks).

In late 1990, MainStreet Ltd. hired a public relations firm and proposed a new approach to revitalization. But merchants vehemently opposed the proposal. Many of the projects proposed were a reaction to the recession. The organization asked the Council for support of a Master Plan for "downtown." In January 1991, in response to objections against MainStreet Ltd., a resident organized a Downtown Property Owners Association (DPOA). Reacting to the movement, MainStreet Ltd. expanded their project area to include all of Orange Avenue.

These world-famous dunes spell out the word, 'CORONADO,' but can only be seen when departing on a flight from Lindbergh Field in San Diego. (CHA)

The 1990 census showed that in ten years the population had increased by 7,750. The median age dropped from 33.6 to 32.5 years. The median price of a home was now $452,500, twice that of San Diego, while the median monthly rental contract was $746. The total population: 26,540 with 17,445 males, and 9,095 females. Naval personnel based on Coronado Island enhanced the number of males. Previous estimates projected the population in the year 2000 would be 18, 835. But, in reality, by 1998 the population had reached 28,537.

In early 1991, the Council voted to go ahead with La Avenida, a 133-room hotel at Orange Avenue and "B" Street. In reaction to the Business Property Owners Association (BPOA), the Council formed a Business Master Plan Committee of 12 people (BMPC). The concept was to give direction. Dean Nelson, Sr., Vice President of the Hotel del Coronado, headed up a group called the Coronado Lodging Association (CLA). The layers and players of public and private committees progressively grew.

The City replaced its only street sweeper, a broken down four-year-old machine, at a cost of $105,870. In July 1991, the City purchased a new police boat, a 24-year-old skipjack. Officer Brian Hardy saw his role as being more instructional, rather than about enforcement. Townspeople approved his authority to reach people who lived on boats, give first aid, enforce speed limits, and retrieve floating debris.

In 1991, the Kiwis (New Zealanders) returned to Coronado to take part in America's 1992 Challenge Cup Race. At first, the Kiwis were turned down when they asked to locate their base on the island, but a mini-America's Cup Village called "Kiwinado," was given new life as the New Zealand headquarters on San Diego Bay. Desafio España Copa America also had its compound on Coronado's bay front. Neighbors complained about the "Spanish Syndicate" at 700 "A" Avenue, where the sailors were quartered "with noisy and rowdy goings on."

The merchants of Coronado raised $50,000 to buy host memberships for the America's Cup Organizing Committee (AOAC), which they said would include perks and free merchandise advertising. The ACOC allegedly oversold their promises and the Coronado merchants felt they were duped. One merchant said he had abstained because he felt "the boys" were "pushing more than their rubber ducks around San Diego's bathtub." By April 15, 1992, the Kiwis won, and then said, "goodbye."

The Council had many agenda items that remained unresolved. The Palm and "D" Steering Committee recommended that the school district build subsidized housing on the site. The location was zoned for Residential Planned Community Development. The idea was tabled. Meanwhile, the Coronado Planning Committee debated affordable housing. The plan of the City to meet federal guidelines for affordable housing for the City's General Plan had been submitted to

One of the things that makes Coronado tick. Students in 2013 gather around the Tiki, symbol of Coronado High School's Islanders, originally donated by the Student Body during the 1961-62 school year. (CHA)

the State. Turned down the first time, a plan was proposed to count housing on the alleys as part of the City's affordable housing plan. On May 30, 1991, a new affordable housing plan was laid out by the Committee to go to Council, then to the Development Agency. (During the alley plan study, the City learned there were 800 "alley" units in the City, many illegally connected to the City's sewer system.) The plan of the City to meet Federal guidelines for affordable housing in the City's General Plan was submitted to the State in late June 1992.

At the end of May, 1991, Ernie Hahn, who had been a prime mover, along with the Centre City Development Corporation, behind the successful redevelopment of downtown San Diego, addressed Coronado's MainStreet Ltd. His advice was:

> "Build a consensus as a step forward, resolving problems and tackling the pricklier issues. Will Coronado decide what it wants to be: a tourist town or a city that looks after its own first, and then worries about the tourists later?"

Revitalization starts with basics: keeping the community pedestrian friendly, and alive with sights, sounds and colors - a vibrant neighborhood -striking the right balance. Knowing where and when to lavish time, money and attention on the community's recreation areas, infrastructure, public facilities, and local businesses.

But from all appearances, Mr. Hahn's straightforward, basic premises were apparently not taken to heart, as far as building consensus was concerned. One performance at City Hall was perhaps the most agonizing, and disorganized, of them all. During an afternoon meeting there was so much haranguing that Council members threatened to leave. Just then, Congressman Duncan Hunter stepped in to say, "Hello." Then the Mayor's birthday party was held. Many items were set aside for a future meeting, including how to reorganize the Coronado Police Department and the City Manager's office.

The 4th of July Parade was a tribute to the men and women who served in "Operation Desert Storm." The summer Sports Fiesta included a Junior Tennis Tournament, a sailing regatta, springboard and synchronized diving, golf-putting tournament, two-person volleyball, youngster fun games, a triathlon, a one-mile cable swim and a 10,000 meter run. The Optimist Club held the Junior World Golf Championship.

In an editorial, the *Coronado Journal* once again called for a new City Hall on Orange Avenue. The existing City Hall had been a gift of the U.S. Navy on December 18, 1959, a 5,900-square-foot building. It proved to be woefully inadequate. Cramped quarters and folding metal chairs must have embarrassed Council members.

Councilmember Patty Schmidt proposed, to the surprise of her colleagues, to place the City Hall issue before the voters in a November referendum that left some of the audience asking, "What is the rush?" The Council moved quickly to a discussion of its plans for a new police station, a city hall and a community center. After 35 years of discussion, Proposition "A" was placed on the ballot in November. The ballot asked, "Shall we relocate City Hall to Seventh and Orange Avenue?"

In August 1991, the City Council went through a 615-page agenda, 3-1/2" thick that took 5-1/2 hours to consider. It included curb painting, use of a park for lacrosse practice, and participation by Coronado in "Rideshare Week." Citizens refused to permit the City Council to let big projects die. They wrestled with equipment storage, the $3 million affordable housing project at Palm and "D," and a subject long believed deceased--the tunnel. One old-timer called Coronado's committees, "a sea of bickering and backbiting."

Loews Coronado Bay Resort opened its doors on October 1, a $90 million, 440-room, Mediterranean-style resort, sitting four miles south of the village of Coronado on a 15-acre peninsula called Crown Isle, adjacent to the Coronado Cays. Not too much earlier, a Crown Isle Defense Fund had been formed by a group of Cays owners who wanted the second harbor entrance.

On October 24, 1991, the Council split 3-2 over the question of the new City Hall. One week later, architects' renderings were unveiled for a new police station, City Hall, and Council Chambers. The Coronado Taxpayers Association called this a wonderful use of property. But on November 7, voters said "NO" by a 2-1 margin. Only 50% of the registered voters cast ballots on one of Coronado's most important opportunities to turn its Civic Center into a superior complex at Orange Avenue and Seventh Street. The Council stated it would honor the advisory vote. Boos and hisses punctuated the Council Chambers.

On November 19, the Council voted to give the Business Area Advisory Committee $66,000 to hire a consultant to restructure downtown planning, and also approved $500,000 in capital improvements, to be paid for by the Coronado Development Agency (CDA), to enhance the Cays and Central Beach. Complaints arose about excessive naval aircraft noise, air quality, and noise from bridge traffic. A pronouncement was made that a Third and Fourth Street Coronado Corridor Action Group (CCAG) had been formed to deal with these problems. For seven years, the CDA had struggled to make its funding understandable to residents. They planned to hold a workshop to explain the role of the redevelopment agency in providing the financing to eliminate "blight" from the City (defined as inadequate public facilities).

Earlier in the year, the newspaper lashed out at the Trustee of the Spreckels Building on Orange Avenue for allowing the 35,000-square-foot building, built by John D. Spreckels in 1917, to decay. A suggestion was made that the City purchase the building and do something good with it. Swift action taken here could have provided a location for all of the City's major public facilities: the City Hall, Community Center, Teen Center, Chamber of Commerce, and some of the City's strong private organizations. Escrow closed on the building before the end of the year 1991. The prime investor was Paul Swerdlove of Beverly Hills who told of his desire to give the building a face-lift, including the corner bank, 13 commercial store spaces, 11 apartments on the second floor, and an extension on Loma Avenue for several shops and the old theatre.

By January 1, 1992, the 80-year-old Coronado Elementary School, was demolished and replaced by Village Elementary School, financed by funds from the CDA. While school construction went on to upgrade other buildings to accommodate more staff and badly needed equipment for the technological age, costs for sports activities appeared to have risen out-of-sight. This did not go unnoticed. The slightest objections to these differences brought rebuttals from the Coronado Unified School District or the School Board. Sports results and stories occupied considerable space in the newspapers. Looking back, the 1941 varsity football team had 30 players, and the JV team that won the major regional Metropolitan League championship had one coach, one assistant coach and a water boy! In 1991, the football team had numerous coaches, coordinators, trainers, JV coaches, and managers with 30 varsity players and 30 JV players. In 1992, high school sports included football, track, tennis, softball, baseball, golf, basketball, handball, swimming, water polo, lacrosse, and soccer. Soon surfing became eligible for academic credit as well. The High School needed a new sports complex, a new football field, and a new track.

For nearly ten years, the Planning Commission had been challenged with finding a traffic solution. In reality, Orange Avenue was a dangerous place to cross on foot. Recreation, new retail shopping, additional condos, housing, and new hotels had increased the vehicle traffic. A Transportation Task Force (TTF) hired Transportation Management Services (TMS) to do a feasibility study. After 20 months of study, the report was widely distributed. Everything revealed was already known. A Traffic Circulation Committee (TCC) plan/decision still eluded the Planning Commission. There had been a 23-year drought of ideas over how to ease congestion on Third and Fourth Streets. The Traffic Circulation Committee could have used a change in membership, since it was the same as it had been 20 years before.

The tunnel idea lived again! A drawing of the proposed tunnel was prepared by Planning Commissioner Thomas Smisek. The Planning Commission recommended the tunnel concept to the Council. At the same time, the Strategic Plan Advisory Committee (SPAC) was preparing its report on protecting and improving Coronado's quality of life. That report was sent to the Council for review of its recommendations.

MainStreet Ltd. planned to work up a Business Area Development Plan (BADP), while the Coronado Transportation Management Association (CTMA) proposed new ways to provide alternatives to single passenger vehicles. MainStreet Ltd. asked, "What could Coronado's downtown look like in the 21st Century?" They speculated about pedestrian-friendly, clean sidewalks, a downtown parking facility, walkways and bike paths, underground utilities, Coronado shuttle, a town square, and mixed-use development! With six commissions and committees working on downtown problems, no mention was made of how all this was going to come about, and there was no plan for funding sources. The business owners complained about chain stores being allowed into town. One businessman declared, "I will resist the economic rape of our neighbors."

The restored 1917 Spreckels Building on Orange Avenue, 1998. For 100 years it has served as the business center of the community. (CHA)

Of new interest were plans for a major rehabilitation of the Hotel del Coronado, presented to City Council in late July 1992, by attorney James R. Dawe, representing the Hotel. The plans would unfold over a 20-year period. Several factors, including the death of owner M. Larry Lawrence, sale of the hotel, and objections by some citizens delayed the master plan's completion.

In the summer of 1992, many special events, involving all citizens, took place in Coronado. The Girl Scouts prepared a paper telling about Troop One, which was organized in 1917. They held their 75th anniversary at Glorietta Bay Park, with 18 original troop members, and more than 300 girls. The 5th Annual "Over the Bridge Run," benefited the Navy-Marine Corps Relief Society.

The Fourth of July celebrations, the Summer Music in Spreckels Park, the Sports Fiesta, and the Farmer's Market were signals that Coronado outdoors was still much better received than indoor Coronado politics.

Had Coronado become too fragmented? A few, but not all, of the commissions or committees in the action included: the ABSLS, BAC, BAAC, BAMP, BRTC, CAB, CAC, CAD, CCP, CHC, CIC, CSC, CCFP, CTMA, DCRAP, DSC, EPB, EDRC, GPCE, GBTA, LBOT, MSLtd, PARB, PC, RAC, RB, SAC #1431, SAC #1432, SPC, STC, and UTC. What is especially intriguing is the overlapping of responsibilities and membership! The Coronado telephone book clearly reflected the sheer volume of community service. There were 77 different service (non-profit) organizations, all of which offered some measure of good to the community. Coronadans could get together and agree about everything except what they wanted for the village.

In August 1992, Mayor Herron gave another "State of the City" address to 95 people. She spoke of the police facility as a stone rolling uphill. Each Coronado agency or department was given kudos for its performances. A group "Coronado Citizens For Progress" (CCFP), meant to foster tourism, mobilize residents, and work for the well being of the community, was formed. When the elections were over in November, Mary Herron won her second term with 60% of the vote. She was joined on the Council by Planning Commission Chair Thomas Smisek and Patty Schmidt. Inflammatory charges were made that money from the Hotel del Coronado was illegally furnished to the campaigns of Herron, Harry Brummitt, and Louis de Beer. Hotel representatives stated their Political Action Committee did contribute $10,000 to Coronado Citizens for Progress (CCP), a committee of small business people organized to independently endorse local candidates. Those who had called attention to the contribution said that was alright, but complained that contributions

The Coronado Cays Yacht Club was formed in 1972 and their spectacular new Clubhouse was opened in 1994. (CHA)

from the Hotel Del and the Coronado Lodging Association had not been filed on time. But State officials showed everything had been filed satisfactorily.

On October 1, 1992, the Fransen Company reported on the "Downtown Coronado Retail Assessment and Plan" (DCRAP). Thirty-four million dollars had been lost in retail revenue. Why? The answer came easily, but it took $27,000 and consultants to figure this out. In brief,

> "A consistent theme of lost opportunities. The village has lost its charm... tired, lonely, neglected...resigned paralysis...merchandising very unprofessional."

With half a dozen committees working under the assumption that there really was a "downtown," one might have assumed there would be some differences of opinion. A beleaguered MainStreet Ltd. laid off some staff.

Councilmembers publicly approved a proposed cutback of the aviation repair facilities at NAS North Island. That move cut 10,000 to 20,000 vehicle trips a day, according to one source. The Council voted 5-0 to inform Congressional representatives of their interest in the loss of the facilities. The backlash thundered from Coronadans who worked at NAS. Ninety-five Coronadans would have lost jobs.

Larry Wade of *The Eagle* did homework on his own, and with a grip on reality, determined the number of vehicles, which were "depot car trips only" was actually 2,800. The errors in traffic figures forced the Council to realize that depot closure would also cause a loss of jobs and business. They wrote to NAS North Island apologizing for their hasty actions, saying their statements had been premature and inappropriate. Once again a proposal was pushed to the Council table, requesting that Council seek land from the U.S. Navy for the golf course. The answer from the U.S. Navy, after 25 years of attempts to obtain the site, was still, "No, thanks!"

The Coronado Schools Foundation, established by concerned parents to augment educational programs, began in 1985. The Foundation raised $395,000 for the Coronado Unified School District. The group organized a number of ways to achieve funding, in part through projects that required considerable volunteer effort.

The Coronado Hospital celebrated its 50th anniversary, having been completed on Christmas Eve 1942. The first hospital was built across from the Hotel Del in 1898; the second hospital was built at 1111 Orange Avenue in 1927. John D. Spreckels had given $10,000 and the property. Coronado boasted a new Police Boat on January 28, 1993, known as "Parker," a 19-foot vessel with a center console, at a cost of $27,000. The older skipjack was traded in for $12,000. This vessel reinforced the need for emergency water enforcement.

In February, 125 sailors of the USS *Coronado* provided relief to the mudslide-stricken Casa de la Esperanza Orfantario. Dentists and medics from various ships gave check-ups to all children in the Tijuana institution. The storm, which also hit the Crown City, surpassed forecasts and exceeded the storm damage of the prior 100 years. Despite day and night efforts by City crews, water seeped into Orange Avenue businesses. Teenagers broke out surfboards and braved the flooded area at Tenth and Alameda.

All during 1992, the City "waffled" on the matter of the police station. Some called the Orange Avenue site a terrible misuse of public property. In March 1993, the Council tabled the project over questions about a design-build concept.

Dean Eckenroth was elected President of the Chamber of Commerce in 1992. By February 1993, he and Mayor Herron kicked off a campaign to promote the City of Coronado Retail Merchants Association (CCRMA).

A Council meeting on March 3 turned ugly during a second hearing about the Glorietta Bay Task Force (GBTF). The argument was about whether this was a sanctioned Committee, or a group of volunteers separate from the government? The "talk" turned into the "most viscous, bitter dogfight of the year." The Council hearings, open to the public, were televised in Coronado by that time, and as the *Coronado Journal* reported, the meeting was a shameless display of "Romper Room Tantrums."

Newspaper headlines, "Fed Up with the School District" opened discussions in March, 1993. Unaccounted for were resignations, community lack of confidence, budgets being hacked, underage drinking, concerns of parents, teachers, and students. A school board meeting bristled with controversy. Most of the heat came from parents. The conclusion was that the School District Administration needed to open its eyes.

Council meetings during March appeared to be unusually full of static. At the March 2nd gathering, "shouting, whistling, jeering, name-calling, and people falling out of chairs brought one Councilman to his feet," saying, "Clean up your act, or stay home and watch T.V." There were simply too many self-labeled "experts" taking up time and space. The Councilmembers never got to the topic of the new police station that had been under consideration since 1972. There appeared to be an old guard of residents, showing a lack of self-control, who consistently badgered the Council to avoid change. On March 25, worried members of the public spoke about "foreigners" from Temecula or Chula Vista using City parks. In April 1993, Gerry MacCartee, co-director of the now renovated Coronado Museum, reported that the Museum was open. Purchased for $267,000, it was now "debt free." In May, presidential candidate Bill Clinton spoke at the Hotel del Coronado to celebrate the 200th birthday of the nation's oldest political party. In May 1993, Lamb's Players began to call Coronado "home," in the old Coronado Theatre, the only full-time artistic ensemble in San Diego.

A City Master Plan was still not in place. The Planning Commission turned down more time-share projects and planned to prepare an ordinance prohibiting such developments. Bay front residents worried about their view being inundated by pedestrians, bikes, cars, and trucks. A month later, after two hours of "testimony," the Council continued the matter. Then, in an unexpected move in May, time-shares were banned. Suddenly, within the month this decision was reversed and the time-share-plan passed as Council realized that the owners of time-shares paid an average of $10,000 a week for their purchase-use, and taxes. Transient Occupancy Taxes did not apply since these were owned properties.

Councilman Tom Smisek proposed a "Talent Bank of Coronado Volunteers"--residents as consultants. He said, "Take our own government and restructure it." True to form, the Council told Mr. Smisek to come back with a plan. His was a sorely needed plan, which never got off the ground; perhaps the plan was ahead of its time. Then Smisek raised another sensible and long-debated issue: Coronado was lacking 100 units of affordable housing. "We [the Council] have avoided affordable housing in Coronado." He was unable to effect action at that meeting.

To hold its position, MainStreet Ltd. reaffirmed its mission, "To revitalize and enhance Coronado's downtown for the benefit of the entire community…eventually to help the Council implement the Master Plan." To help Coronadans understand "downtown," the BAAC hired a consultant to conduct workshops on planning the future of Coronado's business areas and surrounding neighborhoods.

May 1993 was filled with meetings of a Senior Friendship Group, the Alzheimer's Association, a Support Group for Grandparents, and events such as a Widowhood Workshop and a Culture and Arts Celebration, all bringing a refreshing change with much enjoyment. One of Coronado's most respected citizens, Dr. Jim Vernetti, was the Grand Marshall of the July 4th Parade. He had been a Coronado resident since 1937.

> Progress was made at the Coronado Cays Yacht Club, located on Caribe Cays Boulevard North at the northern tip of Grand Caribe Isle, with ground to be broken for a new building in July, 1993. The Cays Yacht Clubhouse was opened in 1994, Coronado's fourth such facility. The Coronado Cays Yacht Club was officially established in June 1972, with Arthur W. (Bud) Holderness as Commodore. Its first race, the Coronado Cays Classic Series, was contested in September 1972.

Progress also seemed to be made when the Council approved a Police Station Design by Drew, Mosher, Watson and Ferguson. An artist's conception appeared in the June 17 issue of the *Coronado Journal*. Progress was not made on the Community Center, as opponents stood against development of a 24,000-square-foot building on Glorietta Bay. In support of this site, the Journal editorial reported the terrible condition of the Playhouse, City Hall, and the Woman's Club, recommending that improvements should get started. A 1963 issue of that same newspaper had asked where is Coronado's Community Center? Thirty years later, the structure had not even made it off the drawing board.

The School District's Master Plan was expected by October. Some money came from unexpected enrollments for the school year. "The Pride Project 93" involved an effort to improve the High School campus. School Board members, families, and students painted rooms, cleaned desks, replaced benches, did some landscaping, and put down carpeting. Over 1,100 people, including service personnel, showed up to do the work. Reports from the School District advised that they would crack down on the Middle School dress code. Hats and shirts reflected gang relations, even though, "We don't have any known gangs in Coronado." The PTA and faculty adopted high school dress codes. Those students who came with inappropriate clothing were sent home. As if to respond, disgusted by the appearance of downtown, which they called "sticky, smelly, with trash-strewn sidewalks," high school students formed a "Broom Brigade" and cleaned up the streets. A City official said that the Public Services Department should not be expected to sweep; this was primarily a sidewalk problem, and up to the property owners.

In November 1993, Babcock Court fell. Spurred temporarily by that effort, the Council moved toward construction of three new public facilities. Was a new City Hall finally in the cards, since facilities along Glorietta Bay might get another facelift? A decision had to be made because new laws governing the Community Development Agency (CDA) stated the Council had to decide before the end of the year. So the City Council asked a Community Center Planning Committee (CCPC) to make a presentation in mid-November about its findings, and to answer the question, "Did Coronado need one, and why?" The CCPC balked. Councilman Joe Talbert insisted, "Move forward with the plan or forget it entirely." Previous objections were renewed--the plan was too big for Coronado's village-like community. The Committee wanted to keep it on Glorietta Bay, an idea that was not popular at all. Everything, but the swimming pool was in the wrong end of town. But after 30 years of contemplation, the Council voted to accept the Community Center in concept, and to request an Request for Quote (RFQ) to draft a space-needs assessment.

Not all the questions of 1993 are reflected here. One controversial matter raised: while other cities were downsizing, some felt the City Council had been implementing a taxpayer-financed welfare program for businesses in Coronado, by providing funds and benefits to three overlapping business organizations: MainStreet Ltd, the Business Advisory Committee, and the Chamber of Commerce. There were tense discussions over a possible merger and/or disbanding of one or two of these groups.

During the first month of 1994, the Naval Amphibious Base celebrated its 50th anniversary, with Secretary of Navy John Dalton attending the ceremonies.

The Coronado Unified School District discovered that planning was more difficult than construction. A sparse turnout forced the Board to cancel a meeting and call for a public workshop. Options proposed at the workshop for the use of Palm and "D" Streets did not include affordable public housing. CUSD vetoed the plan; they had nine other suggestions for the Palm and "D" site. Prompted by completion of Village Elementary and New Strand Hall, architects were to review all school properties and reprioritize the goals. A school discipline code now included students' use of controlled substances, alcohol, firearms or weapons, use of tobacco, graffiti, electronic pagers or telephones, skates, or roller blades, or biking on campus.

Coronadans have always been partial to healthy and environmentally-friendly means of transportation around town, whether by walking our sidewalks, bike-riding or using electric golf carts. Here is an intriguing practical design: a lockable skateboard rack at the High School. (CHA)

In February, ground breaking for the new physical education/sports complex was held. In a total surprise, the announcement was made that the complex would be named for an individual who would, in a moment, announce his retirement from the school. With the demolition of the Carrothers Gymnasium, Coronadans had forgotten that Bob Carrothers was arguably the most important and recognizable athlete ever produced at Coronado High School. He had won numerous National Tennis Championships while still in high school. Some looked in wonderment at the new complex at CUSD, which stood 61 feet high!

In early March 1994, after three years, the Business Area Advisory Committee (BAAC) presented its downtown revitalization program to the City. The comprehensive, ten-chapter report called for improving the Ferry Landing, the Silver Strand Highway, and touched on the many City intersections. The plan was projected to be completed by the year 2000. The BAAC consultant, paid $30,000 for the study, recommended moving City Hall to Tenth and Orange; re-designing Rotary Park; renovating Vons, with subterranean or roof-top parking; and highlighting the Village Theatre--a focal point of the block. "C" Avenue would become a courtyard for special events. Arguments (none of which were new) rose against specific parts of the plan, some personal, some legitimate. Meanwhile, City Council spent $21,655 to spruce up City Hall. Whatever the case, as late as 1998, none of the BAAC's major suggestions had been completed.

To decide what to do about "downtown" or the "business district," the Chamber of Commerce formed a Coordinating Council composed of the following: Coronado MainStreet Ltd., Food and Beverage Association, Lodging Association, Board of Realtors, Visitor Information Center, and other groups. The idea was to facilitate information for the City Council. The Port District gave the City $2.4 million to fund the Glorietta Bay Linear Park, which was still in the "conceptual stage," according to Homer Bludau, City Manager.

Ground was broken for the new police facility, but its location beside the schools and library caused reverberations. At City Hall, the Coronado Playhouse issue resulted in a terrible meeting for the Council as they considered shutting down the facility. The Playhouse was run down and had been virtually used free for many years. Hecklers, led by members of the Playhouse, delivered monologues accusing the Council of hidden agendas, and back door politics, though matters of health and fire safety were tantamount. Asbestos aside, the Council voted 5-0 to allow the Playhouse to remain open. In September 1994, there was another bold move made for a golf course to be built on "Oceanic Lands," in the former Coronado Heights location.

That same month, the Council, in a 4-1 vote, fired City Manager Homer Bludau, who had worked for the City over ten years. The response from the community favored Bludau. Councilmembers said they wanted to move in a new direction, and that the decision resulted from evaluations of Bludau's work over a two-year period. Mayor Herron, the lone dissenter, said the vote was an "abrupt and ill-considered action...." Concern grew over the matter of due process, and in December, a newly elected Council rehired Mr. Bludau. He returned to his job in February 1995.

In a revealing poll, conducted by City staff, Mayor Herron noted that controlled growth was one of Coronado's greatest challenges. Additionally, of those polled, 60% wanted improvements to parks, recreation, police, and fire, as well as a new City Hall. The best things about Coronado were:

Small town	18%	Location	6%
Low Crime	15%	Community Feeling	6%
Atmosphere	11%	Quiet	4%
Weather	10%	Schools	4%
Beach	8%	Beauty	2%
Friendly People	6%	City Service	2%
Other	6%	Clean	2%

A big winter storm hit Coronado in January 1995, felling trees and power lines, and washing boats ashore. This storm was called the worst in the 144-year records of the National Weather Bureau. Two days before, a fire broke out in the 15-story Cabrillo tower at the Coronado Shores, causing little damage.

The New Year brought Councilmember Tom Smisek to the forefront. The first item on his New Year's agenda was a new City Hall. Another Councilmember said Glorietta Bay was the site for a recreation center, with joint use on the Strand for a Community Center, and City Hall. The Council, in sync with the commitment to foster a more business-friendly town, also agreed to update building standards and parking restrictions for hotels and motels as proposed. In March 1995, the Council created a new department to aid facilities planning. The school district decision regarding curving Sixth Street to provide for a regulation-size high school track was put off. The California Interscholastic Federation had ruled that Coronado's track was not standard and, therefore, the school was ineligible to participate in track and field events. One proposed solution had been the Sixth Street curve, which was dropped; Cutler Field was eyed with envy as another possible location. A CUSD task force reported that Village Elementary School, built for 800, could hold a maximum of 1,000 students, and that the Middle School had become too small. A Community/Parent Advisory Committee mapped out an outline to renovate Crown School.

School children had no problem being occupied with sports: they could choose from baseball, softball, swimming, track, lacrosse, tennis, golf, water polo, and a variety of other sports. The teams, which had to play in distant Holtville blamed their losses on the travel. Little League opened in March with 46 teams composed of 575 boys and girls, ages 6-15. At Bradley Field, there were also 11 softball teams with 131 girls in three softball leagues.

The face of the downtown business district was changing, with high-priced rents and a proliferation of restaurants. Some felt the City needed more "mom and pop" shops. Coronado citizens wanted it both ways: numerous businesses, visitors, and income but slow growth and no traffic. An Economic Development Office (EDO) was now on the horizon! A job description for a Director had been touched off by a downturn in Coronado's business, though the City still utilized the Chamber of Commerce and Coronado MainStreet Ltd. Local hotel concierges met with merchants to explain they were sending visitors over the bridge due to a lack of goods and services, extended hours, and public transportation options in town. The Council then voted against fast food franchising, to "save the village from Pizza Hut." A short time later, after McDonald's was denied a franchise in town, the Naval Amphibious Base welcomed the business. Ron Mittag of Shawnee, Kansas, was chosen out of 37 applicants as the Economic Development Director to coordinate the Business Area

An old friend—Cutler Field the site of football games, track meets, soccer, lacrosse and high school graduations, shown here fully packed in the late 1960s. (CHA)

Development Plan (BADP); to assist in maintaining an appropriate business and commercial mix; and to liaise with the business community, interest groups, and perspective business interests.

The Coronado Visitor Bureau, behind the move for the Transient Occupancy Tax (TOT), explained that a raise from seven to eight percent tax brought jobs, clean industry, sponsorship of events, housing of events, donations, educational programs, Christmas lights, restaurants, and a quality of life desired by to the town. Interestingly, no City agency was courting clean light industry, such as bio-tech or medical firms. Why was no agency seeking locations and firms to bring those kinds of research facilities to the island?

After 11 years, the Environmental Impact Report for the Coronado Traffic Plan passed the Council in July 1995. There was no guarantee that the Plan would be carried out. To help with the mounting problems of a variety of crimes, a new Senior Volunteer Patrol, after three months of highly specialized training, assisted the Coronado Police by operating in strict non-confrontational ways: handicapped parking enforcement, vacation house checks, foot and vehicle patrols, answering non-emergency phone calls, and issuing warnings for bike and skateboard infractions.

The City, in August 1995, requested proposals for the development of the Glorietta Bay property, nine acres in size, northeast of Highway 75 between the Chart House and the Naval Amphibious Base. Proposals were to include the Community Center, a new City Hall, a swimming pool complex, a linear park, and the sea wall project.

The final football game was played on Cutler Field on October 9, 1995. The John D. and A.B. Spreckels had deeded the property to Coronado High School 70 years earlier. After more than 500 games, football the following year would be played at the new sports complex, described as "a gym that dwarfed the educational buildings," a vivid illustration of the relationship of sports/recreation to academics.

After five years, residents on Third and Fourth Streets settled a lawsuit against the City out of court. Filed in November 1990, the suit had charged Coronado with environmental neglect along the two streets, due to increased traffic from the bridge. Residents sought damages for air and noise pollution and devalued property. Twenty-three plaintiffs divided the $500,000 payment; $200,000 of which came from CALTRANS, with the City's insurance carriers paying the remainder.

Leaving a documented and respected political legacy, the "Dean of Republican Politics" in the region, Eleanor Reynolds Ring Storrs, passed away. Yet another member of Coronado's "old guard" was gone.

Dormant issues regarding the Navy arose in 1995, and some anxiety developed over the matters. Since 1991, the Navy had been studying the feasibility of accommodating three nuclear-powered aircraft carriers at NAS North Island. Also, for eighteen months, there had been no progress regarding the Navy changing flight patterns. The Council vowed to initiate discussions. Attendees at City Hall voiced cheers and jeers over the Naval aircraft noise; "pure cacophony and hysteria," the majority seemed to say. The California Coastal Commission then approved the U.S. Navy's Environmental Impact Report on the homeporting of three Nimitz Class nuclear-powered aircraft carriers (CVNs) at NAS. "One Concerned Citizen" took out a full-page ad asking people to speak out against "a radioactive Coronado."

In December, Mayor Herron posed mitigation measures to the U.S. Navy regarding traffic, aviation noise, relocation of the main entrance, parking on base, a shuttle service, and barging of equipment and supplies for construction projects. "Recreational access to the Communications Station on the Silver Strand" was a left-handed expression of a desire for a second golf course.

The Environmental Design Review Commission denied a conceptual design for the Public Services Building as not "pedestrian friendly." By year's end, the Council chose Stastny Architects of Portland, Oregon, as the Glorietta Bay Consultants. They led workshops/public discussion groups/

American sailors and Marines have been an important part of Coronado's DNA since the early 1900s. (U.S. Navy Photo)

interest groups, on topics of parking requirements, development of a pedestrian-friendly traffic circulation plan, development of landscaping and amenities, and decisions as to where the new City Hall and Community Center should be placed. Public hearings were held until the end of the year 1996. Detailed plans had to be in place by the end of 1997, with construction starting as early as 1998. On the other side of town, the existing Public Works Project design was delayed, either to be redesigned or scrapped.

An insightful article in the *Coronado Eagle* appeared in October 1995, about the changing face of the island City. For decades, Coronado was portrayed as one of California's last homeowner havens for the wealthy, elderly, and retired military officers. But Coronado had gained a substantial number of dual income-earning parents, as reflected in condominium and home sales in specific ranges. Condos sold for between $100,000 and $700,000. Old timers were selling to "baby boomers" with children. The crime rate had been brought down, schools were excellent, and recreation was a plus.

In early January 1996, Coronadan M. Larry Lawrence, a staunch Democrat and generous philanthropist who had been appointed U.S. Ambassador to Switzerland, died at his home in Berne, Switzerland, at the age of 69. He had purchased the Hotel del Coronado in 1963, from the Alessio family, and had been a staunch preservationist for maintaining Coronado's special quality of life. He was also a heavy booster of the Coronado Schools Foundation, the Coronado Public Library, and the Jewish Community Center. More than 1,000 friends and family members attended Mr. Lawrence's funeral service at the Hotel.

Coronado High School administrators revealed results of a survey by school officials. In 1994-1995, in a 30 day period, 56% of the students had used alcohol; 34% marijuana; 8% crystal meth; 7% LSD; and 4% cocaine. The District had a zero-tolerance policy regarding drugs, alcohol, or weapon possession. The District Board held an expulsion hearing when a student was caught using a controlled substance. Generally, suspension involved community service and involvement with the Coronado Response Group (CRG), which formed a discussion panel to assist kids involved with drugs or alcohol. The CUSD had already paid $44,544 during 1995 to cover student disciplinary actions, $43,220 of which paid attorney fees. Would a teen center help? Students claimed, "We are bored!"

The Navy, which had every intention of meeting the need for a fully conditioned nuclear-carrier base, found support from the City, and from Main Street Ltd., relative to issuance of a dredging permit for the carrier piers at NAS North Island. The Army Corps of Engineers issued a permit to the Navy to dredge in San Diego Bay in anticipation of future berthing of several nuclear-powered aircraft carriers. Richard Guida, Associate Director for Regulatory Affairs for the Naval Nuclear Expansion Program, reassured citizens at a meeting at City Hall, "…their worries [were] misdirected," and gave numerous reasons why. In September 1996, the dredging of the bay to accommodate homeporting of the carriers began, with a May 1997 completion date. Other Navy activities included the West Coast Survival Evasion (SERE) School at North Island being named for Vice Admiral James B. Stockdale, a POW in Vietnam for 7-1/2 years. He and his wife, Sybil, were longtime Coronado residents.

The City was caught unaware that NAS North Island intended to build a facility to clean contaminated soils from U.S. Naval sites around the County, even though trucks had already been hauling soil covered with tarps through the City. The facility was approved after four months of negotiations between City Council and the Navy. Again "Concerned Citizens of Coronado" came forth and continued half and full page ads asking, "Is the Navy Threatening Its Neighbors?" referring to "hot spots, health hazard index elevated PCBs, oil spills, and battlefield nuclear warheads stored in bunkers at NAS North Island."

The new Coronado Police Station opened February 28, at 700 Orange Avenue with a fitting ceremony. The two-story "Spanish-Colonial" building stretches from Seventh and Orange Avenues, two-thirds of the block south towards Eighth. The regularly laid tile roofing, the large arched doors, and windows, typically protected by grillwork, extend the length of the building. Outdoor decorative elements include arched sconces for lighting. The smaller second rectangular area is centered around occupancy for the building. A courtyard stretches the full length of the east facade to the sidewalk. The building has 20,300 square feet of space, with over 34,200 square feet of underground parking. There are 82 parking places and storage space. There are areas for the Investigation, Traffic, Animal Control, Property, Crime Prevention, Public Affairs, and Victim Services Divisions. The architects, familiar to Coronado, were Mosher, Drew, Watson and Ferguson; the general contractor was Kvaas Construction.

The Chamber of Commerce held an "Eggs and Issue Breakfast" in early April 1996. Attendees spoke of the City's relationship with the U.S. Navy, and about future projects, including a new clubhouse at the golf course, a new Public Services building, the Glorietta Bay Masterplan Complex, the new City Hall and teen center, and library expansion. The Glorietta Bay Masterplan, developed by Stastny Architects, was approved by the City Council, with construction to begin in 1999. Citizens vocally expressed concern at the snail's pace with which all of these projects moved.

By September, MainStreet had aggravated some citizens with topiaries installed in gardens on the Orange Avenue median. There was concern about these median gardens expressed at City Council meetings, as discussions focused on the retention of the grassy areas, free of flowers and trees, to keep the view corridor open. MainStreet Ltd was then in a quandary over further garden plans, since donations for future gardens had already been received. One Coronado resident, Ms. Lisa LaPinca, said she wanted to order a 25' by 10' plot in front of the library. Complainants took out ads calling the median gardens a land rights issue, noting that the City was giving away public property. City Council entered the fray and proposed a workshop for further discussion, and then

Large nuclear-powered aircraft carriers based here, have become an important symbol of Coronado for many. (U.S. Navy Photo)

a ballot measure to resolve the issue. Instead of a public vote, the Council placed a moratorium on further median gardens after the already pre-approved garden between "B" and "C" Avenues on the median was in place.

When Police Officer Elizabeth Hirsch was honored by the San Diego Police Officers Association as a member of the Domestic Violence Task Force, she said, "We have a lot of domestic violence in Coronado. I did a two-year study and found our conviction rate was only 30%...often the victim posts bail for the suspect."

The "Over the Bridge Bay Run," begun in 1986 with 800 entrants, fielded 6,000 people in 1996. The race, sponsored by SDG&E and the U.S. Navy, benefited the Naval Amphibious Base quality-of-life programs, and the Navy and Marine Corps Relief Society. The NAB Morale, Welfare and Recreation Department, as a result, offered a variety of services to benefit active-duty personnel, retirees, their dependents and Department of Defense civilians.

President Bill Clinton visited Coronado on June 14, flying into North Island on Sunday afternoon and staying at the Hotel del Coronado. On Monday, he kicked off a mini-Presidential campaign. The President also jogged with the SEALs on the beach, talked about crime at a storefront police station in Hillcrest, and spoke to the San Diego Police Department about illegal immigration. After a visit to Miramar Naval Air Station, he travelled back to the Coronado golf course for a quick round, and then returned to Washington, D.C.

Yet another pitch came to the Council for a second entrance to the bay on June 21, 1996. The main benefit: it would prevent naval vessels from being bottled up in case of emergency. But the new entrance would also be a boon to recreational boaters and sport fishing; improve operations; give an economic shot in the arm to National City, Chula Vista, Imperial Beach, and Coronado; and serve craft of the Amphibious base. Backing this was a non-profit organization, called the "Second Harbor Entrance Project."

The 1996 July 4th celebration, as in years past, included several distance runs, the 38th Rough Water Swim, the USS *Coronado* open house, the two-hour parade, art-in-the park with a concert, and the U.S. Navy air-sea demonstration in Glorietta Bay. Vice Admiral Alexander J. Krekvin served as the Grand Marshal.

In somewhat a surprise move, although the Island grapevine was active, the Hotel del Coronado was sold to an affiliate of Travelers Group. The purchasers, the first new owners in 30 years, vowed to take the Hotel into the next century. Before the ink had dried on the sales contract however, due to serious rumors of changes, busy townspeople were telling Travelers not to "monkey with" the Hotel del Coronado.

After reading all the complaints about the military exchange, the aircraft noise and the traffic, a spunky Navy wife spoke out about how glad her family was when they moved to Coronado. They knew there would be military aircraft, and were grateful for them. Her words caused other Coronadans to speak out, reminding complainers that the military had always been a part of the region, and in time of need, people would be very grateful for their presence.

While dealing with the traffic issue at a Council meeting on October 15th, tempers flared once again. "Concerned City of Coronado Citizens" (CCCC) felt "the quality-of-life was threatened," and provided a phone number to call. They felt that "Coronado was in danger by association with a military/industrial complex, nuclear materials, growing traffic and commuter problems, the mayor's growing power, and a flawed Environmental Impact Report over the nuclear carriers project." They also feared that "the Mayor would kill the Golden Goose, we all call Coronado." On September 27, 1998, the first Nuclear Aircraft Carrier, the USS *John C. Stennis* arrived at its new NAS North Island home, as a very small contingent of environmentalists stood at Harbor View Park swishing their signs.

The attacks on candidates for office grew more personal up to November election time. Thomas Smisek was elected Mayor over Mary Herron 4,460 to 3,439. Smisek wanted the City to refrain from over-development, to preserve the quaint atmosphere and quality of life. Patty Schmidt and Al Ovrom were also elected to the Council. Each election provided something that hinted of improprieties. A political action group, calling themselves "The Muffins," had been meeting quietly every Monday for a year or more, "plotting campaigns for their candidates," as one letter to the editor told the story. They took their nom de plume because they "nibbled on muffins and drank coffee." Their idea was "to change the complexion of the council." Apparently that was alright, but why didn't these people come out in the open and discuss and debate issues? Minutes of the meetings indicated a fair contingent of business people had gotten together. Their minutes accidentally became public, and though the Muffins admitted to meeting, they did not confess to attempting to stack the Council at the next election.

Wilfred C. Seaman was honored by the City with a proclamation. He had given 50 years of involvement and service to Coronado, and to San Diego and Imperial Counties. He had served as a popular principal at Coronado High School for 20 years. Wilf exemplified the redeeming character of Coronado, found in terrific men and women who gave of themselves, often retired, long-time citizens, helping others.

December 1996 was a joyful month. A hayride on the Silver Strand, the Coronado High School Theatre in action, Jazz at the Mexican Village, the VFW Fish Fry, and Brandeis University wine-tasting benefit filled an agenda of fun.

The year could not close out until the Mayor set some goals for the New Year. Glorietta Bay Park was redesigned with a community center, linear park and landscape environment, as a gateway into Coronado. Mayor Smisek, a graduate of Coronado High School in 1962, had been a resident for 26 years. A commercial airline pilot, he used his down time to answer mail and work on other mayoral duties. He wanted to make the island pristine and preserve the village atmosphere. He recognized the community was opposed to big development; expansion would have to be vertical, to which he was adamantly opposed. A fiscal conservative, he believed the major issues were traffic, sidewalks, a good relationship with the Navy, and capital projects. "How much more could he accomplish," asked a number of townspeople, who judged him to be very competent, "if his role were a paid full-time position?"

The new year1997 opened with relative calm, with the pages of the local newspapers brimming with realtors and homes ready for sale. The Chamber of Commerce celebrated its 60th anniversary. The Planning Commission was determined to carry out City Council policy on all proposed projects. The Public Service Yard project crawled forward with a discussion of cost, even though $300,000 had already been spent on an estimated $3.5 million cost for the facility. The area around the current yard, dating from the 1940s, was once the location of the City dump. Referring to the new police station costs, Mayor Smisek pointed out the City didn't want another "Taj Mahal." A not-so-conservative budget for capital expenditures was proposed for the next four years: Public Service Yard renovation at $5,350,000; library expansion at $6 million; and the Community Center Complex on Glorietta Bay at $13,589,500. The latter would include City Hall, the Community Center, pool upgrading, a linear park, and a boat ramp. The money would come from Community Development Agency funds and the general fund.

Much to their distress, local golfers hopeful for a "Coronado Oceanic [Golf] Course" at Coronado Heights, learned their dream might finally be quashed by recent agreements between the Navy and U.S. Fish and Wildlife Service. And plans remained unchanged for the Naval Radio Receiving Station. Viewed with envy, the area was located on the Strand, and known historically as "Coronado Heights." During World War II, Coast Artillery was stationed there in large bunkers. At one time there was a paved road through it, lined with Torrey Pines, and it had a wonderful park and beach area. A month later, despite the Navy's "NO" to the Oceanic Golf Course, the Council approved a proposal to hire a professional consulting firm. Councilwoman Patty Schmidt asked the correct question, when she queried, "What part of the 'NO' don't we understand, when told 'NO'?",

As far as the Community Center Plan was concerned, "Uptown" sites were to be considered for City Hall. Many Coronadans had wanted City Hall in the "center" of town for 40 years. Unimpressed with the size and placement of the new Police Department building at Seventh Street and Orange Avenue, townspeople wanted to consider another location for City Hall that made sense to all citizens, not just those who wanted to drive their cars to the sand dunes on the outskirts of town.

At the start of the New Year, the Truck Traffic Volume Reduction Committee (TTVRC) summed up their report as, "No Progress." Some projects were approved though. On March 28, 1997, approval was given to the Best Western Motel at 275 Orange Avenue, with 36 underground parking spaces and 63 rooms. The power lines on the Silver Strand were to go underground, according to the Silver Strand Beautification Committee (SSBC). Seabees agreed to donate time to assist in the project.

In May, debate continued about City Hall, argued by Mayor Smisek and Councilman Blumenthal. Smisek looked at the projected costs and found there was not enough money for all the desired capital projects, such as the library and Glorietta Bay portion. He wondered if some parts of the project could be moved into the Police Station. Councilman David Blumenthal proposed three plans for the vacated Sixth and Orange police station property. The result of the intense City Council meeting was a hearing to address the City Hall location, considering three alternative sites as well as Glorietta Bay. By a 3-2 vote a week later, Council ruled that City Hall would "Stay on the

Coronado Schools have had a special relationship with the Arts from the very beginning. During the dedication of the High School in 1923, it was touted as "an enduring center of culture for Coronado," well-represented by the theatrical instruction of Clara Bell Cutler in the 1920s and 30s. The Coronado School of the Arts (COSA) continues that tradition today. (CHA)

Bay." The plan called for a two-story, 17,000-sq. ft. City Hall, designed around a courtyard. The Public Services Yard project remained locked in a heated discussion because the Council was divided on cost cutting.

Coronado lost two more grand ladies when Jane Keck Reynolds and Eleanor Spalding Curtis passed away in early 1997. The Fifield Brothers also passed away, as did the Needhams; these long time Coronadans contributed so much to the contracting business, to the Coronado Ferry Company, and to sports and recreation.

The City Attorney said a petition to put a $4 million cap on the Public Services yard project was flawed. The council did choose a skateboard park location at the Tidelands, despite much opposition to the plan. Because of liability to the City and possible attraction of gang members, people were concerned. The fact that the cost for skateboarding was nearly as much as library improvements, and other facilities, raised a large number of questions. Other issues before the City included the existence of Dog Beach, as well as the planting of palm trees or shade trees in the downtown business district. Senior citizens, meanwhile, just smiled and went about having a good time with monthly luncheons, jewelry classes, lawn bowling, bingo games, playing bridge, and learning Spanish. They had been listening with usual wonderment to the City Hall "circus," as one nonagenarian referred to the spectacle.

On June 13, 1997, Coronado's future community and civic center at Glorietta Bay appeared to be a step closer. The Council agreed to start the Environmental Impact Report process, with construction projected to begin by 1998. Meanwhile, planning came to a halt when Travelers Group of New York sold the Hotel del Coronado to Lowe Enterprises, and its Hospitality Management subsidiary, Destination Hotels & resorts.

The Coronado Unified School District asked voters for a new Middle School, and to pay for renovation at other Coronado schools, in the form of a school bond issue that would appear on the November 1997 ballot. The estimated costs were $27,359,000. The new Middle School alone would cost between $12 and $20 million! Scheduled to open in the year 2000, the facility would be built at Cutler Field on Sixth, between "F" and "G." Not all went well. A Coronado resident asked, "Why should taxpayers pay for a new school for inter-district students who don't live in Coronado...even if their parents work here, they pay no taxes." The $27.4 million school bond measure did not get a sufficient "Yes" vote.

Despite occasional political disagreements, Coronado was able to fashion a stunning and intelligent revitalization of its schooling beginning in the early 1990s that featured new facilities for elementary, middle, high school, athletics, and specialty education. Shown here is the entry to the new Coronado High School. (CHA)

The Glorietta Bay Master Plan (GBMP) was now on a fast track. Plans for the new City Hall, Community Center, boat ramp, and yacht club promenade had to be approved after the EIR was completed. Pulling the cover off the GBMP master funding sheet, the Council revealed the total cost to be $22.3 million. City Hall and the Community Center would come from the City's general fund. The Community Development Agency site preparation costs were $1.6 million, and $1.3 million was needed for demolition. City Hall personnel still operated in the quaint old "Hobby Club," as they had since 1953. Conversions had been made at a cost of $14,000, to a building that originally cost $34,757.

There was now no question that the cost of living in Coronado had risen significantly, making life more difficult for retired civilian and military personnel living on fixed incomes. Rentals in the village listed from $650 to $4,000 a month. Rentals in the Cays ranged from $1,700 to $3,000 a month. Rentals at the Shores brought $1,300 to $3,000 a month. Sales of homes included a four-bedroom, four-bath house for $529,000; a 1913 historic landmark with three bedrooms, $1,100,000; and a three-bedroom, three-bath at the Cays, listed for $795,000.

Long-awaited earthquake retrofit work was to begin on the bridge, costing $95 million, and was projected to take four years. The projects would not harm the Barrio Logan murals, district cargo, or Navy ships near the bridge. Problems over traffic delays had been resolved with CALTRANS. Concurrently, the City agreed to fund an initial study for a tunnel, proposed to run from the Bay Bridge into NAS North Island to decrease traffic on Third and Fourth Streets. Though the concept of a tunnel had been voted down in the late 1980s, the City Council formed a Tunnel Proposition Information Group (TPIG) to investigate. The new proposal called for a tunnel boring machine to drill a 39-ft. diameter traffic tunnel pass with three, reversible, 13-ft. wide lanes. The technology was called Earth Pressure Balance Shield (EPBS) tunneling. An important attribute was its ability to handle groundwater. When first proposed by former Mayor Dorman, the cost of a tunnel would have been $60 million. The cost in 1998 was listed at $122 million. Voters would review the tunnel proposal in June.

The Council considered many agenda items in January 1998. The Council received revised library expansion plans. Orange Avenue zoning was reversed; future development of a residential stretch of Orange Avenue was examined to create an R-4 zone (residential, multiple family residences) between Second and Eighth streets. The Council reviewed the major City projects for the coming year, 1998: the Public Services yard; Glorietta Bay Plan, traffic, proposed golf course on the Silver Strand, and pollution problems from storm drain outfall at North Beach. The Council also asked the Coronado Visitors Bureau, the Chamber of Commerce, and Coronado Main Street Ltd. to review hiring processes for a new Economic Development Director. A definition of the position would first be required. That did not take long, since Kevin Ham, Executive Director of the Transportation Management Association (TMA) was named to the position by City Manager Homer Bludau.

Hal Niedermeyer died in 1998, leaving a legacy known in high schools all over the country for sports and academics. A group of his former nationally recognized athletes asked that the new football field be named for him. Niedermeyer coached a number of teams to Southern California and Metro League championships in football, basketball, and track, when Coronado had the smallest enrollment of schools in the region. In August 1998, the school district again placed a proposition on the November ballot to approve a school bond issue. The new plan reduced previous cost estimates, and included more "green space" at the new Middle School. This time around, a private consultant was not hired--a serious mistake made during the previous election. Instead, volunteers were utilized who raised money through a website for voter registration and a bond campaign.

The City Council approved plans for Bradley Field, deemed a Little League "Dream Field." A pitch was made for $26,400 for the design work, with the entire project to cost $400,000.

One of Coronado's police officers, Mitch McKay, was honored by San Diego Crime Stoppers and the San Diego Chapter of MADD, for his exceptional job recovering the most stolen cars, and by the San Diego Auto Theft Association for investigating cases resulting in arrests made of car thieves. Silver Strand Beautification Project (SSBP) volunteers held a re-dedication ceremony for State Highway 75, to bring attention to a scenic highway designation. Their efforts paved the way for future improvements to be made along the road.

In April, the Hotel del Coronado, now owned by Lowe Enterprises, unveiled its preliminary plans for a $50 million renovation and restoration. The plans showed more landscaping and less asphalt, with a high priority given to seismic retrofitting. Emphasizing the Hotel's spirit of preservation and restoration was an announcement of "a new docent program and Archival Project, in keeping with the National Historic Preservation Week," said Michael Hardesty, Managing Director. Due to the popularity of the Hotel's history tours, the resort and the Coronado Historical Association would again collaborate. Cindi Malinick, Executive Director of the Coronado Historical Association, was appointed to seek 50 to 60 volunteers from the Association membership to become docents for the tours. Experienced in archival and museum curatorial work, she also served as an advisor on the Hotel's archival project and exhibition designs.

On May 1st, the City's first "Fast Food Ordinance" was proposed, with "the intent to have it looked at by the public," explained Planning Commissioners, "with public workshops, but Commission-crafted." The definition given "Formula Fast Food," was that which is served in containers and carried out. Citizens were also to observe parking and traffic problems. The Planning Commission was concerned that fast food franchises could overwhelm the village atmosphere, and possibly out-compete existing "Mom and Pop" businesses. One week later, on May 8th, the City said "NO," to fast food businesses, declaring a moratorium; there were already 17 in town. One councilman observed: "We don't want Coronado to look like a Coney Island."

Concerts in Spreckels Park — a beloved Coronado tradition that continues ... (CHA)

In May 1998, Coronado was said to be a "Noise Critical Area," and the City again conducted a study of noise from aircraft, trucks, and traffic. Consultants looked at various areas for a fee of $36,990. The Truck Traffic Reduction Committee (TTRC) and the Blue Ribbon Committee on Traffic (BRCOT) also needed this information. One citizen wrote a "Letter to the Editor," expressing concern about "...the politically and socially incestuous relationship between City leaders, and those pushing development...."

After several years of the City and developers arguing over plans to build La Avenida Center, plans were handed to the Environmental Design Review Commission. They called for razing the 29-room hotel, replacing it with 86 rooms and three retail spaces. One Commission member, poetically inclined, said, "One thing we don't want to see is Fort La Avenida; we want Romantic La Avenida."

The Summer Concert season, planned by Mary Carlin King Ross, was extended to 16 weeks, starting May 31st. This was Ross' 25th year at the helm (with the help of husband Floyd), succeeding Coronado High School teacher Gene Cech in 1973.

The USS *Pearl Harbor* (LSD 52), a Dock Landing Ship, was commissioned at NAS North Island on May 30. Six thousand people attended the ceremonies, including 1,000 members of the Pearl Harbor Survivors Association. Navy Secretary John Dalton and Senator Daniel Inoye spoke, with a message that the "Price of Liberty is expensive, and we should be ready to pay for it." Jessica Myers was one of a number of female sailors assigned to the ship.

The new tunnel proposal moved ahead with wording for the November 1998 ballot. This asked residents whether they wanted the Council to seek local, state, or federal funding for a bored tunnel between the bridge plaza and NAS North Island. In other words, the vote was advisory. This, in effect, left the door open for Council to have the final word: to move ahead with the project, conduct further study, or deny a tunnel.

The 4th of July Parade Committee was led by Andy Szymanski as President. This year was the 50th anniversary, with John Laing, Parade Chairman since 1970. His father, Al Laing, had been parade announcer for 40 years, was well remembered by many friends for his beautiful voice. Louis Dean, one of the originators of the Coronado 4th of July parade, remembered a time when Lone Ranger's horse, "Silver," got loose. "We chased him all over Spreckels Park." Syzymanski remembered another animal chase. "A baby elephant ran through the front yard of someone's house in the staging area."

On August 7, 1998, Eckenroth Communications, which had owned and published the *Coronado Eagle* since 1990, purchased the *Coronado Journal*, which had been reporting local news since 1924. Dean Eckenroth made plans to combine the best parts of both newspapers, and also to print a "Weekender."

Mayor Smisek noted that with the coming election, voters had a chance to determine the future direction of the community. He planned to speak to three issues: the tunnel, the school bond issue, and these unresolved subjects: density, overbuilding, overcrowding, management of tourism, and the efficient use of our public facilities.

Some Reflections on Coronado's Future

In the early 1980s, Coronado contracted with the San Diego County Association of Governments (SANDAG) for an Historic Preservation Element, a program to help Coronado preserve its historic homes. But citizens feared that a "reference only" inventory of historic Coronado properties would infringe upon their property rights. As a result, City Council rejected the four-volume series outright. Sadly, speaking of those who prepared the historic inventory of the City's resources, one Councilmember said, "Those fellows did not know what they were doing. "Those "fellows" were, in reality, 14 of Coronado's most knowledgeable long-time citizens aware of Coronado's architectural history. Attorney Sharon Sherman later wrote a most instructive letter explaining the real purpose of the program: to document and protect Coronado's historic homes voluntarily. A new historic plan was presented in 1998, offering benefits to those who wanted their houses to be protected from future loss by listing them on a local voluntary Inventory.

By 1998, the Coronado Public Library required new space due to all the technology and incentives then bringing grownups and young people alike to Coronado's educational bank. Any rearrangement of the historic Library would not have caused John D. Spreckels to squint one bit.

In 1970, upon retirement after years of service to Coronado, Judge John Richard Goodbody mused that some individuals have shown they are against *any* change whatsoever for business or residents, and that some people believe they own a piece of the Hotel del Coronado, a private enterprise. He was right; years have gone by without a change in Coronado factions.

How will our City support a population of the size towards which Coronado seems to be moving? Not much progress has been made to resolve what the City wants to be, or can be. Coronado seems to have more of everything: traffic and crowds, but fewer available parking places. "One threat is the belief that [Coronado] needs more hotel/motel rooms, which add congestion, and bulky buildings, which cause essential destruction of our village." Mayor Smisek has asked two relative questions, which ought to be resolved. "Do we want to encourage tourism?" and "Should the Transient Occupancy Tax and sales tax be raised?"

Coronadans want to retain their small town atmosphere. They do not want their island to lose its identity. In mid-1998, the population was 28,537, packed within an area of 13.5 square miles. There were 7,612 households, with an average household income of over $67,000. The age group in the highest bracket is 34-54, totaling 9,055 persons. There is an annual visitor population of 2 million. At mid-year 1998, the price of homes in Coronado was second only to Carlsbad in the region. With the economy stronger and interest rates low, local economists believed the community would fare well.

From its inception, Coronado was a resort village for the wealthy and the working classes. John D. Spreckels held strongly to that belief. Coronado's heritage is steeped in its architectural montage, reflecting every decade of age and development. The architects, from the Reid Brothers, to Joseph Falkenham, Harrison Albright, Irving Gill, William Sterling Hebbard, Charles Herreshoff, William Templeton Johnson, Richard Requa, and Sam Hamill, and builders such as Chris Cosgrove, Al Laing, Paul Hathaway, and John Washington, made unique and treasured contributions to the village that are found on every street and avenue. In the future, and in time, the architects and builders of today will be added to that list.

Coronado must be created as a whole—seen from a broader perspective--not in the piece-meal fashion, which has taken decades to resolve. The island is small enough for that to be done. It has not lost its long-term appeal as a village with coastal charm and attractiveness--the very assets earlier developers valued in their planning. Visitors recognize that. Unfortunately, this perspective seems to be in continual tension between residents and the business owners.

The City was too indecisive in creating an attractive focal point that would include a City Hall and a Community Center representing the essential values of the village. Citizens questioned in 1998 were most vocal when observing what they believed to be a village top-heavy in official and unofficial committees. They asked, "Are there not too many people working on the same problems?" Are the political leaders handcuffed because of their part-time positions? Councilwoman Lois Ewen had called for a full-time Mayor in November 1996. Was the City Council too democratic in its

Coronado is the "Birthplace of Naval Aviation," a fact proudly recognized during a year-long Centennial of Naval Aviation celebration in 2011, and highlighted by these eye-catching front-lawn signs, which sprouted up everywhere on the island. (CHA)

processes because its leaders fear community backlash? Has the City relied too much on consultants to do what its administrators should be executing? Should the planning be carried out by Coronado's professional city planners rather than volunteers?

The direction of the year 2000 had to be in the direction of Coronado's Second Century: a premier seacoast village, not like that of the 1920s, but one that could be creatively designed to meet the call of the 21st century. The tangibles that made Coronado legendary are still here - the Hotel del Coronado, the beaches, the parks, the grand old homes and the tiny bungalows...the wide tree-lined avenues and the bright clear bay that need to be preserved.

At the same time, the citizens, as keepers of this unique jewel, must be more considerate of one another, and expect quality developments and creative architecture. Civic buildings must reflect another time, not another place. Public buildings need to reflect a dignity and style that speak of this community's pride and heritage. Efforts to maintain a balance between a resort town and a residential village must never cease, nor must one be permitted to overshadow the other, for it is their successful weaving together that has produced a unique environment. Leave a pristine village for our children and grandchildren, when we are gone. Coronado as it once was is nevermore. The golden days of playboys, polo games, and movie stars will not be again. Yet, the magic can still be felt as the Enchanted Island is still very much here.

(CHA)

(CHA)

The Coronado Almanac
and book of Island facts

SPONSORED BY JANE BRAUN

The City of Coronado is now operated under the council/manager form of government with a City Council of five elected members and a city manager appointed by the council. The City Council selected its mayor from among its members up until 1971, when the people chose to vote for their mayor directly. This came about as a result of hard feelings and controversy among certain members on the Council at the time.

Realtor Rolland M. McNeely became Coronado's first direct-elected mayor. The mayor presides at all council meetings. The Council is the legislative body and, as such, enacts the laws and establishes the policies that govern the activities of the city.

The city manager is responsible for making recommendations to the City Council and for enforcing the laws and carrying out the policies through the employees under his control.

The Council appoints commissions and committees to assist in various aspects of municipal government. The various commissions and committees include: Oversight, Civil Service, Tourism Improvement District, Cultural Arts, Design Review, Historic Resource, Library Board of Trustees, Planning Commission, Street Tree, Traffic Operations, Naval Complexes, and Parks and Recreation Commission. The individuals appointed serve voluntarily in the best interest of the community. Members of the City Council receive a modest salary.

The Council appoints a city attorney to serve as a legal advisor to the City Council, commissions, and the city staff.

City Hall is located at 1825 Strand Way, about a half mile south of Hotel del Coronado. It houses the Council chamber and conference rooms, the Administrative Services, the Community Development Department, the city clerk's office, and that of the City Manager.

The city administration is divided into Administrative Services, Community Development, City Clerk, City Manager, Fire Department, Human Resources, Golf Course, Library, Police Department, Public Services and Engineering, and the Recreation Department.

Elections

Municipal elections are nonpartisan. Held on the first Tuesday after the first Monday in March in the even numbered years.

School Board elections are nonpartisan. Held on the first Tuesday after the first Monday in March in the odd-numbered years.

School financing elections are held the same time as municipal elections.

Initiatives, referenda, and recall elections are held as the particular document designates.

Coronado City Halls

1890-1906:
Hotel Josephine, Third and Orange Avenue - 16 years

1906-1911:
Coronado Beach Co. Bldg., First and Orange Avenue -5 years

1911-1918:
Old Bank of America Bldg.
Corner Orange Ave. & Park Place - 7 years

1918-1953:
1125 Loma Avenue - 35 years

1953-2005:
1278 Strand Way - 52 years

2005- Present:
1825 Strand Way

Presidents of the Board of Trustees

1. E.S. Babcock — Dec. 15, 1890 to March 30, 1891
2. M.R. Vanderkloot — March 30, 1891 to Jan. 15, 1804
3. J.H. Bean — Jan. 15, 1894 to Apr. 16, 1894
4. George Foster — Apr. 16, 1894 to Dec. 30, 1895
5. E.W. Koeppen — Dec. 30, 1895 to Apr. 18, 1898
6. J. Fitzgerald — Apr. 18, 1898 to Dec. 18, 1899
7. C.B. Daggett — Dec. 18, 1899 to Dec. 17, 1900
8. A.L. Reed — Dec. 17, 1900 to May 27, 1901
9. A.S. Childs — May 27, 1901 to Apr. 21, 1902
10. Albert Mathews — Apr. 21, 1902 to July 21, 1902
11. George Holmes — July 21, 1902 to Apr. 15, 1912
12. Wilmot Griffis — Apr. 15, 1912 to Apr. 18, 1916
13. W.C. Harland — Apr. 18, 1916 to Jan. 2, 1918
14. L.S. Chamberlain — Jan. 2, 1918 to Apr. 17, 1922
15. William E. Harper — Apr. 17, 1922 to Apr. 21, 1924
16. J.E. Alcaraz — Apr. 21, 1924 to Apr. 19, 1926

Mayors of the City

17. H.J. Stewart — Apr. 19, 1926 to Apr. 16, 1928
18. W.M. Crose — Apr. 16, 1928 to June 18, 1928
19. J.H. Pendleton — June 18, 1928 to Apr. 21, 1930
20. F.L. Wilson — Apr. 21, 1930 to Apr. 18, 1932
21. Alfred B. Fry — Apr. 18, 1932 to Dec. 4, 1933
22. A.H.S. Black — Dec. 4, 1933 to May 6, 1935
23. Peter MacKenzie — May 6, 1935 to Apr. 20, 1936
24. D.H. Cameron — Apr. 20, 1936 to June 21, 1937
25. J.J. Clausey — June 21, 1937 to Dec. 23, 1937
26. D.H. Cameron — Dec. 23, 1937 to Apr. 18, 1938
27. H.G.S. Wallace — Apr. 18, 1938 to Apr. 15, 1940
28. Carl W. Ince — Apr. 15, 1940 to Apr. 18, 1944
29. Clarence T. Anderson — Apr. 18, 1944 to Apr. 16, 1946
30. Kenneth B. Carson — Apr. 16, 1946 to May 6, 1947
31. Archibald D. Abel — May 6, 1947 to Apr. 20, 1948
32. George Neal — Apr. 20, 1948 to Apr. 18, 1950
33. Emerson G. Stanley — Apr. 18, 1950 to Apr. 15, 1952
34. Keir Brooks — Apr. 15, 1952 to July 29, 1952
35. Lloyd Harmon — Aug. 19, 1952 to Apr. 20, 1954
36. Walter Vestal — Apr. 20, 1954 to Apr. 17, 1956
37. Coleman Gray — Apr. 17, 1956 to Apr. 15, 1958
38. B.R. Harrison — Apr. 15, 1958 to Apr. 19, 1960
39. Robin Goodenough — Apr. 19, 1960 to Apr. 17, 1962
40. W.A. Seavey — Apr. 17, 1962 to Apr. 21, 1964
41. Walter Vestal — Apr. 21, 1964 to Apr. 19, 1966
42. Joseph A. Overton — Apr. 19, 1966 to Apr. 16, 1968
43. Paul Vetter — Apr. 16, 1968 to Apr. 21, 1970
44. Robin Goodenough — Apr. 21, 1970 to Apr. 20, 1971
45. Richard Parker — Apr. 20, 1971 to Apr. 18, 1972
46. Rolland McNeely — Apr. 18, 1972 to Mar. 9, 1976
47. Virginia Bridge — Mar. 9, 1976 to Mar. 14, 1978
48. C. Patrick Callahan — Mar. 14, 1978 to Apr. 17, 1984
49. R.H. Dorman — Apr. 17, 1984 to Nov. 29, 1988

Mayors elected directly by voters for a 4 year term

50. Mary Herron — Nov. 29, 1988 to Nov. 5, 1996
51. Tom Smisek — Nov. 5, 1996 to Nov. 4, 2008
52. Casey Tanaka — Nov. 4, 2008

City Managers

In September 1919, an ordinance creating the office of City Manager, prescribing duties and compensation was presented for the first reading. Coronado had had a city Manager for some time but there was no ordinance creating such a job. The City Engineer served as City Manager for all intents and purposes.

The first official City Manager was selected in 1920:

1. G. Frank Hyatt — 1920
2. T.J. Allen — 1923
3. T.H. Messer — 1926
4. E.A. Ingham — 1929
6. Fred L. Johnson — 1937
7. E.F. Koerner — 1941
8. R.W. Rink — 1942
9. P.B. Wilcox — 1944
10. Howard Fuller — 1945
11. Glenn Wade — 1951
12. Matt W. Slankard — 1954
13. Earl Ketcham — 1955
14. Race Wilt — 1957
15. Robert Winn — 1968
16. Bill Bradley — 1971
17. Warren Benson — 1972
18. Ray Silver — 1979
19. Homer Bludau — 1988
20. Mark Ochenduszko — 1999
21. Blair King — 2010

Superintendents, Coronado Unified School District

1891-1929 Coronado Schools fell under the San Diego County Superintendent of Schools. Coronado Schools occasionally used the title of "Head of Schools" or, even, "Superintendent" but it was only an informal title, frequently the principal of the high school.

1. J. Leslie Cutler   1930*
2. Robert C. Titus   1944
3. A. E. Schaefer   1949
4. Dr. Charles James   1960
5. Dr. Clifford Jordan   1966
6. Dr. Jay Mack   1973
7. William Kinzler   1976
8. David Blumenthal   1984
9. Dr. Rene Townsend   1995
10. Marilyn Wheeler   1998
11. Susan Coyle   2006
12. Dr. Jeff Felix   2008

first to formally carry the title Superintendent

Principals, Coronado High School

1. Professor M. W. Pepper   1891
2. Caroline J. Swyney   1892
3. Charles Stearns   1892
4. Hugh J. Baldwin   1893
5. Henry G. Crocker   1897
6. J. A. Rice   1901
No High School classes   1902-1913
7. Ivan Deach   1913
8. W. A. Pratt   1915
9. E. H. Perry   1918
10. J. Leslie Cutler   1920
11. Benjamin Shoemaker   1935
12. A. E. Schaefer   1940
13. David Michaels   1943
14. Arthur Hearn   1945
15. A. E. Schaefer   1946
16. Wilfred Seamen   1950
17. Dr. Robert Oliver   1967
18. David Blumenthal   1976
19. Hugh Watson   1977
20. Carol Burke Couture   1986
21. Dr. Jeffrey Davis   1993
22. Rick Schmitt   1999
23. Dr. Pam Lewis   2003
24. David Lorden   2004
25. Karl Mueller   2006
26. Jenny Moore   2013

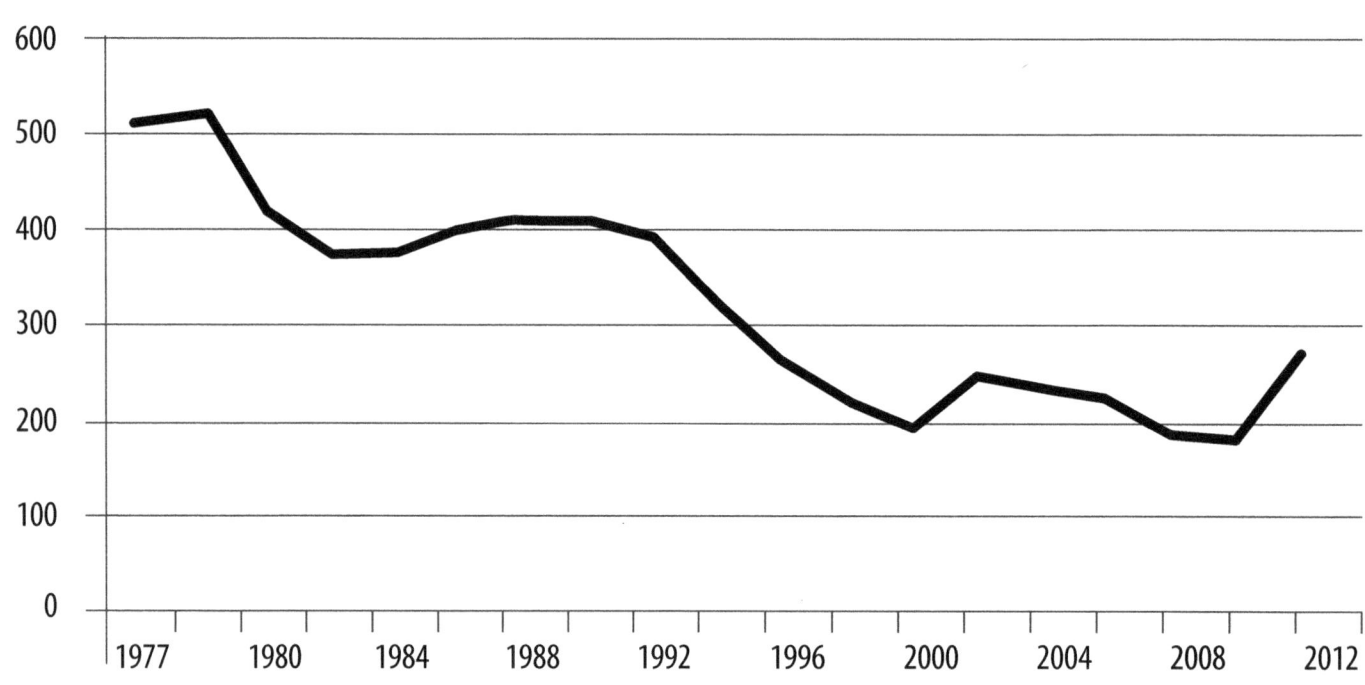

Traffic Accidents in Coronado

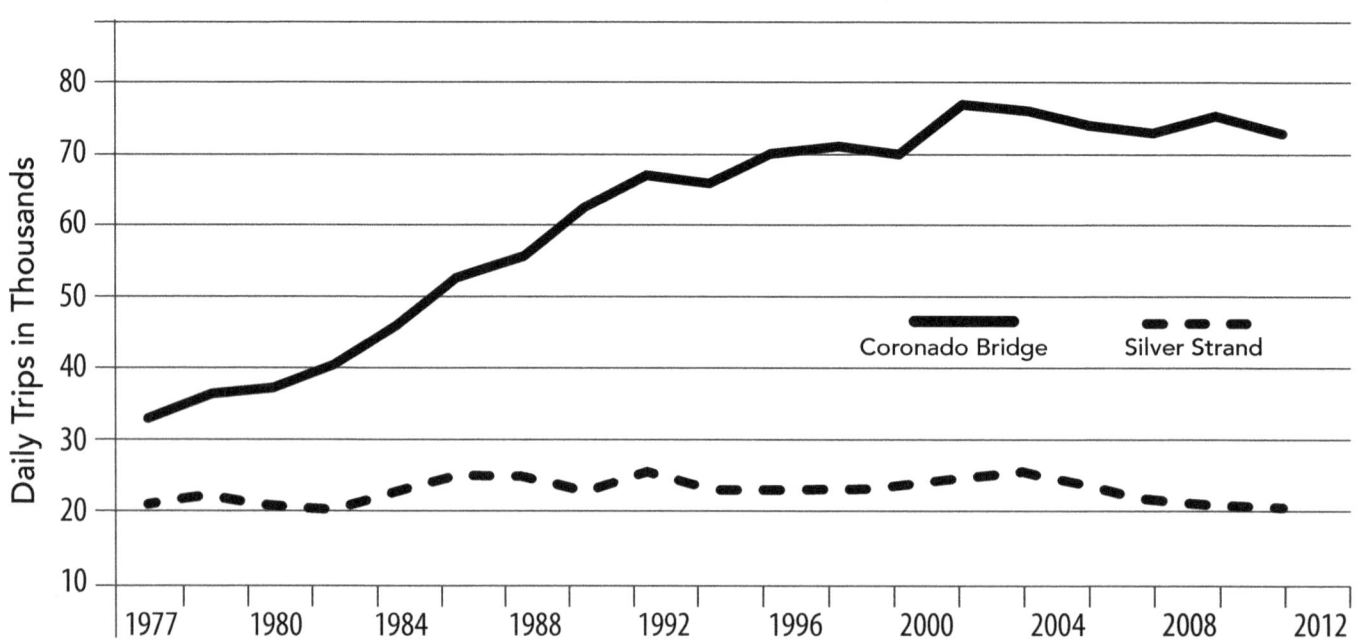

Coronado Traffic: Daily Trips

Fire Chiefs of the Coronado Fire Department

James Waller	1892-1915
Louis Bandel	1915-1918
Sven "Adolph" Johnson	1919-1920
George Sanven	1921-1926
Graham Zimmerman	1926-1934
Lee Thompson	1935-1942
Frank Welch, Jr.	1943-1952
Elgin McCarty	1953-1953
Charles Damren	1953-1958
Edward Kohl	1958-1967
Walter Nettlehorst	1967-1972
Robert Shanahan	1972-1987
James Walker	1987-1996
E. John Traylor	1997-2003
Kim Raddatz	2004-2009
E. John Traylor	2009-2011
Michael Blood	2011-

Coronado Public Library Directors

J. E. Roberts	1893-1894
Mrs. C. M. Crandall	1895-1903
Adaline Baihache	1903-1905
Mary E. Balch	1905-1908
Charles S. Robinson	1909-1910
Mary G. Valentine	1911-1913
Anna Allsebrook	1914-1917
Gabrielle Morton	1918-1951
Evelyn B. Detchon	1951-1955
Merna J. Cox	1956-1974
Mel L. Cantor	1974-1988
Christian R. Esquevin	1988-

City Marshall/Chief of Police, Coronado Police Department

W.w. Stevens	1890 - 1893
F.j. Fisher	1893 - 1894
J.h. Hartupee	1894 - 1900
J.l. Cameron	1900 - 1912
Chas. S. Robinson	1912 - 1916
John H. O'donnell	1916 - 1922
Harry S. Smith	1922 - 1923
Joseph E. Myers	1923 - 1926
M.j. Barron	1926 - 1928
Henry Clay Israel	1928 - 1929
Cletus I. Horvell	1929 - 1931
Ivan J. Smith	1931 - 1937
C.f. Robberson	1937 - 1938
June W. Jordan	1938 - 1943
James J. Traynor	1943 - 1945
June W. Jordan	1946 - 1952
R.h. Manchester	1952 - 1965
B.w. Adams	1965 - 1969
Art Le Blanc	1969 - 1980
Gerald W. Boyd	1981 - 1991
John M. (Jack) Drown	1991 - 1995
Robert S. Hutton	1995 - 2005
Paul W. Crook	2005 - 2007
Louis J. Scanlon	2007 - 2013
Jon Froomin	2013 -

Coronado Floral Association Presidents

1. Harold A. Taylor — 1922-1932
2. Mrs. Dwight Peterson — 1932-1937
3. Mrs. Armand Jessop — 1937-1939
4. Captain H.H. Ritter — 1939-1948
5. Major Ennalls Waggaman — 1948-1950
6. Mrs. Mark Vilim — 1950-1952
7. Major Ennalls Waggaman — 1952-1953
8. Captain R.D. Kirkpatrick — 1953-1955
9. Colonel Donald Spicer — 1955-1957
10. Captain John N. MacInnes — 1957-1959
11. Rear Admiral G.D. Zurmuehlen — 1959-1961
12. Captain Frank T. Sloat — 1961-1963
13. Commander Philip H. Dennler — 1963-1966
14. Captain Richard W. Parker — 1966-1967
15. Commander Philip H. Dennler — 1967-1968
16. Judge Thomas J. Gligorea — 1968-1970
17. Captain George L. Heap — 1970-1972
18. Commander W.T. Finley — 1972-1973
19. Mr. R.L. Hathaway — 1973-1975
20. Captain B.W. Wright — 1975-1977
21. Commander Robert Odiorne — 1978-1979
22. Captain John L. Nichols — 1980-1981
23. Rear Admiral A.S. Goodfellow — 1982-1983
24. Captain George W. Gaienne — 1984
25. Rear Admiral A.S. Goodfellow — 1985
26. Captain Ralph W. Frame — 1986
27. Mrs. Joseph A. Perkins — 1987-1988
28. Captain Oliver Compton — 1989-1990
29. Commander William Williams — 1990-1991
30. Captain Ralph W. Frame — 1992-1994
31. Mrs. Pat Starr — 1994-1995
32. Captain David E. Sigsworth — 1995-1997
33. Captain Thomas Stanley — 1998-1999
34. Linda Stanton — 1999-2000
35. Scott Goodfellow — 2000-2002
36. Sondi Arndt — 2002-2003
37. Mrs. Art Jones — 2003-2004
38. Carvill Veech — 2004-2005
39. Nancy Griffith — 2005-2006
40. Nancy Santos — 2006-2007
41. Tony Santos — 2007-2008
42. Leslie Crawford — 2008-2012
43. Laura Crenshaw — 2012-2014
44. Rob Crenshaw — 2015-2016

Coronado Historical Association Presidents

- Bunny McKenzie — 1969-1972 *(Founder of CHA)*
- Sam Woodhouse — 1972-1974
- Roy McCoy — 1974-1975
- Hilding Weisgerber — 1975-1977
- Wilf Seaman — 1978-1979
- Bob Odiorne — 1979-1981
- Gerry MacCartee — 1981-1990
- Parker Finch — 1990-1991
- Sharon Sherman — 1991-1992
- Mary Ann Chapple — 1995-1997
- Susan Keith — 1997-2000
- Betty Le Moyne — 2000-2003
- Barb DeMichele — 2003-2005
- Phyllis Krause — 2005-2006
- Aileen Oya — 2006-2008
- Whitney Benzian — 2008-2010
- Robert Balfour — 2010-2013
- Carrie O'Brien — 2013-

Coronado Historical Association Executive Directors

- Cindi Malinick — 1999-2002 *(First Executive Director)*
- Page Harrington — 2003-2005
- Joe Ditler — 2005-2008
- Susan Enowitz — 2008-2012
- Bruce Linder — 2012-

Commanding Officers, Naval Air Station, North Island

(Commanding Officer, Naval Air Station, San Diego)
1. LCDR Earl W. Spencer — 1917-1919
2. CAPT James H. Tomb — 1919-1921
3. CDR Frank R. McCrary — 1921-1922
4. CAPT Thomas T. Craven — 1922-1925
5. CAPT Stafford H. R. Doyle — 1925-1927
6. CAPT Frank R. McCrary — 1927-1930
7. CDR Robert R. Paunack — 1930-1932
8. CAPT John H. Hoover — 1932-1934
9. CAPT John H. Towers — 1934-1936
10. CAPT Arthur L. Bristol — 1936-1939
11. CAPT John S. McCain — 1939-1941
12. CAPT Ernest L. Gunthur — 1941-1943
13. RADM Elliot Buckmaster — 1943-1944
14. CAPT George A. Ott — 1944-1945
15. CAPT Leslie E. Gehres — 1945-1948
16. CAPT Lester K. Rice — 1948-1950
17. CAPT William L. Erdmann — 1950-1952
18. RADM Walter F. Rodee — 1952-1954

(Commanding Officer, Naval Air Station, North Island)
19. CAPT Arnold W. McKechnie — 1954-1956
20. CAPT John B. Bowen, Jr. — 1956-1960
21. CAPT William M. Collins — 1960-1962
22. CAPT Robert W. Leeman — 1962-1964
23. CAPT Robert M. Kercheval — 1964-1966
24. CAPT Richard D. Greer, Jr. — 1966-1968
25. CAPT Griffith P. Stokes — 1968-1970
26. CAPT Donald B. Edge — 1970-1972
27. CAPT Robert P. McKenzie — 1972-1973
28. CAPT Francis P. Koval — 1973-1975
29. CAPT Robert C. Kennedy — 1975-1977
30. CAPT David L. Harlow — 1977-1979
31. CAPT Warren E. Aut — 1979-1981
32. CAPT Robert B. Watts — 1981-1983
33. CAPT Russel N. Blatt — 1983-1985
34. CAPT Buddie J. Penn — 1985-1987
35. CAPT Joseph S. Walker — 1987-1989
36. CAPT Joseph R. DeNigro — 1989-1991
37. CAPT Theodore C. Sexton — 1991-1993
38. CAPT James R. Jarrell — 1993-1995
39. CAPT Don E. Steuer — 1995-1997

(Commander, Naval Base Coronado)
39. CAPT Don E. Steuer — 1997-1998
40. CAPT David R. O'Brien — 1998-2001
41. CAPT David R. Landon — 2001-2004
42. CAPT Townsend G. Alexander — 2004-2006
43. CAPT Anthony E. Gaiani — 2006-2009
44. CAPT Yancy B. Lindsey — 2009-2012
45. CAPT Gary A. Mayes — 2012-2013
46. CAPT Christopher E. Sund — 2013-2015
47. CAPT Stephen D. Barnett — 2015-

CORONADO FERRIES

DELLA (or ADELLA)
1885 (Served briefly). Steam-powered launch, frequently pictured towing an open boat for additional passengers

CORONADO
1886 – 1922 (Served infrequently in later years). Steamer, side paddle wheels, wooden hull, room for horse, carriages, foot passengers.

SILVER GATE
1888 – 1890. Built at Coronado Iron Works at Marine Ways on North Island. Steam-powered, early propeller drives, wooden hull. Largely unsuccessful with unresponsive steering and underpowered engines with difficulty in slowing down. Converted into a floating casino, locker hall, and dance pavilion for Tent City. Later purchased by San Diego Yacht Club as their clubhouse and moored in San Diego and Coronado for that purpose. Broken up for scrap during World War I.

BENICIA
1888 – 1903. Built at Martinez, CA 1881 (named after a nearby town). Steam-powered, walking beam drive, side paddle wheels, wooden hull.

RAMONA
1903 – 1932. Built by Risdon Iron Works, Oakland. Steam powered, side paddle wheels, wooden hull. The most successful of the early ferries and a familiar sight to all.

CORONADO
1929 – 1969. Built by Moore Dry Dock Company, Oakland. Specifically designed and built for service with San Diego-Coronado Ferry Company. Retired with opening of Coronado Bridge. Sold in 1973 to a ferry company in Nicaragua, ultimately wrecked on beach at Cosiguina, Nicaragua.

SAN DIEGO
1931 – 1969. Built by Moore Dry Dock Company, Oakland. A near sister ship to Coronado slightly larger with three engines to Coronado's two. Retired with opening of Coronado Bridge. Bought by the Olympic Ferries for the Whidbey Island to Port Townsend run in Puget Sound 1970—1973. She was tied up in Vancouver, British Columbia awaiting a new owner until 1994 when she was towed up the Sacramento River to await conversion to a restaurant at Antioch but was abandoned after a fire near Decker Island in the Sacramento Delta. Scrapped around 2011.

NORTH ISLAND
1938 – 1969. Originally built in 1923 by James Robertson at Alameda and named Golden West, as part of the Golden Gate Ferry Company in San Francisco Bay. After the Bay Area bridge were completed she was acquired in 1938 for use in Coronado. Retired in 1969, the North Island became an abalone processor in Ensenada harbor for years and was eventually abandoned and sank.

SILVER STRAND
1944-1969. Built in 1927 by General Engineering of Alameda. Original name was Golden Shore operating in San Francisco Bay. She was sold to the Puget Sound Navigation Company in 1939 after San Francisco bridges were built and renamed Elwha for the Seattle-Winslow route. When the Navy demanded added ferry capacity in San Diego Bay in 1944, she was renamed Silver Strand and moved to Coronado. She served until 1969 primarily during morning and evening rush hours and many in Coronado disliked her claustrophobic interior. Silver Strand was sold after 1969 she was towed to Los Angeles to be converted to a diving platform but ran aground on the Los Angeles breakwater and was later broken up.

CROWN CITY
1954 – 1969. Built in 1954, Crown City was the last (and largest) ferry in the Coronado fleet. She was efficient, but barge-like in appearance, and never truly loved in Coronado. After 1969 she was purchased by the Washington State Ferries, renamed Kulshan and worked the Clinton-Mukilteo route and on the Hood Canal. She was sold to the Coast Guard in 1982 for a pittance, was renamed Governor and sent to New York City to work between Manhattan and Governor's Island. She was sold again in 1994 to the Martha's Vineyard ferry authority as surplus federal property and used for ferrying autos and large trucks. Crown City was retired in 2015.

Coronado Historic Preservation Program
Sites Designated as Coronado Historic Resources

1886	924 H Ave. — First residential structure completed in Coronado.	1911	744 B Ave. — Craftsman Bungalow style.
c.1886	1000 Eighth St. — Queen Anne Victorian style.	1911	731 C Ave. — Craftsman Bungalow style.
1886	Spreckels Park (East & West Plaza) — Named after J. D. Spreckles. Identified as a Plaza on original 1886 subdivision map	1911	763 C Ave. — Craftsman Bungalow style.
		1911	1100 Orange Ave. — Neo-Classical style. Coronado's first bank.
1886	Star Park — Star shape on original 1886 subdivision map.	1911	801 Tolita Ave. — Tudor style.
		1911	535 Ocean Blvd. — Italian Renaissance style.
1887	930 I Ave. — Folk Victorian style.	1912	427 A Ave. — Craftsman Bungalow style.
1888	279 C Ave. — Queen Anne Victorian style.	1912	600 A Ave. — Craftsman Bungalow style.
c.1888	1112 Churchill Place — Queen Anne Victorian style.	1912	611 A Ave. — Tudor style.
1888	1111 Loma Ave — Folk Victorian style.	1912	476 C Ave. — Craftsman Bungalow style.
1889	823 H Ave. — Folk Victorian style.	1912	909 J Ave. — Craftsman Bungalow style.
1892	760 B Ave. — Queen Anne Victorian style.	1912	1212 Sixth St. — Prairie style.
c.1892	108 D Ave. — Craftsman Bungalow style.	1912	1236 Alameda Blvd. — Italian Renaissance style.
c.1892	576 E Ave. — Foursquare style.	1913	550 A Ave. — Craftsman Bungalow style.
c.1892	720 G Ave. — Folk Victorian style.	1913	975 B Ave. — Craftsman Bungalow style.
c.1892	1015 Flora Ave. — Victorian style.	c.1913	948 D Ave. — Colonial Revival style.
c.1894	917 A Ave. — Craftsman Bungalow.	1913	1027 G Ave. — Craftsman Bungalow style.
1896	1710 Visalia Row — Craftsman style.	1913	812 Third St. Woods.—Craftsman Bungalow style.
1896	718 Visalia Row. — Craftsman style.	1913	1006-1008 Ninth St. — Craftsman Bungalow style.
c.1896	921 A Ave. — Craftsman Bungalow.	1913	1012 Ninth St. — Craftsman Bungalow style.
1896	1022 Park Pl.. — Queen Anne Victorian style	1913	1110 Loma Ave. — Victorian style.
c.1897	1101 Star Park Circle. — Colonial Revival style.	1913	1100 Isabella Ave. — Craftsman Bungalow style.
c.1897	1125 Flora Ave. — Victorian style.	1913	826 Tolita Ave. — Craftsman style.
1898	1022 Adella Ave. — Craftsman Bungalow style.	1913	834 Tolita Ave. — Craftsman Bungalow style.
1898	1106 Fourth St. — Originally at 1038 Orange Ave.	1913	301 Alameda Blvd. — Aeroplane Craftsman style.
c.1898	1126 Loma Ave. — Queen Anne Victorian style.	1914	1111 G Ave. — Craftsman Bungalow style.
1898	1135 Loma Ave. — Craftsman Bungalow style.	1914	1133 Star Park Circle — Estate Wall.
1898	1118 Loma Ln. — French Eclectic style.	1915	803 Adella Ave. — English Revival style.
1901	1000 Adella Ave.. — Relocated from Ocean Blvd. in 1905	1915	824 Adella Ave. — Italianate style.
		1915	1015 Alameda Blvd. — Spanish Eclectic style.
1902	1015 Ocean Blvd. — Tudor style	1915	708 A Ave. — Italian Renaissance style.
1903	1005 Adella Ave. — English Tudor style.	1915	1117 G Ave. — Transitional Ranch style.
c.1903	300 First St. Hawaiian Plantation style.	1915	904 Fifth St.. — Craftsman Bungalow style
1904	941 G Ave. — Craftsman Bungalow style.	1916	1000 Glorietta Blvd. — Pueblo Revival style.
1906	1060 Adella/1404 Ynez — Italianate style.	1918	1003 Alameda Blvd. — Italian Renaissance.
c.1906	723 A Ave. — Tudor style.	1919	848 Glorietta Blvd. — Mediterranean Villa style.
1906	1116 Loma Ave. — Victorian style.	1919	455 B Ave.. — Colonial Revival Bungalow style
1907	1704 Visalia Row. — Tudor style.	1919	1025 E Ave. — Craftsman Bungalow style.
1907	624 First St. — Dutch Colonial Revival style.	1919	961 J Ave. — New Mexico Territorial style.
1908	509 A Ave. — Craftsman Bungalow style.	1919	545 Palm/544 D Ave. — Cubist style.
1908	824 E Ave. — Craftsman Bungalow style.	1919	875 Alameda Blvd. — Spanish Eclectic style.
1908	1043 Ocean Blvd. — Italian Renaissance style.	1919	541 Ocean Blvd. — Foursquare style.
1909	623 A Ave. — Craftsman Bungalow style.	1920	536 A Ave. — Moderne style.
1909	749 C Ave. — Craftsman Bungalow style.	1921	600 Glorietta Blvd.. — Neoclassical style
1909	765 C Ave. — Craftsman Bungalow style.	1921	1001 Olive Ave. — Spanish Bungalow style.
1909	640 Orange Ave. — Public Library Neo-Classical style.	1921	1019 Park Pl. Garden —
1910	726 B Ave. — Craftsman style.	1921	1135 Alameda Blvd. — Colonial Craftsman Cottage style.
1910	754 B Ave. — Craftsman Bungalow style.		
1910	1156 Isabella Ave. — Tudor style.	1923	1027 Adella Ave. — Spanish Colonial Revival style.
1911	700 B Ave. — Craftsman Bungalow style.	1924	1033 Adella Ave. — Prairie style.
1911	738 B Ave. — Craftsman Bungalow style.	1924	721 B Ave. — Mission Revival style.
		1924	927 D Ave. — Tudor style.

Coronado Historic Preservation Program
Sites Designated as Coronado Historic Resources

1924	1127 F Ave. — Mission Revival style.	1930	848 D Ave. — Mediterranean style. "The Monterey"
1924	1038 G Ave.. Craftsman style	1930	900 E Ave. — Spanish Eclectic style.
1924	300 Ninth St. — Mediterranean style.	1930	928 H Ave. — Spanish Colonial Revival.
1924	1030-1032 Olive Ave. — Tudor style.	1931	Bay Circle Park. —
1924	1231 Alameda Blvd. — Tudor style.	1931	1111 Flora Ave. — Italianate style.
1925	940 Glorietta Blvd. — Tudor style.	1931	1010 Olive Ave. — Spanish Colonial Revival style.
1925	526 A Ave. — English Revival style.	1932	323 J Ave. — Spanish Eclectic style.
1925	629 A Ave. — Spanish Moderne style.	1933	1021 Adella Ave. — Spanish Colonial Revival style.
1925	631 A Ave. — Spanish Moderne style.	1933	555 B Ave. — Spanish Eclectic style.
1925	566 B Ave.. —Tudor style.	1933	165 I Ave. — Spanish Eclectic style.
1925	936-954 C Ave. — Mission Revival style.	1933	825 Olive Ave. — Spanish Mediterranean style.
1925	605 Tenth St. — Tudor style.	1934	1027 F Ave. — Spanish Eclectic style.
1925	1119 Flora Ave. — Spanish Colonial Revival style.	1935	1807 Monterey Ave. — Spanish Colonial Revival style.
1925	1115 Loma Ave. — English Country Cottage style.	1935	200 Palm Ave. — Spanish Colonial Revival style.
1925	1241 Alameda Blvd. — Spanish Colonial Revival style.	1935	1026 Flora Ave. — Colonial Revival style.
1925	1244 Alameda Blvd. — English Tudor style.	1935	633 Alameda Blvd. — Spanish Colonial Revival style.
1926	1013 Adella Ave. — English Eclectic style.	1936	777 G Ave. — Spanish Colonial Revival style.
1926	1015 Adella Ave.. Spanish Colonial Revival style.	1936	200 H Ave. — Spanish Eclectic style.
1926	625 A Ave. — Spanish Moderne style.	1936	266 I Ave. — Spanish Hacienda style.
1926	550 B Ave. — Tudor style.	1936	516 I Ave. — Spanish Bungalow style.
1926	909 D Ave. — Mission Revival style.	1936	720 J Ave. — Tudor style.
1926	329 G Ave. —	1936	1427 Fifth St. — Spanish Revival style.
1926	465 G Ave. — Mission Revival style.	1936	320 Seventh St. — French Provincial style.
1926	471 G Ave. — Spanish Bungalow style.	1936	710 Adella Ave. — Beach Cottage style.
1926	601 Fourth St. — Tudor style.	1937	350 D Ave. — Spanish Mission Revival style
1926	1313 Tenth St. — Spanish Colonial Revival.	1937	751-761 G Ave. — Spanish Colonial Revival style.
1926	1017 Park Pl. — Spanish Eclectic. Blue Lantern Inn/ Hotel Marisol	1938	535 Margarita Ave. — Spanish Hacienda style.
1926	1015 Loma Ave. — Mediterranean style.	1938	160 G Ave. — Spanish Hacienda style.
1926	1045 Loma Ave. — Mission Revival style.	1938	555 Alameda Blvd. — Storybook Tudor style.
1926	757 Alameda Blvd. — Spanish Colonial Revival style.	1939	721-727 D Ave — French Normandy style.
1927	1504 Glorietta Blvd. — Spanish Colonial Revival style.	1954	Mathewson Park — Pomona Ave
1927	520 B Ave. — Spanish Colonial Revival.	1955	940 Country Club Ln. — Mid-Century Modern Post and Beam style.
1927	208 C Ave. — Craftsman Bungalow style.	1956	1417 Orange Ave. — Villa Capri Neon Signs.
1927	561 C Ave.. — Spanish Colonial Revival style	1957	Cronan Park — Pomona Ave., Sixth St., and Margarita Ave.
1927	1306 Sixth St. — Italianate style.		
1927	325 Eighth St. — Spanish Eclectic style.	1957	819 First St. — Mid-Century Modern Post and Beam style.
1927	1229 Alameda Blvd. — Spanish Eclectic style.		
1928	1202 Glorietta Blvd. — French Tudor style.	1960	Sunset Park — Ocean Blvd,
1928	575 A Ave. — Moderne style.	1962	1010 Glorietta Blvd. — Mid-Century Modern Post and Beam style.
1928	1125 G Ave. — Spanish Colonial Revival style.		
1928	740 J Ave. — Mission Revival style.	1971	Glorietta Bay Park — Strand Way
1928	941 J Ave. — Spanish Eclectic style.	1976	I Ave. Park, First St. & I Ave.
1928	815 Alameda Blvd., — Spanish Eclectic style.	1976	Palm Park, Third St., Palm Ave., & I Ave.
1928	1043 Ocean Blvd. — Spanish Eclectic style. (Rear House)	1976	Triangle Park, Palm Ave., F Ave, & Fourth St.
1929	450 A Ave. — Tudor style.	1976	Bandel Park, J Ave., Tenth St., & Alameda Blvd.
1929	710 J Ave. — Spanish Colonial Revival.	1984	Vetter Park, Cajon Pl., Guadalupe Ave., & Jacinto Pl.
1929	465 Palm Ave. — Spanish Colonial Revival style.	1986	Centennial Park, Orange Ave. and First St.
1929	416 Ninth St. — Spanish Eclectic style.	1989	Vista del Barco, Glorietta Blvd. & Ynez Pl.

Motion Pictures Filmed in Coronado

1901   *Knights of Pythias Camp*. Probably a documentary and related to the Hotel del Coronado.

1901   *Tent City*. A documentary by J.A. Ramsey.

1901   *Ferryboat Entering Coronado Slip* by J.A. Ramsey.

1912   Documentary by Allan Dwan, *Winter Sports at Coronado.*

1912   Documentary by Allan Dwan, *Curtiss' School of Aviation.*

1913   *In a Japanese Tea Garden*. Short film. Laura Sawyer, Richard Neill, and Ben Wilson. Coronado Beach. Edison Company.

1914   *All at Sea I*. Short Comedy. Eddie Lyons and Victoria Forde. Coronado Beach. Nestor Film Co.

1914   *All at Sea II*. Short Comedy. Keystone Film Co.

1915   *The Lineman's Revenge or Why is Electricity Expensive?* Lubin Studios.

1915   *Retribution*. First Lubin film made in Coronado Studio. Melvin Mayo, Vivian Caples, and Miss Adda Gleason.

1915   *Billy Joins the Navy*. Lubin Company. Stars Billy Reeves. A one reeler slapstick comedy typical of its day. Reeves was Lubin's answer to Charlie Chaplin.

1915   *The Slave of the Harem or Saved from the Harem*, with Lee Schurnway. The film was thought of as a Turkish story and also called "*The Power of Salim Bey*" (USS Colorado and crew landed on beach in front of studio.) Lubin Studios.

1915   *Their Happy Honeymoon*. Short Comedy. Eddie Lyons and Dolly Ohnet. Coronado Beach. Nestor Film Co.

1915   *The Sacred Bracelet*. Lubin Studios.

1915   *The Dragonman*. A two reel play. Lubin Studios.

1915   *Meg of the Cliffs*. Lubin Studios.

1915   *The Vengeance of Cal McCall*. Lubin Studios.

1915   *The Moment Before Death*. Lubin Studios

1915   *The Bond Within*. Lubin Studios.

1915   *The Dusty Gentlemen*. Lubin Studios.

1915   *Two News Items*. Lubin Studios.

1915   *A Delayed Reformation*. Lubin Studios.

1915   *One of the Chosen*. Lubin Studios.

1915   *Out for the Day*. Lubin Studios.

1915   *The Law's Injustice*. Lubin Studios.

1915   *The Embodied Thought*. Lubin Studios.

1915   *His Majesty Plays*. Lubin Studios.

1915   *A Modern Paul*. Lubin Studios.

1915   *Faust*. Lubin Studios. Edward Sloman directed and played the role of Mephistopheles.

1915   *The Hopeless Game*. Lubin Studios.

1915   *Swami Sam*. Lubin Studios.

1916   *The Convict King*. Lubin Studios Production. Starred L.D. Shumxvay, WJ Morley, M. Mayo and Ada Gleason.

1916   *The Redemption of Helene*. Lubin Studios.

1916   *Soldier Sons*. Lubin Studios.

1916   *The Gulf Between*. Lubin Studios.

1916   *A Sister to Cain*. Lubin Studios.

1916   *None So Blind*. 3 reeler, Melvin Mayo, producer. Lubin Studios.

1916   *Jackstraws*. 3 reeler, Melvin Mayo, producer. Lubin Studios.

1916   *Gethsemane*. Melvin Mayo, producer. Lubin Studios.

1916   *The Stolen Master*. Lubin Studios.

1916   *The Black Sheep*. Lubin Studios.

1916   *Sons of the Sea*. Lubin Studios.

1916   *The Green Fairy*. Lubin Studios.

1916   *The Code of the Hills*. Lubin Studios.

1916   *Love's Law*. Lubin Studios.

1916   *The Return of John Boston*. Lubin Studios.

1916   *The Rough Neck*. Lubin Studios.

1918	*The Married Virgin.* (Aka *Frivolous Wives.*) Drama. Vera Sisson and Rudolph Valentino. Hotel del Coronado and Coronado Beach. Maxwell Productions.
1919	*The Dragon Painter* starring Sessue Hayakawa. Filmed at Japanese Tea Gardens.
1919	*It Pays to Advertise.* Comedy. Bryant Washburn and Lois Wilson. Paramount Pictures.
1927	*Love My Dog*, a Hal Roach Our Gang comedy with Johnny Downs
1928	*Telling the World,* MGM with Anita Page
1929	*The Flying Fleet.* Ramon Navarro, Anita Page, Ralph Graves. Written by Lt. Comdr. Frank Wead, USN. Melodrama of Naval Air Exploits.
1932	*Suicide Fleet.* Ginger Rogers and Bill Boyd. Directed by Albert S. Rogell. RKO, 87 min.
1935	*Coronado.* (Sometimes titled *Going to Coronado.*) Johnny Downs, Betty Burgess, Jack Haley and Andy Devine. Song, dance, and slapstick.
1935	*Devil Dogs of the Air.* James Cagney and Pat O'Brien. Released 1935. Warners, 86 min. sound 16mm black and white.
1936	*Mr. Cinderella.* Sometimes the film is titled *Movie Struck.* Jack Haley, Betty Furness, Rosina Lawrence and Arthur Treacher. (Spreckels Mansion.) Movie may have had Stan Laurel, Oliver Hardy and Patsy Kelly. Hal Roach producer, 80 min. sound 16mm. black and white.
1936	*Yours for the Asking.* Sometimes titled Moon over Miami. Dolores Costello, George Raft, Ida Lupino, Edward Kennedy, and John Barrymore. At Hotel del Coronado, and at the Flowerland.
1937	*Submarine D-1.* Pat O'Brien, George Brent, Wayne Morris. Filmed in part at Coronado Beach. Warner Bros.
1938	*Wings of the Navy.* George Brent, Olivia de Haviland. At North Island, bit parts by 3 daughters of admirals. Directed by Lloyd Bacon. Warners 89 min. sound 16mm black and white.
1939	*Dive Bomber.* Errol Flynn, Fred MacMurray, Alexis Smith. Warners 137 min sound 16mm color. Rental MGM/United.
1939	*Thunder Afloat.* Wallace Beery and Chester Morris. Metro-Goldwyn-Mayer.
1940	*Eyes of the Navy.* Short documentary. Warren McCollum and Frank Whitbeck. Filmed in part on North Island. Metro-Goldwyn-Mayer.
1947	*Repeat Performance.* Joan Leslie, Louis Hayward and Richard Basehart. Directed by Alfred M. Werber. Eagle Lion, 90 min. sound 16mm black and white. Filmed on Coronado Ferry boat.
1953	*Panther Squadron 8.* Frank Lovejoy, Van Johnson, Walter Pidgeon. Filmed aboard the USS Princeton. Commander Paul W. Gray was technical advisor.
1955	*Francis Joins the Navy.* Donald O'Connor, Martha Hyer and Francis the talking mule. Made at Amphib. base. Directed by Arthur Lubin. Universal, 80 min. sound 16mm black and white.
1955	*Battle-Stations.* Starred John Lund, William Bendix and Richard Boone. Filmed aboard the USS Princeton.
1956	*The Brothers Rico.* Starred Richard Conte, filmed by Columbia Studios with scenes on Glorietta Boulevard. The script was written by Paul Gallico.
1956	*Highway Patrol.* Syndicated 1956. Broderick Crawford and William Boyett. Experiences of California Highway Patrol Office. Number of shots taken at 432 "B" Ave. [House cine moved to 10th & B]
1957	*Underwater Warriors.* Featured Dan Daily, Claire Kelly and filmed by MGM.
1958	*Some Like It Hot.* Marilyn Monroe, Tony Curtis, Jack Lemmon. Hotel del Coronado. 120 min. sound 16mm. video tape version. MGM/United and Festival Films.
1960	*Cry for Happy.* Columbia film shot at Hotel del Coronado and on board ships. Glenn Ford and Donald O'Connor. Directed by George Marshall. Columbus, 100 min. sound 16mm color.
1960	*Coronado 9.* Syndicated 1960. Rod Cameron's exploits as a naval officer turned detective.
1964	*The Easy Way*, Lana Turner, Jane Fonda. Hotel del Coronado.
1964	*Robrioz Ring*, episode of Kraft Suspense Theater TV Series. Robert Loggia and Julie Harris. Filmed in part at Hotel del Coronado.
1965	*Family Jewels*, Directed by Jerry Lewis. Stars Donna Butterworth and Sabastian Cook and Jerry Lewis. Paramount Studios, 100 min. sound 16mm color. Filmed at Coronado Ferry Landing and on ferryboat.

1971	*Lovin Man*. Star, Fabion Forte. Shooting at Lot One, the former Coronado Ferry Landing.
1972	*Wicked Wicked*. James Mead, Diane McBain, Edd Byrnes, Tiffany Bolling. United General Pictures. This is a must – a real murder mystery at Hotel del Coronado. Directed by Richard Bare. MGM (Anamorphic), 95 min. Sound 16mm color.
1972	*Ghost Story*. Miniseries. Stella Stevens, Pamela Franklin, Gena Rowland, Karen Black. 13 episodes. Plights of people with supernatural experiences. NBC.
1975	*Somewhere in Time*. From book Bid Time Return filmed entirely at Hotel del Coronado. Christopher Reeve and Jane Seymour.
1976	*Captains and Kings*. Miniseries. Richard Jordan, Patty Duke Astin, Perry King, Henry Fonda, Ray Bogler. Struggles of strong willed Irishman immigrant as he fights for wealth. NBC.
1976-1977	*Rich Man, Poor Man*. Series about 3 brothers. Nick Nolte, Peter Strauss, Susan Blakely, Ed Asner, Dorothy McGuire, Kay Lenz. 12 hours on ABC.
1979-1984	*Hart to Hart*. Robert Wagner. Wealthy industrialist and wife Jennifer an artist, who help people in trouble. Series, ABC.
1980	*Alien 2 On Earth*. Belinda Mayne and Mark Bodin. Filmed in part on Coronado.
1980	*The Girl, the Gold Watch and Everything*. Robert Hayes, Pam Dawber, Jill Ireland, Maurice Evans. Tale revolved around magic watch, and event watch brings out.
1980	*The Stunt Man*. Peter O'Toole, Barbara Hershey. A fugitive Steve Railsback stumbles onto movie set where he accidentally causes death of their ace stuntman. Filmed at Hotel del Coronado.
1982	*Neuron Suite*. TV Documentary. James Burke. Hotel del Coronado. Beach Media.
1982-1984	*Simon & Simon*. Jameson Parker, Gerald Ed Barth and Jeannie Wilson. A.J. and Rick, private eyes. CBS. Filmed in Coronado and various parts of county. Series.
1984	*Space*, TV Miniseries. North Island, Coronado and selected homes in Coronado and on North Island. From James Michener's novel. James Garner, Harry Hamlin, Lloyd Bridges, Bruce Dern.
1986	*Star Trek IV*. (In Search of Spock) U.S.S. Enterprise in 20th Century. Return of Spock from Genesit. Leonard Nimoy, Walter Koenig, Michelle Nichols. Filmed on the U.S.S Ranger and the U.S.S. Enterprise.
1986	*Top Gun*. Tom Cruise, Tim Robbins, Kelly McGillis. Filmed in part at North Island. Paramount Pictures.
1989	*K-9*. James Belushi. Filmed in part at the Coronado Beach and Hotel del Coronado. Universal Pictures.
1990	*My Blue Heaven*. Steve Martin, Rick Moranis, Joan Cusack. Warner Bros.
1990	*Ladies of Sweet Street*, Gloria DeHaven & Doris Roberts. TV. ABC pilot film. Filmed at Star Park Circle.
1990	*Tora, Tora, Tora*, Jason Robards, Martin Balsam, Joseph Cotten and E.G. Marshall. Filmed in part at North Island. 20th Century Fox.
1990	*Flight of the Intruder*. Danny Glover, William Dafoe and Brad Johnson. Filmed in part on U.S.S. Independence & U.S.S. Ranger. Paramount Pictures.
1991	*The Legend of Kate Morgan*. Filmed in part at old Armory. TV film.
1991	*Operation Petticoat*. Universational-International.
1992	*L.A. Connections*. Siegal Productions.
1992	*Plan of Attack*, with Loni Anderson and Anthony Denison. Filmed at Le Meridian. CBS Television.
1992	*Who Speaks for Jonathan?* JoeBeth Williams and Chris Burke, NBC Television.
1993	*Baywatch* Episode at Hotel del Coronado and on Beach.
1996	*Mr. Wrong*. (Shot at Hotel del Coronado)
1996	*What Love Sees*. TV Movie of the Week – Shot at Hansen House.
1996	*Wise Guy* with Ellen DeGeneris.
1996	*Wiseguy*. Ken Wahl, Debrah Farentino, Ted Levine. Filmed in part on Coronado. Stephen J. Cannell Productions.
1996	*Flirting with Disaster*. Ben Stiller and Patricia Arquette. Scene on Orange Ave. with Villa Capri in background. Miramax.
1997	Episodes of *Renegade* with Lorenzo Llamas.

1997	*Pensacola NAS*, Film shot on Silver Strand State Beach.
2002	*Antwone Fisher*. Denzel Washington, Derek Luke, Joy Bryant. Filmed in part on Coronado. Fox Searchlight Pictures.
2003	*Hotel del Coronado*, episode of Great Hotels TV Series.
2003	*Ghosts of California*. Documentary. Lori Brosnan, Derek Bodkin, and Kathryn Dial. Filmed in part at the Hotel del Coronado. Kinetic Pictures.
2004	*Anchorman the Legend of Ron Burgundy*. Will Ferrell. Scene on Coronado Bridge. DreamWorks.
2005	*Clash of the Tritons*, episode of TV show Veronica Mars. Kristen Bell and Jason Dohring. Scenes with Coronado Bridge. Silver Pictures TV.
2005	*Ordinary Miracles*. Jaclyn Smith and Lyndsy Fonseca. Filmed in part on Coronado. Hallmark Entertainment.
2005	*Stealth*. Jamie Foxx, Jessica Biel, Josh Lucas. Filmed in part at North Island and on the USS Abraham Lincoln. Columbia Pictures Corporation.
2006	*Airplane Disasters*. Joshua Fisher P. Anderson and Monica Young. Jive at Five Films.
2007	*Depression in Paradise*. Short Comedy. Kyle Lorenson and Will Turner. Turner Cinematography.
2008	*Lucidity*. Short Drama. Nikki Blotner, Andrew Friedman, Tassanee Sukramule. Filmed in part on Coronado. Smart Carbon Productions.
2008	*Proud American*. Michael G. Davis and Cecelia Antoinette. Slowhand Cinema.
2008	*Grim Abdication*. Short film. Ayla Bryan and Bill Cobbs.
2009	*A Call to Arms*. Documentary. Michael Douglas, Linda Hamilton, Scott Miller. Filmed in part at North Island. Scott Miller & Co.
2009	*Transformers Revenge of the Fallen*. Shia LaBeouf, Megan Fox, Josh Duhamel. Filmed in part in Coronado. DreamWorks and Paramount Pictures.
2010	*Jeopardy!*, Episode 26.93. Alex Trebek. Filmed at Coronado Naval Amphibious Base. Columbia TriStar Television.
2011	Roxy King and Lia Marie in San Diego Dogs. Short film. Coronado Beach and Old Ferry Landing. Surfs Up Studios.
2012	*Coronado*, Episode of What's Local San Diego TV Series, Season 1, Episode 2. Austin Auger, Adam Brick.
2012	*Act of Valor*. Filmed in part in Coronado. Relativity Media.
2014	*Navy Seals Their Untold Story*
2014	*Crossroads*. Rydell Danzie and Shannan Leigh Reeve. Filmed in part on Coronado. Ynot/SinPelo Entertainment.
2015	*La Migra*. Michael Copon and Antoinette Kalaj. Filmed in part on Coronado. Angelic Pictures and Happy Dance Productions.
2015	*The Right Eye*. Emily Bowen, Jaclyn Winters, Marie Oldenbourg. Filmed in part in Coronado. Nuclear Breakthrough Productions.
2016	*Nadoland*. Randy Davidson, Mark Anthony Cox, Jennifer Scibetta. Coronado School of the Arts.

BIBLIOGRAPHY

Adams, H. Austin. *The Man John D. Spreckels*. San Diego, CA: Press of Frye and Smith, 1924.

Babcock Court / Coronado Historical Association. Coronado, CA: Coronado Historical Association, 1991.

Baird, Robert W. "*A History of the Coronado Hospital*," n.d., n.p.

Barkley, Winfield. "*Coronado.*" *San Diego Magazine*, September 1927.

Bates, Cheryl Lei. "The Life and Times of Gilbert Aubrey Davidson." MA Thesis, University of San Diego, 1995.

Becker, Robert H. *Diseños of California Ranchos, Maps of Thirty-Seven Land Grants, 1822-1846*. San Francisco, CA: The Book Club of California, 1964.

Bemmelmans, Ludwig. *To The One I Love The Best*. New York, NY: The Viking Press, 1955.

Black, Samuel E. S*an Diego County, California: a record of settlement, organization, progress and achievement*. Chicago, IL: S. J. Clarke Company, 1913.

Boyd, Ann. *Our first one hundred years: Christ Episcopal Church Coronado, California 1888-1988*. Coronado, CA: Christ Episcopal Church, 1988.

Brandes, Ray and Catherine Eitzen Carlin. *Coronado: The Enchanted Island*. Coronado, CA: Coronado Historical Association, 1987.

— C*oronado: We Remember*. Coronado, CA: Coronado Historical Association, 1993.

— "Historical Report, Richards/Dupee House, Mr. & Mrs. M. Larry Lawrence." 1984.

— "Report on the History of the Coronado Bank Building for the Schulman Family." 1986. Coronado, CA: City of Coronado, 1978.

— *San Diego: An Illustrated History*. Beverly Hills, CA: Rosebud Press, 1981.

— translator and editor. *The Costansó Narrative of the Portolá Expedition: First Chronicle of the Spanish Conquest of California*. Newhall, CA: Hogarth Press, 1972.

— with James R. Moriarty and Susan H. Carrico. *New Town: San Diego*. San Diego, CA: San Diego Science Foundation, 1985.

Breitenbach, Marjorie. "Coronado's Personal History." *San Diego Magazine*, June 1949.

Brennan, Frederick Hazlitt. "Coronado Fever." *Collier's*, October 7, 1939.

Brown, Christian, "Hey-Day of the N.C. and O." *Journal of San Diego History*, April 1958.

Buckley, Marcie. *The Crown City's Brightest Gem*. Coronado, CA: Hotel del Coronado, 1975.

Buckley, Marcie. *Hotel Del Coronado, A National Landmark: Official Illustrated History*. Coronado, CA: Hotel Del Coronado, l983.

Building the dream: the design and construction of the Hotel del Coronado. Coronado, CA: Hotel Del Coronado Heritage Dept., 2008.

Burns, Bob, director. *A Concert in the park: Coronado homecoming for Nick Reynolds*. El Cajon, CA: Compadre Video, 1989. Film

Burton, Richard. "Coronado's Poem." *The Outlook*, June 29, 1901.

Busch, Noel E. "Sun Shines on San Diego." *Readers Digest,* October 1975.

"California in the Eighties as Pictured in the Letters of Anne Seward." *California Historical Society Quarterly*, March 1938.

BIBLIOGRAPHY

Caltrans. Coronado Transportation Study. San Diego, CA: Caltrans, District 2, November 1971.

Campbell, Allen A. *The Flats of Coronado.* Coronado, CA: Alice Crittenden, 1994.

Carrillo, Leo. *The California I Love.* Englewood Cliffs, NJ: Prentice-Hall 1961.

Celebrating Over A Century Of Romance At The Hotel Del Coronado. Coronado, CA: Hotel del Coronado, 2012.

Chandler, William. "San Diego Interiors, 1880-1930." *Journal of San Diego History*, Fall 1979.

"Coronado." *The Golden Era,* Vol. 27, No.4, April 1888.

"Coronado." *San Diego Magazine*, April 1930.

"Coronado Centennial, 1886-1986 A Brief Pictorial History and Tour Guide." Coronado, CA: Coronado Historical Association, 1986.

"Coronado Historical Tour Guide: Eighty-Six Homes and Sites / compiled by Katherine E. Carlin and Bunny MacKenzie." Coronado, CA: Coronado Historical Association 1981.

Crawford, Leslie Hubbard. Coronado. Charleston, SC: Arcadia Publishing, 2011.

Crosby, Walter W. "A City-Wide Tree Plan and Street Tree Map in Coronado, California." *The American City*, December 1930.

"Cutting Corners in Coronado." *The American City*, November 1930.

Dodge, Richard V. "Rails of the Silver Gate." *Pacific Railway Journal*, 1960.

Donovan, Christine. *Coronado, California: Hometown, Homeport, Home Away From Home.*

Coronado, CA: Island Bound Press, 2011.

Dutton, Davis, editor. *San Diego and the Back Country.* New York, NY: Ballentine Books, 1972.

Duvall, Lucille Clark. "William Kettner, San Diego's Dynamic Congressman." *Journal of San Diego History,* Summer 1979. This is an excerpt from her Master's Thesis for the University of San Diego.

Dyle, Bill. "Seventy-five Years of Light." *Journal of San Diego History Society*, July 1956.

Englund, Vi. *The Strand.* Lexington Park, MD: Golden Owl Publishers, 1977.

Engstrand, Iris. *San Diego: California's Cornerstone.* Tulsa, OK: Continental Heritage Press, 1980.

Ethington, Freda and Mary Jane. "A History of Imperial Beach." as a supplement to The Reminder, July 14, 1976.

Fairbank, Jim. "San Diego-Coronado Bay Bridge." Los Angeles, CA: University of Southern California Institute of Safety and Systems Management, October 1967.

Fisher, C. Allan Jr. "San Diego, California's Plymouth Rock." *The National Geographic*, July 1969.

Flanigan, Sylvia Kathleen. "William Sterling Hebbard, Consummate California Architect, 1888-1910." Master's Thesis, University of San Diego, 1985.

From New York to San Diego: Experiences of a Traveler in Search of Health-Resorts in Southern California." *Leslie's Illustrated Newspape*r, December 22, 1888.

Gibson, R.K., Letter to R.L. Regal, Spreckels Union Bldg., San Diego, January 14, 1932, re. James Reid was the landscaper for the Hotel del Coronado. Hotel del Collection, Coronado Historical Association.

BIBLIOGRAPHY

Giebner, Robert C. "Historical American Building Survey, San Diego, 1971." *Journal of San Diego History*, Fall 1971.

Girardot, Terry. *The Ghost of the Hotel del Coronado: The True Story Of Kate Morgan*. Dallas, TX: DME Creative Services, 2001.

Gunn, Guard D. "The Old Mexican Rancho That Became Coronado and North Island." *The Southern California Rancher*, April 1946.

Hall, J. Austin. "San Diego." *California Illustrated Magazine,* February 1883: 379

Harris, Ben L. "An early history of the Coronado Roundtable." Coronado, CA: 1991.

Harris, Carol. "Coronado Modern: Inside Story." *San Diego Magazine*, June 1949.

"The Hotel Del Coronado across the Bay." *San Diego Magazine*, February-March 1951.

Hotel Del Coronado Centennial Gala. Coronado, CA: Hotel del Coronado, 1996. Film Documentary

Hotel Del Coronado History. Coronado, CA: Hotel del Coronado, 2013.

Hotel del Coronado: San Diego, California. Wheeling, IL: Film Ideas, Inc., 2004. Historic Hotels of America, Film Series.

Hotel Del Coronado: The History of a Legend. Coronado, CA: Hotel del Coronado, 1997.

Hunt, Rockwell D., editor. *California and Californians*. Los Angeles, CA: The Lewis Publishing Company, 1926. 5 vols.

Huser, Elizabeth. *Our first 100 years: the Graham Memorial Presbyterian Church*. Coronado, CA: Graham Memorial Presbyterian Church, 1988.

"Incorporation of City of Coronado and Boundaries, see File 3054, in the Coronado City Clerk's Office for a typewritten statement of the Incorporation request. Coronado City Hall.

Johnson, Lucius. "Snug Harbor." *Magazine Sun Diego*, December 1951.

Jordan, J. Wilbur. "Coronado Cops." *San Diego Magazine*, August and November 1974.

Keen, Harold. "Behind the Bridge Battle." *San Diego Magazine*, June 1964.

Klenner, Patricia E. "Robert Decatur Israel, San Diego Pioneer and Keeper of the Light, 1826-1908." Master's Thesis, University of San Diego, 1983.

Kuhn, Gerald G. and Francis P. Shepard. *Sea Cliffs, Beaches and Coastal Valleys of San Diego County: Some Amazing Histories and some Horrifying Implications*. Berkeley, CA: University of California Press, 1980.

La Avenida Murals are featured in *Art News*, May 1946 and June 1946, and in *Christian Science Monitor* magazine, October 12, 1946.

Larsen, Kenneth James. "The Island or Peninsula of San Diego, 1846-1890." Master's Thesis, University of San Diego, 1971.

Leberthon, T.T. and A. Taylor (editors). *The City and County of San Diego. San Diego*, CA: Leberthon and Taylor, 1888.

Lee, Laurence B. "William E. Smythe and San Diego, 1901-1908." *Journal of San Diego History*, Winter 1973.

BIBLIOGRAPHY

Linder, Bruce. *San Diego's Navy*. Annapolis, MD: Naval Institute Press, 2001.

— *The Navy in San Diego*. Charleston, SC: Arcadia Publishing, 2007.

— *San Salvador: Cabrillo's Galleon of Discovery*. San Diego, CA: Maritime Museum of San Diego. 2011.

MacMullen. "The *Silver Gate*, Coronado's Wonderful Steamboat." *The Automobile Club of Southern California Westways*, March 1945.

— "Tenting on the Old Camp Ground." *The Automobile Club of Southern California Westways*, June 1949; reprinted September 1951.

— *They Came By Sea*. San Diego, CA: The Ward Ritchie Press, with the Maritime Museum Association of San Diego, 1969.

MacPhail, Elizabeth C. *The Story of New San Diego and of its Founder, Alonzo E. Horton*. San Diego, CA: Pioneer Press, 1969.

— *Kate Sessions: Pioneer Horticulturist*. San Diego, CA: San Diego Historical Society, 1976.

Makovic, Patrice, director. *San Diego - Coronado Bay Bridge*. La Mesa, CA: Village Videography, 2009. Film

Malinick, Cynthia. "The Lives and Works of the Reid Brothers, Architects, 1852-1943." Master's Thesis, University of San Diego, 1992.

Malinick, Cynthia. "Classicism and Concrete: Harrison Albright's Architectural Contribution to Coronado." *The Journal of San Diego History*, Spring 1997.

Marbury, Elizabeth. *My Crystal Ball: Reminiscences*. New York, NY: Boni and Liveright Publishers, 1923.

May, Alan M. *The Legend of Kate Morgan: the hunt for the haunt of the Hotel del Coronado*. San Diego, CA: May, Alan M., 1989.

McGrew, Clarence Alan. *City of San Diego and San Diego County: The Birthplace of California*. New York, NY: The American Historical Society, 1922. 2 vols.

Middlebrook, R.P. "The High Iron to La Jolla." *San Diego History Center Quarterly*, January 1961.

— and R.V. Dodge. "San Diego's First Railroad." *Journal of San Diego History,* January 1956.

Mills, James. "Southern California's First Light." *Journal of San Diego History,* October 1954.

Morrow, Thomas J. *Hotel Del Coronado*. Coronado, CA: Hotel del Coronado, 1984.

Nebergall, James. "Site of San Diego Whaling Station." Ms for State of California, 1940.

Newspapers (dates are inclusive of their publication time):

Coronado Evening Mercury, daily except Sunday, from May 16, 1887 v.1 no.1 - August 14, 1888 v.3 no. 76, continued as The Coronado Mercury.

The Coronado Mercury, weekly, August 21, 1888 v.1 no.1 - December 27, 1890 v.4 no.13, ceased publication May 16, 1891. Publication replaced by The Mercury.

The Mercury, weekly, May 23, 1891 v.5 no.2 – August, 27, 1892 v.6 no.14, continued by Seaport News, September 3, 1892, published in San Diego after January 1, 1893.

Seaport News, September 3, 1892 - ?

BIBLIOGRAPHY

The Coronado Mercury, weekly, resumed publication January 4, 1893 v.7 no.33 - July 25, 1896 v.10 no.10.

Coronado Ozone, 1897 weekly, no newspapers of record except for Coronado Ozone was published in Coronado from August 1896 - May 1912.

The Coronado Strand, weekly, May 24, 1912 v.1 no.1 - October 28, 1922 v.11 no.25

El Patio, weekly, August 21, 1920 v.1 no.1 - September 24, 1921 v.3 no.8, continued as The Sun Dial.

The Sun Dial, weekly, October 1, 1921 v.1 no.1 - February 18, 1922 v.1 no.21, published in San Diego after February 18, 1922.

Coronado Saturday Night, weekly, April. 1, 1922 v.1 no.6 - April 29, 1922 v.1 no.10; May 13, 1922 v.1 no.12 - May 20, 1922 v.1 no.13; August 19, 1922 v.1 no.26; December 30, 1922 v.1 no.34; January 6, 1923 v.11 no.37 - August 25, 1923 v.12 no.16.

Coronado Journal, weekly, September 1, 1923 v.12 no.17 - June 30, 1949 v.37 no. 26, continued as

Coronado Journal – Compass.

Coronado Citizen, weekly, November 4, 1937 v.1 no.1 - March 27, 1942 v.5 no.22, absorbed by the Coronado Journal.

Coronado Compass, weekly, October 31, 1946 v.1 no.1 - December 29, 1948 v.3 no.77, merged with Coronado Journal and Coronado Citizen.

Coronado Journal - Compass, weekly, July 7, 1949 v.37 no.27 - November 27, 1952 v.39 no.48, continued as Coronado Journal.

Coronado Journal, weekly, December 4, 1952 v.39 no.49 - August 7, 1998 v.88 no.32

Coronado Eagle, weekly, July 4 - 17, 1990 v.1 no.1 - August 18, 1998 v.9 no.32, purchased the

Coronado Journal and became the *Coronado Eagle and Journal.*

Coronado Eagle and Journal, weekly, August 26, 1998 v.88 no.35 – Current.

Island Inquirer, especially June 26, 1979.

San Diego Evening Tribune

San Diego Sun, especially July 31, 1911.

San Diego Union, especially issues of the January 1st each year for a summary of what occurred in each previous year. Also articles in issues of March 11, 1962, September 7, 1969, August 1, 1980, and August 6, 1998.

Seaport News, San Diego, 1903-1908.

Nolte, Linda M. Pearce. "Yachting - Its History in San Diego." *Journal of San Diego History*, Fall 1974.

Ogden, Adele. *The California Sea Otter Trade, 1784-1848*. Berkeley, CA: The University of California Press, 1941.

Ormsby, Burke. "The Lady Who Lives By the Sea." *Journal of San Diego History*, January 1946.

"Orthotropic Bridge Links San Diego and Coronado." *The American City,* September 1969.

Parks Of Coronado. Coronado, CA: Coronado Historic Resource Commission, 2005.

BIBLIOGRAPHY

Pescador, Katrina. *San Diego's North Island, 1911-1941.* San Francisco, CA: Arcadia Pub., 2007.

Peterson, Harold J. *The Coronado Story.* Coronado, CA: Coronado Federal Savings and Loan, 1954; reprinted, 1959.

Phillips, Irene. "Don Pedros Cattle Ranch." *Journal of San Diego History*, July 1956.

Pomeroy, C.P. *Reports of Cases Determined in the Supreme Court of the State of California Volume 77.* San Francisco, CA: Bancroft-Whitney Company, 1889: 511 "City of San Diego v. J.W. Granniss."

Pomeroy, C.P. *Reports of Cases Determined in the Supreme Court of the State of California, Volume 85.* San Francisco, CA: Bancroft-Whitney Company, 1906. "The People ex. rel. O.C. Miller v. The Common Council of the City of San Diego 1890."

Pomeroy, C.P. *Reports of Cases Determined in the Supreme Court of the State of California, Volume 85.* San Francisco, CA: Bancroft-Whitney Company, 1906. "People v. Douglas Gunn 1890."

Pope, Vernon and Paul Dorsey. "Island of Navy Wives." *Saturday Evening Post*, September 5, 1942.

Pourade, Richard. *History of San Diego.* San Diego, CA: Copley Press, 7 volumes between 1960 and 1977.

Powell, Tim, director. Coronado, *Building a Dream.* San Diego, CA: Powell Films, 2007. Film

Press, Ben. *100 Years of Tennis at the Hotel Del Coronado, Playground of the Stars.* Carlsbad, CA: Kales Press, *2010.*

Report of the Commissioner of the General Land Office in the Case of the Contested Survey of the Pueblo Lands of San Diego, Containing this Decision on the questions of Law and Fact involved in the Contest. Washington, DC: Government Printing Office, 1871.

Richards, Bartlett I. and Ruth Van Ackeren. *Bartlett Richards: Nebraska Sandhills Cattlemen.* Lincoln, NE: Nebraska State Historical Society, 1980.

Ridgely, Roberta. "Rebuilding a Tradition." *San Diego Magazine*, May 1961.

Rink, R.W. "Incineration—The City's Housekeeper." *The American City,* October 1943.

Robinson, Alfred. *Life in California.* Oakland, CA: Reprint by Bio Books, 1947.

Robinson, Martha Ingersoll. "A Day's Possibilities in the San Diego Region." *Sunset Magazine*, August 1900.

Rodecape, Lois Foster. "Quand Meme - A Few Footnotes to the Biography of Sara Bernhardt." *California Historical Society Quarterly*, June 1941.

Roorbach, Eloise. "Creating Atmosphere in the Gardens; illustrated by a Japanese half-acre in California." *The Craftsman*, September 1913.

Rush, Philip S. "Historic Ranchos: Peninsula of San Diego." *The Southern California Rancher*, July-August 1961.

— A History of the California, San Diego, CA: Neyenesch Printers 1958.

Sack, Ed. *The development of the Coronado shores: A history. Coronado,* CA: E.A. Sack, 2005.

BIBLIOGRAPHY

San Diego Telephone Directories 1887-1925
    <https://archive.org/search.php?query=collection%3A%22sandiegopubliclibrary%22>

"San Diego's Pictorial Past...to Progressive Present." *Union Title-Trust Topics.* January-February, 1959.

San Diego State University Special Collections and Archives:
    <http://library.sdsu.edu/scua>
        Babcock, E.S. Jr., Correspondence
        Coronado Chamber of Commerce (1974-)
        Hotel del Coronado (1888-1995)
        San Diego and Coronado Ferry Company (1886-1969)

Schlenker, Gerald. "The Internment of the Japanese of San Diego County during the Second World War." *Journal of San Diego History,* Winter 1972.

Scott, Ed. *San Diego County Soldier-Pioneers, 1846-1866.* National City, CA: County of San Diego Bicentennial Project, Crest Printing Company, 1969.

Senn, Thomas J. "Coronado-1846-1946." *Union Title-Trust Topics,* December 1946 - January 1947.

Serhan, Diana L. *Coronado: The Marketing of Paradise.* MA Thesis, University of San Diego, 2001.

Sheridan, Bob. "The Decision to Build the Bay Bridge: A Look at the Power Politics," Ms., University of San Diego, 1986.

Simpich, Frederick. "San Diego Can't Believe It." *National Geographic,* June 1942.

Simpson, Ernest E. "John D. Spreckels, Miracle-maker." *Sunset, The Pacific Monthly*, February 1913.

Slankard, M.W. "Coronado Ties All Purchases to the Budget." *The American City,* June 1955.

Smith, Bertha H. "Charm of Coronado's Sunset." *The Pacific Monthly,* March 1912 and May 1916.

Smith, Helen Huntington. "Port of Navy Wives." *Saturday Evening Post,* February 20, 1943.

Statistics of Coronado Beach Company Sale of Lots from November 13, 1886 to 15th Day of October 1887, $2,650,488.23. San Diego, CA: Ferguson, Bumgardner & Company, 1887.

Statutes of California Passed at the Twenty-First Session of the Legislature, 1875-1876. Sacramento, CA: State Printing Office, 1876.

Statutes of California and Amendments to the Codes Passed at the Twenty-Eighth Session of the Legislature, 1889. Sacramento, CA: State Printing Office, 1889.

Stanford, Leland. "San Diego's Medico-legal History, 1850-1900." *Journal of San Diego History,* Spring 1970.

Stewart, Don M. *Frontier Port.* Los Angeles, CA: The Ward Ritchie Press, 1965.

Strandgaard, Lise Graham. "Coronado: The Image of the Island." Master's Thesis, San Diego State University, 1984.

Stockdale, James. "On the armed forces' appreciation of Coronado: a talk at the Coronado Library." Coronado, CA: Coronado Public Library, 1990. Transcript of a talk given May 2, 1990

—- with Sybil Stockdale. *In Love and War: The Story of a Family's Ordeal and Sacrifice During the Vietnam Years.* New York: Harper & Row. 1984.

BIBLIOGRAPHY

Sudsbury, Elretta. *Jackrabbits to Jets: The History of North Island, San Diego, California*. San Diego, CA: Neyenesch Printers, 1967.

Sullivan, William. "Coronado: The Rolls Royce of Beaches." *Coast Magazine*, February, 1977.

Taschner, Mary. "Richard Requa, Southern California Architect, 1881-1941." Master's Thesis, University of San Diego, 1982.

Taylor, Bayard. *Eldorado or Adventures in the Path of Empire*. New York, NY: Putnam, 1857.

"Tent City." *The Automobile Club of Southern California Westways*, September 1959.

"There is Another Coronado." *Sunset Magazine*, June 1979.

Thomas, William H. *On Land and Sea, or California in the Years 1843,'44 and '45*. Boston, MA: DeWolfe, Fiske, 1885.

Thomas, William H. *Lewey and I; or Sailor Boy's Wanderings*. Boston, MA: DcWolfe, Fiske, 1885.

United States Navy. Pamphlet concerning the Naval Radio Receiving Facility at Imperial Beach, n.d., n.p.

University of San Diego. "Directory of San Diego Architects, 1868-1939." Department of History, Public History Graduate Students, Spring 1984.

University of San Diego. "Can You Read My Lips! A Guide to the Silent Film Industry in San Diego, 1898-1930." Department of History, Public History Graduate Students, Spring 1982.

Van Deman, R.H. "Harbor of the Sun—San Diego, California." *Civil Engineering*, July 1941.

Van der Pas, Peter W. "Hugh de Vries Visits San Diego." *Journal of San Diego History*, Summer 1971.

Van Dyke, Thomas S. "A Newly Discovered Land." Overland Monthly, December 1887.

— "Around San Diego Bay," Overland Monthly, February 1888.

Vogt, Walter. "Tax Base Sharing Implications from San Diego County." *Journal of the American Planning Association*, April 1979.

Webster, Karna. "Architects William, Charles, and Edward Quayle and their Buildings." Master's Thesis, University of San Diego, 1984.

"Where do the Admirals Go?" *Newsweek*, April 15, 1963.

Weegar, Sally Diane. "A History of the Coronado Public Library." MA Thesis, University of San Diego, 2009.

Wilson, Edmund. "The Jumping Off Place." *The New Republic*, December 23, 1931.

Wish You Were Here: Vintage Postcards from the Hotel Del Coronado. Coronado, CA: Hotel Del Coronado, 2001.

Witty, Bob. "Coronado Island." *The Automobile Club of Southern California Westways*, August 1969.

— "A Southern Principality," *Out West*, March 1902.

Yorke, John. *Coronado, California: Photography by John Yorke & Friends*. Coronado, CA: John Yorke Photography. 2000.

Young, Laura E. "The Silent Sentinel; Samuel Wood Hamill, FAIA." Master's Thesis, University of San Diego, 1984.

INDEX

A
Adams, H. Austin *128, 159*
Air raid drills *185*
Albright, Harrison *89, 118, 119, 173, 295*
Alessio Family *227-228, 239, 285*
American Women's Voluntary Services *186, 197*
America's Cup *274*
Anderson, Clarence *193*
Anderson's Bakery *69*
A & P Market *182, 194*
Archeology *3*
Armstrong, R.E. *41*
Army *118, 120*
    Fort Emory *191*
    Rockwell Field *99, 117, 120, 121, 124, 126-127, 147, 149, 171, 177*
    Signal Corps Aviation *99, 111*
Arnold, Henry "Hap" *117*
Aspinwall, William H. *8-9*
Averill, S. Hoyte *41, 44*

B
Babcock Court *142, 261, 266, 271, 281*
Babcock Jr., Elisha S. *15, 22, 33, 35, 39, 41, 48, 52, 53, 56, 58, 67, 71, 79, 83, 100, 119, 154*
    lot sales *19, 21, 30*
    partnership *10-11*
    schools *43*
    water *18, 37*
Baldwin, Hugh J. *68-69, 80*
Bandel, K. W. *179*
Bandel, Louis C. *79, 102, 122, 136, 173*
Bandstand *60, 90*
Bank of America *95, 265*
Bank of Commerce and Trust *94-95, 96*
Bank of Coronado *118, 142*
Baseball *41, 153, 166, 167*
Basketball *151, 166, 180, 182, 218, 222, 248, 268*
Baum, L. Frank *104, 109, 228*
BayBerry Tree Gift Shop *138*
Beach Company Nursery *31*
Bennington, (steel gunboat) *86*
Best Western Motel *267, 289*
Biltmore Hotel *132, 222*
Blackout ordinance *184*
Bludau, Homer *282, 292*
Blue Lantern Cafe *132*
Blue Lantern Inn *132, 160*
Blumenthal, David *289*
Board of Trustees *57, 59-60, 65-67, 70, 79, 81, 82, 84-85, 88, 90, 92, 96, 101, 104, 106, 110, 118-119, 121, 143, 250*
    bathing suits *114*
    land issues *60, 72*
    segregation *67-68*
Bologna Park *110*
Booth, William *182, 217*
Bowman's City Market *194*
Boyd, William *131*
Boy Scouts of America *117, 122, 134*
Brickyard Cove *97, 206*
Bridge *171, 209, 223, 235, 239, 240, 246, 255, 257, 259, 261, 291.* See also Tunnel
    construction *242, 244-245, 247, 253*
    early plans *145, 152-153, 158, 161*
    naming *250*
    opening *252-253*
    tolls *254, 270*
    traffic *259, 261, 265, 267, 275, 291*
Brown, Dayton Reginald Eugene *138*

C
Carrillo, Pedro C. *6-7*
Cabrillo, Juan Rodríguez *1*
CALTRANS *242, 259, 265, 272, 284, 291*
Carlin, Katherine Eitzen *195*
Carrothers, Bob *179, 181*
Carrothers Gym *178, 281*
Carter, Jimmy *262*
Cech, Gene *293*
Centennial of Naval Aviation *295*
Centennial Park *269*
Central Drug Store *95-96, 176*
Chamber of Commerce *202, 238, 276, 279, 281, 282, 283, 289, 292*
Chapin, Sidney D. *119*
Chaplin, Charlie *130-132, 144*
Chew, Ed *185*
Chew, R.L. *116*
Childs, A.S. *79*
Christensen School of Music *117*
Christmas *84*
Churches *67*
    Baptist *61*
    Baptist Church (Southern) *221*
    Catholic *58, 61-62, 184, 239*
    Christian Science *114-115, 137*
    Episcopal *61-62, 72, 173, 236*
    First Baptist *216*
    Methodist *61-62, 106, 144, 198, 236*
    Presbyterian *59, 61, 65, 252*
Churchill, Mendal *72, 80-81, 165*
City Council *121*
City Defense Council *184*
City Hall *95-96, 202, 204, 207, 212, 216, 271, 275, 280, 282, 283, 290, 291*
Clinton, Bill *279, 287*
Cohen, Ben *236*
Collett, Josephus *11, 67*
Community and Club building *179*
Community Development *269, 271*
Community Development Agency *281, 289, 291*
Concert in the Park *293*
Constellation (aircraft carrier) *232*
Copley, Ira C. *86, 145*
Copley, James S. *207*
Corbett, A. W. *59*
Coronado
    75th Anniversary *241, 244*
    annexation threat *114, 264*
    city bounderies *52, 207, 229, 264, 272*
    city planning *128, 138, 148, 158, 174, 177, 194, 204, 206, 209, 212, 240, 265, 274, 276, 277, 279, 289*
    incorporation *42, 44, 51-52, 54, 56-57, 67*
    land sales *8-10, 20-21, 28, 37*
    name *16*
    preservation *232, 241*
    the Flats *147*
    zoning *128, 240*
Coronado "9" *225*
Coronado Athletic Club *41, 59*
Coronado Beach Company *11, 14-15, 18-22, 24-26, 28-29, 32-33, 35, 36, 43, 44, 48, 52, 53, 74, 92, 100, 125, 142*
    auctions *20-22, 32, 36*
Coronado Beach Railroad. *See Railroads*
Coronado Boathouse *28, 39, 57, 65, 83, 103, 106, 164*

Coronado Brick Company *23*
Coronado Cays *221-222, 257, 260, 275, 280*
Coronado Chamber of Commerce *172, 175*
Coronado Citizen Committee on Survival, *234*
Coronado Community Center *280, 281, 283, 289, 291*
Coronado Company *270*
Coronado Dairy Farm *25, 50*
Coronado Department Store *207*
Coronado Flower Show *134, 266*
Coronado Furniture *200*
Coronado Heights *18, 36, 68, 119, 129, 142, 152, 191, 243, 262, 282, 289*
    Wullenweber antenna *243*
Coronado High School *68, 105, 110, 129, 133, 142, 144, 151, 154, 165, 176, 182, 192, 224, 230-231, 248, 262, 276, 280, 284, 285, 288, 290-291*
    current school *291*
    demolition *229-230*
    first class *105*
    first high school *135*
    new school *230, 236*
    Tiki *236, 274*
Coronado Historical Association *95, 160, 245, 251, 266, 268, 292*
Coronado International Film Festival *234, 237*
Coronado Island Marriott Hotel *264*
Coronado Islands (Las Islas Coronadas) *2*
Coronado MainStreet *268*
Coronado MainStreet Ltd. *282, 283, 292*
Coronado Masonic Lodge *241*
Coronado Milling Company *39*
Coronado Motor Car agency *100*
Coronado Motor Inn *216*
Coronado Museum *94-95, 266, 279*
Coronado peninsula ("the Peninsula") *6-9, 42*
Coronado Plaza *262*
Coronado Point *262*
Coronado Public Library *59, 60, 64, 70, 72, 74, 89, 101, 119, 124, 137, 166, 184, 222, 233, 261, 268, 285, 292, 294*
Coronado Public Works Department *251*
Coronado Realty Board *201*
Coronado School District *68, 181, 268, 276, 281, 290. Also Coronado Unified School District*
    School Board *69-70, 125, 129, 185, 236, 245-247, 252, 276, 280*
    school bonds *129*
Coronado School of the Arts *290*
Coronado Schools Foundation *278, 285*
Coronado Shores *215, 240, 249, 254, 259, 282*
Coronado Sport and Hobby Shop *200*
Coronado Taxpayers Association *275*
Coronado Texaco *207*
Coronado Towers *231, 239*
Coronado Upholstery & Drapery Shop *200*
Coronado Visitor Bureau *284, 292*
Coronado Water Company *18, 37, 52. See also Water*
    Coronado Waukesha Water *37, 69*
Coronado Woman's Club *85, 203*
Coronado Yacht Club *26, 41, 106, 164, 179, 182, 199, 204, 236, 239-240, 271*
Coronado Youth Club *202*
Cosgrove, Chris A. *159, 168, 174, 295*
Country Club Estates *207-209, 212, 218, 251*
Crandall, C.M. *80*
Crown Shops *200*
Curtis, Eleanor Spalding *290*
Curtiss Aviation School *98-99, 107, 116*
Curtiss, Glenn *92, 98-100*
Cutler, Clara Bell *132, 144, 165*
Cutler, J. Leslie *144, 181*
Cyane (sloop of war) *7*

D
Davidson, G. Aubrey *95, 113, 141*
Davis, Rod *263*
Depression *137, 154, 157, 160, 167, 178*
Desch, Ivan *104*
Devon Hotel *218*
Dirigible *126*
Dog Beach *290*
Doolittle, Jimmy *120, 127*
Dorman, R.H. *263, 264, 267, 269*
Downs, Johnny *132, 144, 171*
Dredging *170, 175-176, 178, 180, 232, 261, 286*
    Glorietta Bay *24, 39, 82, 161, 164, 176, 218, 241*
    Spanish Bight *24*
Dupee, Walter H. *102, 109*

E
Eckenroth, Dean *279, 294*
Edward, Prince of Wales *130*
Edwards, William A. *59, 73-74, 79*
Eisenhower, Dwight D. *229*
El Cordova Hotel *154, 161, 166, 222, 237, 239*
Elections *50, 57, 65, 202, 220, 229, 230, 245-246, 263, 269, 275, 288, 290*
Ellyson, Theodore *98-99*
Ervast, Andrew *72, 79, 104, 110*
Estoppey, Eugene M. *117*

F
Falkenham, Joseph *295*
Fallout shelters *234*
Fast Food Ordinance *292*
Fenton, Henry G. *101*
Ferries *242*
    Benicia (ferry) *39, 50*
    Coronado (ferry) *19-20, 24, 152, 254*
    Coronado Ferry Company *19, 133*
    Crown City (ferry) *217, 251*
    Della (ferry) *13-14*
    Morena (ferry) *129*
    nickel snatcher *178, 250, 254*
    North Island (ferry) *230*
    Ramona (ferry) *82-83, 86, 94, 108, 122, 133, 144, 145*
    San Diego (ferry) *152, 254*
    Silver Gate (ferry) *26, 78, 106, 107*
    Silver Strand (ferry) *194*
Ferry Landing *26-28, 44, 129, 264, 265, 282*
Filipino Sporting Club *166*
Films *107, 116, 144-145, 150-151, 152, 154, 171, 173, 175, 176, 216, 220, 222, 223*
Fire Department *51, 58, 81, 88-89, 124, 132, 133, 136-137, 142, 143, 176, 200, 260*
Fisher, M. Bert *206*
Fitch, Herbert R. *101, 104*
Fitch III, Walter *114*
Fleming, Sara Braithwaite *81*
Flyover *122, 124, 150*
Football *80, 110, 153, 166, 168, 180, 264, 268, 276, 284*
Forney, Max *208*
Fourth of July Parade *49, 57, 127, 219, 244, 271, 275, 277, 280, 288, 294*
Francis, Merle R. *203*
Free Brothers Market *191, 200*
Fuller, Howard *208*

G

Garbage 97, 205-206, 212. See Hog Ranch
Gerry's Restaurant 182
Gill, Irving John 80, 82, 114-115, 295
Gise, Bill 176
Glorietta Bay (also Glorietta Bight) 23-24, 26, 41, 152, 169
Glorietta Bay Inn 90
Glorietta Bay Masterplan 286
Glorietta Bay Master Plan 291, 292
Golf 132, 134, 138, 164, 206, 241, 262, 282, 284, 287, 289
    Coronado Country Club (also Coronado Golf Club) 75-76, 87, 102, 110, 117, 126, 138-139, 166, 192, 207
    Coronado Municipal 218, 223, 240, 245, 259, 264
    first golf course 71-72, 75
Goodbody, J.R. 235, 238, 240, 258, 294
Goodenough, Robin 215, 224, 228, 260
Goodhue, Bertram Grosvenor 125
Gophers 72
Government Family housing 190, 212, 214-215, 222, 245, 247-248
Grampus (submarine) 93-94
Granniss, George W. 9-11, 22, 42
Gray, Coleman 223, 238
Greene, Frank "Toady" 151, 168, 208, 218
Gruendike, Jacob 10-11, 18, 67
Gun batteries 68, 70, 71, 191, 289
Gunn, William A. 152

H

Hahn, Ernie 274
Haines, Robbie 263
Hakes, L.B. 104
Hansen, Leo 230
Haralson, Helen Smith 246
Harland, W.C. 121
Hartmann's Beauty Shop 171
Hathaway, Paul 241, 295
Hernan, J.J. 106, 127
Herron, Mary 263, 268, 269, 271, 277, 282, 284, 288
Higgs Jewelers 200
Hinde, Charles T. 62, 65, 70
Historic preservation 227, 271, 292, 294
Hog Ranch 204-207. See Garbage
Holabird, W.H. 19-21, 47
Holbrook, Lillie Spreckels 129
Holderness, Arthur W. (Bud) 280
Holland's Bicycle Shop 134, 146
Holly, Charles F. 9

Holmes, George 80, 121
Hord, Donal 178
Horse Show 87, 139, 176, 179
Hospitals 81, 88, 184, 279
    1111 Orange Ave 138
    Coronado Emergency Hospital 147
    Coronado Hospital 201, 215, 221, 258, 279
    early 41, 73-74, 79, 96, 138-139
    North Island Family Hospital 184
    Rockwell Field Hospital 127
Hotel del Coronado 21-22, 28, 33, 36-52, 59, 61, 64-65, 68, 74, 84, 87, 95, 97, 102, 131, 133, 148, 160, 171, 175, 187, 205, 212, 227, 234, 237, 239, 254, 259, 261, 277, 287, 290, 292
    ballroom 230
    Bath House 47
    Circus Room 230
    construction 23-24, 33, 40, 43, 44
    Crown Room 45-46, 130
    Del Coronado Sands 240
    electricity 24, 44, 224
    harborette 141-142
    opening 46, 48
    pier 58, 86, 133
    pool 59, 164, 169
    Spreckels acquisition 53, 57
    The Plunge 168
Hotel Josephine 29, 33, 47, 60, 72, 111
Hotel Marisol Coronado 160
Huffman, Leon 235
Hydroaeroplanes 98, 124

I

Il Fornaio Italian Restaurant 265
Ince, Carl W. 190, 193
Indians. See Native Americans
Influenza epidemic 123
Ingham, Edwin A. 171
Ingle, Herbert 11, 22, 67
Israel, Henry Clay 114
Ivy Pool Hall 166
Ivy's Tea Garden 103

J

Jackson, Richard Harrison 245
Japanese-American families 185-186
Japanese Tea Garden 76-77, 86, 207
Jean Jurad's Dance Studio 182
Jessop, Alonzo 117
Jessop, Armand 101, 104
Jessop, Joseph 3, 87
John C. Stennis (aircraft carrier) 288
Johnson, Lyndon B. 258
Johnson, William Templeton 219, 295

Jones, Herbert Charpiot 183-184
Josephine Hotel. See Hotel Josephine
J. R. Robertson's Chevrolet 207
J.R. Townsend Studebaker 194

K

Kahn, Albert 126
Keith, Susan Ring 184, 245, 270
Keller, Walter S. 115
Kellogg, Giles 72, 84
Kingston Trio 224, 271
Kitty Hawk (ship) 232
Klass and Parisienne Cafe 100
Kneedler, William L. 84, 86

L

La Avenida Motel 218, 220, 273, 293
La Avenida Restaurant 161, 205
Laing, Al 294, 295
Laing's Appliances 200
Lancaster, Maude Carson 147
Langley (aircraft carrier) 140, 169
Larson, Don 234, 237
Lawrence, M. Larry 28, 239, 240, 268, 285
Le Meridien Hotel 263
Lewis, George J. 132
Lindbergh, Charles 147-148
Liquor 47, 118, 124
Loews Coronado Bay Resort 275
Lubin Motion Picture Company 116, 143
Lubin, Siegmund 116-117
Lumber yard 28
Lurline (yacht) 30
Lyons, Johnny 165, 168

M

MacCartee, Gerry 279
MacMullen, James D. 117
MainStreet Ltd. 270-272, 274, 276, 280, 281, 286
Marco's Italian restaurant 95
Marine Railway (also Marine Works, Coronado Iron Works) 26, 35, 36, 50, 92
Marines 7, 55, 100, 111, 140, 143, 149, 184
Marriott Hotel 215
Marsh, George T. 76, 86
Martin, Edward H. 260
Martínez, Alfredo Ramos 161
Mathewson, Arthur 80, 110, 169, 185, 229
Mathewson, J. A. 25, 41, 51, 167
May, Cliff 166
McKenzie, B.W. 118

McLean, W. J. *43*
McNeeley, Roland *260*
Messer, T.H. *146, 148, 149*
Mexican Era *4, 6*
Mexican Village *58, 62, 200, 213, 236, 288*
Military Draft *180, 181, 188, 208*
Millen, Louis de Ryk *135, 201, 207, 232*
Miller, Ben S. *28*
Miller, Herman *206*
Mitchell Art Gallery *114, 137–138*
Mitchell, John W. *136, 137*
Monte Carlo (gambling ship) *173–174, 181*
Morton, Gabrielle *89, 124*
Mosher, Robert *245*
Moson, Frank B. *100, 103*
Municipal pool *223*
Mustin, Henry *127*

N

Nadeau House *29, 59*
Native Americans *3–4*
Natural History Museum *9, 47*
Navy *73, 95, 118, 120, 143, 145, 168, 285*
   amphibious warfare *237*
   Army-Navy land swap *171*
   destroyers *93, 136*
   Great White Fleet *90–91*
   Naval Air Station *120, 124, 140, 146, 149, 171, 177, 190, 199, 221, 233, 246, 264, 284, 288*
   Naval Amphibious Base *180, 189–190, 204, 217–218, 238, 265, 281*
   nuclear aircraft carriers *284–288*
   Pacific Squadron *55, 93, 97*
   PBY Catalina flying boat *187*
   radio compass station *191*
   SEAL *211, 234, 235, 287*
   seaplane *98, 221–222*
   Shenandoah (airship) *139–140*
   Station ITEM *191*
   submarines *93–95*
   UDT *211, 234, 235*
   USS Coronado *245, 265, 279, 288*
   WAVES barracks *189*
Neal, George F. *205*
Newspapers
   Coronado Citizen *187*
   Coronado Compass *201*
   Coronado Eagle *272, 278, 285, 294*
   Coronado Evening Mercury *25, 31, 39, 66, 69–70*
   Coronado Journal *100, 136, 240, 279, 294*
   Coronado News *87*
   Coronado Ozone *71*
   Coronado Reminder *246*
   Coronado Saturday Night *134*
   Coronado Shopping News *201*
   Coronado Strand *100, 103, 133, 134*
   El Patio *128, 130, 134*
   Seaport News *66*
   Sun Dial *132, 134*
   Tent City News *118*
Niedermeyer, Hal *172, 182, 292*
Nixon, Richard M. *258*
Nordhoff, Charles *60, 70, 79*
North Beach *205*
North Island *2, 7, 13, 26, 36, 67, 92, 93, 97, 98–100, 111, 120, 122, 125–126, 139–140, 168, 170, 178, 187, 192–193, 199*
   causeway *122*
   Eleventh Naval District *127*
   federal takeover *100, 119*
   hide houses *5*
   Navy's interest *54, 56*
   Whaler's Bight *5*
   whaling *5, 9*
   World War I *120*

O

Oakwood Garden *257*
Ohlmeyer, Henry *81, 108*
Old Armory building *271*
Optimist Club *275*
Oscar's Drivein *200*
Oscars Drive-In *231*
Ostrich Farm *33, 50, 84*
Ovrom, Al *288*
Oxford Hotel *14, 20, 28, 41, 50, 59, 162, 205*

P

Padway, Barney *228, 236, 239*
Palmer-Built Homes Inc. *193*
Panama-California Exposition *113–114, 117*
Parade *56, 90, 122, 134, 253, 258*
Parent Teachers Association *114, 172, 187, 224, 280*
Peachy, Archibald *7–8*
Pearl Harbor attack *183–184*
Pendleton, Joseph H. *111, 143, 149*
Perkins Flowers *200*
Peterson, William A. *254*
Pickford, Roy *142*
Piers *61, 93–94, 119*
Pike (submarine) *93–94*
Plane crash *151, 177, 212, 230, 242*
Plevinsky, Reuben *212*
Police Department *58, 67, 96–97, 101, 102, 106, 121, 122, 127, 132, 136–137, 146, 166, 187, 218, 219, 220, 247, 270–271, 279, 280, 286, 289*
Polo *64, 69, 87, 92–93, 99, 102, 104, 117, 123, 124, 131–132, 139, 144, 147, 209*
Population *92, 111, 119, 127, 128, 157, 179, 197, 209, 227, 241, 247, 257, 294*
Port District *235–236, 238, 240, 244, 249, 282*
Post Office *22, 25–26, 29, 51, 92, 95, 121, 190, 202*
Pratt, W. A. *111, 117*
Prien, Henry F. *51*
Prohibition *124, 129*
Property *190*
Public Services *271, 280, 289, 292*

Q

R

Railroads *49, 252*
   Belt Line *18, 36, 39, 48, 66, 70, 72, 87, 190, 191, 260*
   Coronado Beach Railroad *16, 18, 32, 45, 57*
   Pomona Avenue line *18*
   San Diego Electric Railway Company *66*
   streetcars *18, 28, 47, 56, 60, 66, 87, 90, 126–127, 129, 133, 181, 202*
   trestle bridge *18*
Rancho Carrillo *206, 209, 216–217, 219, 221, 228, 231, 238, 240, 242, 244–245, 248*
Ranger (aircraft carrier) *171*
Rationing, World War II *188–189*
Reagan, Ronald *253, 258*
Realty Board *128*
Recreation committee *198*
Red Cross *123, 161, 182, 185, 193, 197*
Reed, A.L. *79*
Reed, H.W. *203*
Reid Brothers (architects) *22–23, 29, 44, 47, 61, 176*
Requa, Richard *124, 137, 219, 295*
Residential Association *235, 239*
Reynolds, Jane Keck *184, 290*
Reynolds, Nick *224*
Rice, Thomas M. *194*
Richards, Bartlett J. *81–82, 84, 109*
Riddell, Richard M. *201*

Ring, Eleanor *184, 241, 245, 284*
Rink, Russell W. *192*
Ritter, William Emerson *82-83*
Ritz Hotel *132*
Roach, Hal *144*
Robinson, Charles S. *89*
Rocks *56, 67, 72, 87, 101, 141-142, 164*
Roehrig, Frederick Louis *109*
Rogan, Nat *118, 128, 139*
Roosevelt, Franklin D. *171-172*
Roosevelt, Mrs. Franklin Delano *188*
Ross, Colin *123, 131, 132, 139*
Ross, Mary Carlin King *293*
Rotary Club *132, 169, 173*
Rotary Park *282*

S

Safeway *147*
Sailing *152*
San Carlos Hotel *218*
SANDAG *263, 294*
Sandarger (freighter) *241*
San Diego Unified Port District *236*
San Diego Yacht Club *106*
Sand Spit *56, 66, 70, 168*
San Salvador (galleon) *1*
Saratoga (aircraft carrier) *183*
Schaefer, Amos E. *181, 208-209*
Schmidt, Patty *275, 277, 288-289*
Schools *80, 125, 144. See also Coronado High School, Coronado School District*
    1888 Schoolhouse *42-43, 68, 96, 111*
    Coronado Beach School *64, 105*
    Coronado School (also Central Elementary School) *104, 105, 111, 246, 247, 276*
    Crown School *218*
    Cutler Field *167, 178, 179, 283-284*
    first public school *25*
    Glorietta School *215*
    Junior High School *224-225*
    La Escuela de Coronado *165*
    Middle School *272, 280, 283, 290*
    Public School Tent *25, 43*
    Sacred Heart *202*
    Silver Strand Elementary School *241*
    Village Elementary School *276, 281, 283*
Schumann-Heink, Madame Ernestine *117, 123, 161, 173*
Scrap Metal Drive
    World War II *162*
Scripps Institute of Oceanography *82*

Seaman, William C. *288*
Seavey, William *235*
Seawall *110, 115, 259*
Seghers, John B. *33, 36*
Sessions, Kate *31, 103, 159*
Sewer *92, 232*
Shaefer, A.E. *203*
Sherman, Sharon *294*
Shoreland Motor Hotel *216*
Silver Stand Highway *282*
Silver Strand *2, 9, 150, 152, 159, 175-176, 207, 237*
    bay entrance *180, 220, 287*
    channel *264, 270*
    Fiddler's Cove *244*
    highway construction *220*
Silver Strand Beautification Committee *289*
Silver Strand Skyport *201-202*
Silver Strand State Park *152, 159, 174, 176, 206*
Simmons, Bezer *7*
Smisek, Thomas *276-277, 280, 282, 288-289, 294*
Snell, Ivan H. *148, 164, 184*
Society of Military Widows *208*
Sosnoski, Harry A. *241*
Southern California Soap Company *59*
Southern Trust and Commerce Bank *142*
Spanish-American War *72*
Spanish Bight *5-6, 87, 98-99, 122, 178, 180, 191, 195*
Spanish Era
    California frontier *3, 5*
    land grants *6*
Spencer, Earl Winfield *120*
Spencer, Wallis Warfield *120, 130*
Spreckels, Adolph *30*
Spreckels Brothers Commercial Company *30, 35, 70, 85*
Spreckels Building *118-119, 121, 276-277*
Spreckels, Claus *30, 145*
Spreckels Companies *133*
Spreckels, John D. *30, 39, 53, 54, 66, 74, 87, 89, 113-114, 117, 121, 127, 145, 159*
    beach cottage *89*
    mansion *53, 55, 90*
Spreckels Railroad Company *126*
Springs *2-3, 60, 251*
    Russian Spring *3, 5, 7*
Stables *20, 57, 64, 127, 167, 209*
Stanley, E.G. *206*
Stark, William R. *260*
Star Park *81, 143, 238*

Stewart, William Wallace *26*
Stingray Point *39*
Stockdale, James *240, 260, 286*
Stockdale, Sybil *260, 286*
Storms *85-86, 87, 115, 119, 141, 146, 170, 176, 179, 192, 208, 218, 224, 262, 266-267, 279, 282*
Story, Hampton L. *10-11, 13, 15, 19, 22, 33, 36, 39, 42, 48, 53, 67*
Strand Realty Company *201*
Strauss, Harold *177*
Streets *15-16, 36, 39, 85, 92, 101, 138, 143, 153*
    Cabrillo Esplanade *17, 143*
    Dead Man's Curve *129*
    Fourth Street tunnel *265, 267, 269, 276, 291, 293*
    Glorietta Boulevard *115*
    house numbering *82*
    Mullinnix Drive *192, 215*
    Ocean Boulevard *86-87, 115, 168*
    parking meters *198*
    Pendleton Road *149*
    Rotary Circle *84*
    speed limits *84*
    Star Park Circle *17*
    Strand Highway *138, 142*
    traffic *129, 135, 158, 178, 194, 199-200, 219, 242, 259, 265, 268, 276, 278, 284, 288, 289, 292, 293, 294*
    traffic signal *257*
Surfing *228, 267, 276*
Swan, Harold A. *118*
Swimming *241*

T

Talbert, Joe *281*
Tarbuck, Ray A. *238*
Taylor, Harold A. *134*
Telephone *26, 67, 85, 107, 121, 134, 160, 194*
Tennis *47, 139, 166, 175, 231, 239, 241, 252, 268*
Tent City *24, 78-79, 81, 94, 106, 108, 114, 127, 132, 136, 150, 152, 167, 173, 180*
    Camp Coronado *76*
    carousel *106-108*
    dog show *139*
Theaters
    Coronado Community Theatre *225*
    Coronado Playhouse *224, 271, 280, 282*
    Coronado Theatre *161, 194, 207, 212, 279*
    Lamb's Players *279*

Silver Strand *118, 123, 128, 161, 165*
The Palms *199*
The Star *103*
Village Theater *208, 234, 237, 282*
The Deb Shop *200*
The Landing *264*
The Yarn Mart *200*
Thompson, Gus A. *57*
Tidelands *193, 218, 220, 225, 235, 236, 240, 244-245, 249*
Tidelands Park *215, 264, 290*
Tiedemann, Ernest R. *241*
Titus, Harry L. *10, 85, 89, 134, 173*
Tomb, J. Harvey *127*
Tomlinson, Daniel *143*
Towers, Mrs. John Henry (Pierette) *191*
Town & Country Shop *200*
Transient Occupancy Tax *280, 284, 294*
Trevelyan, Eddie *263*
Troxel's Variety Store *121, 167*
Tunnel *158, 161, 172, 209, 217, 219, 223-224, 232. See also Bridge* opposition *158*
Turquand, William A. *132, 134*

U
U.S.O. Club *187, 202-203*

V
Vizcaíno, Sebastian *2*
Vanderkloot, M.R. *65*
Van Valkenburg, Frank *185*
Venetia (yacht) *66, 121, 133, 145*
Vernetti, Jim *280*
Vestal, Walter *174, 236, 240, 244*
Vetter, Paul *240, 253, 263*
Vilar, Louis Henry *270*
Village Inn *132*
VJ Day *199*

W
Wade, Larry *278*
Walker, Greg *270*
Wallace, Henry G.S. *176*
War Salvage Committee *187*
Water *60, 65, 90, 92, 180. See also Coronado Water Company*
Water polo *59, 70, 72, 102, 276*
Waters, John C. *203*
Water tower *210*
Wead, Frank ("Spig") *150*
Wegeforth, Arthur B. *138*
Wegeforth, Harry *147*
Wegeforth, Milton *138*
Wegeforth, Paul *96, 129, 148*

Welles, Roger *127*
Wells Fargo and Company *44*
Western Salt Company *100-101*
Weston, Henry G. *164*
Weston, John M. *249*
Whaling. *See North Island*
White Elephant Shop *142*
Wilhelmina House *29*
Williams, George K. *206, 212, 217, 223, 233, 252, 260*
Wilson, Bob *239*
Windsor Cottage *268*
Woman's Club *280*
Woman's Section of the Navy League *115*
Women's Ambulance and Transport Corps *182*
Women's Christian Temperance Union *115*
Women's rights *70*
Works Progress Administration (WPA) *178-179*

X

Y
Yachting *41, 164. See also Coronado Yacht Club, Sailing*
Coronado Cays Yacht Club *278, 280*
San Diego Naval Sailing Club *244*
Young, Cassin *188*

Z
Zacharias, Ellis M. *176, 188, 194, 212*
Zuñiga Jetty *56, 67, 68, 71-73, 87, 170, 174*
Zuñiga Point *55, 56*

www.ingramcontent.com/pod-product-compliance
Lightning Source LLC
Chambersburg PA
CBHW061152010526
44118CB00027B/2947